Middle School 3-1

기말고사 완벽대비

적중 100

영어 기출 문제집

중 3

천재 | 정사열

Best Collection

구성과 특징

교과서의 주요 학습 내용을 중심으로 학습 영역별 특성에 맞춰 단계별로 다양한 학습 기회를 제공하여
단원별 학습능력 평가는 물론 중간 및 기말고사 시험 등에 완벽하게 대비할 수 있도록 내용을 구성

Words & Expressions

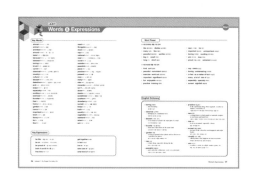

Step1 Key Words 단원별 핵심 단어 설명 및 풀이
Key Expression 단원별 핵심 숙어 및 관용어 설명
Word Power 반대 또는 비슷한 뜻 단어 배우기
English Dictionary 영어로 배우는 영어 단어

Step2 실력평가 단원별 수시평가 대비 주관식, 객관식 문제풀이

Step3 서술형 대비 학업성취도 및 수행능력평가 대비 서술형 문제풀이

Conversation

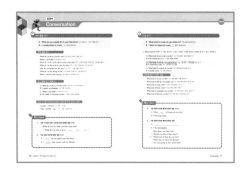

Step1 핵심 의사소통 소통에 필요한 주요 표현 방법 요약
핵심 Check 기본적인 표현 방법 및 활용능력 확인

Step2 대화문 익히기 교과서 대화문 심층 분석 및 확인

Step3 교과서 확인학습 빈칸 채우기를 통한 문장 완성 능력 확인

Step4 기본평가 시험대비 기초 학습 능력 평가

Step5 실력평가 단원별 수시평가 대비 주관식, 객관식 문제풀이

Step6 서술형 대비 학업성취도 및 수행능력평가 대비 서술형 문제풀이

Grammar

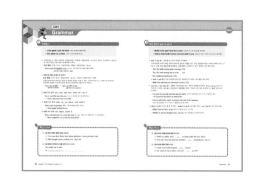

Step1 주요 문법 단원별 주요 문법 사항과 예문을 알기 쉽게 설명
핵심 Check 기본 문법사항에 대한 이해 여부 확인

Step2 기본평가 시험대비 기초 학습 능력 평가

Step3 실력평가 단원별 수시평가 대비 주관식, 객관식 문제풀이

Step4 서술형 대비 학업성취도 및 수행능력평가 대비 서술형 문제풀이

Reading

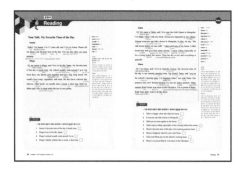

Step1 구문 분석 단원별로 제시된 문장에 대한 구문별 분석과 내용 설명
확인문제 문장에 대한 기본적인 이해와 인지능력 확인

Step2 확인학습A 빈칸 채우기를 통한 문장 완성 능력 확인

Step3 확인학습B 제시된 우리말을 영어로 완성하여 작문 능력 키우기

Step4 실력평가 단원별 수시평가 대비 주관식, 객관식 문제풀이

Step5 서술형 대비 학업성취도 및 수행능력평가 대비 서술형 문제풀이
교과서 구석구석 교과서에 나오는 기타 문장까지 완벽 학습

Composition

|영역별 핵심문제|

단어 및 어휘, 대화문, 문법, 독해 등 각 영역별 기출문제의 출제 유형을 분석하여 실전에 대비하고 연습할 수 있도록 문제를 배열

|단원별 예상문제|

기출문제를 분석한 후 새로운 시험 출제 경향을 더하여 새롭게 출제될 수 있는 문제를 포함하여 시험에 완벽하게 대비할 수 있도록 준비

|서술형 실전 및 창의사고력 문제|

학교 시험에서 점차 늘어나는 서술형 시험에 집중 대비하고 고득점을 취득하는데 만전을 기하기 위한 학습 코너

|단원별 모의고사|

영역별, 단계별 학습을 모두 마친 후 실전 연습을 위한 모의고사

교과서 파헤치기

- **단어Test1~3** 영어 단어 우리말 쓰기, 우리말을 영어 단어로 쓰기, 영영풀이에 해당하는 단어와 우리말 쓰기
- **대화문Test1~2** 대화문 빈칸 완성 및 전체 대화문 쓰기
- **본문Test1~5** 빈칸 완성, 우리말 쓰기, 문장 배열연습, 영어 작문하기 복습 등 단계별 반복 학습을 통해 교과서 지문에 대한 완벽한 습득
- **구석구석지문Test1~2** 지문 빈칸 완성 및 전문 영어로 쓰기

Contents

Lesson 3

Laugh First and Then Think

 의사소통 기능

- 기대 표현하기
  I'm looking forward to seeing you at the race.
- 기원하기
  I'll keep my fingers crossed!

 언어 형식

- enough to
  Is this research project good **enough to** win a Nobel Prize?
- not only ~ but also ...
  Not only the winners' fun studies **but also** the ceremony makes people laugh.

Words & Expressions

Key Words

- **accept** [æksépt] 동 받아들이다
- **actually** [ǽktʃuəli] 부 실제로, 사실은
- **afraid** [əfréid] 형 두려운
- **award** [əwɔ́ːrd] 동 수여하다 명 상
- **backward** [bǽkwərd] 부 뒤로 형 뒤의
- **bomb** [bɑm] 명 폭탄
- **brave** [breiv] 형 용감한
- **ceremony** [sérəmòuni] 명 의식, 식
- **cheer** [tʃiər] 동 응원하다
- **cross** [krɔːs] 동 교차하다 명 십자가
- **discovery** [diskʌ́vəri] 명 발견
- **eager** [íːgər] 형 열렬한, 간절히 바라는
- **economics** 명 경제학
- **feeder** [fíːdər] 명 모이통
- **field trip** 명 현장 학습, 수학여행
- **float** [flout] 동 뜨다
- **guess** [ges] 동 추측하다
- **honor** [ɑ́nər] 동 존중하다 명 명예
- **imaginative** [imǽdʒənətiv] 형 창의적인, 상상력이 풍부한
- **interest** [íntərəst] 명 관심
- **invent** [invént] 동 발명하다
- **invention** [invénʃən] 명 발명, 발명품
- **join** [dʒɔin] 동 참가하다
- **laughable** [lǽfəbl] 형 웃기는
- **live** [laiv] 형 살아 있는
- **lovely** [lʌ́vli] 형 귀여운
- **magnet** [mǽgnit] 명 자석
- **maybe** [méibiː] 부 아마도
- **mistake** [mistéik] 명 실수
- **navy** [néivi] 명 해군
- **nervous** [nə́ːrvəs] 형 긴장한, 초조한
- **opening** [óupəniŋ] 명 개막
- **peace** [piːs] 명 평화
- **perform** [pərfɔ́ːrm] 동 공연하다
- **practice** [prǽktis] 동 연습하다 명 연습
- **present** [prizént] 동 수여하다
- **prize** [praiz] 명 상
- **project** [prɑ́dʒekt] 명 과제
- **race** [reis] 명 경주, 달리기
- **receive** [risíːv] 동 받다
- **repeatedly** [ripíːtidli] 부 반복적으로
- **research** [risə́ːrtʃ] 명 연구, 조사 동 조사하다
- **sailor** [séilər] 명 선원
- **solve** [sɑlv] 동 풀다, 해결하다
- **store** [stɔːr] 동 저장하다
- **study** [stʌ́di] 명 연구
- **tradition** [trədíʃən] 명 전통
- **trillion** [tríljən] 명 1조
- **university** [jùːnəvə́ːrsəti] 명 대학, 대학교
- **unusual** [ənjúːʒuəl] 형 드문, 특이한
- **useful** [júːsfəl] 형 유용한
- **while** [hwail] 접 ~하는 동안, ~인 반면에
- **winner** [wínər] 명 수상자
- **worth** [wəːrθ] 명 가치 형 ~의 가치가 있는

Key Expressions

- **a number of** 얼마간의, 다수의
- **be eager to** ~을 (열렬히) 하고 싶어 하다
- **be filled with** ~로 가득 차다
- **can't wait for** ~를 몹시 기다리다
- **closing speech** 폐막 연설
- **get bored** 지루해지다
- **get out of** ~에서 떠나다, 나가다
- **How about ~?** ~하는 것이 어때?
- **instead of** ~ 대신에
- **keep A from -ing** A가 ~하지 못하게 하다
- **keep -ing** 계속 ~하다
- **keep one's fingers crossed** 행운을 빌다
- **laugh out loud** 큰 소리로 웃다
- **less than** ~ 이하, ~보다 적은
- **look forward to** ~을 기대하다
- **run away** 달아나다
- **sense of humor** 유머 감각
- **succeed in** ~에 성공하다
- **take part in** ~에 참여하다
- **talent show** 장기 자랑

Word Power

※ 서로 비슷한 뜻을 가진 어휘

- □ accept 받다 : obtain 얻다
- □ cheer 응원하다 : encourage 장려하다
- □ actually 실제로 : really 사실은
- □ imaginative 상상력이 풍부한 : original 독창적인

※ 서로 반대의 뜻을 가진 어휘

- □ accept 받다 ↔ reject 거절하다
- □ backward 뒤로 ↔ forward 앞으로
- □ opening 개막 ↔ closing 폐막
- □ usual 일상적인 ↔ unusual 드문, 특이한
- □ float 뜨다 ↔ sink 가라앉다
- □ nervous 불안한 ↔ calm 차분한
- □ present 수여하다 ↔ receive 받다
- □ useful 유용한 ↔ useless 쓸모없는

※ 형용사 – 명사

- □ dark 어두운 – darkness 어두움
- □ happy 행복한 – happiness 행복
- □ sad 슬픈 – sadness 슬픔
- □ eager 열렬한 – eagerness 열망
- □ kind 친절한 – kindness 친절
- □ soft 부드러운 – softness 부드러움

English Dictionary

- □ accept 받아들이다
  → to take something offered 제안된 어떤 것을 취하다
- □ award 수여하다
  → to give a prize 상을 주다
- □ backward 뒤의
  → looking or facing in the direction that is behind you 뒤쪽 방향을 보거나 향하고 있는
- □ discovery 발견
  → the act of finding something for the first time 처음으로 어떤 것을 발견하는 행위
- □ eager 열렬한, 간절히 바라는
  → wanting very much to do or have something 어떤 것을 하거나 갖기를 매우 원하는
- □ float 뜨다, 띄우다
  → to be on a liquid and not sink 액체의 위에 있고 가라앉지 않다
- □ honor (명) 명예
  → something you are proud to do 하기를 자랑스러워하는 어떤 것
  (동) 존경하다
  → to show great respect for someone, esp. in public 특히 공공연히 누군가에 대한 대단한 존경을 보여주다
- □ imaginative 창의적인, 상상력이 풍부
  → having or showing new and exciting ideas 새롭고 흥미로운 생각을 갖거나 보여주는
- □ invent 발명하다
  → to make, design, or think of a new type of thing 새로운 것을 만들거나 디자인하거나 생각해 내다
- □ live 살아 있는
  → not dead 죽지 않은
- □ magnet 자석
  → a piece of metal that attracts other iron 다른 철을 끌어당기는 금속 조각
- □ navy 해군
  → a military force made up of boats and ships 배와 함선으로 이루어진 군대
- □ research 연구, 조사
  → the study of something to discover new facts 새로운 사실들을 발견하기 위한 어떤 것의 연구
- □ sailor 선원
  → someone who works on a ship 배에서 일하는 사람
- □ trillion 1조
  → the number 1,000,000,000,000 1,000,000,000,000이라는 수
- □ university 대학
  → an educational institution at the highest level, where you study for a degree 학위를 받기 위해서 공부하는 가장 높은 수준의 교육 기관

01 다음 글의 빈칸에 〈영어 설명〉에 알맞은 단어를 쓰시오.

> Finding the new land was an amazing _____.
>
> <영어 설명> the act of finding something for the first time

중요

02 다음 빈칸에 공통으로 들어갈 말로 가장 적절한 것은?

> • The friendship between the cat and the dog is quite _____.
> • Some people keep _____ pets such as pigs, iguanas, and even snakes.

① ugly   ② unusual
③ popular   ④ useful
⑤ wonderful

[03~04] 다음 영어 설명에 해당하는 단어를 고르시오.

03

> an educational institution at the highest level, where you study for a degree

① navy   ② honor
③ bomb   ④ university
⑤ research

04

> someone who works on a boat or ship

① sail   ② peace
③ nurse   ④ navy
⑤ sailor

05 다음 우리말에 맞게 주어진 단어를 이용하여 쓰시오.

> 아이들은 어서 수업을 마치고 놀기 시작하고 싶어 했다. (eager / finish)

➡ The children _____ class and start playing.

06 다음 빈칸에 공통으로 들어갈 말로 알맞은 것은?

> (A) On July 16, the Korean _____ contest was held in California, U.S.
> (B) The boy gave a _____ in front of the class.

① rcscarch   ② science
③ speech   ④ trillion
⑤ ceremony

07 다음 짝지어진 단어의 관계가 같도록 알맞은 말을 쓰시오.

> sad – sadness : dark – _____

중요

08 다음 빈칸에 들어갈 말이 바르게 짝지어진 것은?

> (A) The gate _____ people from entering the park.
> (B) The paintings of Leonardo da Vinci are _____ a lot of money.

① keeps – worth
② keeps – eager
③ receives – worth
④ gets – unusual
⑤ gets – eager

01 〈보기〉에서 알맞은 단어를 선택하여 문장의 빈칸을 완성하시오. (필요하면 변형하여 쓰시오.)

┌─ 보기 ─┐
receive repeated bore number
└───────┘

(1) Bring games on an airplane not to get _____.

(2) The kids sang their favorite song _____.

(3) _____ of students failed the test.

(4) He _____ a special card from his grandfather last Christmas.

02 대화의 빈칸에 〈영영 풀이〉에 해당하는 단어를 쓰시오.

B: Minji, you're a happy girl. I think you'll get the Ms. Cheerful _____. I'll keep my fingers crossed!
G: Oh, thank you, Jiho.

〈영영 풀이〉 a prize or other marks of recognition given in honor of an achievement

➡ _____

03 영영 풀이에 해당하는 단어를 〈보기〉에서 찾아 첫 번째 빈칸에 쓰고, 두 번째 빈칸에는 우리말 뜻을 쓰시오.

┌─ 보기 ─┐
ceremony magnet invent navy
└───────┘

(1) _____: a military force made up of boats and ships: _____

(2) _____: a piece of metal that attracts other iron: _____

(3) _____: to make, design, or think of a new type of thing: _____

(4) _____: a formal public event with special traditions: _____

04 다음 우리말에 맞게 주어진 글의 빈칸에 알맞은 단어를 쓰시오.

이것은 '커피 애호가를 위한 우산'입니다. 당신은 그것을 우산뿐만 아니라 컵 걸이로도 사용할 수 있습니다. 이 발명품은 당신의 삶을 훨씬 더 편안하게 할 정도로 충분히 유용합니다.

➡ This is the Umbrella for Coffee Lovers. You can use it _____ as an umbrella _____ as a cup holder. This _____ is _____ to make your life much easier.

05 다음 글의 빈칸에 주어진 철자로 시작하는 알맞은 단어를 쓰시오.

(1) The workers at this company didn't a_____ any gifts from customers.

(2) I think I have a good sense of h_____.

(3) I will study e_____ at university to become a banker.

(4) The large box is f_____ with warm clothes for the poor.

(5) The writer of the children's story is very i_____.

Conversation

1 기대 표현하기

> • I'm looking forward to seeing you at the race. 나는 경기에서 너를 보기를 기대해.

■ 앞으로 일어날 일이나 하고 싶은 일에 대한 기대를 표현할 때 '~을 기대한다'의 의미로 'I'm looking forward to ~.'나 'I look forward to ~.'의 표현을 사용한다. '빨리 ~하고 싶다, ~을 너무 하고 싶다.'의 뜻으로 'I can't wait for ~.', 'I am dying to ~.', 'I'm expecting to ~.'라고 하기노 한다.

■ '~을 기대하다'라는 의미의 'look forward to'에서 to가 전치사이기 때문에 그 뒤에 명사나 동명사가 온다. 'I can't wait for ~.'는 원하던 일이 다가오고 있어 빨리하고 싶은 기대감을 나타내는 표현이며, 직역의 의미는 '~하는 것을 기다릴 수 없다.'이고, 보통 '당장 ~하고 싶다, 빨리 ~했으면 좋겠다.'로 해석한다. to 뒤에는 동사원형의 형태가 오는데, 뒤에 명사구가 올 경우에는 'I can't wait for+명사[명사구]'의 형태로 쓰기도 한다.

■ '기대하다'라는 의미의 expect를 써서 'I'm expecting to 동사원형 ~.'이라고 하거나 '열망하다'라는 의미의 동사 long을 써서 'I'm longing to+동사원형', 'I'm longing for+명사'라고 하거나, 형용사 eager(열망하는)를 써서 'I'm eager to+동사원형', 'I'm eager for+명사'의 형태로 나타내기도 한다.

기대 표현하기

- I'm looking forward to+명사(구) (~을 기대한다.)
- I can't wait for+명사/to+동사원형 (빨리 ~했으면 좋겠다.)
- I am expecting to+동사원형 (~하기를 기대한다.)
- I am longing for+명사/to+동사원형 (~하기를 열망한다.)
- I am eager for+명사/to+동사원형 (~하기를 기대한다.)

핵심 Check

1. 다음 우리말과 일치하도록 주어진 단어를 포함하여 적절한 형태로 빈칸에 알맞은 말을 쓰시오.

A: We're going on a field trip next Tuesday. What are you going to do in the talent show, Jimin?

B: I'm going to talk like our teachers do in class and tell some jokes.

A: Wow! _____. (나는 정말로 그것이 기대가 돼.) (be, really, forward, it)

B: Will everyone like my show? I'm not sure.

➡ _____

② 기원하기

• I'll keep my fingers crossed. 행운을 빌어.

■ 상대가 하는 일이 잘 되기를 기원하면서 '행운을 빌어!'라고 할 때 'I'll keep my finger's crossed (for you)!'라고 한다. 'keep one's fingers crossed'란 집게손가락 위에 가운데 손가락을 교차시켜서 소원이 이루어지도록(= hope for something) 행운을 비는 동작을 묘사한 말로 '기도하다, 좋은 결과나 행운을 빌어준다'라는 의미이다.

■ 흔히 상대에게 행운을 비는 말은 'Good luck!'이고, 'Have a nice ~!'도 상대에게 행운을 기원하는 말이다. 기원이나 기대를 나타내는 wish, expect, hope, pray를 사용하여 행운을 기원하기도 한다. 'Break a leg!(행운을 빌어!)'라는 표현은 주로 공연이나 행사, 경기 등을 앞두고 있는 사람에게 '행운을 빌어!'라고 격려할 때 자주 쓰인다.

■ 긴장한 상대에게 긴장을 풀어주는 표현 'Don't worry.', 'Don't be worried.', 'Just relax.', 'Take it easy.', 'Loosen up.', 'Don't be too nervous.'(긴장 풀어. 너무 긴장하지 마.)에 이어서 행운을 빌어주는 표현을 쓰는 경우가 많다. '기원하다'라는 의미의 'wish'는 'wish+명사, wish+주어+동사'의 형태이다.

기대 표현하기

• I'll keep my fingers crossed (for you)! (행운을 빌게!)

• Let's keep our fingers crossed for you. (행운을 빌어.)

• Good luck! / Good luck to you! (행운을 빌어!)

• I wish you luck! (행운이 함께 하기를 빌어!)

• I wish/hope/pray ~. (나는 ~하길 바란다.)   • Break a leg! (행운을 빌어!)

• I wish you all the best. (행운이 있기를 빌어.)

• I hope everything goes well with you. / Everything will be okay. (다 잘 될 거야.)

핵심 Check

2. 다음 주어진 말에 이어지는 대화의 순서를 바르게 배열하시오.

W: Soyun, are you going to take part in any races on the sports day?

(A) Just do your best. I'll keep my fingers crossed!

(B) Wow, I'm looking forward to seeing you at the race.

(C) But, Mom, I'm not sure I'll win the race.

(D) Sure. I'm going to run a 100 meter race at the end of the day.

➡ _____

Step Up – Real-life Scene

Miso: We're going on a field trip next Tuesday. ❶What are you going to do in the talent show, Jimin?

Jimin: I'm going to talk like our teachers ❷do in class and tell some jokes.

Miso: Wow! I'm really ❸looking forward to it.

Jimin: Will everyone like my show? I'm not sure.

Miso: Don't worry. I'm sure you'll do great. I'll ❹keep my fingers crossed!

Jimin: Thank you, Miso. ❺Let me show you one part of my act. Guess who? "Goood Jooob!"

Miso: Ha-ha, you sound like our English teacher.

Jimin: Do I? I'm going to show you more at the show.

Miso: Great! You always ❻make us laugh out loud.

미소: 다음 주 화요일에 수학여행을 갈 거야. 지민아, 너는 장기 자랑에서 뭘 할 거니?

지민: 나는 수업 시간에 선생님들이 말하는 것을 흉내 내고 농담도 할 거야.

미소: 와! 정말 기대되는데.

지민: 모든 사람이 나의 쇼를 좋아할까? 잘 모르겠어.

미소: 걱정하지 마. 나는 네가 잘 할 거라고 확신해. 행운을 빌어 줄게!

지민: 고마워, 미소야. 내가 나의 연기의 한 부분을 보여 줄게. 누군지 맞힐 수 있겠니? "잘~ 했어~요!"

미소: 하하. 우리 영어 선생님처럼 들리는데.

지민: 그래? 장기 자랑에서 더 많이 보여 줄게.

미소: 멋지다! 너는 항상 우리를 웃게 만들어.

❶ 미래의 계획을 물을 때 사용하는 표현으로 "무엇을 할 예정이니?"의 의미이다.

❷ 앞 문장의 'talk'을 대신하는 대동사이다.

❸ 앞으로 일어날 일이나 하고 싶은 일에 대한 기대를 표현하는 말로, 'look forward to+명사/동명사' 형태이다.

❹ 행운을 빌어줄 때 사용하는 표현으로 '동사(keep)+목적어(my fingers)+목적보어(crossed: 과거분사)'의 5형식 구문이다.

❺ 'let+목적어+동사원형'은 '…가 ~하게 하다'라는 의미이다.

❻ 'make(사역동사)+목적어+목적보어(동사원형)' 구문으로 '…가 ~하게 하다'라는 의미이다.

Check(√) True or False

(1) Miso is looking forward to Jimin's show.　　　　　　　　　T ☐ F ☐

(2) Miso is not sure whether Jimin will do great.　　　　　　　T ☐ F ☐

Start Off – Listen & Talk A 1

G: Mom, ❶I can't wait for the sports day.

W: What are you going to do on that day, Minji?

G: I'm going to play basketball for my class. ❷We've practiced hard for a few weeks.

W: Oh, I'm looking forward to your game.

G: Actually, ❸I'm a little worried. I'm afraid I'll make a mistake.

W: Don't worry. You'll do a good job. I'll keep my fingers crossed!

G: 엄마, 체육 대회가 정말 기다려져요.

W: 민지야, 너는 그날 무엇을 할 거니?

G: 저는 학급을 대표해서 농구를 할 거예요. 우리는 몇 주간 열심히 연습해 왔어요.

W: 오, 너의 경기가 기대되는구나.

G: 사실은, 전 조금 걱정이 돼요. 제가 실수를 할까봐 겁나요.

W: 걱정하지 마. 넌 잘할 거야. 행운을 빌어 줄게!

❶ '~이 정말 기다려져'의 뜻으로 기대를 표현할 때 사용한다.

❷ 현재완료(have practiced)는 기간을 나타내는 for a few weeks와 함께 사용되어 과거부터 현재까지의 계속적인 일을 나타낸다.

❸ '걱정하다'라는 표현으로 'be worried'를 사용한다. a little은 '약간, 조금'의 의미로 과거분사 worried를 수식한다.

Check(√) True or False

(3) Minji is looking forward to the sports day.　　　　　　　T ☐ F ☐

(4) Minji's mother is afraid Minji will make a mistake.　　　　T ☐ F ☐

Start Off – Listen & Talk B

G: Mom, ❶are you coming to the sports day?

W: Sure. I'm going to play the game Kick a Shoe. This will be the first time ❷for me to try it.

G: Don't worry. I'm sure you'll ❸do great. I'll keep my fingers crossed for you!

W: Thank you. I'm also going to perform a funny dance with some other mothers.

G: ❹That sounds fun. I'm looking forward to watching you on the stage.

G: 엄마, 체육 대회에 오실 거예요?

W: 물론이지. 나는 'Kick a Shoe' 게임에 참가할 거야. 이번에 처음 해 보는 거야.

G: 걱정하지 마세요. 엄마는 잘 하실 거예요. 행운을 빌어 드릴게요!

W: 고맙다. 나는 다른 엄마들과 코믹 댄스도 할 거야.

G: 재밌겠네요. 무대에 선 엄마 모습을 보는 것이 기대돼요.

❶ 'are coming(현재진행형)'은 미래 시점과 사용이 될 때 미래의 일을 나타낼 수 있다.

❷ 'for me(for+목적격)'는 to부정사의 의미상의 주어로 '내가'로 해석한다. to부정사 'to try it'은 'the first time'을 수식하는 형용사 용법이다. it = the game Kick a Shoe

❸ do great: 잘하다

❹ 'sound+형용사'로 '~처럼 들리다'라는 뜻이다.

Check(√) True or False

(5) The girl's mom have played the game Kick a Shoe before.   T ☐   F ☐

(6) The girl is looking forward to watching her mom on the stage.   T ☐   F ☐

🔖 **Fun Time**

A: I'm going to travel to Jejudo next week.

B: Wow! That sounds great.

A: Yeah, I'm really looking forward to it.

A: I'm going to ❶enter the dance contest next week, but ❷I'm worried about it.

B: Don't worry. You'll do great. I'll keep my fingers crossed.

A: Thank you.

A: 나는 다음 주에 제주도를 여행할 거야.

B: 와! 멋지다.

A: 응, 난 그것이 정말 기대돼.

A: 난 다음 주에 춤 대회에 나갈 건데, 걱정이 된다.

B: 걱정하지 마. 넌 잘할 거야. 행운을 빌어 줄게.

A: 고마워.

❶ enter는 타동사이므로 전치사 없이 목적어를 취한다.

❷ 'be worried about ~'은 '~에 관해 걱정하다'라는 뜻이다.

Check(√) True or False

(7) A will travel to Jejudo next week.   T ☐   F ☐

(8) B hopes A will do great at the dance contest next week.   T ☐   F ☐

Get Ready 2

(1) G: You solved ❶a lot of problems in class. I'm sure you'll win the Class Brain award.

B: Do you really think so?

G: Of course. I'll keep my fingers crossed for you, Sangjun!

(2) B: The winner of the Oh So Sweet award will get some candies.

G: Oh, I ❷want to get the prize.

B: ❸I'm sure you'll get the prize this time. Good luck, Jiu!

(3) B: ❹I'm looking forward to the Best Joker award this time.

G: Ha-ha. You always ❺make us laugh out loud. So you'll get the prize, Yunki. Good luck.

B: Thank you.

(4) B: Minji, you're a happy girl. I think you'll get the Ms. Cheerful award. I'll keep my fingers crossed!

G: Oh, thank you, Jiho.

❶ 여기서 'a lot of'는 'many'의 의미로 'lots of, plenty of'로 바꾸어 쓸 수 있다.
❷ 'want'는 목적어로 'to-V'를 취한다.
❸ '~을 확신하다'라는 표현으로 'I'm sure (that)+주어+동사 ~'를 사용한다.
❹ 앞으로 일어날 일에 대한 기대를 표현하는 말로 'to'는 전치사로 뒤에 명사나 동명사가 온다.
❺ 'make(사역동사)+목적어+목적보어(동사원형)' 구문으로 '…가 ~하게 하다'라는 의미이다.

Start Off – Listen & Talk A 2

W: Soyun, ❶are you going to take part in any races on the sports day?

G: Sure. ❷I'm going to run a 100 meter race at the end of the day.

W: Wow, ❸I'm looking forward to seeing you at the race.

G: But, Mom, I'm not sure I'll win the race.

W: Just do your best. I'll keep my fingers crossed!

❶ 'take part in ~'은 '~에 참가하다'라는 의미이고, 의문문에서는 '어떤'의 의미로 'any'를 사용한다.
❷ 'be going to+동사원형'은 '~할 예정이다'라는 미래의 일을 나타낼 때 사용한다.
❸ 'look forward to+동명사(seeing)'는 '~을 기대하다'라는 뜻이다.

Start Off – Speak Up

A: I'm looking forward to the model airplane contest tomorrow. Are you ready?

B: Well, ❶I think so, but I'm nervous.

A: You will do well. ❷I'll keep my fingers crossed!

❶ I think so = I think (that) I'm ready
❷ 상대가 하는 일이 잘 되기를 기원하면서 "행운을 빌어!"라고 할 때 사용하는 표현이다.

Express Yourself A

1. G: Can you tell me something about your invention?

B: They are ❶a pair of special shoes. You can also clean the floor with them.

G: Great! I'm sure you'll win a prize. I'll keep my fingers crossed!

2. B: This ❷looks interesting. Is this a cutting board or a bird feeder?

G: It is ❸not only a cutting board but also a bird feeder. You can do two things ❹at the same time.

B: That's a great idea!

G: Do you really think so?

B: Yes. ❺I'm really looking forward to using it.

❶ '신발 한 켤레'를 나타낼 때는 'a pair of shoes'를 쓴다.
❷ 'look+형용사'로 '~처럼 보이다'라는 의미이다.
❸ 'not only A but also B'는 'A뿐만 아니라 B도'의 의미이다.
❹ at the same time: 동시에
❺ 'look forward to+동명사(using)'는 '~을 기대하다'라는 뜻이다.

● 다음 우리말과 일치하도록 빈칸에 알맞은 말을 쓰시오.

Get Ready 2

(1) G: You _____ _____ _____ _____ problems in class. _____ _____ you'll win the Class Brain _____.

　　B: Do you really _____ _____?

　　G: Of course. I'll _____ my fingers _____ for you, Sangjun!

(2) B: The _____ of the Oh So Sweet _____ will get some candies.

　　G: Oh, I want _____ _____ the _____.

　　B: _____ _____ you'll get the prize this time. _____ _____, Jiu!

(3) B: I'm _____ _____ _____ the Best Joker award this time.

　　G: Ha-ha. You always _____ us _____ out loud. So you'll _____ _____ _____, Yunki. Good luck.

　　B: Thank you.

(4) B: Minji, you're a happy girl. I think you'll get the Ms. Cheerful award. I'll _____ _____ _____ _____!

　　G: Oh, thank you, Jiho.

Start Off – Listen & Talk A

1. G: Mom, I _____ _____ _____ the sports day.

　 W: _____ are you _____ _____ _____ on that day, Minji?

　 G: I'm going to play basketball for my class. We've _____ hard _____ a few weeks.

　 W: Oh, I'm _____ _____ _____ your game.

　 G: _____, I'm _____ _____. I'm _____ I'll _____ a _____.

　 W: _____ _____. You'll _____ a good _____. I'll keep _____ _____ _____!

2. W: Soyun, are you going to _____ _____ _____ any races on the sports day?

　 G: Sure. I'_____ _____ _____ run a 100 meter race at the _____ of the day.

　 W: Wow, I'm looking _____ to _____ you at the race.

　 G: But, Mom, I'm not _____ I'll _____ the race.

　 W: Just _____ _____ _____. I'll _____ _____ _____ _____!

Start Off – Listen & Talk B

G: Mom, _____ _____ _____ to the sports day?

W: Sure. I'm _____ to play the game Kick a Shoe. This will be the first time _____ _____ _____ _____ it.

G: Don't worry. I'm _____ you'll _____ _____. I'll _____ my fingers _____ for you!

W: Thank you. I'm also going to _____ a funny dance with some _____ mothers.

G: That _____ _____. I'm _____ _____ to _____ you on the _____.

Start Off – Speak Up

A: I'm _____ _____ _____ the _____ airplane contest tomorrow. Are you _____?

B: Well, I think _____, but I'm _____.

A: You will _____ _____. I'll _____ my fingers _____!

Step Up – Real-life Scene

Miso: We're going on a _____ _____ next Tuesday. What are you going to do in the _____ _____, Jimin?

Jimin: I'm going to talk _____ our teachers _____ in class and tell some _____.

Miso: Wow! I'm really _____ _____ _____ _____.

Jimin: Will everyone like my _____? I'm not _____.

Miso: Don't _____. I'm sure you'll _____ _____. I'll _____ _____ _____ _____!

Jimin: Thank you, Miso. _____ me _____ you one part of my act. _____ who? "Goood Jooob!"

Miso: Ha-ha, you _____ _____ our English teacher.

Jimin: Do I? I'm going to _____ you more at the show.

Miso: Great! You always _____ us _____ _____ _____.

해석

G: 엄마, 체육 대회에 오실 거예요?

W: 물론이지. 나는 'Kick a Shoe' 게임에 참가할 거야. 이번에 처음 해 보는 거야.

G: 걱정하지 마세요. 엄마는 잘하실 거예요. 행운을 빌어 드릴게요!

W: 고맙다. 나는 다른 엄마들과 코믹 댄스도 할 거야.

G: 재밌겠네요. 무대에 선 엄마 모습을 보는 것이 기대돼요.

B: 나는 내일 모형 비행기 대회가 기대돼. 너는 준비됐니?

G: 음, 그런 것 같아. 하지만 긴장돼.

B: 너는 잘할 거야. 내가 행운을 빌어 줄게!

미소: 다음 주 화요일에 수학여행을 갈 거야. 지민아, 너는 장기 자랑에서 뭘 할 거니?

지민: 나는 수업 시간에 선생님들이 말하는 것을 흉내 내고 농담도 할 거야.

미소: 와! 정말 기대되는데.

지민: 모든 사람이 나의 쇼를 좋아할까? 잘 모르겠어.

미소: 걱정하지 마. 나는 네가 잘할 거라고 확신해. 행운을 빌어 줄게!

지민: 고마워, 미소야. 내가 나의 연기의 한 부분을 보여 줄게. 누군지 맞힐 수 있겠니? "잘~ 했어~요!"

미소: 하하. 우리 영어 선생님처럼 들리는데.

지민: 그래? 장기 자랑에서 더 많이 보여 줄게.

미소: 멋지다! 너는 항상 우리를 웃게 만들어.

Fun Time

A: I'_____ _____ _____ travel to Jejudo next week.

B: Wow! That _____ _____.

A: Yeah, I'_____ _____ _____ _____ _____ it.

A: I'm going to _____ the dance contest next week, but I'_____ _____ _____ it.

B: Don't worry. You'll do great. I'll _____ _____ _____ _____.

A: Thank you.

Express Yourself A

1. **G:** _____ _____ _____ _____ something about your _____?

   B: They are _____ _____ _____ _____ shoes. You can also _____ the _____ with them.

   G: Great! I'm sure you'll _____ _____ _____. I'll _____ my fingers crossed!

2. **B:** This looks _____. Is this a _____ _____ or a bird _____?

   G: It is _____ _____ a cutting _____ _____ _____ a bird _____. You can do two things _____ _____ _____ _____.

   B: That's a great _____!

   G: Do you really think so?

   B: Yes. I'm really _____ _____ to _____ it.

해석

A: 나는 다음 주에 제주도를 여행할 거야.
B: 와! 멋지다.
A: 응, 난 그것이 정말 기대돼.

A: 나 다음 주에 춤 대회에 나갈 거데, 걱정이 된다.
B: 걱정하지 마. 넌 잘할 거야. 행운을 빌어 줄게.
A: 고마워.

1. G: 너의 발명품에 관해 이야기를 좀 해 줄래?
   B: 그것은 특별한 신발이야. 너는 그것으로 바닥을 청소할 수도 있어.
   G: 멋지다! 네가 상을 탈 거라고 확신해. 행운을 빌게!

2. B: 이것은 흥미로워 보여. 도마니, 아니면 새 모이통이니?
   G: 그것은 도마일 뿐만 아니라 새 모이통이기도 해. 너는 동시에 두 가지를 할 수 있어.
   B: 멋진 아이디어야!
   G: 정말 그렇게 생각하니?
   B: 응. 난 그것을 사용해 보는 게 정말 기대가 되는 걸.

Conversation 시험대비 기본평가

01 다음 우리말에 맞도록 주어진 단어를 활용하여 4단어로 쓰시오.

> 행운을 빌어. (keep, fingers, cross)

➡ I'll _____ .

02 다음 대화의 빈칸에 들어갈 말로 알맞은 것은?

> B: I'm looking forward to the Best Joker award this time.
> G: Ha-ha. _____ So you'll get the prize,
>   Yunki. Good luck.
> B: Thank you.

① We've practiced hard for a few weeks.

② I'm looking forward to seeing your photos.

③ You always make us laugh out loud.

④ That sounds great.

⑤ Joker is my favorite movie of all.

03 다음 대화의 빈칸에 들어갈 말로 적절한 것은?

> B: The winner of the Oh So Sweet award will get some candies.
> G: Oh, I want to get the prize.
> B: _____ Good luck, Jiu!

① Eating too many candies isn't good for your teeth.

② I'm sure you'll like the candies.

③ Why don't you bring some sweets to your classmates?

④ I don't think so.

⑤ I'm sure you'll get the prize this time.

04 다음 대화의 빈칸에 들어갈 말로 알맞은 것은?

> A: I'm looking forward to the model airplane contest tomorrow.
>   Are you ready?
> B: Well, I think so, but I'm _____ .
> A: You will do well.

① proud   ② nervous   ③ funny

④ cheerful   ⑤ useful

[01~02] 다음 대화를 읽고 물음에 답하시오.

W: Soyun, are you going to take part in any races on the sports day?

G: Sure. I'm going to run a 100 meter race at the end of the day.

W: Wow, I'm looking forward to ___(A)___ (see) you at the race.

G: But, Mom, I'm not sure I'll win the race.

W: Just do your best. I'll keep my fingers ___(B)___ (cross)!

서답형

01 위 대화의 빈칸 (A)와 (B)에 주어진 단어를 알맞은 형태로 고치시오.

➡ (A) _____ (B) _____

02 위 대화의 내용과 일치하지 않는 것은?

① They are talking about the sports day.

② Soyun is going to run a 100 meter race.

③ Soyun's mom wants to run the race.

④ Soyun is not sure she'll win the race.

⑤ Soyun's mom hopes that Soyun will do her best.

[03~05] 다음 대화를 읽고 물음에 답하시오.

G: Mom, are you coming to the sports day?

W: Sure. I'm going ⓐto play the game Kick a Shoe. This will be the first time ⓑfor me to try it.

G: Don't worry. I'm sure you'll ⓒdo great. (A) I'll keep my fingers crossed for you!

W: Thank you. I'm also going to perform a funny dance with some ⓓother mothers.

G: That sounds fun. I'm looking forward ⓔto watch you on the stage.

중요

03 위 대화의 밑줄 친 ⓐ~ⓔ 중 어법상 어색한 것은?

① ⓐ   ② ⓑ   ③ ⓒ   ④ ⓓ   ⑤ ⓔ

04 위 대화의 밑줄 친 (A)와 바꾸어 사용할 수 없는 표현은?

① Let's keep our fingers crossed for you.

② Good luck to you!

③ I wish you all the best.

④ Don't be worried. Just relax.

⑤ Break a leg!

서답형

05 위 대화를 읽고 다음 질문에 영어로 답하시오.

Q: What is Mom going to take part in?

➡ She is going to take part in _____

_____ .

[06~07] 다음 대화를 읽고 물음에 답하시오.

B: This looks interesting. Is this a cutting board or a bird feeder?

G: _____(A)_____ You can do two things at the same time.

B: That's a great idea!

G: Do you really think so?

B: Yes. (B)난 그것을 사용해 보는 게 정말 기대가 되는 걸.

06 위 대화의 빈칸 (A)에 들어갈 말로 알맞은 것은?

① It is either a cutting board or a bird feeder.

② You can use it only as a bird feeder.

③ It is neither a cutting board nor a bird feeder.

④ It is only a cutting board.

⑤ It is not only a cutting board but also a bird feeder.

서답형

07 위 대화의 밑줄 친 (B)의 우리말에 맞게 주어진 단어를 활용
하여 영어로 쓰시오.

> be, really, forward, use, it

➡ _____

[08~09] 다음 대화를 읽고 물음에 답하시오.

> Miso: We're going on a field trip next
> Tuesday. What are you going to do in the
> talent show, Jimin? (①)
> Jimin: I'm going to talk like our teachers do
> in class and tell some jokes. (②)
> Miso: Wow! I'm really looking forward to it.
> Jimin: Will everyone like my show? I'm not
> sure.
> Miso: Don't worry. (③) I'm sure you'll do
> great. I'll keep my fingers crossed!
> Jimin: Thank you, Miso. (④) Guess who?
> "Goood Jooob!" (⑤)
> Miso: Ha-ha, you sound like our English
> teacher.
> Jimin: Do I? I'm going to show you more at
> the show.
> Miso: Great! You always make us laugh out
> loud.

08 위 대화의 (①)~(⑤) 중 주어진 문장이 들어갈 위치로 알맞
은 것은?

> Let me show you one part of my act.

①   ②   ③   ④   ⑤

09 위 대화를 읽고 답할 수 없는 질문은?

① What are Jimin and Miso talking about?

② When is the field trip?

③ What is Jimin going to do in the talent
show?

④ Why is Miso looking forward to Jimin's
show?

⑤ How many times has Jimin ever taken
part in a talent show?

[10~11] 다음 대화를 읽고 물음에 답하시오.

> G: Mom, _____(A)_____
> W: What are you going to do on that day,
> Minji?
> G: I'm going to play basketball for my class.
> We've practiced hard for a few weeks.
> W: Oh, (B)너의 경기가 기대되는구나.
> G: Actually, I'm a little worried. I'm afraid I'll
> make a mistake.
> W: Don't worry. You'll do a good job. I'll
> keep my fingers crossed!

중요

10 위 대화의 빈칸 (A)에 들어갈 말로 알맞은 것은?

① are you going to take part in any races
on the sports day?

② are you coming on the sports day?

③ I think I'll get the Ms. Cheerful award.

④ I can't wait for the sports day.

⑤ are you ready?

서답형

11 위 대화의 밑줄 친 (B)의 우리말에 맞게 주어진 단어를 활용
하여 영작하시오.

(be / look / to / your game)

➡ _____

[01~02] 다음 대화를 읽고 물음에 답하시오.

Miso: We're going on a field trip next Tuesday. What are you going to do in the talent show, Jimin?

Jimin: I'm going to talk like our teachers do in class and tell some jokes.

Miso: Wow! _____ (A)

Jimin: Will everyone like my show? I'm not sure.

Miso: Don't worry. I'm sure you'll do great.
_____ (B)

Jimin: Thank you, Miso. Let me show you one part of my act. Guess who? "Goood Jooob!"

Miso: Ha-ha, you sound like our English teacher.

Jimin: Do I? I'm going to show you more at the show.

Miso: Great! You always make us laugh out loud.

01 위 대화의 빈칸 (A)와 (B)에 들어갈 말을 〈조건〉에 맞게 영어로 쓰시오.

┌─ 조건 ┐
(A) • 기대를 표현하는 말을 쓸 것.
   • 현재진행형과 대명사 'it'을 사용할 것.
(B) • 기원을 표현하는 말을 쓸 것.
   • 'keep'과 'cross'를 활용할 것.
└────────┘

➡ (A) _____
  (B) _____

02 위 대화를 읽고 다음 물음에 영어로 답하시오.

Who did Jimin talk like in the dialog?

➡ _____

03 다음 대화의 밑줄 친 부분과 같은 의미가 되도록 주어진 단어를 써서 문장을 다시 쓰시오.

B: This looks interesting. Is this a cutting board or a bird feeder?

G: It is a bird feeder as well as a cutting board.(only, also) You can do two things at the same time.

B: That's a great idea!

G: Do you really think so?

B: Yes. I'm really looking forward to using it.

➡ _____

[04~05] 다음 대화를 읽고 물음에 답하시오.

G: Mom, (a)체육 대회가 정말 기다려져요.

W: What are you going to do on that day, Minji?

G: I'm going to play basketball for my class. We've practiced hard for a few weeks.

W: Oh, I'm looking forward to your game.

G: Actually, I'm a little worried.
_____ (A)

W: Don't worry. You'll do a good job.

04 위 대화의 흐름상 빈칸 (A)에 들어갈 말을 주어진 단어를 이용하여 영작하시오.

(afraid, a mistake)

➡ _____

05 위 대화의 밑줄 친 (a)의 우리말을 주어진 〈조건〉을 이용하여 영작하시오.

┌─ 조건 ┐
• 'wait'을 이용할 것.
• the sports day
└────────┘

➡ _____

Grammar
교과서

① enough to

> • Is this research project good **enough to** win a Nobel Prize?
> 이 연구 과제는 노벨상을 받을 정도로 훌륭할까?

■ 형태: 형용사/부사+enough to+동사원형
  의미: '~할 만큼 충분히 ~한/하게'

■ 'enough'는 형용사/부사 뒤에 위치한다.

  • My bag is big **enough to** hold as many as 5 books.
  나의 가방은 책을 5권이나 담을 수 있을 만큼 충분히 크다.

■ to부정사의 의미상 주어가 문장의 주어와 다를 경우 to부정사 앞에 'for+목적격'을 쓴다.

  • The weather was warm **enough for the kids to play** outside.
  날씨가 아이들이 밖에 나가서 놀 수 있을 만큼 충분히 따뜻했다.

■ 'so+형용사/부사+that+주절의 주어(또는 의미상 주어)+can+동사원형(+목적어)'으로 바꾸어 쓸 수 있다.

  • She is **smart enough to understand** the difficult question.

  = She is **so smart that she can understand** the difficult question.
  그녀는 그 어려운 문제를 이해할 만큼 충분히 똑똑하다.

  • This soup tastes **good enough for me to enjoy**.

  = This soup tastes **so good that I can enjoy it**.
  이 수프는 내가 즐기기에 충분히 맛이 좋다.

핵심 Check

1. 다음 괄호 안에서 알맞은 것을 고르시오.

 (1) I'm (enough strong / strong enough) to carry the big box.

 (2) Did you work hard enough (winning / to win) the contest?

 (3) This textbook is easy enough (for young students / of young students) to read.

② not only ~ but also ...

> • **Not only** the winners' fun studies **but also** the ceremony makes people laugh.
>
> 수상자들의 재밌는 연구들뿐만 아니라 시상식도 또한 사람들을 웃게 만든다.

- 형태: not only ~ but also …
  의미: ~뿐만 아니라 …도

- 두 단어가 짝을 이루어 하나의 접속사 역할을 하는 상관접속사로, 상관접속사로 연결되는 두 어구의 형태를 일치시킨다.

  • Jack is **not only** kind **but also** smart. (형용사)
  Jack은 친절할 뿐만 아니라 똑똑하기도 하다.

  • We can **not only** meet the singer **but also** take a picture with him. (동사원형)
  우리는 그 가수를 만날 수 있을 뿐만 아니라 그와 사진을 찍을 수도 있다.

- '… as well as ~'로 바꾸어 쓸 수 있다.

  • This coffee **not only** tastes fresh **but also** has rich aromas.

  = This coffee has rich aromas **as well as** tastes fresh.
  이 커피는 맛이 신선할 뿐만 아니라 풍부한 향을 가지고 있다.

- 'Not only ~ but also …'가 주어로 쓰일 경우 수의 일치는 'but also'와 쓰인 주어에 맞춘다.

  • **Not only** Jenny **but also** her parents were born in New Zealand.
  Jenny뿐만 아니라 그녀의 부모님들도 뉴질랜드에서 태어났다.

핵심 Check

2. 다음 괄호 안에서 알맞은 것을 고르시오.

(1) The dancers performed not only beautifully but also (intense / intensely).

(2) This vegetable is not only nutritious (and / but) also delicious.

(3) Not only (they are / are they) dangerous but also they can harm the environment.

01 다음 우리말에 맞게 괄호 안에 주어진 단어를 이용하여 문장을 완성하시오.

(1) 그 밴드는 상을 수상할 정도로 충분히 인기 있다. (popular, win, award)

➡ The band is _____.

(2) 우리의 노래들은 부르기에 충분히 쉽다. (easy, sing)

➡ Our songs _____.

(3) 그는 용감할 뿐만 아니라 매우 친절하다. (brave, nice)

➡ He is not only _____.

(4) Ann은 사랑스러울 뿐만 아니라 똑똑하다. (lovely, smart)

➡ Ann _____.

02 다음 문장에서 어법상 <u>어색한</u> 부분을 바르게 고쳐 쓰시오.

(1) Their music is enough great to make their fans excited.

➡ _____

(2) Their fans are excited enough crying out.

➡ _____

(3) Pinocchio is not only popular but also very nicely.

➡ _____

(4) I know not only the meaning of "eager" but also "eagerness".

➡ _____

03 다음 〈보기〉의 문장을 참고하여 주어진 두 문장을 한 문장으로 바꾸어 쓰시오.

┌─ 보기 ─
│ My mom is brave. She can climb the high mountain.
│ → My mom is brave enough to climb the high mountain.
└

(1) The singer is tall. She can reach the shelf.

➡ _____

(2) The flower is big. It can cover the woman's face.

➡ _____

01 다음 빈칸에 'enough'가 들어갈 수 <u>없는</u> 하나를 고르시오.

① She is rich _____ to have a fancy car.
② Ann is brave _____ to catch the bug.
③ I have _____ time to meet you.
④ Do we have _____ paint for the wall?
⑤ Leslie is _____ shy to raise her hand.

02 다음 두 문장을 한 문장으로 바르게 바꾸면?

> • I teach German to the students.
> • Oliver teaches German to the students, too.

① Either I or Oliver teaches German to the students.
② Not only I but also Oliver teach German to the students.
③ Oliver as well as I teaches German to the students.
④ Neither I nor Oliver teaches German to the students.
⑤ Both I and Oliver teaches German to the students.

03 다음 빈칸에 들어갈 말로 적절한 것은?

> It was warm _____ for children to play soccer outside.

① so　　　② very　　　③ too
④ enough　　　⑤ as

04 다음 중 어법상 어색한 문장을 고르시오.

① He is not only kind but also intelligent.
② I like to play soccer as well as baskctball.
③ Not only Tom but also Susie will take part in the contest.
④ You as well as he have a sister.
⑤ He enjoys not only cooking but also to eat.

05 다음 문장의 뜻이 나머지 넷과 <u>다른</u> 것은?

① Because it was so cold, we stayed in the classroom.
② It was so cold that we stayed in the classroom.
③ It was very cold, so we stayed in the classroom.
④ It was cold enough for us to stay in the classroom.
⑤ It was too cold for us to stay in the classroom.

06 빈칸에 들어갈 말을 순서대로 바르게 연결한 것은?

> • The movie was _____ touching that I almost cried.
> • She was _____ sad to go to the party.

① so　　　– so
② so　　　– enough
③ so　　　– too
④ enough　– too
⑤ enough　– so

서답형

07 다음 괄호 안에 주어진 어구를 바르게 배열하여 문장을 다시 쓰시오.

> The room is (enough, up to 100 people, to accommodate, big).

➡ _____

_____

08 다음 문장과 같은 뜻을 가진 것은?

> She is so tall that she can reach the ceiling.

① She is tall enough that she can reach the ceiling.
② She is too tall to reach the ceiling.
③ She is enough tall to reach the ceiling.
④ She is tall enough to reach the ceiling.
⑤ She is so tall to reach the ceiling.

서답형

09 다음 문장에서 어법상 어색한 것을 바르게 고쳐 다시 쓰시오.

(1) He was so diligent that he can finish the work.

➡ _____

_____

(2) Tom as well as his parents are eating chicken.

➡ _____

_____

서답형

10 다음 두 문장을 'enough to'를 사용하여 한 문장으로 바꿔 쓰시오.

> • The puzzle was so easy.
> • I could solve it.

➡ _____

중요

11 다음 중 어법상 어색한 문장을 고르시오.

① Not only my dad but also my uncle are going to quit smoking.
② Harry as well as you is very famous now.
③ Not only children but also adults like the movie *Frozen*.
④ Not only you but also he was interested in the game.
⑤ Not only the teacher but also her students try their best.

서답형

12 다음 괄호 안에서 알맞은 말을 고르시오.

(1) The girl was (enough nice / nice enough) to help the poor.
(2) The box is (too / enough) big to put in the car.
(3) The princess was brave enough (to fight / fighting) the monster.
(4) This coat is so warm that I (wear / wear it) in winter.
(5) The computer is so fast that (to run / it can run) the program.

13 다음 밑줄 친 우리말을 영어로 바르게 옮긴 것은? (2개)

> Mary뿐만 아니라 John도 joined the drama club.

① Not only Mary but also John
② Not John but Mary
③ Neither Mary nor John
④ John as well as Mary
⑤ Either John or Mary

14 다음 괄호 안에 주어진 어구를 바르게 배열하여 문장을 다시 쓰시오.

> This building (to survive / is / strong / a heavy storm / enough).

➡ _____

_____

15 주어진 어휘를 이용하여 다음 우리말을 영어로 쓰시오.

> 그 책은 여러 번 읽을 만큼 충분히 흥미롭다. (interesting, several times)

➡ _____

_____

16 다음 중 내용상 어색한 문장을 고르시오.

① He was so young that he couldn't go to school.
② It was so hot that we went to the pool.
③ She was brave enough to stand up for the truth.
④ He was too strong to carry all the books.
⑤ The box is light enough for a young child to lift up.

17 빈칸에 들어갈 말을 순서대로 바르게 연결한 것은?

> • Both Tom and Ann _____ late.
> • I'm hungry _____ to eat all the food.

① were – too   ② was – enough
③ were – so   ④ was – too
⑤ were – enough

18 주어진 어휘를 이용하여 다음 우리말을 영어로 쓰시오.

> 그 강은 거대한 배가 항해할 수 있을 만큼 충분히 깊다. (a huge ship, enough, sail on, deep)

➡ _____

19 다음 두 문장을 한 문장으로 바르게 옮긴 것은?

> • He is very smart.
> • He can put a 500-piece puzzle together.

① He is too smart to put a 500-piece puzzle together.
② He is so smart to put a 500-piece puzzle together.
③ He is smart enough to put a 500-piece puzzle together.
④ He is smart so that he can put a 500-piece puzzle together.
⑤ He is smart so that he can't put a 500-piece puzzle together.

20 대화의 빈칸에 적절한 말을 주어진 단어를 알맞은 형태로 바꾸어 써 넣으시오.

(1) A: I think Winnie the Pooh is very heavy. What do you think?
    B: He is not only heavy but also very _____. (love)
(2) A: I think Hong Gildong is very fast. What do you think?
    B: He is not only fast but also very _____. (strength)

01 'not only ~ but also ...'를 이용하여 두 문장을 한 문장으로 쓰시오.

(1) • Eric is kind.
   • Eric is smart.
   ➡ _____

(2) • Jake is a student.
   • You are a student.
   ➡ _____

(3) • She was hardworking.
   • She was honest.
   ➡ _____

(4) • You run fast.
   • He runs fast.
   ➡ _____

(5) • You are going to join our club.
   • He is going to join our club.
   ➡ _____

02 다음 우리말을 주어진 어휘를 이용하여 영어로 옮기시오.

(1) 이 발명품은 너의 삶을 훨씬 쉽게 만들어 줄 만큼 충분히 유용하다. (invention, useful, enough, make, much easier)
   ➡ _____
   _____

(2) 너의 미소는 교실을 밝혀줄 만큼 충분히 환하다. (smile, bright, enough, light up)
   ➡ _____
   _____

(3) 너는 우리를 행복하게 만들 뿐만 아니라 우리가 잘 지내도록 도와준다. (not only, make, help, get along well)
   ➡ _____
   _____

03 다음 문장을 괄호 안의 어구를 써서 문장을 다시 쓰시오.

(1) You can use it not only as a door but also as a table for playing table tennis. (as well as)
   ➡ _____
   _____

(2) She was so kind that she showed me how to use chopsticks. (enough to)
   ➡ _____
   _____

04 잘못된 부분을 바르게 고쳐 문장을 다시 쓰시오.

(1) Mark visited not only his mother also his friends.
   ➡ _____
   _____

(2) This building is strong enough surviving a heavy storm.
   ➡ _____

(3) He is enough tall to touch the ceiling.
   ➡ _____
   _____

(4) They sell not only eggs but also to milk.
   ➡ _____
   _____

(5) The box is too heavy for the girl to move it.
   ➡ _____
   _____

05 다음 두 문장을 'enough to부정사'를 이용하여 한 문장으로 바르게 바꿔 쓰시오.

> • The water is very clean.
> • We can drink it.

➡ _____

⑥6 (중요) 다음 그림을 보고 괄호 안의 단어를 활용하여 문장을 완성하시오.

(1)

Umbrella for Coffee Lovers

> This is the Umbrella for Coffee Lovers. You can use it not only as an umbrella _____. (but also, cup holder)

(2)

Magic Stairs

> These are Magic Stairs. You can use them not only for going up and down _____. (but also, store, things)

(3)

LED Shoes

> These are LED Shoes. You can use them not only as shoes _____. (but also, lights)

07 다음 (A), (B) 문장을 괄호 안의 지시대로 바꿔 쓰시오.

> (A) He is not only a teacher but also a painter. (as well as를 써서)
> (B) She looks wise as well as friendly. (not only ~ but also를 써서)

➡ (A) _____
　 (B) _____

08 (고난이도) 다음 문장을 어법에 맞게 고쳐 쓰시오.

(1) He is tall very to be a basketball player.

➡ _____
_____

(2) Sumin ran enough fast to get there on time.

➡ _____
_____

(3) The girl was brave too to speak in front of many people.

➡ _____
_____

(4) It is warm enough plays outside.

➡ _____
_____

(5) He's cheerful enough making us feel happy.

➡ _____
_____

Reading

교과서

The Ig Nobel Prize

"What happens when you walk backward while you are carrying a cup of coffee?" Han Jiwon, a Korean high school student, did research on this topic in 2015. Is this research project good enough to win a Nobel Prize? Maybe not. But how about an Ig Nobel Prize? He won one in 2017 for this fun research.

The Ig Nobel Prizes are awarded for discoveries that "first make one laugh and then think." They were started in 1991 by *AIR* magazine to increase people's interest in science by honoring the unusual and the imaginative.

The prizes are presented by real Nobel winners in Sanders Theater at Harvard University. The room is usually filled with people who are eager to cheer for the brave scientists with their "laughable" research.

The U.K. Navy won the Ig Nobel Prize for Peace in 2000. To save money, the Navy made its sailors shout, "Bang!" instead of using real bombs. Is that funny enough for you to laugh out loud?

Andre Geim also won an award that year. He succeeded in floating a live frog in the air by using magnets. "In my experience, if people don't have a sense of humor, they are usually not very good scientists," he said when he accepted his award.

---

magnet 자석
float 뜨다, 띄우다
research 연구, 조사
award 상; 수여하다
discovery 발견
increase 증가시키다, 늘리다
honor 명예; 존경하다
unusual 특이한, 색다른
imaginative 창의적인, 상상력이 풍부한
university 대학교
be filled with …로 가득 차다
eager 열렬한, 간절히 바라는
be eager to …을 (열렬히) 하고 싶어 하다
peace 평화
sailor 선원
instead of … 대신에
bomb 폭탄
navy 해군
succeed 성공하다
sense 감각
humor 유머, 익살
accept 받아들이다

 확인문제

● 다음 문장이 본문의 내용과 일치하면 T, 일치하지 <u>않으면</u> F를 쓰시오.

1 Han Jiwon won an Ig Nobel Prize in 2017 for this fun research. ☐

2 The Ig Nobel Prizes are awarded for discoveries that "first make one think and then laugh." ☐

3 *AIR* magazine started the Ig Nobel Prizes in 1991. ☐

4 The Ig Nobel Prizes are presented by former Ig Nobel winners. ☐

5 The U.K. Navy won the Ig Nobel Prize for Peace in 2000. ☐

If that still does not bring a smile to your face, how about this?
= what about

In 2005, Gauri Nanda won the Ig Nobel Prize in Economics
in: [성질·능력·기예 등의 분야를 한정하여] ···에서

for inventing an alarm clock. It keeps running away until the sleeper
for: [이유·원인] ··· 때문에, ···으로 (인하여)   keep ~ing: 계속해서 ~하다

finally gets out of bed.
– at last

Not only the winners' fun studies but also the ceremony for the Ig
not only A but also B = B as well as A: A뿐만 아니라 B도

Nobel Prizes makes people laugh. There are a number of interesting
make(×)   a number of: 많은. the number of: ~의 수

things that keep people from getting bored. The opening and closing
keep/stop/prevent/prohibit A from ~ing: A가 ~하지 못하게 하다

speeches are just two words each: "Welcome. Welcome." and

"Goodbye. Goodbye." If someone talks for too long, an eight-year-

old girl called Miss Sweetie Poo shouts repeatedly, "Please stop! I'm
called 앞에 주격 관계대명사 who와 be동사가 생략되어 있다.   = over and over (again)

bored." Each winner receives ten trillion Zimbabwean dollars, which
boring(×)

is worth less than one U.S. dollar. Throwing paper planes is another
be worth: ~의 가치가 있다   동명사 주어   are(×)

fun tradition.

The Ig Nobel Prize ceremony ends with the words, "If you didn't
end with: ···으로 끝나다   = Unless you won

win a prize — and if you did — better luck next year!" The winners do
'won a prize'를 대신하는 대동사

not receive lots of money. And the awards are not great honors like the
= much   ···와 (똑)같이[마찬가지로]

Nobel Prizes. But the Ig Nobel Prizes make science a lot more fun!
비교급을 강조

economics 경제학
get out of ···에서 떠나다, 나가다
ceremony 의식, 식
a number of 얼마간의, 다수의
keep ... from ···가 ~하지 못하게 하다
get bored 지루해지다
speech 연설, 담화
repeatedly 반복적으로
receive 받다
trillion 1조
worth ···의 가치가 있는

확인문제

● 다음 문장이 본문의 내용과 일치하면 T, 일치하지 <u>않으면</u> F를 쓰시오.

1 In 2005, Gauri Nanda won the Ig Nobel Prize in Economics for inventing an alarm clock. ☐

2 The alarm clock keeps running after the sleeper until the sleeper finally gets out of bed. ☐

3 The ceremony for the Ig Nobel Prizes as well as the winners' fun studies makes people laugh. ☐

4 There are a number of things that keep people bored. ☐

5 The opening and closing speeches are just two words each. ☐

6 Ten trillion Zimbabwean dollars is worth more than one U.S. dollar. ☐

● 우리말을 참고하여 빈칸에 알맞은 말을 쓰시오.

1 The _____ _____ Prize

2 "What _____ when you walk _____ while you are carrying a cup of coffee?"

3 Han Jiwon, a Korean high school student, _____ _____ on this topic in 2015.

4 Is this research project good _____ _____ win a Nobel Prize?

5 _____ not.

6 But _____ _____ an Ig Nobel Prize?

7 He won _____ in 2017 for this fun research.

8 The Ig Nobel Prizes _____ _____ _____ discoveries that "first make one _____ and then _____."

9 They were started in 1991 by *AIR* magazine to increase people's interest in science _____ _____ _____ _____ and _____ _____.

10 The prizes _____ _____ _____ real Nobel winners in Sanders Theater at Harvard University.

11 The room _____ usually _____ _____ people who are eager to cheer for the brave scientists with their "_____" research.

12 The U.K. Navy won the Ig Nobel Prize _____ Peace in 2000.

13 _____ _____ money, the Navy made its sailors shout, "Bang!" _____ _____ using real bombs.

14 Is that funny enough for you to _____ _____ _____?

15 Andre Geim also _____ _____ _____ that year.

16 He _____ _____ _____ a live frog in the air by using magnets.

---

1 이그노벨상

2 "당신이 커피 한 잔을 들고 가면서 뒤로 걸을 때 무슨 일이 일어날까?"

3 한국의 한 고등학생인 한지원은 2015년에 이 주제에 관해 연구했다.

4 이 연구 과제는 노벨상을 받을 정도로 훌륭할까?

5 아마도 아닐 것이다.

6 하지만 이그노벨상은 어떤가?

7 그는 이 재미있는 연구로 2017년에 상을 탔다.

8 이그노벨상은 '먼저 웃기고 나서 다음에 생각하게 하는' 발견에 수여된다.

9 그것은 특이하고 창의적인 사람들을 높이 평가함으로써 과학에 대한 사람들의 흥미를 늘리기 위해 AIR 잡지에 의해 1991년에 시작되었다.

10 그 상들은 하버드 대학의 Sanders 극장에서 진짜 노벨상 수상자들에 의해 수여된다.

11 그 방은 대개 '웃기는' 연구를 한 용감한 과학자들을 열렬히 격려하고자 하는 사람들로 가득 찬다.

12 영국 해군은 2000년에 이그노벨 평화상을 탔다.

13 돈을 아끼기 위해, 해군에서는 선원들에게 진짜 폭탄을 사용하는 대신에 "쾅!"이라고 소리치게 했다.

14 그것이 당신이 큰 소리로 웃을 정도로 우스운가?

15 Andre Geim도 그해에 상을 탔다.

16 그는 자석을 이용해서 살아 있는 개구리를 공중에 띄우는 데 성공했다.

17 "In my experience, if people don't have _____ _____ _____ _____, they are usually not very good scientists," he said when he accepted his award.

18 If that still does not _____ a smile _____ your face, how about this?

19 In 2005, Gauri Nanda won the Ig Nobel Prize _____ Economics _____ inventing an alarm clock.

20 It _____ _____ _____ until the sleeper finally gets out of bed.

21 _____ _____ the winners' fun studies _____ _____ the ceremony for the Ig Nobel Prizes _____ people laugh.

22 There are _____ _____ _____ interesting things that _____ people _____ _____ _____.

23 The opening and closing speeches are just _____ _____ _____: "Welcome. Welcome." and "Goodbye. Goodbye."

24 If someone talks for too long, _____ _____ _____ Miss Sweetie Poo shouts repeatedly, "Please stop! I'm bored."

25 Each winner receives ten trillion Zimbabwean dollars, which is _____ _____ _____ one U.S. dollar.

26 _____ paper planes _____ another fun tradition.

27 The Ig Nobel Prize ceremony _____ _____ the words, "If you didn't win a prize — and if you _____ — better luck next year!"

28 The winners _____ _____ _____ lots of money.

29 And the awards are not _____ _____ _____ the Nobel Prizes.

30 But the Ig Nobel Prizes make science _____ _____ _____ _____!

17 그는 상을 받을 때, "내 경험상, 사람들이 유머 감각이 없다면, 그들은 대개 별로 훌륭한 과학자가 아니다."라고 말했다.

18 그것이 아직도 당신의 얼굴에 미소를 띠게 하지 않는다면, 이것은 어떤가?

19 2005년에 Gauri Nanda는 자명종을 발명해서 이그노벨 경제학상을 받았다.

20 그것은 잠자는 사람이 결국 침대 밖으로 나올 때까지 계속 도밍을 다닌다.

21 수상자들의 재미있는 연구뿐만 아니라 이그노벨상 시상식도 또한 사람들을 웃게 만든다.

22 사람들이 지루해하지 않도록 하는 재미있는 것들이 많이 있다.

23 개회사와 폐회사는 단지 두 마디이다: "환영합니다. 환영합니다."와 "안녕. 안녕."

24 만일 누군가가 너무 오랫동안 말을 하면, Miss Sweetie Poo라고 하는 여덟 살짜리 여자아이가 "제발 멈춰요! 지루해요."라고 계속 외친다.

25 각 수상자는 10조의 짐바브웨 달러를 받는데, 그것은 미국의 1달러보다 가치가 낮다.

26 종이비행기를 날리는 것은 또 다른 재미있는 전통이다.

27 이그노벨상 시상식은 "만일 당신이 상을 타지 못했다면 – 그리고 만일 탔다면 – 내년에는 좀 더 많은 행운이 있기를!"이라는 말로 끝이 난다.

28 수상자들은 많은 상금을 받지 않는다.

29 그리고 그 상은 노벨상같이 훌륭한 영광은 아니다.

30 하지만 이그노벨상은 과학을 훨씬 더 재미있게 만든다!

● 우리말을 참고하여 본문을 영작하시오.

1 이그노벨상

➡ _____

2 "당신이 커피 한 잔을 들고 가면서 뒤로 걸을 때 무슨 일이 일어날까?"

➡ _____

3 한국의 한 고등학생인 한지원은 2015년에 이 주제에 관해 연구했다.

➡ _____

4 이 연구 과제는 노벨상을 받을 정도로 훌륭할까?

➡ _____

5 아마도 아닐 것이다.

➡ _____

6 하지만 이그노벨상은 어떤가?

➡ _____

7 그는 이 재미있는 연구로 2017년에 상을 탔다.

➡ _____

8 이그노벨상은 '먼저 웃기고 나서 다음에 생각하게 하는' 발견에 수여된다.

➡ _____

9 그것은 특이하고 창의적인 사람들을 높이 평가함으로써 과학에 대한 사람들의 흥미를 늘리기 위해 AIR 잡지에 의해 1991년에 시작되었다.

➡ _____

_____

10 그 상들은 하버드 대학의 Sanders 극장에서 진짜 노벨상 수상자들에 의해 수여된다.

➡ _____

11 그 방은 대개 '웃기는' 연구를 한 용감한 과학자들을 열렬히 격려하고자 하는 사람들로 가득 찬다.

➡ _____

12 영국 해군은 2000년에 이그노벨 평화상을 탔다.

➡ _____

13 돈을 아끼기 위해, 해군에서는 선원들에게 진짜 폭탄을 사용하는 대신에 "쾅!"이라고 소리치게 했다.

➡ _____

14 그것이 당신이 큰 소리로 웃을 정도로 우스운가?

➡ _____

15 Andre Geim도 그해에 상을 탔다.

➡ _____

16 그는 자석을 이용해서 살아 있는 개구리를 공중에 띄우는 데 성공했다.

➡ _____

17 그는 상을 받을 때, "내 경험상, 사람들이 유머 감각이 없다면, 그들은 대개 별로 훌륭한 과학자가 아니다."라고 말했다.

➡ _____

18 그것이 아직도 당신의 얼굴에 미소를 띠게 하지 않는다면, 이것은 어떤가?

➡ _____

19 2005년에 Gauri Nanda는 자명종을 발명해서 이그노벨 경제학상을 받았다.

➡ _____

20 그것은 잠자는 사람이 결국 침대 밖으로 나올 때까지 계속 도망을 다닌다.

➡ _____

21 수상자들의 재미있는 연구뿐만 아니라 이그노벨상 시상식도 또한 사람들을 웃게 만든다.

➡ _____

22 사람들이 지루해하지 않도록 하는 재미있는 것들이 많이 있다.

➡ _____

23 개회사와 폐회사는 단지 두 마디이다: "환영합니다. 환영합니다."와 "안녕. 안녕."

➡ _____

24 만일 누군가가 너무 오랫동안 말을 하면, Miss Sweetie Poo라고 하는 여덟 살짜리 여자아이가 "제발 멈춰요! 지루해요."라고 계속 외친다.

➡ _____

_____

25 각 수상자는 10조의 짐바브웨 달러를 받는데, 그것은 미국의 1달러보다 가치가 낮다.

➡ _____

26 종이비행기를 날리는 것은 또 다른 재미있는 전통이다.

➡ _____

27 이그노벨상 시상식은 "만일 당신이 상을 타지 못했다면 – 그리고 만일 탔다면 – 내년에는 좀 더 많은 행운이 있기를!"이라는 말로 끝이 난다.

➡ _____

_____

28 수상자들은 많은 상금을 받지 않는다.

➡ _____

29 그리고 그 상은 노벨상같이 훌륭한 영광은 아니다.

➡ _____

30 하지만 이그노벨상은 과학을 훨씬 더 재미있게 만든다!

➡ _____

[01~03] 다음 글을 읽고 물음에 답하시오.

"What happens when you walk backward while you are carrying a cup of coffee?" (①) Han Jiwon, a Korean high school student, did research ___ⓐ___ this topic in 2015. (②) Is this research project good enough to win a Nobel Prize? (③) But how about an Ig Nobel Prize? (④) He won one in 2017 ___ⓑ___ this fun research. (⑤)

The Ig Nobel Prizes are awarded for discoveries that "first make one laugh and then think." They were started in 1991 by *AIR* magazine to increase people's interest in science by honoring the unusual and the imaginative.

01 위 글의 빈칸 ⓐ와 ⓑ에 들어갈 전치사가 바르게 짝지어진 것은?

	ⓐ	ⓑ			ⓐ	ⓑ
①	on	–	in	②	about	–	of
③	about	–	in	④	at	–	for
⑤	on	–	for			

02 위 글의 흐름으로 보아, 주어진 문장이 들어가기에 가장 적절한 곳은?

> Maybe not.

① ② ③ ④ ⑤

03 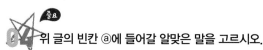 According to the passage, which is NOT true?

① Han Jiwon was a Korean high school student.

② Han Jiwon studied about the topic "What happens when you walk backward while you are carrying a cup of coffee?"

③ Han Jiwon won an Ig Nobel Prize in 2017.

④ The Ig Nobel Prizes are awarded for discoveries that "first make one think and then laugh."

⑤ The Ig Nobel Prizes were started in 1991 by *AIR* magazine.

[04~06] 다음 글을 읽고 물음에 답하시오.

The prizes are presented by real Nobel winners in Sanders Theater at Harvard University. The room is usually filled with people who (A)are eager to cheer for the brave scientists with their "laughable" research.

The U.K. Navy won the Ig Nobel Prize for Peace in 2000. (B)To save money, the Navy made its sailors shouting, "Bang!" instead of using ___ⓐ___. Is that funny enough for you to laugh out loud?

04 위 글의 빈칸 ⓐ에 들어갈 알맞은 말을 고르시오.

① real knives   ② fake blows

③ fake bombs   ④ artificial knives

⑤ real bombs

05 위 글의 밑줄 친 (A)와 바꿔 쓸 수 없는 말을 고르시오.

① are anxious to cheer

② long to cheer

③ are anxious about cheering

④ long for cheering

⑤ are dying to cheer

서답형

06 위 글의 밑줄 친 (B)에서 어법상 틀린 부분을 찾아 고치시오.

_____ ➡ _____

[07~09] 다음 글을 읽고 물음에 답하시오.

The U.K. Navy won the Ig Nobel Prize for Peace in 2000. To save money, the Navy made its sailors shout, "Bang!" instead of using real bombs. ⓐIs that _____ out loud?

Andre Geim also won an award that year. He succeeded in floating a ⓑlive frog in the air by using magnets. "In my experience, if people don't have a sense of humor, they are usually not very good scientists," he said when he accepted his award.

서답형

07 위 글의 문장 ⓐ의 빈칸에 알맞은 단어를 넣어 다음 문장과 같은 뜻이 되도록 하시오. (여섯 단어)

Is that so funny that you can laugh out loud?

➡ _____

서답형

08 When did Andre Geim win the Ig Nobel Prize? Answer in English in a full sentence. (5 words)

➡ _____

09 위 글의 밑줄 친 ⓑlive와 같은 의미로 쓰인 것을 고르시오.

① The doctors said he only had six months to live.
② The show is going out live.
③ We saw a real live rattlesnake!
④ The club has live music most nights.
⑤ Their names live in our memory.

[10~12] 다음 글을 읽고 물음에 답하시오.

Not only the winners' fun studies but also the ceremony for the Ig Nobel Prizes makes people laugh. There are a number of interesting things that keep people from getting bored. The opening and closing speeches are just two words each: "Welcome. Welcome." and "Goodbye. Goodbye." If someone talks for too long, an eight-year-old girl called Miss Sweetie Poo shouts ⓐrepeatedly, "Please stop! I'm bored." ⓑEach winner receives ten trillion Zimbabwean dollars, which are worth less than one U.S. dollar. Throwing paper planes is another fun tradition.

10 위 글의 밑줄 친 ⓐrepeatedly와 바꿔 쓸 수 없는 말을 모두 고르시오.

① again and again
② over and over
③ all of a sudden
④ all at once
⑤ over and over again

서답형

11 위 글의 밑줄 친 ⓑ에서 어법상 틀린 부분을 찾아서 고치시오.

_____ ➡ _____

중요

12 다음 중 이그노벨상 시상식의 재미있는 전통에 해당하지 않는 것은?

① The opening speech is "Welcome. Welcome."
② The closing speech is "Goodbye. Goodbye."
③ The winners must give a long speech.
④ Miss Sweetie Poo is an eight-year-old girl.
⑤ The prize money is ten trillion Zimbabwean dollars.

[13~15] 다음 글을 읽고 물음에 답하시오.

> The Ig Nobel Prize ceremony ends with the words, "If you didn't win a prize — and if you (A)did — better luck next year!" The winners do not receive lots of money. And the awards are not great honors (B)like the Nobel Prizes. But the Ig Nobel Prizes make science ___ⓐ___ more fun!

13 위 글의 빈칸 ⓐ에 들어갈 수 <u>없는</u> 말을 고르시오.

① much ② very ③ even
④ a lot ⑤ still

14 위 글의 밑줄 친 (A)did와 바꿔 쓸 수 있는 말을 쓰시오. (세 단어)

➡ _____

15 위 글의 밑줄 친 (B)like와 같은 의미로 쓰인 것을 고르시오.

① How did you <u>like</u> the movie?
② She responded in <u>like</u> manner.
③ I don't <u>like</u> the way he's looking at me.
④ He ran <u>like</u> the wind.
⑤ <u>Like</u> I said, you're always welcome to stay.

[16~18] 다음 글을 읽고 물음에 답하시오.

> The prizes are (A)presented by real Nobel winners in Sanders Theater at Harvard University. The room is usually filled with people who are eager to cheer for the brave scientists with their "laughable" research.
> The U.K. Navy won the Ig Nobel Prize for Peace in 2000. To save money, the Navy made its sailors shout, "Bang!" ___ⓐ___ using real bombs. Is that funny enough for you to laugh out loud?

16 위 글의 빈칸 ⓐ에 들어갈 알맞은 말을 고르시오.

① besides ② instead of
③ along with ④ in spite of
⑤ in addition to

17 위 글의 밑줄 친 (A)presented와 바꿔 쓸 수 있는 단어를 철자 a로 시작하여 쓰시오.

➡ _____

18 위 글을 읽고 'the Ig Nobel Prize'에 대해 알 수 <u>없는</u> 것을 고르시오.

① 상의 수여자 ② 시상식 장소
③ 시상식 참여자 ④ 시상식 시기
⑤ 2000년 수상자

[19~21] 다음 글을 읽고 물음에 답하시오.

> Andre Geim also won an award that year. He succeeded in floating a live frog in the air by using magnets. "In my experience, if people don't have a sense of humor, they are usually not very good scientists," he said when he accepted his award.
> If that still does not bring ___ⓐ___ to your face, how about this? In 2005, Gauri Nanda won the Ig Nobel Prize in Economics for inventing an alarm clock. It keeps ___ⓑ___ away until the sleeper finally gets out of bed.

19 위 글의 빈칸 ⓐ에 들어갈 가장 알맞은 말을 고르시오.

① some comfort ② your regret
③ some respect ④ inner peace
⑤ a smile

서답형
20 위 글의 빈칸 ⓑ에 run을 알맞은 형태로 쓰시오.

➡ _____

서답형
21 How did Andre Geim succeed in floating a live frog in the air? Fill in the blanks with suitable words.

He accomplished it by _____ _____.

[22~24] 다음 글을 읽고 물음에 답하시오.

The Ig Nobel Prize ceremony ends (A)[up / with] the words, "(A)If you didn't win a prize — and if you (B)[did / were] — better luck next year!" The winners do not receive lots of money. And the awards are not great honors (C)[alike / like] the Nobel Prizes. But the Ig Nobel Prizes make science a lot more fun!

서답형
22 위 글의 괄호 (A)~(C)에서 문맥이나 어법상 알맞은 낱말을 골라 쓰시오.

➡ (A) _____ (B) _____ (C) _____

서답형
23 위 글의 밑줄 친 (A)를 Unless를 사용하여 고치시오.

➡ _____

서답형
24 본문의 내용과 일치하도록 다음 빈칸 (A)~(C)에 알맞은 단어를 쓰시오. (한 칸에 두 단어도 가능)

Though the prize money of the (A)_____ Prize is not big and the winners don't gain great honors like the (B)_____ Prize winners, the (C)_____ Prizes make science much more fun.

[25~27] 다음 글을 읽고 물음에 답하시오.

"What happens when you walk backward while you are carrying a cup of coffee?" Han Jiwon, a Korean high school student, did research on this topic in 2015. Is this research project good enough ⓐto win a Nobel Prize? Maybe not. But how about an Ig Nobel Prize? He won one in 2017 for this fun research.

The Ig Nobel Prizes are awarded for discoveries that "first make one laugh and then think." ⓑThey were started in 1991 by *AIR* magazine to increase people's interest in science by honoring ⓒthe unusual and ⓓthe imaginative.

25 위 글의 밑줄 친 ⓐto win과 to부정사의 용법이 같은 것을 고르시오.

① He cannot be a gentleman to do such a thing.
② She is studying English to get a good job.
③ He worked too slowly to finish it in time.
④ He left his native country never to return.
⑤ She smiled to see the monkey.

서답형
26 위 글의 밑줄 친 ⓑThey가 가리키는 것을 본문에서 찾아 쓰시오.

➡ _____

서답형
27 위 글의 밑줄 친 ⓒthe unusual, ⓓthe imaginative와 바꿔 쓸 수 있는 말을 각각 두 단어로 쓰시오.

➡ ⓒ _____ ⓓ _____

[01~03] 다음 글을 읽고 물음에 답하시오.

"What happens when you walk backward while you are carrying a cup of coffee?" Han Jiwon, a Korean high school student, did research on this topic in 2015. ⓐ이 연구 과제는 노벨상을 받을 정도로 훌륭할까? Maybe not. But how about an Ig Nobel Prize? He won one in 2017 for this fun research.

The Ig Nobel Prizes are (A)[awarded / rewarded] for discoveries that "first make one laugh and then think." They were started in 1991 by *AIR* magazine to increase people's interest in science by (B)[honoring / ignoring] the unusual and the imaginative.

01 위 글의 괄호 (A)~(B)에서 문맥상 알맞은 낱말을 골라 쓰시오.

➡ (A) _____ (B) _____

02 위 글의 밑줄 친 ⓐ의 우리말에 맞게 주어진 어휘를 알맞게 배열하시오.

> a Nobel Prize / enough / research project / good / this / to win / is / ?

➡ _____

_____

03 다음 빈칸 (A)와 (B)에 알맞은 단어를 넣어 Han Jiwon에 대한 소개를 완성하시오.

> He was a Korean high school student and won an (A)____ ____ ____ in 2017 because of the (B)____ research that he had done in 2015.

[04~06] 다음 글을 읽고 물음에 답하시오.

ⓐThe prizes are presented by real Nobel winners in Sanders Theater at Harvard University. The room is usually filled with people who are eager to cheer for the brave scientists with their "laughable" research.

The U.K. Navy won the Ig Nobel Prize for Peace in 2000. To save money, the Navy made its sailors shout, "Bang!" instead of using real bombs. Is ⓑthat funny enough for you to laugh out loud?

04 위 글의 밑줄 친 ⓐ를 능동태로 고치시오.

➡ _____

_____

05 Why did the U.K. Navy make its sailors shout, "Bang!" instead of using real bombs? Fill in the blanks with suitable words.

> Because it wanted to ____ ____ .

06 위 글의 밑줄 친 ⓑthat이 가리키는 것을 본문에서 찾아 쓰시오.

➡ _____

_____

[07~08] 다음 글을 읽고 물음에 답하시오.

Andre Geim also won an Ig Nobel Prize that year. He succeeded in floating a live frog in the air by using magnets. "In my experience, ⓐif people don't have a sense of humor, they are usually not very good scientists," he said when he accepted his award.

07 위 글의 밑줄 친 ⓐ를 unless를 사용하여 고치시오.

➡ _____

08 다음 빈칸 (A)와 (B)에 알맞은 단어를 넣어 Andre Geim에 대한 소개를 완성하시오.

> Andre Geim was successful in (A)_____ a live frog in the air by using magnets, and won an Ig Nobel Prize. In his acceptance speech, he referred to (B)_____ _____ _____ _____ as an essential qualification of a good scientist.

[09~10] 다음 글을 읽고 물음에 답하시오.

> ⓐNot only the winners' fun studies but also the ceremony for the Ig Nobel Prizes makes people laugh. There are ⓑa number of interesting things that keep people from getting bored. The opening and closing speeches are just two words each: "Welcome. Welcome." and "Goodbye. Goodbye." If someone talks for too long, an eight-year-old girl called Miss Sweetie Poo shouts repeatedly, "Please stop! I'm bored." Each winner receives ten trillion Zimbabwean dollars, which is worth less than one U.S. dollar. Throwing paper planes is another fun tradition.

09 위 글의 밑줄 친 ⓐ를 as well as을 사용하여 고치시오.

➡ _____
_____

10 위 글의 밑줄 친 ⓑ에 해당하는 것을 우리말로 쓰시오. (네 가지)

➡ _____
_____
_____
_____

[11~12] 다음 글을 읽고 물음에 답하시오.

> "What happens when you walk backward while you are carrying a cup of coffee?" Han Jiwon, a Korean high school student, did research on this topic in 2015. Is this research project good enough to win a Nobel Prize? ⓐ Maybe not. But how about an Ig Nobel Prize? He won one in 2017 for this fun research.
>
> The Ig Nobel Prizes are awarded for discoveries that "first make one laugh and then think." They were started in 1991 by *AIR* magazine to increase people's interest in science by honoring the unusual and the imaginative.

11 위 글의 밑줄 친 ⓐ에 생략된 부분을 넣어 완전한 문장으로 쓰시오.

➡ _____
_____

12 Why did *AIR* magazine start the Ig Nobel Prizes? Fill in the blanks with suitable words.

> *AIR* magazine started them to increase people's _____ _____ by honoring the unusual and the imaginative.

구석구석

Self-study Guide

- New words again!

- He showed great eagerness to learn new things.
  명사를 수식하는 형용사 용법

- Oh, I get the meaning of "-ness."
  = understand

- Now I know not only the meaning of "eager" but also the meaning of "eagerness."

구문해설 • eagerness: 열정 • meaning: 의미 • not only A but also B: A뿐만 아니라 B도
• eager: 열렬한, 간절히 바라는

• 또 새 단어네!

• 그는 새로운 것들을 배우고자 하는 열정을 보여주었다.

• 오, 나는 '-ness'의 의미를 알았어.

• 이제 나는 'eager'의 뜻뿐만 아니라 'eagerness'의 뜻도 알아.

Express Yourself C

Magic Stairs

These are Magic Stairs. You can use them not only for going up and down
not only A but also B = B as well as A: A뿐만 아니라 B도 동명사
but also for storing things. This invention is useful enough to make your life
동명사   ~ enough to = so ~ that ... can
much easier.
비교급 강조(훨씬)

구문해설 • stair: 계단 • store: 저장[보관]하다 • invention: 발명

마법의 계단

이것은 '마법의 계단'입니다. 당신은 그것을 올라가고 내려가기 위해서 뿐만 아니라 물건을 보관하기 위해서도 사용할 수 있습니다. 이 발명품은 당신의 삶을 훨씬 더 편안하게 할 정도로 충분히 유용합니다.

Link to the World

The Nobel Prize

The Nobel Prize was named after Alfred Nobel, a Swedish scientist. It is
be named after: ~의 이름을 따서 짓다   동격
awarded to people who have done great work for the world.
수동태   주격 관계대명사
Of all the winners, Malala Yousafzai is the youngest. She won the Nobel Prize
~ 중에서
at the age of 17 because she had fought for women's and children's rights.
~의 나이에   과거완료
The Curie family received the Nobel Prize three times. Not only Marie Curie
but also her daughter was awarded the Nobel Prize.
= Her daughter as well as Marie Curie

구문해설 • be named after: ~의 이름을 따서 짓다 • Swedish: 스웨덴의 • award: 수여하다
• right: 권리

노벨상

노벨상은 스웨덴 과학자인 Alfred Nobel의 이름을 따서 지었다. 그 상은 세계를 위해 위대한 일을 행한 사람들에게 수여된다.

모든 수상자들 중에서, Malala Yousafzai가 최연소이다. 그녀는 여성과 어린이의 권리를 위해서 싸웠기 때문에 17세의 나이에 노벨상을 수상했다.

Curie 가족은 노벨상을 3번 수상했다. Marie Curie뿐만 아니라 그녀의 딸도 노벨상을 수상했다.

영역별 핵심문제

01 다음 주어진 두 단어의 관계가 같도록 빈칸에 알맞은 단어를 쓰시오.

> useful – useless : usual – _____

02 다음 문장의 빈칸 (a)와 (b)에 들어갈 단어가 바르게 짝지어진 것은?

> • We had to ____(a)____ the swimming pool as it rained.
> • The nation's president hoped to end the war and bring ____(b)____.

① wait for – peace
② get into – discovery
③ get out of – peace
④ get out of – discovery
⑤ wait for – honor

03 다음 대화의 빈칸에 들어갈 말을 〈영영 풀이〉를 참고하여 대화에 나오는 한 단어를 이용하여 쓰시오.

> A: I'm going to enter the dance contest next week, but I'm _____ about it.
> B: Don't worry. You'll do great. I'll keep my fingers crossed.
> A: Thank you.

> 〈영영 풀이〉 unhappy because you are thinking about problems or unpleasant things that might happen

➡ _____

[04~05] 다음 영영 풀이에 해당하는 것을 고르시오.

04

> to be on a liquid and not sink

① fill ② volunteer
③ hang ④ represent
⑤ float

05

> something you are proud to do

① honor ② humor
③ sense ④ trillion
⑤ sailor

06 다음 중 밑줄 친 부분의 뜻이 잘못된 것은?

① Everyone went underground before the bomb went off. (폭탄)
② He wanted to join the navy instead of the army. (해군)
③ The student did research on the Internet to learn about King Sejong. (조사)
④ The writer of the children's story is very imaginative. (가상의)
⑤ The store increased the price of toys. (증가시키다, 늘리다)

07 다음 대화에서 어법상 어색한 부분을 찾아 바르게 고치시오.

> B: I'm looking forward to the Best Joker award this time.
> G: Ha-ha. You always make us laughing out loud. So you'll get the prize, Yunki. Good luck.
> B: Thank you.

➡ _____

08 다음 짝지어진 대화 중 어색한 것은?

① A: What kind of prize did Han Jiwon win in 2017?

B: He won an Ig Nobel Prize.

② A: I'm going to travel to Jejudo next week.

B: Wow! That sounds great.

③ A: I'm going to enter the speech contest tomorrow.

B: Me, too. I'm looking forward to it.

④ A: I'm going to join the dance contest next Friday.

B: Are you? I'm looking forward to watching you dance.

⑤ A: I'm looking forward to the funny dance contest tomorrow. Are you ready?

B: Well, I think so, but I'm confident.

[09~11] 다음 대화를 읽고 물음에 답하시오.

Miso: We're going on a field trip next Tuesday. What are you going to do in the talent show, Jimin?

Jimin: I'm going to talk like our teachers do in class and tell some jokes.

Miso: Wow! I'm really ⓐlooking forward to it.

Jimin: Will everyone like my show? I'm not sure.

Miso: Don't worry. I'm sure you'll do great. I'll ⓑkeep my fingers crossed!

Jimin: Thank you, Miso. ⓒLet me to show you one part of my act. Guess who? "Goood Jooob!"

Miso: Ha-ha, you ⓓsound like our English teacher.

Jimin: Do I? I'm going to show you more at the show.

Miso: Great! You always make us ⓔlaugh out loud.

09 위 대화의 밑줄 친 부분 중 어법상 틀린 것은?

① ⓐ ② ⓑ ③ ⓒ ④ ⓓ ⑤ ⓔ

10 위 대화의 제목으로 가장 적절한 것은?

① Difficulty of Imitating Teachers' Voice
② Doing the Show Which Everyone likes
③ Choosing the Place of a Field Trip
④ Looking Forward to the Talent Show
⑤ Making Others Laugh out Loud

11 위 대화의 내용과 일치하지 않는 것을 고르시오.

① They are talking about the talent show.
② The field trip is next Tuesday.
③ Miso is going to talk like the teachers do in class and tell some jokes.
④ Jimin always makes Miso laugh out loud.
⑤ Jimin talked like his English teacher.

Grammar

12 주어진 문장의 밑줄 친 that과 용법이 같은 것은?

The dinner at that famous restaurant was so nice that I couldn't forget it.

① I hope that I can see your face.
② The report shows that we need to have healthier food.
③ The money that you saved will be used to buy a bike.
④ That is the jacket that my aunt made for me.
⑤ The old lady is so wise that we always get advice from her.

13 다음 글에서 어법상 <u>어색한</u> 부분을 찾아 바르게 고치시오.

The Curie family received the Nobel Prize three times. Not only Marie Curie but also her daughter were awarded the Nobel Prize.

➡ _____

_____

14 다음 주어진 우리말과 의미가 <u>다른</u> 하나를 고르시오.

방이 너무 어두워서 나는 책을 읽을 수 없었다.

① It was so dark in the room that I couldn't read books.
② Because it was so dark in the room, I couldn't read books.
③ It was dark enough in the room for me to read books.
④ It was too dark in the room for me to read books.
⑤ It was very dark in the room, so I wasn't able to read books.

15 다음 중 어법상 <u>어색한</u> 문장의 개수로 알맞은 것은?

a. Kate not only runs fast but also jump high.
b. Mike drinks a lot as well as eats a lot.
c. She is such smart that she can make those decisions.
d. This is not only an umbrella but also a coffee holder.
e. It is useful enough making my life much easier.
f. He was clever enough to understand the question.

① 1개 ② 2개 ③ 3개 ④ 4개 ⑤ 5개

16 주어진 문장과 같은 뜻이 되도록 'as well as'를 써서 바꿔 쓸 때 빈칸에 알맞은 말을 쓰시오.

We communicate not only on the phone but also by email.
= We communicate _____.

➡ _____

17 다음 우리말을 주어진 어휘를 이용하여 영어로 옮기시오.

(1) Ted는 나의 가방을 들어줄 만큼 충분히 친절했다. (kind, enough, carry)
➡ _____

(2) Vivian은 많은 돈을 저축할 만큼 충분히 열심히 일했다. (hard, to save, lots)
➡ _____

(3) 그 마당은 매우 커서 우리 모두 자전거를 탈 수 있다. (yard, so big, bikes, in)
➡ _____

18 다음 우리말을 영어로 바르게 옮긴 것은?

Mary는 불을 끌 수 있을 정도로 키가 크다.

① Mary is tall enough to turn on the light.
② Mary is tall enough to turn off the light.
③ Mary is so tall that she can't turn off the light.
④ Mary is so tall that she can turn on the light.
⑤ Mary is too tall not to turn off the light.

Reading

[19~20] 다음 글을 읽고 물음에 답하시오.

Not only the winners' fun studies but also the ceremony for the Ig Nobel Prizes makes people laugh. There are a number of interesting things that keep people from getting bored. The opening and closing speeches are just two words each: "Welcome. Welcome." and "Goodbye. Goodbye." If someone talks for too long, an eight-year-old girl ⓐcalled Miss Sweetie Poo shouts repeatedly, "Please stop! I'm bored." Each winner receives ten trillion Zimbabwean dollars, which is worth less than one U.S. dollar. ⓑThrowing paper planes is another fun tradition.

19 위 글의 밑줄 친 ⓐcalled 앞에 생략된 말을 쓰시오.

➡ _____

20 아래 〈보기〉에서 위 글의 밑줄 친 ⓑThrowing과 문법적 쓰임이 같은 것의 개수를 고르시오.

┤ 보기 ├
① We stopped throwing paper planes.
② They are throwing paper planes.
③ Do you know the boys throwing paper planes?
④ They are fond of throwing paper planes.
⑤ I saw them throwing paper planes.

① 1개　② 2개　③ 3개　④ 4개　⑤ 5개

[21~23] 다음 글을 읽고 물음에 답하시오.

"What happens when you walk backward while you are carrying a cup of coffee?" Han Jiwon, a Korean high school student, did research on this topic in 2015. (A)Is this research project good enough to win a Nobel Prize? Maybe not. But how about an Ig Nobel Prize? He won (B)one in 2017 for this fun research.

The Ig Nobel Prizes are awarded for discoveries that "first make (C)one laugh and then think." They were started in 1991 ___ⓐ___ AIR magazine to increase people's interest in science ___ⓑ___ honoring the unusual and the imaginative.

21 위 글의 빈칸 ⓐ와 ⓑ에 공통으로 들어갈 알맞은 전치사를 쓰시오.

➡ _____

22 다음 빈칸에 알맞은 단어를 넣어 위 글의 밑줄 친 (A)를 복문으로 고치시오.

➡ Is this research project _____ good _____ it _____ win a Nobel Prize?

23 아래 〈보기〉에서 위 글의 밑줄 친 (B)one, (C)one과 같은 의미로 쓰인 것을 각각 고르시오.

┤ 보기 ├
① One must obey one's parents.
② I'd like an ice cream. Are you having one, too?
③ One can be glad and sorry at the same time.
④ I don't have a pen. Can you lend me one?
⑤ Do you have a watch? — Yes, I have one.

➡ (B) one: _____　(C) one: _____

[24~25] 다음 글을 읽고 물음에 답하시오.

Andre Geim also won an award that year. He succeeded in floating a live frog in the air by using magnets. "In my experience, if people don't have a sense of humor, they are usually not very good scientists," he said when he accepted his award.

If that still does not bring a smile to your face, how about this? In 2005, Gauri Nanda won the Ig Nobel Prize in Economics for inventing an alarm clock. It keeps running away until the sleeper ⓐfinally gets out of bed.

24 위 글의 밑줄 친 ⓐfinally와 바꿔 쓸 수 없는 말을 모두 고르시오.

① at last
② in the end
③ above all
④ at least
⑤ in the long run

25 다음 중 위 글에 대한 설명을 바르게 하지 못한 사람을 고르시오.

① 형규: Andre Geim은 자석을 사용해서 살아 있는 개구리를 공중에 띄울 수 있었어.
② 수희: Andre Geim에 따르면, 대체로 아주 훌륭한 과학자가 되려면 유머 감각이 필요하다고 해.
③ 민수: 2005년에 Gauri Nanda가 이그노벨상을 탔어.
④ 세진: 응, 자명종을 발명해서 이그노벨 경제학상을 받은 거야.
⑤ 나리: 그 자명종은 잠자는 사람이 깨어날 때까지 쫓아다닌대.

[26~28] 다음 글을 읽고 물음에 답하시오.

Umbrella for Coffee Lovers

This is the Umbrella for Coffee Lovers. You can use it not only ⓐas an umbrella but also as a cup holder. ⓑThis invention is useful enough to make your life much easier.

Magic Stairs

These are Magic Stairs. ⓒYou can use them not only for going up and down but also for storing things. This invention is useful enough to make your life much easier.

26 위 글의 밑줄 친 ⓐas와 같은 의미로 쓰인 것을 고르시오.

① As he is honest, he is trusted by everyone.
② This box will serve as a table.
③ Susan is not as pretty as Jane.
④ As I entered the room, they cried.
⑤ Her anger grew as she talked.

27 위 글의 밑줄 친 ⓑ를 복문으로 고치시오.

➡ _____

_____

28 다음 중 위 글의 밑줄 친 문장 ⓒ와 의미가 같지 않은 문장을 고르시오.

① You can use them not just for going up and down but also for storing things.
② You can use them not simply for going up and down but also for storing things.
③ You can use them for storing things as well as for going up and down.
④ You can use them not for going up and down but for storing things.
⑤ You can use them not only for going up and down but for storing things as well.

출제율 90%

01 다음 짝지어진 단어의 관계가 같도록 빈칸에 알맞은 말을 쓰시오.

> backward – forward : sink – _____

출제율 95%

02 다음 영영 풀이에 해당하는 단어는?

> a weapon made of material that will explode

① magnet ② navy ③ bomb
④ army ⑤ science

출제율 100%

03 다음 대화를 읽고 B의 빈칸에 들어갈 말을 〈조건〉에 맞게 쓰시오.

> ┌── 보기 ──┐
> • 행운을 빌어주는 표현을 쓸 것.
> • 'leg'를 사용할 것.

> A: I'm going to enter the dance contest next week, but I'm worried about it.
> B: Don't worry. You'll do great. _____!
> A: Thank you.

➡ _____

[04~05] 다음 대화를 읽고 물음에 답하시오.

> Miso: We're going on a field trip next Tuesday. What are you going to do in the talent show, Jimin?
> Jimin: I'm going to talk like our teachers do in class and tell some jokes.
>
> (A) Will everyone like my show? I'm not sure.
> (B) Thank you, Miso. Let me show you one part of my act. Guess who? "Goood Jooob!"
> (C) Ha-ha, you sound like our English teacher.
> (D) Don't worry. I'm sure you'll do great. I'll keep my fingers crossed!
> (E) Wow! I'm really looking forward to it.
>
> Jimin: Do I? I'm going to show you more at the show.
> Miso: Great! You always make us laugh out loud.

출제율 100%

04 위 대화의 (A)~(E) 중 흐름상 네 번째 위치할 대화는?

① (A) ② (B) ③ (C) ④ (D) ⑤ (E)

출제율 90%

05 위 대화를 읽고 다음 질문에 영어로 답하시오.

> Q: What is Jimin going to do in the talent show?

➡ _____
_____

출제율 95%

06 다음 대화의 빈칸에 들어갈 말로 어색한 것은?

> A: I'm looking forward to the model airplane contest tomorrow. Are you ready?
> B: Well, I think so, but I'm nervous.
> A: You will do well. _____

① I'll keep my fingers crossed!
② Good luck!
③ Don't give up!
④ I wish you all the best.
⑤ Don't be worried.

07 대화에서 단어의 쓰임이 <u>어색한</u> 곳을 찾아 바르게 고치시오. (2개)

> B: This looks interesting. Is this a cutting board and a bird feeder?
>
> G: It is not only a cutting board but also a bird feeder. You can do one thing at the same time.
>
> B: That's a great idea!
>
> G: Do you really think so?
>
> B: Yes. I'm really looking forward to using it.

_____ ➡ _____ , _____ ➡ _____

[08~09] 다음 대화를 읽고 물음에 답하시오.

> G: Mom, I can't wait for the sports day.
>
> W: What are you going to do on that day, Minji?
>
> G: I'm going to play basketball for my class. We've practiced hard for a few weeks.
>
> W: Oh, I'm looking forward to your game.
>
> G: Actually, I'm a little worried. I'm afraid I'll make a mistake.
>
> W: Don't worry. You'll do a good job. _____(A)_____ !

08 위 대화의 빈칸 (A)에 들어갈 알맞은 말을 주어진 단어를 이용하여 쓰시오.

> (keep, fingers, crossed)

➡ _____

09 위 대화의 내용과 일치하지 <u>않는</u> 것은?

① They are talking about the sports day.
② Minji will play basketball for her class.
③ Minji is looking forward to the sports days.
④ Minji's mom is expecting to play basketball.
⑤ Minji is afraid she'll make a mistake.

10 다음 대화의 빈칸에 들어갈 말로 <u>어색한</u> 것은?

> (A) B: The winner of the Oh So Sweet award will get some candies.
>
> G: Oh, I want to get the prize.
>
> B: I'm sure you'll get the prize this time. _____ , Jiu!
>
> (B) B: I'm looking forward to the Best Joker award this time.
>
> G: Ha-ha. You always make us laugh out loud. So you'll get the prize, Yunki. _____ .
>
> B: Thank you.

① Good luck
② I knock on wood for you
③ I hope everything goes well with you
④ I'll keep my fingers crossed for you
⑤ I can't wait to get the prize

11 다음 문장에서 어법상 <u>어색한</u> 부분을 찾아 바르게 고치시오.

> You can use it not only putting on your back but also for controlling the TV.

_____ ➡ _____

12 다음 빈칸에 들어갈 말로 적절하지 <u>않은</u> 것을 고르시오.

> He gave me not _____ clothes but also money.

① only
② just
③ rather
④ simply
⑤ merely

13 우리말과 같은 뜻이 되도록 괄호 안에 주어진 말과 'not only ~ but also ...'를 사용하여 한 문장으로 쓰시오.

(1) Tommy는 힘이 셀뿐만 아니라 현명하기도 해. (strong, wise)

➡ _____

(2) 그녀는 지식뿐만 아니라 용기도 가지고 있다. (knowledge, courage)

➡ _____

(3) 나는 춤추는 것뿐만 아니라 노래도 잘한다. (good at, dancing, singing)

➡ _____

(4) 너뿐만 아니라 그도 그 영화를 보고 싶어 한다. (want, see the movie)

➡ _____

[14~16] 다음 글을 읽고 물음에 답하시오.

"What happens when you walk backward while you are carrying a cup of coffee?" Han Jiwon, a Korean high school student, did research on ⓐthis topic in 2015. Is this research project good enough to win a Nobel Prize? Maybe not. But how about an Ig Nobel Prize? He won one in 2017 for this fun research.

The Ig Nobel Prizes are awarded for discoveries ⓑthat "first make one laugh and then think." ⓒThey were started in 1991 by *AIR* magazine to increase people's interest in science by honoring the unusual and the imaginative.

14 위 글의 밑줄 친 ⓐthis topic이 가리키는 것을 본문에서 찾아 쓰시오.

➡ _____

_____

15 위 글의 밑줄 친 ⓑthat과 문법적 쓰임이 같은 것을 모두 고르시오.

① Look at that man over there.
② Who was the first man that came here?
③ The trouble is that we are short of money.
④ This is my sister and that is my cousin.
⑤ Is this the farm that they spoke of?

16 위 글의 밑줄 친 ⓒ를 능동태로 고치시오.

➡ _____

[17~18] 다음 글을 읽고 물음에 답하시오.

Andre Geim also won an award that year. He (A)succeeded in floating a live frog in the air by using magnets. "In my experience, if people don't have a sense of humor, they are usually not very good scientists," he said when he accepted his award.

If that still does not bring a smile to your face, how about this? In 2005, Gauri Nanda won the Ig Nobel Prize ⓐ Economics ⓑ inventing an alarm clock. It keeps running away until the sleeper finally gets out of bed.

17 위 글의 빈칸 ⓐ와 ⓑ에 들어갈 전치사가 바르게 짝지어진 것은?

	ⓐ	ⓑ		ⓐ	ⓑ
①	for	– at	②	in	– at
③	in	– for	④	to	– by
⑤	to	– for			

18 위 글의 밑줄 친 (A)를 다음과 같이 바꿔 쓸 때, 빈칸에 들어갈 알맞은 단어를 쓰시오.

➡ was _____ in floating

[19~21] 다음 글을 읽고 물음에 답하시오.

	Since 1991
The 27th	First make one
Ig Nobel	laugh and
Prize Ceremony	then think

Thursday, September 14, 2017 6:00 PM
in Sanders Theater at Harvard University
Join us for the awarding of 10 new Ig Nobel Prizes
Winners of 2017:
Han Jiwon, Korea
"How to Carry Your Coffee"

출제율 100%

19 위 글의 종류로 알맞은 것을 고르시오.

① diary ② summary ③ article
④ invitation ⑤ advertisement

출제율 90%

20 To win an Ig Nobel Prize, which is more important, making one laugh or making one think? Fill in the blanks (A) and (B) with suitable words.

> To win an Ig Nobel Prize, making one
> (A)_____ is more important than
> making one (B)_____.

출제율 95%

21 위 글을 읽고 답할 수 없는 질문을 고르시오.

① When was the Ig Nobel Prize started?
② What is the condition of winning the prize?
③ When will the ceremony be held?
④ Where will the ceremony be held?
⑤ Who will present the prizes?

[22~24] 다음 글을 읽고 물음에 답하시오.

Not only the winners' fun studies but also the ceremony for the Ig Nobel Prizes makes people laugh. There are a number of interesting things that ⓐkeep people from getting bored. The opening and closing speeches are just two words each: "Welcome. Welcome." and "Goodbye. Goodbye." If someone talks for too long, an eight-year-old girl called Miss Sweetie Poo shouts repeatedly, "Please stop! I'm bored." Each winner receives ten trillion Zimbabwean dollars, which is worth less than one U.S. dollar. ⓑThrowing paper planes is another fun tradition.

출제율 90%

22 위 글의 밑줄 친 ⓐkeep과 바꿔 쓸 수 있는 말을 모두 고르시오.

① stop ② prevent ③ prohibit
④ allow ⑤ encourage

출제율 95%

23 밑줄 친 ⓑ를 다음과 같이 바꿔 쓸 때 빈칸에 들어갈 알맞은 말을 두 단어로 쓰시오.

➡ It is another fun tradition _____
_____ paper planes.

출제율 100%

24 According to the passage, which is NOT true?

① The winners' fun studies make people laugh.
② The ceremony for the Ig Nobel Prizes also makes people laugh.
③ There are many interesting things that keep people interested.
④ The opening speeches are just four words: "Welcome. Welcome." and "Goodbye. Goodbye."
⑤ Miss Sweetie Poo is eight years old.

01 다음 대화의 우리말에 맞게 주어진 단어를 활용하여 영어로 쓰시오.

G: Mom, are you coming to the sports day?

W: Sure. I'm going to play the game Kick a Shoe. This will be the first time for me to try it.

G: Don't worry. I'm sure you'll do great. I'll keep my fingers crossed for you!

W: Thank you. I'm also going to perform a funny dance with some other mothers.

G: That sounds fun. 무대에 선 엄마 모습을 보는 것이 기대돼요. (I'm / look / watch / on the stage)

➡ _____

02 다음 대화를 읽고 요약문을 완성하시오.

A: We're going on a field trip next Tuesday. What are you going to do in the talent show, Jimin?

B: I'm going to talk like our teachers do in class and tell some jokes.

A: Wow! I'm really looking forward to it.

B: Will everyone like my show? I'm not sure.

A: Don't worry. I'm sure you'll do great. I'll keep my fingers crossed!

B: Thank you, Miso. Let me show you one part of my act. Guess who? "Goood Jooob!"

A: Ha-ha, you sound like our English teacher.

B: Do I? I'm going to show you more at the show.

A: Great! You always make us laugh out loud.

Jimin and Miso are talking about the _____. Jimin is going to _____ their teachers do in class and _____. Miso is _____ his show.

03 대화의 흐름상 빈칸에 들어갈 문장을 〈조건〉에 맞게 쓰시오.

W: Soyun, are you going to take part in any races on the sports day?

G: Sure. I'm going to run a 100 meter race at the end of the day.

W: Wow, _____

G: But, Mom, I'm not sure I'll win the race.

W: Just do your best. I'll keep my fingers crossed!

┤ 조건 ├

• 진행형을 이용하여 '기대를 표현하는 말'을 쓸 것.

• look / see / you / at the race를 사용할 것.

➡ _____

04 다음 글에서 어법상 틀린 곳의 기호를 쓰고 바르게 고쳐 쓰시오. (3개)

The Nobel Prize

The Nobel Prize (a)named after Alfred Nobel, a Swedish scientist. It (b)is awarded to people who (c)has done great work for the world.

The Curie family (d)received the Nobel Prize three times. Not only Marie Curie but also her daughter (e)were awarded the Nobel Prize.

➡ _____

"What happens when you walk backward while you are carrying a cup of coffee?" Han Jiwon, a Korean high school student, did research on this topic in 2015. Is this research project good enough to win a Nobel Prize? Maybe not. ⓐBut how about an Ig Nobel Prize? He won one in 2017 for this fun research.

The Ig Nobel Prizes are awarded for discoveries that "first make one laugh and then think." They were started in 1991 by *AIR* magazine to increase people's interest in science by honoring ⓑ특이하고 창의적인 사람들.

05 위 글의 밑줄 친 ⓐ를 다음과 같이 바꿔 쓸 때 빈칸에 들어갈 알맞은 말을 두 단어로 쓰시오.

➡ But is this research project _____ _____ to win an Ig Nobel Prize?

06 위 글의 밑줄 친 ⓑ의 우리말에 맞게 주어진 단어를 사용하여 5 단어로 영작하시오. (unusual, imaginative)

➡ _____

07 다음 빈칸 (A)와 (B)에 알맞은 단어를 넣어 the Ig Nobel Prizes에 대한 소개를 완성하시오.

AIR magazine started them in 1991 for the purpose of increasing people's interest in science. If a discovery first makes one (A)_____ and then (B)_____, it can award the prize.

Not only the winners' fun studies but also the ceremony for the Ig Nobel Prizes (A) [make / makes] people laugh. ⓐ사람들이 지루해하지 않도록 하는 재미있는 것들이 많이 있다. The opening and closing speeches are just two words each: "Welcome. Welcome." and "Goodbye. Goodbye." If someone talks for too long, an eight-year-old girl called Miss Swcctic Poo shouts repeatedly, "Please stop! I'm bored." Each winner receives ten trillion Zimbabwean dollars, which (B)[is / are] worth less than one U.S. dollar. Throwing paper planes (C)[is / are] another fun tradition.

08 위 글의 괄호 (A)~(C)에서 어법상 알맞은 낱말을 골라 쓰시오.

➡ (A) _____ (B) _____ (C) _____

09 위 글의 밑줄 친 ⓐ의 우리말에 맞게 주어진 어휘를 이용하여 13 단어로 영작하시오.

a number of, keep, bored

➡ _____
_____

10 What is the closing speech of the Ig Nobel Prizes? Answer in English in a full sentence. (4 words)

➡ _____

01 〈보기〉의 (A)는 기대를 표현하는 대화이고, (B)는 기원을 표현하는 대화이다. 〈보기〉를 보고 (A), (B)의 표현을 써서 대화를 완성하시오.

(A)	(B)
• travel to Jejudo	• have a basketball game
• go camping with my parents	• enter the dance contest
• club festival	• join the invention contest
• see a musical	• have an important meeting

┤ 보기 ├

(A) A: I'm going to travel to Jejudo next week.

　　B: Wow! That sounds great.

　　A: Yeah, I'm really looking forward to it.

(B) A: I'm going to enter the dance contest next week, but I'm worried about it.

　　B: Don't worry. You'll do great. I'll keep my fingers crossed.

　　A: Thank you.

02 〈보기〉에 주어진 표현을 사용하여 'not only ~ but also ...' 또는 'enough to부정사'의 문장을 쓰시오.

┤ 보기 ├

understand the novel	buy the building	speak English	speak Chinese
interested in basketball	interested in volleyball	watch the drama	play the game

rich　clever　young　old　careful　foolish　cheap　expensive

(1) _____

(2) _____

(3) _____

(4) _____

단원별 모의고사

01 다음 단어에 대한 영어 설명이 <u>어색한</u> 것은?

① backward: looking or facing in the direction that is behind you

② imaginative: having or showing new and exciting ideas

③ live: not dead

④ million: the number 1,000,000,000,000

⑤ university: an educational institution of learning of the highest level

02 다음 짝지어진 단어의 관계가 같도록 빈칸에 알맞은 말을 쓰시오.

> happy – happiness : eager – _____

03 다음 영영풀이에 해당하는 단어를 고르시오.

> to achieve something that you planned to do

① reach   ② accept   ③ succeed

④ fill   ⑤ throw

[04~05] 다음 대화의 빈칸에 들어갈 말로 알맞은 것을 고르시오.

04

> A: I'm going to enter the dance contest next week, but I'm worried about it.
> B: _____ I'll keep my fingers crossed.
> A: Thank you.

① Why don't you practice dancing hard?

② Don't worry. You'll do great.

③ Who will take part in the dance contest?

④ I'm looking forward to it.

⑤ Wow! That sounds great.

05

> B: _____ award this time.
> G: Ha-ha. You always make us laugh out loud. So you'll get the prize, Yunki. Good luck.
> B: Thank you.

① I'm looking forward to the Best Joker

② I'm looking forward to the Class Brain

③ I'm looking forward to Oh So Sweet

④ I'm looking forward to the Ms. Cheerful

⑤ I'm looking forward to the Best Note Keeper

06 다음 중 짝지어진 대화가 <u>어색한</u> 것은?

① A: These are special shoes. I hope to win a prize with this invention.
   B: I'm sure you will.

② A: I'm looking forward to the funny dance contest tomorrow. Are you ready?
   B: Well, I think so, but I'm nervous.

③ A: I'm going to enter the photo contest tomorrow.
   B: Are you? I'll keep my fingers crossed!

④ A: I'm going to go camping with my parents next week.
   B: Wow! That sounds great.

⑤ A: Minho always makes us laugh out loud.
   B: Don't worry. You'll do great. I'll keep my fingers crossed.

07 대화의 흐름상 밑줄 친 ①~⑤ 중 어휘의 쓰임이 어색한 것은?

> G: Mom, I ①can't wait for the sports day.
>
> W: What are you going to do on that day, Minji?
>
> G: I'm going to play basketball for my class. We've ②practiced hard for a few weeks.
>
> W: Oh, ③I'm looking forward to your game.
>
> G: Actually, ④I'm little worried. I'm afraid I'll make a mistake.
>
> W: Don't worry. You'll do a good job. I'll ⑤keep my fingers crossed!

①   ②   ③   ④   ⑤

[08~09] 다음 대화를 읽고 물음에 답하시오.

> G: Mom, are you coming to the sports day?
>
> W: Sure. I'm going to play the game Kick a Shoe. (①) This will be the first time for me to try it. (②)
>
> G: Don't worry. I'm sure you'll do great. I'll keep my fingers ___(A)___ (cross) for you! (③)
>
> W: Thank you. (④)
>
> G: That sounds fun. (⑤) I'm looking forward to ___(B)___ (watch) you on the stage.

08 위 대화의 (①)~(⑤) 중 주어진 문장이 들어갈 위치로 알맞은 곳은?

> I'm also going to perform a funny dance with some other mothers.

①   ②   ③   ④   ⑤

09 위 대화의 (A)와 (B)에 주어진 단어를 알맞은 형태로 쓰시오.

➡ (A) _____   (B) _____

[10~12] 다음 대화를 읽고 물음에 답하시오.

> Miso: We're going on a field trip next Tuesday. What are you going to do in the talent show, Jimin?
>
> Jimin: I'm going to talk like our teachers (A)do in class and tell some jokes.
>
> Miso: Wow! I'm really looking forward to it.
>
> Jimin: Will everyone like my show? I'm not sure.
>
> Miso: Don't worry. I'm sure you'll do great. I'll keep my fingers crossed!
>
> Jimin: Thank you, Miso. Let me show you one part of my act. Guess who? "Goood Jooob!"
>
> Miso: Ha-ha, you sound like our English teacher.
>
> Jimin: (B)Do I? I'm going to show you more at the show.
>
> Miso: Great! You always make us laugh out loud.

10 위 대화의 내용과 일치하도록 Jimin의 장기 자랑 계획을 영어로 쓰시오. (to부정사로 문장을 시작하시오.)

➡ Jimin's Plan for the Talent Show

(1) _____

(2) _____

11 위 대화의 밑줄 친 (A)의 'do'가 의미하는 바로 알맞은 것은?

① teach   ② like   ③ talk

④ make   ⑤ go

12 위 대화의 밑줄 친 (B)의 'Do I?'를 완전한 문장으로 쓰시오.

➡ _____

[13~15] 괄호 안에 주어진 표현을 사용하여 우리말을 영어로 완성하시오.

13 (as well as, nice)

A: I think Pinocchio is popular. What do you think?

B: 그는 친절할 뿐만 아니라 인기 있어.

➡ _____

14 (both ~ and ..., lovely)

A: I think Rapunzel is very beautiful. What do you think?

B: 그녀는 예쁘고 사랑스러워.

➡ _____

15 (neither ~ nor ..., creative)

A: I think Ms. Marple is very smart. What do you think?

B: 그녀는 똑똑하지도 창의적이지도 않아.

➡ _____

16 다음 중 어법상 어색한 문장을 고르시오.

① This hall is big enough to hold 1,000 people.

② Mr. Kim is old enough to drive a car.

③ Jimin was smart enough to solve the difficult problem.

④ Sue sings not only beautifully but also happy.

⑤ He teaches not just English but science.

17 다음 두 문장을 한 문장으로 바르게 옮긴 것을 모두 고르시오.

> • The lake is deep.
> • You can't swim in the lake.

① The lake is so deep that you can't swim in the lake.

② The lake is so deep for you to swim in the lake.

③ The lake is too deep for you to swim in the lake.

④ The lake is too deep for you to swim in.

⑤ The lake is so deep that you can't swim in.

18 다음 중 어법상 어색한 문장의 개수로 알맞은 것은?

> a. You can use it not only for holding paper but also to put your phone on it.
> b. She not only sang well but also dance perfectly.
> c. The cat was not only tired but also hungry.
> d. This water is so clean that we could drink it.
> e. Her voice was loud enough to wake the boy up.

① 1개　② 2개　③ 3개　④ 4개　⑤ 5개

[19~22] 두 문장이 같은 뜻이 되도록 괄호 안의 어구를 사용하여 문장을 쓰시오.

19 We were so brave that we faced the strong enemy. (enough to)

➡ _____

20 Ted is old enough to talk about the topic. (so ... that ~ can)

➡ _____

21 He has experience as well as knowledge. (not only ~ but also ...)

➡ _____

22 I must not only feed the animals but also look after the children. (as well as)

➡ _____

23 다음 문장에서 밑줄 친 우리말을 영어로 옮기시오.

> You can use it not only for (1)피자를 자르기 (2)피자 한 조각을 집기 위해서도.

➡ (1) _____
　 (2) _____

24 주어진 〈보기〉를 참고하여 두 문장을 하나의 문장으로 쓰시오.

> ─ 보기 ─
> You like the movie.
> + Eric likes the movie, too.
> → Not only you but also Eric likes the movie.

(1) She has to leave here.
　 + You have to leave here, too.
　 ➡ _____

(2) I like to play with dogs.
　 + My brothers like to play with dogs, too.
　 ➡ _____

(3) I am from Busan.
　 + My best friend is from Busan, too.
　 ➡ _____

[25~26] 다음 글을 읽고 물음에 답하시오.

"What happens when you walk backward while you are carrying a cup of coffee?" Han Jiwon, a Korean high school student, did research on this topic in 2015. Is this research project good enough to win a Nobel Prize? Maybe not. But how about an Ig Nobel Prize? He won ⓐone in 2017 for ⓑthis fun research.

ⓒThe Ig Nobel Prizes are awarded for discoveries that "first makes one laugh and then think." They were started in 1991 by *AIR* magazine to increase people's interest in science by honoring the unusual and the imaginative.

25 위 글의 밑줄 친 ⓐone이 가리키는 것을 본문에서 찾아 쓰고, ⓑthis fun research의 조사 내용을 우리말로 쓰시오.

➡ ⓐ _____

ⓑ _____

26 위 글의 밑줄 친 ⓒ에서 어법상 틀린 부분을 찾아 고치시오.

_____ ➡ _____

[27~28] 다음 글을 읽고 물음에 답하시오.

The prizes are presented by real Nobel winners in Sanders Theater at Harvard University. The room is usually filled with people who are eager ⓐto cheer for the brave scientists with their "laughable" research.

The U.K. Navy won the Ig Nobel Prize for Peace in 2000. To save money, the Navy made its sailors shout, "Bang!" instead of using real bombs. Is that funny enough for you to laugh out loud?

27 아래 〈보기〉에서 위 글의 밑줄 친 ⓐto cheer와 to부정사의 용법이 같은 것의 개수를 고르시오.

┤ 보기 ├
① To hear him talk, you would take him for a fool.
② My plan is to go to the movies tonight.
③ The mother was pleased to see her son well.
④ He didn't live to see the work finished.
⑤ What a fool she is to believe such a thing!

① 1개   ② 2개   ③ 3개   ④ 4개   ⑤ 5개

28 According to the passage, which is NOT true?

① The prizes are presented by real Ig Nobel winners.
② The prizes are presented in Sanders Theater at Harvard University.
③ People who are eager to cheer for the brave scientists with their "laughable" research usually fill the room.
④ The U.K. Navy won the Ig Nobel Prize for Peace in 2000.
⑤ To save money, the Navy made its sailors shout, "Bang!" instead of using real bombs.

[29~30] 다음 글을 읽고 물음에 답하시오.

Andre Geim also won an award that year. He succeeded in floating a live frog in the air by using magnets. "In my experience, if people don't have a sense of humor, they are usually not very good scientists," he said when he accepted his award.

If that still does not bring a smile to your face, how about this? In 2005, Gauri Nanda won the Ig Nobel Prize in Economics for inventing an alarm clock. It keeps running away until the sleeper finally gets out of bed.

29 본문의 내용과 일치하도록 다음 빈칸에 알맞은 단어들을 쓰시오.

According to Andre Geim, _____ _____ _____ _____ is usually a necessary condition to be a very good scientist.

30 다음 빈칸 (A)와 (B)에 알맞은 단어를 넣어 Gauri Nanda에 대한 소개를 완성하시오.

Gauri Nanda won the Ig Nobel Prize in Economics in 2005 because she invented (A)_____ _____ _____ which the sleeper can stop only after he or she finally (B)_____ _____ _____ _____.

[31~32] 다음 글을 읽고 물음에 답하시오.

Not only the winners' fun studies but also the ceremony for the Ig Nobel Prizes makes people laugh. ⓐThere are the number of interesting things that keeps people from getting bored. The opening and closing speeches are just two words each: "Welcome. Welcome." and "Goodbye. Goodbye." If someone talks for too long, an eight-year-old girl called Miss Sweetie Poo shouts repeatedly, "Please stop! I'm bored." Each winner receives ten trillion Zimbabwean dollars, ⓑ그것은 미국의 1달러보다 가치가 낮다. Throwing paper planes is another fun tradition.

31 위 글의 밑줄 친 ⓐ에서 어법상 틀린 부분을 찾아 고치시오. (두 군데)

_____ ➡ _____

_____ ➡ _____

32 위 글의 밑줄 친 ⓑ의 우리말에 맞게 주어진 어휘를 알맞게 배열하시오.

one U.S. dollar / worth / than / which / less / is

➡ _____

Dreaming of My Future

🎙 의사소통 기능

- 슬픔, 불만족, 실망의 원인에 대해 묻기
  Why are you disappointed?

- 충고 구하기
  Do you think I should keep trying?

🎙 언어 형식

- 분사구문
  Hearing this, I felt really sorry for her.

- 관계대명사 'what'
  That's **what** I need to learn from her.

Words & Expressions

Key Words

- a white school 백인학교
- ability [əbíləti] 명 능력
- accept [æksépt] 동 받아들이다
- African-American 명 아프리카계 미국인
- against [əgénst] 전 ~에 반대하여, ~에 맞서
- allow [əláu] 동 허락하다
- as [æz] 전 ~처럼
- audition [ɔːdíʃən] 명 오디션
- baker [béikər] 명 제빵사
- career [kəríər] 명 직업, 직장 생활
- case [keis] 명 소송 사건
- character [kǽriktər] 명 등장인물
- colored [kʌ́lərd] 형 색깔이 있는, 유색 인종의
- competition [kàmpətíʃən] 명 대회, 시합
- control [kəntróul] 동 조종하다
- cook [kuk] 명 요리사
- courage [kə́ːridʒ] 명 용기
- decorate [dékərèit] 동 장식하다
- disappointed [dìsəpɔ́intid] 형 실망한
- engineer [èndʒiníər] 명 기술자, 엔지니어
- expert [ékspəːrt] 명 전문가
- face [feis] 동 (상황에) 직면하다
- figure [fígjər] 명 (중요한) 인물, 거물, 숫자, 피규어(모형 장난감)
- grade [greid] 명 성적
- hanger [hǽŋər] 명 옷걸이
- hidden [hídn] 형 숨겨진, 비밀의

- impress [imprés] 동 감명을 주다, 깊은 인상을 주다
- install [instɔ́ːl] 동 설치하다
- job festival 진로 박람회, 직업 설명회
- judge [dʒʌdʒ] 명 판사
- later [léitər] 부 나중에, 후에
- laughter [lǽftər] 명 웃음(소리)
- line [lain] 명 (연극, 영화 등의) 대사
- lose [luːz] 동 지다, 패배하다
- magic trick 마술 묘기
- magician [mədʒíʃən] 명 마술사
- manager [mǽnidʒər] 명 관리자, 경영자
- match [mætʃ] 명 시합, 경기
- matter [mǽtər] 동 중요하다, 문제가 되다
- offer [ɔ́ːfər] 명 제의, 제안
- permission [pərmíʃən] 명 허락
- presentation [prèzəntéiʃən] 명 발표
- programmer [próugræmər] 명 프로그래머
- recognize [rékəgnàiz] 동 알아보다, 인정하다
- record [rékɔːrd] 명 기록
- reporter [ripɔ́ːrtər] 명 기자
- rocket [rákit] 명 로켓
- space [speis] 명 우주
- speech [spiːtʃ] 명 연설, 말
- tip [tip] 명 조언
- useful [júːsfəl] 형 유용한
- Your Honor 판사님, 재판장님

Key Expressions

- a little 약간, 조금
- be afraid of ~을 두려워하다
- be against ~에 반대하다
- break down ~을 부수다
- get over ~을 극복하다
- get upset 기분이 상하다
- give permission 허가하다
- give up 포기하다
- have no choice but to ~할 수밖에 없다
- How about -ing? ~하는 것이 어때?
- keep ~ in mind ~을 명심하다

- keep -ing 계속 ~하다
- laugh at ~을 비웃다
- look down 우울해 보이다
- make a suggestion 제안하다
- prepare for ~을 준비하다
- set a goal 목표를 정하다
- stand up for ~을 옹호하다, 지지하다
- take a class 수업을 받다
- Take it easy. 걱정하지 마., 진정해.
- thanks to ~ 덕분에
- Why don't you ~? ~하는 게 어때?

Word Power

※ 서로 비슷한 뜻을 가진 어휘

- □ **ability** 능력 : **capability** 능력
- □ **competition** 대회, 시합 : **match** 시합
- □ **hidden** 숨겨진, 비밀의 : **veiled** 숨겨진
- □ **recognize** 알아보다 : **perceive** 인식하다

- □ **allow** 허락하다 : **permit** 허락하다
- □ **courage** 용기 : **bravery** 용기
- □ **matter** 중요하다 : **count** 중요하다
- □ **reporter** 기자 : **journalist** 기자

※ 서로 반대의 뜻을 가진 어휘

- □ **accept** 받아들이다 ↔ **reject** 거절하다
- □ **colored** 유색 인종의 ↔ **white** 백인의
- □ **expert** 전문가 ↔ **novice** 초보자
- □ **lose** 지다, 패배하다 ↔ **win** 이기다
- □ **useful** 유용한 ↔ **useless** 쓸모없는

- □ **allow** 허락하다 ↔ **forbid** 금지하다
- □ **courage** 용기 ↔ **cowardice** 비겁함
- □ **install** 설치하다 ↔ **remove** 제거하다
- □ **permission** 허락 ↔ **prohibition** 금지

※ 동사 – 명사

- □ **accept** 받아들이다 – **acceptance** 수용
- □ **compete** 경쟁하다 – **competition** 대회, 시합
- □ **impress** 깊은 인상을 주다 – **impression** 인상
- □ **prepare** 준비하다 – **preparation** 준비

- □ **allow** 허락하다 – **allowance** 허용
- □ **decorate** 장식하다 – **decoration** 장식
- □ **permit** 허가하다 – **permission** 허락
- □ **recognize** 인정하다 – **recognition** 인식

English Dictionary

- □ **allow** 허락하다
  → to let someone do something
  어떤 사람이 무엇을 하도록 내버려 두다
- □ **career** 직업, 직장 생활
  → the series of jobs that you do during your working life 직장 생활 동안 하는 일련의 직업
- □ **colored** 유색 인종의
  → of a race other than white 백인종을 제외한 인종의
- □ **courage** 용기
  → the ability to control your fear in a dangerous or difficult situation
  위험하거나 어려운 상황에서 두려움을 조절하는 능력
- □ **engineer** 기술자, 엔지니어
  → a person who designs, builds, or maintains machines
  기계를 설계하고, 만들고 또는 유지하는 사람
- □ **expert** 전문가
  → a person with a high level of knowledge or skill in a particular area
  어떤 특정한 분야에서 높은 수준의 지식 또는 기술을 가진 사람
- □ **face** (상황에) 직면하다
  → to deal with a difficult situation 어려운 상황을 처리하다

- □ **figure** (중요한) 인물, 거물
  → a well-known person 잘 알려진 사람
- □ **hidden** 숨겨진, 비밀의
  → not easy to find 찾기가 쉽지 않은
- □ **judge** 판사
  → the person in a court who decides how criminals should be punished
  법정에서 범죄자들이 어떻게 처벌 받아야 하는지를 결정하는 사람
- □ **laughter** 웃음(소리)
  → the act or sound of laughing 웃는 행동 또는 소리
- □ **manager** 관리자, 경영자
  → a person who is responsible for controlling an organization 조직을 통제할 책임이 있는 사람
- □ **permission** 허락
  → the action of allowing someone to do something
  누군가에게 무엇을 하도록 허용해 주는 행위
- □ **space** 우주
  → the region beyond the Earth's atmosphere or beyond the solar system
  지구의 대기 또는 태양계 너머의 지역

서답형

01 다음 글의 빈칸에 〈영어 설명〉에 맞게 두 단어로 쓰시오.

> They _____ me when I made a mistake.
> <영어 설명> to show that you think someone or something is stupid

02 다음 빈칸에 공통으로 들어갈 말로 가장 적절한 것은?

> • The _____ sentenced him to three years in prison.
> • It's very wrong to _____ people by their skin color.

① cook
② judge
③ report
④ grade
⑤ expert

[03~04] 다음 설명에 해당하는 단어를 고르시오.

03
> the region beyond the Earth's atmosphere or beyond the solar system

① permission
② rocket
③ engineer
④ university
⑤ space

04
> the ability to control your fear in a dangerous or difficult situation

① programmer
② peace
③ courage
④ permission
⑤ laughter

서답형

05 다음 우리말에 맞게 주어진 단어를 이용하여 쓰시오.

> 그는 실패를 두려워하지 않을 만큼 충분히 대담했다. (afraid)

➡ He was bold enough not to _____ failure.

06 다음 빈칸에 들어갈 말이 바르게 짝지어진 것은?

> (A) Did you _____ the new program on your computer?
> (B) The dancer _____ her teacher with her excellent dance skills.

① offer – faced
② offer – recognized
③ install – impressed
④ break down – allowed
⑤ install – offered

서답형

07 다음 짝지어진 단어의 관계가 같도록 알맞은 말을 쓰시오.

> accept – acceptance : allow – _____

08 다음 빈칸에 공통으로 들어갈 말로 알맞은 것은?

> (A) Walt Disney is an important cultural _____ in history.
> (B) The _____ is lower than the OECD average of $6,741.

① figure
② match
③ programmer
④ laughter
⑤ suggestion

01 〈보기〉에서 알맞은 단어를 선택하여 문장의 빈칸을 완성하시오. (필요하면 변형하고 단어를 추가하여 쓰시오.)

┌─ 보기 ┐
later   thank   laugh   engineer

(1) _____ his brother's advice, Minho could become a doctor.

(2) How many _____ designed this bridge?

(3) _____, the poor boy became the President.

(4) I believe that _____ is the best medicine.

02 대화의 빈칸에 〈영영풀이〉에 해당하는 단어를 주어진 철자로 쓰시오.

A: Why are you d_____?
B: I lost the tennis game. Do you think I should practice harder?
A: Yes, I think so.

<영영풀이> sad because something is not as good as you expected, or because something did not happen

➡ _____

03 다음 우리말과 같도록 문장의 빈칸에 주어진 철자로 시작하는 한 단어를 쓰시오.

(1) 그런 상황에서, 어떻게 미래 직업을 준비할 수 있는가?

➡ In such conditions, how should one prepare for his or her future c_____?

(2) 어쨌든 우주에는 숨겨진 보석이 있었다.

➡ There was a h_____ gem in the universe after all.

(3) 세계는 한글이 매우 독창적이고 과학적이라고 인정합니다.

➡ The world r_____ that Hangul is very unique and scientific.

04 영영풀이에 해당하는 단어를 〈보기〉에서 찾아 첫 번째 빈칸에 쓰고, 두 번째 빈칸에는 우리말 뜻을 쓰시오.

┌─ 보기 ┐
permission   expert   manager   face

(1) _____: to deal with a difficult situation: _____

(2) _____: a person with a high level of knowledge or skill in a particular area: _____

(3) _____: the action of allowing someone to do something: _____

(4) _____: a person who is responsible for controlling an organization: _____

05 빈칸에 주어진 철자로 시작하는 알맞은 단어를 쓰시오.

(1) Do you have your own way to g_____ over the cold?

(2) One eighth of the whole population in the U.S. was c_____ slaves.

(3) A spelling bee is a spelling c_____ in the U.S.

Conversation

1 슬픔, 불만족, 실망의 원인에 대해 묻기

> • **Why are you disappointed?** 너는 왜 실망하고 있니?

■ 'Why are you disappointed?(너는 왜 실망하고 있니?)'는 실망하고 있는 상대방에게 그 이유를 묻는 표현이다. 상대방이 뭔가에 불만족하거나 실망하고 있는 것을 보고 사용하는 표현으로, 그 원인을 물을 때 'What's the matter (with you)?(무슨 일 있니?)'라고 물을 수 있다.

■ 'Why are you disappointed?'처럼 상대방의 걱정, 슬픔이나 불만족, 실망의 원인에 대해 물을 때 사용되는 일반적인 표현으로 'What's the matter (with ~)?'가 쓰이며 '무슨 일 있니?'라는 뜻으로 다음 표현으로 바꿔 쓸 수 있다. (What's wrong? = What's the problem? = Is there anything wrong? = What happened? = Why the long face?)

■ 걱정이나 두려움을 나타내는 표현으로는 'be anxious about ~(~에 대해 걱정하다)', 'be worried about ~', 'be concerned about ~(~에 대해 걱정이다)' 등이 있고, 상대방의 걱정, 염려, 슬픔, 불만족, 실망에 대해, Don't worry. / I'm sorry to hear that. / That's too bad. / Cheer up! 등과 같은 위로하는 표현을 쓸 수 있다.

슬픔, 불만족, 실망의 원인에 대해 묻는 표현

- Why are you disappointed? 너는 왜 실망하고 있니?
- What's the matter? 무슨 문제가 있니?
- What's wrong? 뭐가 잘못되었니?
- What's the problem? 무슨 문제 있니?
- Why the long face? 왜 그렇게 우울한 얼굴이니?
- What makes you sad/depressed/disappointed? 무엇 때문에 슬프니/우울하니/실망했니?
- Is there anything wrong? 잘못된 일 있니?

핵심 Check

1. 다음 밑줄 친 (A) 대신 쓰기에 적절하지 <u>않은</u> 것은?

G: You look down today. (A) <u>What's the matter?</u>

B: I want to take dance classes, but my father doesn't like that idea. He thinks that boys should play sports.

G: I'm sorry to hear that.

① Why are you disappointed?   ② What matters the most?

③ What's wrong?   ④ What's the problem?

⑤ Why the long face?

② 충고 구하기

> • Do you think I should keep trying? 너는 내가 계속 노력해야 한다고 생각하니?

■ 'Do you think I should ~?(너는 내가 ~해야 한다고 생각하니?)'는 상대방으로부터 충고를 구하는 표현이다. 이 질문에 대해 'Yes.'나 'No.'로 대답한 후, '(I think) You should[had better] ~(내 생각에는 ~해야 해.)', 'Why don't you ~?(~하는 것이 어떠니?)', 'How[What] about -ing?(~하는 것이 어떨까?)' 등과 같이 부연해서 조언해 줄 수 있다.

충고를 구하는 표현

- Do you think I'd better ~? 너는 내가 ~해야 한다고 생각하니?
- If you were me, would you ~? 네가 나라면 너는 ~할 거니?
- What would you do if you were in my shoes? 네가 내 입장이라면 너는 무엇을 할래?
- What should I do? 내가 무엇을 해야 할까?
- What do you think I should do? 너는 내가 무엇을 해야 한다고 생각하니?
- What would you advise me to do? 너는 나에게 무엇을 하라고 충고할 거니?

■ 실망하거나 낙담한 상대방에게 처음부터 조언이나 충고를 하는 것보다는 위로나 위안의 말을 먼저 건네는 것이 더 자연스러운 대화가 될 수 있다.

위로 · 위안의 표현

- Come on. 힘 내.
- Take it easy. 진정해.
- I'm sorry to hear that. 그 말을 들으니 유감이다.
- Everything will be fine. 다 잘 될 거야.

핵심 Check

2. 다음 대화의 내용으로 보아, 빈칸에 들어가기에 적절한 것은?

G: Why are you disappointed?

B: I'm preparing for the ski competition, but my record is not good. _____

G: I think you should keep practicing more. I'm sure you'll get better and better.

① What's the matter?　　② I'm sorry to hear that.

③ What would you do?　　④ Will you do me a favor?

⑤ What should I do?

Step Up – Real-life Scene

Jisu: ❶Why are you so disappointed, Ryan?

Ryan: My parents won't ❷let me enter Superstar 101, a singing competition.

Jisu: ❸I'm sorry to hear that. Why are they against it?

Ryan: ❹They want me to study hard and be a doctor. ❺They're always worried about my grades.

Jisu: Did you tell your parents you really want to be a singer?

Ryan: Not yet. ❻Do you think I should talk with them about it?

Jisu: Yes. Just show them ❼how much you love singing. ❽Why don't you sing the songs you made in front of them?

Ryan: Okay. I'll try. Thank you for your advice, Jisu.

지수: 너는 왜 그렇게 실망하고 있니, Ryan?

Ryan: 부모님은 내가 노래 경연 대회인 슈퍼스타 101에 참가하는 걸 허락하지 않으실 거야.

지수: 그 말을 들으니 유감이구나. 왜 부모님은 그것에 반대하시니?

Ryan: 부모님은 내가 열심히 공부해서 의사가 되기를 원하셔. 항상 내 성적을 걱정하시지.

지수: 부모님께 네가 정말로 가수가 되고 싶다고 말씀드렸니?

Ryan: 아니 아직. 너는 내가 부모님께 그것에 대해 말씀드려야 한다고 생각하니?

지수: 응. 그냥 부모님께 네가 얼마나 노래 부르는 것을 좋아하는지 보여 드려. 부모님 앞에서 네가 만든 노래를 부르는 건 어때?

Ryan: 알았어. 시도해 볼게. 조언해 줘서 고마워, 지수야.

❶ 'disappoint'는 '실망시키다'라는 뜻의 동사로 사람이 실망한 것은 과거분사 'disappointed'를 사용한다.
❷ '사역동사+목적어+동사원형'의 형태로 '…가 ~하도록 허락하다'라는 뜻이다.
❸ 상대방의 좋지 않은 일에 대해 유감을 표현하는 말이다.
❹ '동사(want)+목적어(me)+목적보어(to부정사)'의 5형식 구문으로 '…가 ~하기를 원하다'로 해석한다.
❺ 'be worried about'은 '~에 관해 걱정하다'라는 뜻이다.
❻ 'Do you think I should ~?(너는 내가 ~해야 한다고 생각하니?)'는 상대방으로부터 충고를 구하는 표현이다.
❼ 동사 'show'의 직접목적어로 '의문사(how much)+주어(you)+동사(love)' 어순의 '간접의문문'이다.
❽ 'Why don't you+동사원형?'은 '~하는 게 어떠니?'라는 뜻으로 제안할 때 사용한다.

Check(√) True or False

(1) Ryan is disappointed because he failed a singing competition.　　T ☐ F ☐

(2) Jisu wants Ryan to tell his parents about his dream.　　T ☐ F ☐

Start Off A – Listen & Talk 1

B: You don't ❶look happy. Why are you disappointed?

G: We lost the basketball game ❷because of my mistake.

B: Come on. ❸Everyone makes mistakes.

G: Do you think I should practice more?

B: Well, yes. You know, practice makes perfect.

B: 너는 기분이 좋아 보이지 않는구나. 왜 실망하고 있니?
G: 내 실수 때문에 우리가 농구 시합에서 졌어.
B: 괜찮아. 모든 사람은 실수하기 마련이야.
G: 내가 더 연습해야 한다고 생각하니?
B: 음, 그래. 너도 알다시피, 연습이 완벽을 만들잖아.

❶ 'look+형용사'로 '~처럼 보이다'라는 의미이다.
❷ '~ 때문에'라는 의미로 'because of+명사(구)' 또는 'because+주어+동사'를 사용할 수 있다. 즉, because of my mistake는 because I made a mistake.로 바꾸어 쓸 수 있다.
❸ 'Everyone'은 '모든 사람들'의 의미로 단수 취급한다.

Check(√) True or False

(3) Because everyone makes mistakes, the girl isn't disappointed.　　T ☐ F ☐

(4) The boy advises the girl to practice more.　　T ☐ F ☐

Get Ready 2

(1) **G:** You look down today. ❶What's the matter?
B: I want to take dance classes, but my father doesn't like that idea. He thinks ❷ that boys should play sports.
G: I'm sorry to hear that.

(2) **G:** Why are you disappointed?
B: I'm preparing for the ski jumping competition, but my record is not good. What should I do?
G: ❸I think you should keep practicing more. I'm sure ❹you'll get better and better.

(3) **B:** I want to be a cook, but everybody laughs at me. Do you think I should give up my dream?
G: No, never give up. I think you're really good at cooking. You'll be a great cook!
B: Thank you.

❶ 실망이나 불만족하는 원인을 물 때 사용하는 표현이다.
❷ 'that'은 동사 'think'의 목적어를 이끄는 접속사이다.
❸ 'I think' 뒤에는 목적어를 이끄는 접속사 'that'이 생략되어 있다. 'keep -ing(동명사)'는 '계속 ～하다'라는 의미이다.
❹ 'get+비교급 and 비교급'은 '점점 더 ～해지다'라는 의미이다.

Start Off – Listen & Talk A 2

G: Why are you disappointed?
B: I didn't give a good presentation.
G: ❶Take it easy. Your speech was a little fast, but I liked your presentation.
B: Do you think I should speak more slowly?
G: Yes. It will ❷help your classmates understand you better.

❶ 위로·위안의 표현으로 '괜찮아.', '진정해.' 등의 의미로 해석할 수 있다.
❷ 'help+목적어+동사원형'으로 '…가 ～하는 데 도움이 되다'로 해석한다.

Start Off – Listen & Talk B

G: Junsu, you look down today. ❶Why are you disappointed?
B: I lost the cooking competition.
G: I'm sorry to hear that. I know you tried hard.
B: Yeah, but maybe that wasn't enough. ❷Do you think I should learn more cooking tips?
G: Yes. I think they will help. ❸How about getting useful tips from cooking shows online?
B: Okay. I'll try. Thank you for your advice, Mina.
G: You're welcome. Just remember I'm a fan of your dishes.

❶ 'What makes you disappointed?'로 바꾸어 쓸 수 있다.
❷ 'Do you think I should ～?(너는 내가 ～해야 한다고 생각하니?)'는 상대방으로부터 충고를 구하는 표현이다.
❸ 'How about+동명사 ～?'는 '～하는 게 어때?'라는 뜻으로 제안할 때 사용한다.

Start Off – Speak Up

B: ❶Why are you disappointed?
G: I failed the audition for the Mapo Youth Band. Do you think I should keep trying?
B: Sure. Don't give up. You'll do better next time.
G: Thank you.

❶ 슬픔, 불만족, 실망의 원인에 대해 묻는 표현으로 'What's the matter?', 'What's the problem?' 등으로 바꾸어 쓸 수 있다.

Express Yourself A

1. **W:** You don't look happy. Why are you disappointed?
B: I ❶want to be a wonderful magician like you, but I failed the magic competition. Do you think I should give up?
W: No. Practice hard every day and you'll get better and better. ❷It's important to keep trying.
B: Okay, I'll try. Thank you for your advice.

2. **W:** Please come in. ❸Are you interested in designing things?
B: Yes, I want to be a product designer. Do you think I should go to design school?
W: I think that will help, but ❹it's more important to practice drawing every day. ❺Reading design magazines will also help you.
B: Thank you. I'll keep that in mind.

❶ 'want'는 to부정사를 목적어로 취하는 동사이다.
❷ 가주어(It) ～ 진주어(to keep trying) 구문으로 가주어는 '그것'으로 해석하지 않는다.
❸ 'be interested in'은 '～에 관심이 있다'라는 의미로 전치사 뒤에 동명사(designing)가 온다.
❹ 가주어(it) ～ 진주어(to practice) 구문이다. 'practice'는 동명사를 목적어로 취하는 동사이다.
❺ 동명사(Reading) 주어로 '읽는 것은'으로 해석한다.

Learning Diary – Listen & Speak 1

B: You look down today, Minji. Why are you disappointed?
G: We lost the soccer game ❶because I made a mistake.
B: Don't be so sad. It can happen to anyone.
G: Do you think I should practice more?
B: Well, yes. I can help you if you want. You know, I'm a good soccer player.
G: Really? Thank you, Seho.

❶ because는 접속사로 '주어+동사'가 나온다.

● 다음 우리말과 일치하도록 빈칸에 알맞은 말을 쓰시오.

Get Ready 2

(1) G: You _____ _____ today. What's _____ _____?
   B: I want _____ _____ dance classes, but my father doesn't like _____ _____. He thinks _____ boys _____ play sports.
   G: I'm _____ _____ _____ _____ _____.

(2) G: Why are you _____?
   B: I'm _____ for the ski jumping _____, but my _____ is not good. _____ should I do?
   G: I think you should _____ _____ more. I'm _____ you'll _____ _____ _____ _____ _____.

(3) B: I want _____ _____ a _____, but everybody _____ _____ me. Do you think I should _____ _____ my dream?
   G: No, _____ _____ _____. I think you're really _____ _____ _____. You'll be a great _____!
   B: Thank you.

Start Off – Listen & Talk A

1. B: You don't _____ happy. _____ are you _____?
   G: We _____ the basketball game _____ _____ my _____.
   B: Come on. Everyone _____ _____.
   G: Do you think I should _____ more?
   B: Well, yes. You know, _____ _____ _____ _____.
2. G: Why_____ _____ _____?
   B: I didn't _____ a good _____.
   G: _____ it _____. Your _____ was _____ _____ fast, but I liked your _____.
   B: Do you think I should speak _____ _____?
   G: Yes. It will _____ your classmates _____ you better.

Start Off – Listen & Talk B

G: Junsu, you _____ _____ today. Why are you _____?
B: I _____ the cooking _____.
G: I'm _____ _____ _____ _____ _____. I know you tried _____.
B: Yeah, but _____ that wasn't _____. Do you think I should learn more _____ _____?
G: Yes. I think they will help. _____ _____ _____ _____ tips from cooking shows online?
B: Okay. I'll _____. Thank you _____ your _____, Mina.
G: You're welcome. Just _____ I'm a fan of your _____.

(1) G: 너는 오늘 우울해 보이는구나. 무슨 일이니?
   B: 나는 춤 수업을 듣고 싶은데, 아버지는 그 생각을 마음에 들어하지 않으셔. 아버지는 남자아이들은 운동을 해야 한다고 생각하셔.
   G: 그것 참 안됐구나.
(2) G: 너는 왜 실망하고 있니?
   B: 스키 점프 대회를 준비하고 있는데, 내 기록이 좋지 않아. 내가 무엇을 해야 할까?
   G: 네가 계속 더 많이 연습해야 한다고 생각해. 난 네가 점점 더 나아질 거라고 확신해.
(3) B: 나는 요리사가 되고 싶은데, 모두 나를 비웃어. 너는 내가 꿈을 포기해야 한다고 생각하니?
   G: 아니, 절대 포기하지 마. 나는 네가 정말 요리를 잘한다고 생각해. 너는 훌륭한 요리사가 될 거야!
   B: 고마워.

1. B: 너는 기분이 좋아 보이지 않는구나. 왜 실망하고 있니?
   G: 내 실수 때문에 우리가 농구 시합에서 졌어.
   B: 괜찮아. 모든 사람은 실수하기 마련이야.
   G: 내가 더 연습해야 한다고 생각하니?
   B: 음, 그래. 너도 알다시피, 연습이 완벽을 만들잖아.
2. G: 너는 왜 실망하고 있니?
   B: 나는 발표를 잘하지 못했어.
   G: 괜찮아. 너의 발표는 약간 빨랐지만, 나는 너의 발표가 마음에 들었어.
   B: 너는 내가 더 천천히 말해야 한다고 생각하니?
   G: 응. 그러면 너의 학급 친구들이 네 말을 더 잘 이해하게 될 거야.

G: 준수야, 너 오늘 우울해 보이는구나. 왜 실망하고 있니?
B: 요리 대회에서 떨어졌어.
G: 그것 참 안됐구나. 네가 열심히 노력했다는 걸 알아.
B: 응, 하지만 아마 그게 충분하지는 않았나 봐. 너는 내가 더 많은 요리 요령들을 배워야 한다고 생각하니?
G: 응. 나는 그것이 도움이 될 거라고 생각해. 온라인 요리 영상에서 유용한 조언들을 얻는 게 어때?
B: 알았어. 시도해 볼게. 조언해 줘서 고마워, 미나야.
G: 천만에. 내가 네 요리의 팬이라는 것만 기억해.

Start Off – Speak Up

B: _____ are you _____?
G: I _____ the _____ for the Mapo Youth Band. Do you think I should _____ _____?
B: Sure. _____ _____ _____. You'll do _____ next time.
G: Thank you.

Start Up – Real-life Scene

Jisu: Why are you so _____, Ryan?
Ryan: My parents _____ _____ me _____ Superstar 101, a singing competition.
Jisu: I'm _____ _____ _____ that. Why are they _____ it?
Ryan: They want me _____ _____ hard and be a doctor. They're always _____ _____ my grades.
Jisu: Did you tell your _____ you really want _____ _____ a singer?
Ryan: _____ _____. Do you think I should _____ _____ them about it?
Jisu: Yes. Just show them _____ _____ you love singing. _____ _____ _____ _____ the songs you made _____ _____ _____ them?
Ryan: Okay. I'll try. _____ _____ _____ your advice, Jisu.

Express Yourself A

1. W: You don't look happy. Why are you _____?
   B: I want to be a wonderful _____ _____ you, but I _____ the magic _____. Do you think I should _____ _____?
   W: No. _____ every day and you'll _____ and _____. It's important _____ _____ _____.
   B: Okay, I'll try. Thank you for _____ _____.
2. W: Please _____ _____. _____ you _____ _____ _____ things?
   B: Yes, I want to be a _____ _____. Do you think I should go to _____ school?
   W: I think that will help, but _____ more important _____ _____ _____ every day. _____ design _____ will also help you.
   B: Thank you. I'll _____ _____ _____ _____ _____ _____.

Learning Diary– Listen & Speak 1

B: You _____ _____ today, Minji. _____ _____ _____ _____ _____?
G: We _____ the soccer game _____ I made a mistake.
B: _____ _____ so sad. It can _____ to _____.
G: Do you think I should _____ _____?
B: Well, yes. I can help you _____ you want. _____ _____, I'm a good soccer player.
G: Really? Thank you, Seho.

해석

B: 너는 왜 실망하고 있니?
G: 나는 마포 청소년 밴드 오디션에서 떨어졌어. 너는 내가 계속 노력해야 한다고 생각하니?
B: 물론이지. 포기하지 마. 너는 다음번에 더 잘할 거야.
G: 고마워.

지수: 너는 왜 그렇게 실망하고 있니, Ryan?
Ryan: 부모님은 내가 노래 경연 대회인 슈퍼스타 101에 참가하는 걸 허락하지 않으실 거야.
지수: 그 말을 들으니 유감이구나. 왜 부모님은 그것에 반대하시니?
Ryan: 부모님은 내가 열심히 공부해서 의사가 되기를 원하셔. 항상 내 성적을 걱정하시지.
지수: 부모께 네가 정말로 가수가 되고 싶다고 말씀드렸니?
Ryan: 아니 아직. 너는 내가 부모께 그것에 대해 말씀드려야 한다고 생각하니?
지수: 응. 그냥 부모님께 네가 얼마나 노래 부르는 것을 좋아하는지 보여 드려. 부모님 앞에서 네가 만든 노래를 부르는 건 어때?
Ryan: 알았어. 시도해 볼게. 조언해 줘서 고마워, 지수야.

1. W: 기분이 안 좋아 보이네요. 왜 실망하고 있나요?
   B: 저는 당신처럼 멋진 마술사가 되고 싶은데, 마술 대회에서 떨어졌어요. 제가 포기해야 한다고 생각하나요?
   W: 아뇨. 매일 열심히 연습하면 점점 더 나아질 거예요. 계속 노력하는 것이 중요해요.
   B: 네, 노력해 볼게요. 조언해 주셔서 감사합니다.
2. W: 어서 들어오세요. 물건을 디자인하는 것에 관심이 있나요?
   B: 네, 저는 상품 디자이너가 되고 싶어요. 제가 디자인 학교에 가야 한다고 생각하나요?
   W: 그것이 도움이 될 거라고 생각해요. 하지만 매일 그림을 연습하는 것이 더 중요해요. 디자인 잡지를 읽는 것도 도움이 될 거예요.
   B: 감사합니다. 그 점을 명심할게요.

B: 오늘 우울해 보이는구나, 민지야. 왜 실망하고 있니?
G: 내가 실수를 해서 우리가 축구 시합에서 졌거든.
B: 너무 슬퍼하지 마. 그런 일은 누구에게나 일어날 수 있어.
G: 넌 내가 더 연습해야 한다고 생각하니?
B: 음, 그래. 네가 원한다면 내가 너를 도와줄 수 있어. 너도 알다시피, 내가 축구를 잘하잖아.
G: 정말이니? 고마워, 세호야.

01 다음 우리말에 맞도록 주어진 단어를 활용하여 빈칸을 채우시오.

> 너는 왜 실망하고 있니? (disappoint)

➡ Why _____ you _____?

02 다음 대화의 빈칸에 들어갈 말로 어색한 것은?

> G: You look down today. _____
>
> B: I want to take dance classes, but my father doesn't like that idea. He thinks that boys should play sports.
>
> G: I'm sorry to hear that.

① What's wrong?　　　　② Is there anything wrong?

③ What's the matter?　　④ Why the long face?

⑤ Do you think I should keep trying?

03 다음 대화의 빈칸에 들어갈 말로 적절한 것은?

> B: I want to be a cook, but everybody laughs at me. _____
>
> G: No, never give up. I think you're really good at cooking. You'll be a great cook!
>
> B: Thank you.

① Does anybody want to share your ideas?

② Do you think I should keep trying?

③ Do you think I should give up my dream?

④ Everything will be fine.

⑤ Do you think I should learn more cooking tips?

04 다음 대화의 밑줄 친 말의 의도로 알맞은 것은?

> A: Do you think I should have a role model for my future?
>
> B: Yes. I think that will help.

① 관심 표현하기　　　　② 충고 구하기

③ 의견 표현하기　　　　④ 위로 표현하기

⑤ 실망의 원인에 대해 묻기

[01~02] 다음 대화를 읽고 물음에 답하시오.

B: You look down today, Minji. Why are you (a)disappointed?

G: We lost the soccer game (b)because of I made a mistake.

B: (c)Don't be so sad. It can (d)happen to anyone.

G: _____ (A) _____

B: Well, yes. I can help you (e)if you want. You know, I'm a good soccer player.

G: Really? Thank you, Seho.

01 위 대화의 빈칸 (A)에 들어갈 말로 알맞은 것은?

① Do you think I should go to design school?

② Do you think I should give up?

③ Are you happy with your team?

④ Do you think I should practice more?

⑤ Should I want to be a soccer player?

서답형

02 위 대화의 (a)~(e) 중 어법상 틀린 것을 찾아 바르게 고치시오. (1개)

➡ 틀린 것: _____

➡ 고치기: _____ ➡ _____

[03~04] 다음 대화를 읽고 물음에 답하시오.

W: Please come in. Are you interested in designing things?

B: Yes, I want to be a product designer. _____ (A) _____ go to design school?

W: I think that will help, but it's more important to practice drawing every day. Reading design magazines will also help you.

B: Thank you. _____ (B) _____

03 위 대화의 빈칸 (A)에 들어갈 말로 알맞은 것은?

① Do you have to

② Do you want to

③ Do you think I should

④ Why do I have to

⑤ Do I think you should

중요

04 위 대화의 흐름상 (B)에 들어갈 알맞은 표현은?

① Let's keep our fingers crossed for you.

② I'll keep that in mind.

③ I wish you all the best.

④ You can be what you act.

⑤ Break a leg!

[05~06] 다음 대화를 읽고 물음에 답하시오.

G: Junsu, you look (a)down today. Why are you disappointed?

B: I lost the cooking competition.

G: I'm (b)pleased to hear that. I know you tried hard.

B: Yeah, but maybe that wasn't (c)enough. Do you think I should learn more cooking tips?

G: Yes. I think they will help. How about getting useful tips from cooking shows online?

B: Okay. I'll try. Thank you for your (d)advice, Mina.

G: You're welcome. Just (e)remember I'm a fan of your dishes.

05 위 대화의 (a)~(e) 중 흐름상 어휘의 쓰임이 어색한 것은?

① (a) ② (b) ③ (c) ④ (d) ⑤ (e)

06 위 대화에서 요리 대회에 떨어진 Junsu에게 해줄 수 있는 조언으로 알맞은 것은?

① Killing two birds with one stone.
② Birds of a feather flock together.
③ Curiosity killed the cat.
④ Every failure is a step closer to success.
⑤ Actions speak louder than words.

07 다음 대화의 빈칸에 들어갈 단어를 주어진 영영풀이를 보고 쓰시오.

> B: Why are you disappointed?
> G: I failed the _____ for the Mapo Youth Band.

> <영영풀이> a short performance that someone gives to try to get a job as an actor, musician, dancer, etc.

➡ _____

[08~09] 다음 대화를 읽고 물음에 답하시오.

Jisu: Why are you so disappointed, Ryan?
Ryan: My parents won't let me (a)enter Superstar 101, a singing competition.
Jisu: I'm sorry (b)to hear that. Why are they against it?
Ryan: They want me (c)to study hard and be a doctor. They're always worried about my grades.
Jisu: Did you tell your parents you really want to be a singer?
Ryan: Not yet. Do you think I should talk with them about it?
Jisu: Yes. Just show them (d)how many you love singing. (e)Why don't you sing the songs you made in front of them?
Ryan: Okay. I'll try. Thank you for your advice, Jisu.

08 위 대화를 읽고 답할 수 없는 질문은?

① Why is Ryan disappointed?
② What is Superstar 101?
③ Why are Ryan's parents against his entering Superstar 101?
④ What does Ryan want to be?
⑤ How many songs did Ryan make?

09 위 대화의 (a)~(e) 중 어법상 어색한 것은?

① (a)　② (b)　③ (c)　④ (d)　⑤ (e)

[10~11] 다음 대화를 읽고 물음에 답하시오.

> B: You don't look happy. Why are you disappointed?
> G: We lost the basketball game because of my mistake.
> B: Come on. _____(A)_____
> G: Do you think I should practice more?
> B: Well, yes. You know, _____(B)_____.

10 위 대화의 빈칸 (A)에 들어갈 말로 알맞은 것은?

① Everyone makes mistakes.
② Faith without deeds is useless.
③ We give advice, but we cannot give conduct.
④ Habit is second nature.
⑤ When you are in trouble, you find out who your real friends are.

서답형
11 위 대화의 흐름상 빈칸 (B)에 들어갈 말을 주어진 단어를 이용하여 영어로 쓰시오.

> practice / perfect

➡ _____

Conversation **서술형 시험대비**

[01~02] 다음 대화를 읽고 물음에 답하시오.

Jisu: _____(A)_____, Ryan?

Ryan: My parents won't let me enter Superstar 101, a singing competition.

Jisu: I'm sorry to hear that. Why are they against it?

Ryan: They want me to study hard and be a doctor. They're always worried about my grades.

Jisu: Did you tell your parents you really want to be a singer?

Ryan: Not yet. _____(B)_____ talk with them about it?

Jisu: Yes. Just show them how much you love singing. Why don't you sing the songs you made in front of them?

Ryan: Okay. I'll try. Thank you for your advice, Jisu.

01 위 대화를 읽고 다음 물음에 영어로 답하시오. (Because를 사용할 것)

Q: Why are Ryan's parents against his entering Superstar 101?

➡ _____

02 위 대화의 빈칸 (A)와 (B)에 들어갈 말을 〈조건〉에 맞게 영어로 쓰시오.

┤ 조건 ├

(A) • 실망하고 있는 상대방에게 그 이유를 묻는 표현을 쓸 것.
   • 'disappoint'와 'so'를 이용할 것.
(B) • '너는 내가 ~해야 한다고 생각하니?'의 의미가 되도록 상대방으로부터 충고를 구하는 표현을 쓸 것.

➡ (A) _____
  (B) _____

03 다음 대화의 빈칸 (A)에 들어갈 표현을 주어진 〈조건〉에 맞게 쓰시오.

G: Junsu, you look down today. Why are you disappointed?

B: I lost the cooking competition.

G: _____(A)_____ I know you tried hard.

B: Yeah, but maybe that wasn't enough. Do you think I should learn more cooking tips?

G: Yes. I think they will help.

┤ 조건 ├

• 'sorry'와 'that'을 이용하여 유감이나 동정을 나타내는 표현을 쓸 것.

➡ _____

[04~05] 다음 대화를 읽고 물음에 답하시오.

W: Please come in. (A)물건을 디자인하는 것에 관심이 있나요?

B: Yes, I want to be a product designer. Do you think I should go to design school?

W: I think that will help, but (B)매일 그림을 연습하는 것이 더 중요해요. Reading design magazines will also help you.

B: Thank you. I'll keep that in mind.

04 위 대화에서 (A)의 우리말을 'interest'와 'design things'를 활용하여 영작하시오.

➡ _____

05 위 대화의 (B)의 우리말에 맞게 주어진 어구를 알맞은 순서로 배열하시오.

more / to / it / practice / is / drawing / important / every day

➡ _____

Grammar

교과서

① 분사구문

> • **Hearing** this, I felt really sorry for her. 이 말을 듣고서, 나는 그녀가 정말로 안됐다고 느꼈다.

- 형태: '접속사+주어+동사'를 현재분사(동사원형+-ing)를 써서 간략하게 나타낸 것
  의미: 때, 이유, 동시동작, 연속상황, 조건 등의 뜻을 나타내는 일종의 부사구

- **분사구문 만드는 법**
  (1) 접속사를 생략
  (2) 접속사절의 반복 주어를 생략
  (3) 접속사절의 동사를 현재분사(Ving)로 바꿈
  (4) 주절은 그대로 둠
  - As I felt sick, I went to bed early. → **Feeling** sick, I went to bed early. (이유)
    아파서, 나는 일찍 잠자리에 들었다.

- 분사구문에서 Being이나 Having been은 보통 생략한다.
  - As my friend was embarrassed by his mistake, he couldn't say anything.
    → (Being) **Embarrassed** by his mistake, my friend couldn't say anything. (이유)
    자신의 실수에 당혹스러워서, 내 친구는 아무 말도 하지 못했다.

- 부사절과 주절의 주어가 다를 때는 부사절의 주어를 생략하지 않고 사용한다.
  - If it rains tomorrow, we will play futsal indoors.
    → **It raining** tomorrow, we will play futsal indoors. (조건)
    내일 비가 오면, 우리는 실내에서 풋살을 할 거야.

- 분사구문으로 바꿀 부사절이 부정문이면 'not+현재분사'의 형태로 쓴다.
  - As I don't know what to say, I will keep silent.
    → **Not knowing** what to say, I will keep silent.
    무슨 말을 해야 할지 모르기 때문에, 나는 계속 조용히 있을 거야.

핵심 Check

1. 다음 두 문장이 같은 뜻이 되도록 분사구문을 사용하여 빈칸에 알맞은 말을 쓰시오.
   (1) As my daughter had her leg broken, she couldn't walk.
      = _____ her leg broken, my daughter couldn't walk.
   (2) If you turn left, you can see my house next to the post office.
      = _____ left, you can see my house next to the post office.

② 관계대명사 'what'

- That's **what** I need to learn from her. 그것이 내가 그녀에게서 배울 필요가 있는 점이다.
- The judge was impressed by **what** she said and finally gave her permission.
  판사는 그녀가 말한 것에 감명을 받고 마침내 그녀에게 허락해 주었다.

■ 형태: what = the thing(s) that[which]
  의미: (…하는) 것

■ 선행사 the thing(s)을 포함한 관계대명사로 명사절의 역할(주어, 목적어, 보어)을 한다.

- **What you broke** is my mom's favorite dish. (주어)
  네가 깨트린 것은 우리 엄마가 가장 좋아하는 접시야.

- I understand **what you said**. (목적어)
  나는 네가 말한 것을 이해한다.

- This is what **I recommended to you**. (보어)
  이것이 내가 너에게 추천했던 것이다.

■ 선행사를 포함하는 관계대명사이므로 앞에 명사(선행사)가 나오면 안 된다.

- You should get ready for the thing what lies ahead of you.   (×)

  → You should get ready for ~~the thing~~ what lies ahead of you. (○)
  너는 네 앞에 놓여 있는 것에 대비해야 한다.

핵심 Check

2. 다음 괄호 안에서 알맞은 것을 고르시오.

(1) I agree with the thing (what / that) you said.

(2) This is (what / that) I'd like to buy.

(3) (What/ That) he said was true.

01 다음 우리말에 맞게 괄호 안에 주어진 단어를 이용하여 문장을 완성하시오.

(1) 돈이 없어서, 그들은 먹을 것을 살 수 없다. (having, money)

➡ ＿＿＿＿＿＿＿＿＿＿＿＿＿＿＿, they can't buy anything to eat.

(2) 거리를 걸으면서, 그는 지도를 보았다. (walking, street)

➡ ＿＿＿＿＿＿＿＿＿＿＿＿＿＿＿, he looked at the map.

(3) 네가 원하는 것을 나에게 말해 줘. (what, want)

➡ Tell me ＿＿＿＿＿＿＿＿＿＿＿＿＿.

(4) 우리에게 필요한 것은 약간의 공간이다. (what, need)

➡ ＿＿＿＿＿＿＿＿＿＿＿＿＿ is a little space.

02 다음 문장에서 어법상 <u>어색한</u> 부분을 바르게 고쳐 다시 쓰시오.

(1) Feel tired, he sat on a bench.

➡ ＿＿＿＿＿＿＿＿＿＿＿＿＿＿＿＿＿＿＿＿＿

(2) Watched the news, she called her mom.

➡ ＿＿＿＿＿＿＿＿＿＿＿＿＿＿＿＿＿＿＿＿＿

(3) Let me tell you that I heard yesterday.

➡ ＿＿＿＿＿＿＿＿＿＿＿＿＿＿＿＿＿＿＿＿＿

(4) Show me the things what you have in your pocket.

➡ ＿＿＿＿＿＿＿＿＿＿＿＿＿＿＿＿＿＿＿＿＿

03 다음 〈보기〉의 문장을 참고하여 빈칸을 완성하시오.

┌─ 보기 ├─

When I heard the news, I ran to my teacher.

= Hearing the news, I ran to my teacher.

(1) As he was surprised at his test result, he dropped the cup.

= ＿＿＿＿＿＿＿＿＿＿＿＿＿＿＿＿＿＿＿, he dropped the cup.

(2) If you feel happy with what you are doing, don't let anything stop you from doing it.

= ＿＿＿＿＿＿＿＿＿＿＿＿＿＿＿＿＿＿＿, don't let anything stop you from doing it.

01 다음 빈칸에 들어갈 말이 나머지와 다른 하나를 고르시오.

① The detective believed _____ Tim told her.

② I can't remember _____ time we should meet in front of this building.

③ I think _____ impressed me most in this book is his courage.

④ It is believed _____ hundreds of wild animals still survive in the forest.

⑤ Have you decided _____ to buy for her?

02 다음 밑줄 친 부분을 바꾸어 쓸 때 가장 적절한 것은?

Being on a diet, he doesn't eat any bread.

① Though he is on a diet, he doesn't eat any bread.

② As he is on a diet, he doesn't eat any bread.

③ Before he was on a diet, he doesn't eat any bread.

④ Because he was on a diet, he doesn't eat any bread.

⑤ If he is on a diet, he doesn't eat any bread.

03 다음 빈칸에 들어갈 말로 적절한 것을 모두 고르시오.

Climbing the mountain, he ran into a grizzly bear.
= _____ he was climbing the mountain, he ran into a grizzly bear.

① As   ② Though   ③ If
④ While   ⑤ Until

04 다음 중 어법상 어색한 문장을 고르시오.

① What I want is the smartphone.

② What you should do is to check all the e-mails.

③ I think what she said is not true.

④ Leaving this crowded city is all what I want.

⑤ I remember what you did to me last night.

05 다음 중 어법상 어색한 것은?

① When she arrived at home, she found out that she had left her bag at the party.

② Arriving at home, she found out that she had left her bag at the party.

③ As she arrived at home, she found out that she had left her bag at the party.

④ When arrived at home, she found out that she had left her bag at the party.

⑤ When arriving at home, she found out that she had left her bag at the party.

서답형
06 다음 괄호 안에 주어진 단어들을 바르게 배열하여 문장을 완성하시오.

I'm sorry, but this (we, not, ordered, what, is).

➡ _____

07 빈칸에 들어갈 말을 순서대로 바르게 연결한 것은?

> • This is _____ I want to read.
> • I couldn't believe the things _____ I saw yesterday.

① what – what
② what – that
③ which – what
④ that – what
⑤ that – which

08 다음 문장과 같은 의미의 문장으로 바꿔 쓴 것으로 어법상 어색한 것은?

> This book is what I bought yesterday.

① This book is the thing I bought yesterday.
② This book is the thing that I bought yesterday.
③ This book is the thing which I bought yesterday.
④ This is the book that I bought yesterday.
⑤ This is the book what I bought yesterday.

09 다음 중 어법상 어색한 문장을 고르시오.

① Not knowing the password, I couldn't go into the house.
② I did my homework, listening to the radio.
③ Being angry at him, the woman shouted.
④ Stayed in New York, he had a chance to eat the famous burger.
⑤ Tired after the long walk, my grandma decided to take a rest on the bench.

서답형

10 다음 문장에서 어법상 어색한 것을 바르게 고쳐 다시 쓰시오. (선행사를 사용하지 말 것)

(1) That he said is true.

➡ _____

(2) I know which you did yesterday.

➡ _____

서답형

11 다음 두 문장을 관계대명사 'what'을 사용하여 한 문장으로 쓰시오.

> • This bag is the thing.
> • I want to buy it.

➡ _____

서답형

12 다음 괄호 안에서 알맞은 말을 고르시오.

(1) I watched a TV show, (eat / eating) fried chicken.
(2) (Cooked / Cooking) dinner, he sang a song.
(3) He listened to music, (did / doing) his homework.
(4) (Say / Saying) good-bye, he left the classroom.
(5) (Get / Getting) up early, and you will be on time.

서답형

13 다음 괄호 안에 주어진 단어들을 바르게 배열하여 문장을 완성하시오.

> The boy (sad, loudly, cried, feeling).

➡ _____

14 다음 우리말을 영어로 바르게 옮긴 것은?

> 내 남동생은 원하는 것을 받았다.

① My brother got that he wanted.
② My brother got the thing he wanted it.
③ My brother got what he wanted.
④ My brother got the thing what he wanted.
⑤ My brother got what he wanted it.

서답형

15 다음 우리말을 주어진 어휘를 이용하여 빈칸을 채우시오.

> 오늘 할 수 있는 것을 내일로 미루지 마라. (do / what / today)

➡ Don't put off _____.

16 다음 중 어법상 <u>어색한</u> 문장을 고르시오.

① Reaching the top of the mountain, I took a picture of myself there.
② Feeling not well, I went to see a doctor.
③ It being nice, we had a nice family trip.
④ Knowing how to fix it, he helped me with my copying machine.
⑤ Talking on the phone, Dad kept smoking.

서답형

17 두 대화에 공통으로 들어갈 말을 두 대화 중에 쓰인 단어들을 이용하여 쓰시오.

(1) A: Is this bed what you want?
   B: No. That's not _____. This is what I need.
(2) A: Do you like this ball?
   B: Yes. That's exactly _____.

18 대화의 빈칸에 들어갈 말을 순서대로 바르게 연결한 것은?

> A: Is this book _____ you are looking for?
> B: Yes, that is the book _____ I am looking for.

① what – which
② what – what
③ that – what
④ that – that
⑤ which – what

서답형

19 주어진 어휘를 이용하여 다음 우리말을 영어로 쓰시오.

> 그들은 음악에 맞춰 춤을 추면서, 길을 건넜다. (to, crossed, dancing, the street, they, the music)

➡ _____

_____

20 다음 두 문장을 한 문장으로 바르게 옮긴 것은?

> • I opened the box.
> • I found a gift in it.

① When I open the box, I found a gift in it.
② Open the box, I found a gift in it.
③ Opened the box, I found a gift in it.
④ Opening the box, I found a gift in it.
⑤ I opened the box, I found a gift in it.

21 다음 중 어법상 <u>어색한</u> 문장의 개수로 알맞은 것은?

> a. This book is what I needed.
> b. I couldn't understand what he said.
> c. What you did were very brave.
> d. Writing in Chinese, the letter was difficult to read.
> e. Hearing the news, he was surprised.

① 1개 ② 2개 ③ 3개 ④ 4개 ⑤ 5개

01 'what'을 이용하여 두 문장을 한 문장으로 쓰시오.

(1) • Don't always believe the things.
   • You see them.

   ➡ _____

(2) • Never put off the things.
   • You can do them today.

   ➡ _____

(3) • The thing is your health.
   • It is the most important.

   ➡ _____

(4) • I'm not interested in the things.
   • He showed them to me.

   ➡ _____

(5) • The thing was eating spicy food.
   • I get used to it in Korea

   ➡ _____

02 다음 우리말을 괄호 안에 주어진 어휘를 이용하여 분사구문으로 시작하는 영어 문장으로 쓰시오.

(1) TV를 보다가, 그는 잠이 들었다. (watch, fall, asleep)

   ➡ _____

(2) 노래를 부르면서, 그녀는 행복하게 춤을 추었다. (a song, happily)

   ➡ _____

(3) 파일럿으로 일하기 때문에, 그는 여행을 많이 한다. (work, a pilot, travel, a lot)

   ➡ _____

03 주어진 문장을 의미가 같도록 분사구문을 이용하여 다시 쓰시오.

(1) She left the room, as she was singing a song.

   ➡ _____
   _____

(2) As there were no tickets left, we couldn't go to the concert.

   ➡ _____
   _____

04 잘못된 부분을 바르게 고쳐 문장을 다시 쓰시오.

(1) She walked in the park, she ate bread.

   ➡ _____
   또는 _____

(2) Is this cap that you wanted?

   ➡ _____

(3) This key is what I was looking for it.

   ➡ _____

(4) Had no money, I can't help you.

   ➡ _____

(5) I humming a song, I vacuumed the floor.

   ➡ _____

(6) I hope he remembers that I did for him.

   ➡ _____

05 다음 두 문장을 분사구문을 이용하여 하나의 문장으로 쓰시오.

- I didn't know what to say.
- I just stood around like a fool.

➡ _____

_____

06 우리말과 같은 뜻이 되도록 괄호 안의 단어들을 바르게 배열하시오.

사과를 먹으면서, Amy는 그녀의 개를 산책시켰다.
(an, Amy, walked, apple, dog, her, eating)

➡ _____

_____

07 다음 그림을 보고 괄호 안의 단어를 활용하여 빈칸에 알맞은 분사구문을 쓰시오.

(1)

_____, Katherine solved a very difficult math problem. (write, board)

(2)

_____, Charlie walked with Snoopy. (hold, flower)

(3)

_____, the dog enjoyed the summer. (swim, pool)

08 주어진 〈보기〉를 참고하여 같은 뜻의 문장을 쓰시오.

보기
When I visited Busan, I met my cousin.
→ Visiting Busan, I met my cousin.

(1) While I was climbing a mountain, I fell down.

➡ _____

_____

(2) As he dislikes watching TV, he only listens to music.

➡ _____

_____

(3) Although I don't have time to see the movie "*Frozen*", I know who the Olaf is.

➡ _____

_____

(4) Dad took me to the kitchen, and showed me what he had cooked.

➡ _____

_____

교과서
Reading

The Hidden Figures of NASA

I watched the movie *Hidden Figures* last weekend. It was a movie about three African-American women who worked at NASA. They began their career in the 1960s as "human computers." However, they dreamed of becoming space experts at NASA and tried hard to get over difficulties.

Katherine Johnson was one of the three "hidden figures" in this movie. She worked hard and showed a talent in math, and her manager Al Harrison recognized her ability. One day, he got upset when Katherine was missing from her desk for too long. Al asked where Katherine had been, and she answered.

Katherine: The bathroom. There are no COLORED bathrooms in this building. I have to run half a mile away just to use the bathroom.

Hearing this, I felt really sorry for her. However, I was glad that she had courage to talk to the manager about the problem. This made Al Harrison break down the "Colored Ladies Room" sign.

Mary Jackson was the character I liked the most of the three. She wanted to learn more about rocket science, but she wasn't allowed to go to a white school. So, she asked a judge to give her permission.

hidden 숨겨진, 비밀의
figure (중요한) 인물, 거물, 숫자, 피규어
(모형 장난감)
career 직업, 직장 생활
space 우주
expert 전문가
get over ~을 극복하다
manager 관리자, 경영자
recognize 알아보다, 인정하다
ability 능력
colored 색깔이 있는, 유색 인종의
courage 용기
break down ~을 부수다
rocket 로켓
allow 허락하다
judge 판사
permission 허락

 확인문제

- 다음 문장이 본문의 내용과 일치하면 T, 일치하지 <u>않으면</u> F를 쓰시오.

1 *Hidden Figures* was a movie about three African-American women who worked at NASA. ☐

2 The three African-American women began their career in the 1960s as computer programmers. ☐

3 Katherine Johnson worked hard and showed a talent in math. ☐

4 Katherine Johnson had to run half a mile away just to use the bathroom. ☐

5 Mary Jackson wanted to learn more about rocket science, and she was allowed to go to a white school. ☐

Mary: I can't change the color of my skin. So ... I have no choice but to be the first. Your Honor, of all the cases you'll hear today, which one will matter in a hundred years? Which one will make you the "first?"

The judge was impressed by what she said and finally gave her permission. Mary stood up for herself and for other African-Americans. That was what impressed me most in the movie. Finally, she became the first African-American woman engineer at NASA.

Dorothy Vaughan was the last "hidden figure." When IBM computers were installed at NASA in 1961, she was worried the "human computers" would lose their jobs. She studied a new programming language, FORTRAN. She also taught it to her team members. Later, when she was asked to be the leader of a new IBM team, she made a suggestion.

Dorothy: I'm not accepting the offer if I can't bring my ladies with me. We need a lot of people to program that machine. I can't do it alone. My girls are ready.

Thanks to Dorothy, her team members could become programmers. She wasn't afraid of change and used it as a chance. That's what I need to learn from her.

Watching this movie, I could learn how to face challenges in life. I won't forget the tears and laughter of Katherine, Mary, and Dorothy.

---

have no choice but to ~할 수밖에 없다

impress 감명을 주다, 깊은 인상을 주다

stand up for ~을 옹호하다, 지지하다

engineer 기술자, 엔지니어

inctall 설치하다

later 나중에, 후에

offer 제의, 제안

thanks to ~ 덕분에

programmer 프로그래머

be afraid of ~을 두려워하다

face (상황에) 직면하다

laughter 웃음(소리)

확인문제

● 다음 문장이 본문의 내용과 일치하면 T, 일치하지 않으면 F를 쓰시오.

1 Mary had no choice but to be the first. ☐

2 Mary stood up for herself and for other American women. ☐

3 Mary became the first African-American woman engineer at NASA. ☐

4 When IBM computers were installed at NASA in 1961, Dorothy Vaughan lost her job. ☐

5 Dorothy Vaughan studied a new programming language, FORTRAN. ☐

6 Thanks to Dorothy, her team members could become human computers. ☐

● 우리말을 참고하여 빈칸에 알맞은 말을 쓰시오.

1 The _____ _____ of NASA

2 I watched the movie *Hidden Figures* _____ _____ .

3 It was a movie about three _____ women who worked at NASA.

4 They began their career _____ _____ _____ _____ "human computers."

5 However, they dreamed of becoming _____ at NASA and tried hard _____ _____ _____ _____ .

6 **Katherine Johnson** was one of the _____ " _____ _____ " in this movie.

7 She worked hard and _____ _____ _____ _____ math, and her manager Al Harrison recognized her ability.

8 One day, he _____ _____ when Katherine was missing from her desk for too long.

9 Al asked _____ _____ _____ _____ , and she answered.

10 Katherine: The _____ .

11 There are no _____ _____ in this building.

12 I have to run half a mile away _____ _____ _____ the bathroom.

13 _____ _____ , I felt really sorry for her.

14 However, I was glad that she _____ _____ _____ _____ to the manager about the problem.

15 This made Al Harrison _____ _____ the "Colored Ladies Room" sign.

16 **Mary Jackson** was the _____ I liked the most of the three.

17 She wanted to learn more about rocket science, but she _____ _____ _____ go to a white school.

18 So, she asked a judge _____ _____ _____ _____ .

19 Mary: I _____ _____ the color of my skin.

1 NASA의 숨겨진 인물들

2 나는 지난 주말에 〈히든 피겨스〉라는 영화를 보았다.

3 그것은 NASA에서 일했던 세 명의 아프리카계 미국인 여성들에 대한 영화였다.

4 그들은 1960년대에 '인간 컴퓨터(계산원)'로 일을 시작했다.

5 하지만 그들은 NASA에서 우주 전문가가 되기를 꿈꾸었고 어려움을 극복하기 위해 열심히 노력했다.

6 Katherine Johnson은 이 영화에서 세 명의 '숨겨진 인물들' 중 한 명이었다.

7 그녀는 열심히 일했고 수학에서 재능을 보였으며, 그녀의 상사인 Al Harrison은 그녀의 능력을 알아차렸다.

8 어느 날, 그는 Katherine이 너무 오래 자리를 비웠을 때 화가 났다.

9 Al은 Katherine에게 어디에 갔었는지 물었고 그녀는 대답했다.

10 Katherine: 화장실요.

11 이 건물에는 유색 인종 전용 화장실이 없어요.

12 저는 단지 화장실을 사용하기 위해 반 마일을 달려가야 해요.

13 이 말을 듣고서, 나는 그녀가 정말로 안됐다고 느꼈다.

14 그러나 나는 그 문제에 대해 상사에게 말한 그녀의 용기를 보고 기뻤다.

15 이것은 Al Harrison으로 하여금 '유색 여성 화장실' 표지판을 부수게 만들었다.

16 Mary Jackson은 셋 중에 가장 나의 마음에 드는 인물이었다.

17 그녀는 로켓 공학에 대해 더 많이 배우고 싶었지만 백인 학교에 다니는 것이 허락되지 않았다.

18 그래서 그녀는 판사에게 허락해 달라고 요청했다.

19 Mary: 저는 제 피부색을 바꿀 수 없어요.

20 So ... I _____ _____ _____ _____ _____ be the first.

21 Your Honor, of all the cases you'll hear today, which one will matter _____ _____ _____ _____?

22 _____ _____ will make you the "first?"

23 The judge was _____ by _____ she said and finally gave her permission.

24 Mary _____ _____ _____ herself and for other African-Americans.

25 That was _____ _____ _____ _____ _____ in the movie.

26 Finally, she became the _____ _____ _____ _____ at NASA.

27 **Dorothy Vaughan** was _____ _____ "hidden figure."

28 When IBM computers _____ _____ at NASA in 1961, she was worried the "human computers" _____ _____ their jobs.

29 She studied a _____ _____ _____, FORTRAN.

30 She also _____ _____ to her team members.

31 Later, when she _____ _____ _____ be the leader of a new IBM team, she made a suggestion.

32 **Dorothy:** _____ _____ _____ the offer if I can't bring my ladies with me.

33 We need a lot of people _____ _____ that machine.

34 I can't do it _____.

35 My girls _____ _____.

36 _____ _____ Dorothy, her team members could become programmers.

37 She _____ _____ _____ change and used it _____ _____ _____.

38 That's _____ _____ _____ _____ _____ _____ _____ from her.

39 Watching this movie, I could learn _____ _____ _____ _____ in life.

40 I won't forget the _____ _____ _____ of Katherine, Mary, and Dorothy.

---

20 그래서⋯ 저는 '최초'가 되는 것 이외에는 선택이 없어요.

21 판사님, 당신이 오늘 들을 모든 사건 중에서, 백 년 뒤에 어느 것이 중요할까요?

22 어느 것이 판사님을 '최초'로 만들까요?

23 판사는 그녀가 말한 것에 감명을 받고 마침내 그녀에게 허락해 주었다.

24 Mary는 그녀 자신과 다른 아프리카계 미국인들의 편에 섰다.

25 그것은 영화에서 나를 가장 감동하게 한 점이었다.

26 마침내 그녀는 NASA에서 최초의 아프리카계 미국인 여성 공학자가 되었다.

27 Dorothy Vaughan은 마지막 '히든 피겨(숨은 인물)'였다.

28 1961년 NASA에 IBM 컴퓨터가 설치되었을 때, 그녀는 '인간 컴퓨터(계산원)'들이 직업을 잃을까봐 걱정했다.

29 그녀는 새로운 프로그래밍 언어인 포트란을 공부했다.

30 그녀는 또한 그것을 그녀의 팀원들에게 가르쳤다.

31 나중에 그녀가 새 IBM 팀의 리더가 되도록 요청받았을 때, 그녀는 제안했다.

32 Dorothy: 저는 저의 여성 팀원들을 데려올 수 없다면 그 제안을 받아들이지 않겠습니다.

33 그 기계의 프로그램을 짜기 위해서는 많은 사람이 필요합니다.

34 저는 그것을 혼자 할 수 없습니다.

35 제 여성 팀원들은 준비가 되어 있습니다.

36 Dorothy 덕분에, 그녀의 팀원들은 프로그래머가 될 수 있었다.

37 그녀는 변화를 두려워하지 않고 그것을 기회로 이용했다.

38 그것이 내가 그녀에게서 배울 필요가 있는 점이다.

39 이 영화를 보면서, 나는 삶에서 어떻게 도전에 직면해야 하는지 배울 수 있었다.

40 나는 Katherine, Mary, 그리고 Dorothy의 눈물과 웃음을 잊지 않을 것이다.

● 우리말을 참고하여 본문을 영작하시오.

1 NASA의 숨겨진 인물들
➡ _____

2 나는 지난 주말에 〈히든 피겨스〉라는 영화를 보았다.
➡ _____

3 그것은 NASA에서 일했던 세 명의 아프리카계 미국인 여성들에 대한 영화였다.
➡ _____

4 그들은 1960년대에 '인간 컴퓨터(계산원)'로 일을 시작했다.
➡ _____

5 하지만 그들은 NASA에서 우주 전문가가 되기를 꿈꾸었고 어려움을 극복하기 위해 열심히 노력했다.
➡ _____

6 Katherine Johnson은 이 영화에서 세 명의 '숨겨진 인물들' 중 한 명이었다.
➡ _____

7 그녀는 열심히 일했고 수학에서 재능을 보였으며, 그녀의 상사인 Al Harrison은 그녀의 능력을 알아차렸다.
➡ _____

8 어느 날, 그는 Katherine이 너무 오래 자리를 비웠을 때 화가 났다.
➡ _____

9 Al은 Katherine에게 어디에 갔었는지 물었고 그녀는 대답했다.
➡ _____

10 Katherine: 화장실요.
➡ _____

11 이 건물에는 유색 인종 전용 화장실이 없어요.
➡ _____

12 저는 단지 화장실을 사용하기 위해 반 마일을 달려가야 해요.
➡ _____

13 이 말을 듣고서, 나는 그녀가 정말로 안됐다고 느꼈다.
➡ _____

14 그러나 나는 그 문제에 대해 상사에게 말한 그녀의 용기를 보고 기뻤다.
➡ _____

15 이것은 Al Harrison으로 하여금 '유색 여성 화장실' 표지판을 부수게 만들었다.
➡ _____

16 Mary Jackson은 셋 중에 가장 나의 마음에 드는 인물이었다.
➡ _____

17 그녀는 로켓 공학에 대해 더 많이 배우고 싶었지만 백인 학교에 다니는 것이 허락되지 않았다.
➡ _____

18 그래서 그녀는 판사에게 허락해 달라고 요청했다.
➡ _____

19 Mary: 저는 제 피부색을 바꿀 수 없어요.
➡ _____

20 그래서… 저는 '최초'가 되는 것 이외에는 선택이 없어요.

➡ _____

21 판사님, 당신이 오늘 들을 모든 사건 중에서, 백 년 뒤에 어느 것이 중요할까요?

➡ _____

22 어느 것이 판사님을 '최초'로 만들까요?

➡ _____

23 판사는 그녀가 말한 것에 감명을 받고 마침내 그녀에게 허락해 주었다.

➡ _____

24 Mary는 그녀 자신과 다른 아프리카계 미국인들의 편에 섰다.

➡ _____

25 그것은 영화에서 나를 가장 감동하게 한 점이었다.

➡ _____

26 마침내 그녀는 NASA에서 최초의 아프리카계 미국인 여성 공학자가 되었다.

➡ _____

27 Dorothy Vaughan은 마지막 '히든 피겨(숨은 인물)'였다.

➡ _____

28 1961년 NASA에 IBM 컴퓨터가 설치되었을 때, 그녀는 '인간 컴퓨터(계산원)'들이 직업을 잃을까 봐 걱정했다.

➡ _____

_____

29 그녀는 새로운 프로그래밍 언어인 포트란을 공부했다.

➡ _____

30 그녀는 또한 그것을 그녀의 팀원들에게 가르쳤다.

➡ _____

31 나중에 그녀가 새 IBM 팀의 리더가 되도록 요청받았을 때, 그녀는 제안했다.

➡ _____

32 Dorothy: 저는 저의 여성 팀원들을 데려올 수 없다면 그 제안을 받아들이지 않겠습니다.

➡ _____

33 그 기계의 프로그램을 짜기 위해서는 많은 사람이 필요합니다.

➡ _____

34 저는 그것을 혼자 할 수 없습니다.

➡ _____

35 제 여성 팀원들은 준비가 되어 있습니다.

➡ _____

36 Dorothy 덕분에, 그녀의 팀원들은 프로그래머가 될 수 있었다.

➡ _____

37 그녀는 변화를 두려워하지 않고 그것을 기회로 이용했다.

➡ _____

38 그것이 내가 그녀에게서 배울 필요가 있는 점이다.

➡ _____

39 이 영화를 보면서, 나는 삶에서 어떻게 도전에 직면해야 하는지 배울 수 있었다.

➡ _____

40 나는 Katherine, Mary, 그리고 Dorothy의 눈물과 웃음을 잊지 않을 것이다.

➡ _____

[01~03] 다음 글을 읽고 물음에 답하시오.

I watched the movie *Hidden* (A)*Figures* last weekend. It was a movie about three African-American women who worked at NASA. They began their career in the 1960s as "human computers." ____ⓐ____, they dreamed of becoming space experts at NASA and tried hard to get over difficulties.

중요

01 위 글의 빈칸 ⓐ에 들어갈 알맞은 말을 고르시오.

① For example ② However
③ Therefore ④ That is
⑤ In addition

02 위 글의 밑줄 친 (A)*Figures*와 같은 의미로 쓰인 것을 고르시오.

① She figures if she takes the night train, she can be in Scotland by morning.
② Tell me the latest sales figures.
③ Inflation is in double figures.
④ He figures the attendance at 1,500.
⑤ I met many leading figures in the music industry.

중요

03 According to the passage, which is NOT true?

① The writer watched the movie *Hidden Figures* last weekend.
② *Hidden Figures* was a movie about three African-American women who worked at NASA.
③ The three women began their career in the 1960s as "human computers."

④ The three women dreamed of becoming space astronauts at NASA.
⑤ The three women tried hard to get over difficulties.

[04~06] 다음 글을 읽고 물음에 답하시오.

Katherine Johnson was one of the three "hidden figures" in this movie. She worked hard and showed a talent ____ⓐ____ math, and her manager Al Harrison recognized her ability. One day, he got upset when Katherine was missing from her desk for too long. Al asked where Katherine had been, and she answered.

Katherine: The bathroom. There are no COLORED bathrooms in this building. I have to run half a mile away just to use the bathroom.

Hearing (A)this, I felt really sorry ____ⓑ____ her. However, I was glad that she had courage to talk to the manager about the problem. This made Al Harrison break down the "Colored Ladies Room" sign.

04 위 글의 빈칸 ⓐ와 ⓑ에 들어갈 전치사가 바르게 짝지어진 것은?

　　ⓐ　ⓑ　　　　　　ⓐ　ⓑ
① of – for　　② in – for
③ in – of　　④ for – on
⑤ of – on

서답형

05 위 글의 밑줄 친 (A)this가 가리키는 내용을 우리말로 쓰시오.

➡ _____

_____

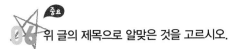 위 글의 제목으로 알맞은 것을 고르시오.

① The Three "Hidden Figures" at NASA

② Katherine's Wonderful Ability

③ Al Harrison Got Upset

④ No More "Colored Ladies Room"

⑤ Al Harrison, a Strict Manager

[07~09] 다음 글을 읽고 물음에 답하시오.

Mary Jackson was the character I liked the most of the three. She wanted to learn more about rocket science, but she wasn't allowed to go to a white school. So, she asked a judge to give her ⓐ .

Mary: I can't change the color of my skin. So ... I have no choice but to be the first. Your Honor, of all the cases you'll hear today, which one will matter in a hundred years? Which one will make you ⓑthe "first?"

The judge was impressed by what she said and ⓒfinally gave her permission. Mary stood up for herself and for other African-Americans. That was what impressed me most in the movie. Finally, she became the first African-American woman engineer at NASA.

[서답형]

07 위 글의 빈칸 ⓐ에 permit을 알맞은 형태로 쓰시오.

➡ _____

[서답형]

08 다음 빈칸 (A)와 (B)에 알맞은 단어를 넣어, 밑줄 친 ⓑthe first가 무엇을 의미하는지 완성하시오.

It means the first judge who allowed a (A)_____ student to take classes with (B)_____ students.

09 위 글의 밑줄 친 ⓒfinally와 바꿔 쓸 수 없는 말을 고르시오.

① eventually　　② after all

③ in the end　　④ at least

⑤ in the long run

[10~12] 다음 글을 읽고 물음에 답하시오.

I watched the movie *Hidden Figures* (A) [last / latest] weekend. It was a movie about ⓐ세 명의 아프리카계 미국인 여성들 who worked at NASA. They began their career in the 1960s as "human computers." However, they dreamed of becoming space (B)[experts / exports] at NASA and tried (C)[hard / hardly] ⓑto get over difficulties.

[서답형]

10 위 글의 괄호 (A)~(C)에서 문맥상 알맞은 낱말을 골라 쓰시오.

➡ (A) _____ (B) _____ (C) _____

[서답형]

11 위 글의 밑줄 친 ⓐ의 우리말에 맞게 3 단어로 영작하시오.

➡ _____

12 위 글의 밑줄 친 ⓑto get over와 to부정사의 용법이 다른 것을 모두 고르시오.

① I want to know how to get over difficulties.

② He was too weak to get over difficulties.

③ It is the fastest way to get over difficulties.

④ I tried to get over difficulties.

⑤ She was relieved to get over difficulties.

[13~14] 다음 글을 읽고 물음에 답하시오.

ⓐWatching this movie, ⓑI could learn how to face challenges in life. I won't forget the tears and laughter of Katherine, Mary, and Dorothy.

13 위 글의 밑줄 친 ⓐWatching과 문법적 쓰임이 같은 것을 고르시오.

① He was fond of watching movies.

② Do you know the man watching a movie there?

③ My brother was watching a movie.

④ Who enjoys watching the movie?

⑤ His hobby is watching movies.

서답형

14 위 글의 밑줄 친 ⓑ를 다음과 같이 바꿔 쓸 때 빈칸에 들어갈 알맞은 말을 두 단어로 쓰시오.

➡ I could learn how _____ face challenges in life.

[15~17] 다음 글을 읽고 물음에 답하시오.

(ⓐ) **Dorothy Vaughan** was the last "hidden figure." (ⓑ) When IBM computers were installed at NASA in 1961, she was worried ①the "human computers" would lose ②their jobs. (ⓒ) She also taught it to ③her team members. (ⓓ) Later, when she was asked to be the leader of a new IBM team, she made a suggestion. (ⓔ)

Dorothy: I'm not accepting the offer if I can't bring ④my ladies with me. ⑤We need a lot of people to program that machine. I can't do it alone. My girls are ready.

Thanks to Dorothy, her team members could become programmers. She wasn't afraid of change and used it as a chance. That's what I need to learn from her.

15 위 글의 흐름으로 보아, 주어진 문장이 들어가기에 가장 적절한 곳은?

She studied a new programming language, FORTRAN.

① ⓐ　　② ⓑ　　③ ⓒ　　④ ⓓ　　⑤ ⓔ

16 위 글의 밑줄 친 ①~⑤ 중에서 가리키는 대상이 나머지 넷과 다른 것은?

①　　②　　③　　④　　⑤

중요

17 According to the passage, which is NOT true?

① When IBM computers were installed at NASA in 1961, Dorothy Vaughan was worried the "human computers" would lose their jobs.

② Dorothy Vaughan studied a new programming language, FORTRAN.

③ Dorothy Vaughan taught FORTRAN to her team members.

④ Thanks to Dorothy, her team members could become programmers.

⑤ Dorothy Vaughan was afraid of using the change as a chance.

[18~21] 다음 글을 읽고 물음에 답하시오.

Katherine Johnson was one of the three "hidden figures" in this movie. She worked hard and showed a talent in math, and her manager Al Harrison recognized her ability. One day, he got ___ⓐ___ when Katherine was missing from her desk for too long. Al asked where Katherine had been, and she answered.

Katherine: The bathroom. (①) There are no COLORED bathrooms in this building. (②) I have to run half a mile away just to use the bathroom. (③)

Hearing this, I felt really sorry for her. (④) This made Al Harrison break down the "Colored Ladies Room" sign. (⑤)

18 위 글의 빈칸 ⓐ에 들어갈 알맞은 말을 고르시오.

① ashamed ② satisfied ③ upset
④ relieved ⑤ embarrassed

19 위 글의 흐름으로 보아, 주어진 문장이 들어가기에 가장 적절한 곳은?

> However, I was glad that she had courage to talk to the manager about the problem.

①   ②   ③   ④   ⑤

20 위 글을 읽고 알 수 없는 것을 고르시오.

① Who are the three "hidden figures" in the movie?
② In what did Katherine Johnson show a talent?
③ Who was Al Harrison?
④ Why did Al Harrison get upset?
⑤ Why was Katherine missing from her desk for too long?

서답형

21 다음 빈칸에 알맞은 단어를 넣어 Katherine Johnson에 대한 소개를 완성하시오.

> Katherine Johnson was a _____ _____ who made Al Harrison break down the "Colored Ladies Room" sign.

[22~24] 다음 글을 읽고 물음에 답하시오.

Mary Jackson was the character I liked the most of the three. She wanted to learn more about rocket science, but she wasn't allowed to go to a white school. So, she asked a judge to give her permission.

Mary: I can't change the color of my skin. So ... I have no choice but to be the first. Your Honor, of all the cases you'll hear today, which one will ⓐmatter in a hundred years? Which one will make you the "first?"

The judge was impressed by what she said and finally gave her ⓑpermission. Mary stood up for herself and for other African-Americans. That was what impressed me most in the movie. Finally, she became the first African-American woman engineer at NASA.

22 위 글의 밑줄 친 ⓐmatter와 같은 의미로 쓰인 것을 고르시오.

① They had an important matter to discuss.
② He wants to study the properties of matter.
③ It doesn't matter whether you are rich or not.
④ She didn't approve of their choice of reading matter.
⑤ Is anything the matter?

서답형

23 위 글의 밑줄 친 ⓑpermission 뒤에 생략된 말을 본문에서 찾아 쓰시오.

➡ _____

24 위 글의 종류로 알맞은 것을 고르시오.

① essay ② anecdote ③ review
④ article ⑤ book report

[01~03] 다음 글을 읽고 물음에 답하시오.

I watched the movie *Hidden Figures* last weekend. ⓐIt was a movie about three African-American women who worked at NASA. They began their career in the ⓑ 1960s as "human computers." However, they dreamed of becoming space experts at NASA and tried hard to ⓒget over difficulties.

01 위 글의 밑줄 친 ⓐIt이 가리키는 것을 본문에서 찾아 쓰시오.

➡ _____

02 위 글의 밑줄 친 ⓑ1960s를 영어로 읽으시오.

➡ _____

03 위 글의 밑줄 친 ⓒget over와 바꿔 쓸 수 있는 단어를 쓰시오.

➡ _____

[04~07] 다음 글을 읽고 물음에 답하시오.

Katherine Johnson was one of the three "hidden figures" in this movie. She worked hard and showed a talent in math, and her manager Al Harrison recognized her ability. One day, he got upset when Katherine was missing from her desk for too long. Al asked where Katherine had been, and she answered.

Katherine: The bathroom. There are no COLORED bathrooms in this building. I have to run half a mile away just to use the bathroom.

ⓐHearing this, I felt really sorry for her. However, I was glad that she had courage to talk to the manager about the problem. ⓑ This made Al Harrison to break down the "Colored Ladies Room" sign.

04 Why did Katherine have to run half a mile away just to use the bathroom? Answer in English beginning with "Because". (9 words)

➡ _____

_____

05 위 글의 밑줄 친 ⓐHearing this를 부사절로 고치시오.

➡ _____

06 위 글의 밑줄 친 ⓑ에서 어법상 틀린 부분을 찾아 고치시오.

_____ ➡ _____

07 다음 빈칸에 알맞은 단어를 넣어 위 글을 읽고 추론할 수 있는 내용을 완성하시오.

In the past, the colored people faced the racial discrimination. For example, even such a smart woman as Katherine could not use the _____ bathrooms with whites and was forced to use separate bathrooms.

*racial discrimination: 인종차별

[08~10] 다음 글을 읽고 물음에 답하시오.

Mary Jackson was the character I liked the most of the three. She wanted to learn more about rocket science, but she wasn't allowed to go to a white school. So, she asked a judge to give her permission.

Mary: I can't change the color of my skin. So ...

ⓐI have no choice but to be the first. Your Honor, of all the cases you'll hear today, which one will matter in a hundred years? Which one will make you the "first?"

The judge was impressed by what she said and finally gave her permission. Mary stood up for herself and for other African-Americans. ⓑ그것이 영화에서 나를 가장 감동하게 한 것이었다. Finally, she became the first African-American woman engineer at NASA.

08 위 글의 밑줄 친 ⓐ를 다음과 같이 바꿔 쓸 때 빈칸에 들어갈 알맞은 단어를 쓰시오.

➡ I cannot help _____ the first. = I cannot but _____ the first.

09 위 글의 밑줄 친 ⓑ의 우리말에 맞게 주어진 어휘를 이용하여 9 단어로 영작하시오.

> That, impressed, most

➡ _____

10 다음 빈칸 (A)와 (B)에 알맞은 단어를 넣어 Mary Jackson에 대한 소개를 완성하시오.

> Mary Jackson learned more about (A)_____ _____ at a white school, and became the first African-American woman (B)_____ at NASA.

[11~13] 다음 글을 읽고 물음에 답하시오.

Dorothy Vaughan was the last "hidden figure." When IBM computers were installed at NASA in 1961, she was worried the "human computers" would lose their jobs.

She studied a new programming language, FORTRAN. She also taught it to her team members. Later, when she was asked to be the leader of a new IBM team, she made a suggestion.

Dorothy: I'm not accepting the offer ⓐif I can't bring my ladies with me. We need a lot of people to program that machine. I can't do it alone. My girls are ready.

Thanks to Dorothy, her team members could become programmers. She wasn't afraid of change and used it as a chance. ⓑThat's what I need to learn from her.

Watching this movie, I could learn how to face challenges in life. I won't forget the tears and laughter of Katherine, Mary, and Dorothy.

11 위 글의 밑줄 친 ⓐ를 unless를 사용하여 고치시오.

➡ _____

12 위 글의 밑줄 친 ⓑThat이 가리키는 것을 본문에서 찾아 쓰시오.

➡ _____

13 다음 빈칸 (A)와 (B)에 알맞은 단어를 넣어 Dorothy Vaughan에 대한 소개를 완성하시오.

> Dorothy Vaughan was a hidden figure who studied a (A)_____ _____ _____, FORTRAN, and helped her team members become (B)_____ by teaching them FORTRAN.

교과서 구석구석

해석

Express Yourself C

1. I had a good time with the baker. He told me about his job, decorating some
   분사구문으로 '~하면서'로 해석한다.
   cupcakes. I will not forget what he said, "Make what your family love."
   관계대명사   Make의 목적어로 사용된 관계대명사절
2. I had a good time with the actor. He told me about his job, saying his
   동시동작의 분사구문
   famous lines. I will not forget what he said, "You can be what you act."
   forget의 목적어로 사용된 관계대명사절   be동사의 보어로 사용된 관계대명사절

구문해설 • baker: 제빵사 • decorate: 장식하다 • forget: 잊다 • actor: 배우 • line: 대사

1. 저는 제빵사와 즐거운 시간을 보냈습니다. 그는 컵케이크에 장식하며 그의 직업에 대해 말해 주었습니다. 저는 그가 말한 것을 잊지 않을 것입니다. "가족이 좋아하게 될 것을 만드세요."
2. 저는 그 배우와 즐거운 시간을 보냈습니다. 그는 자신의 유명한 대사를 말하면서 그의 직업에 대해 말해 주었습니다. 저는 그가 말한 것을 잊지 않을 것입니다. "당신은 자신이 연기하는 것이 될 수 있습니다."

After You Read A

Katherine Johnson: I made my manager break down the "Colored Ladies
                                                    to break(×)
Room" sign.

Mary Jackson: I asked the judge to allow me to study at a white school.
                     ask+목적어+to부정사   allow+목적어+to부정사

Dorothy Vaughan: I studied a new programming language to prepare for
                                                          to부정사의 부사적 용법(목적)
change.

구문해설 • manager: 관리자, 경영자 • break down: ~을 부수다 • colored: 색깔이 있는, 유색 인종의
• judge: 판사 • allow: 허락하다 • prepare for: ~을 준비하다

Katherine Johnson: 나는 나의 상사로 하여금 '유색 여성 화장실' 표지판을 부수게 만들었다.

Mary Jackson: 나는 판사에게 백인 학교에서 공부하도록 허락해 달라고 요청했다.

Dorothy Vaughan: 나는 변화에 대비해 준비하기 위하여 새로운 프로그래밍 언어를 공부했다.

Link to the World

Q1 What do you do at this restaurant?

A1 I make various Italian dishes and desserts.

Q2 What is difficult about your job?

A2 I have so many things to do other than cooking. I have to buy fresh meat
                                 형용사적 용법 : ~해야 할
and vegetables every day. I also wash the dishes and keep my kitchen clean.
                                                      keep   목적어   목적보어(형용사)
Q3 Are you happy with your job?

A3 Yes, I am. It's a tough job, but I love what I do. I feel proud, seeing people
                                      선행사를 포함한 관계대명사: ~하는 것   분사구문: ~하면서
enjoy my dishes.

구문해설 • various: 다양한 • dessert: 후식 • other than: ~ 이외에도 • tough: 힘든

Q1. 당신은 이 식당에서 무엇을 합니까?
A1. 저는 다양한 이탈리아 요리와 후식을 만듭니다.
Q2. 당신 직업의 어려운 점은 무엇입니까?
A2. 저는 요리 외에도 할 일이 많습니다. 저는 매일 신선한 고기와 채소를 사야 합니다. 또한 설거지하고 주방을 깨끗이 유지합니다.
Q3. 당신은 당신의 직업에 만족합니까?
A3. 네, 그렇습니다. 힘든 직업이지만, 저는 제가 하는 일을 좋아합니다. 저는 사람들이 제 요리를 즐기는 것을 보면서 자부심을 느낍니다.

Words & Expressions

01 다음 주어진 두 단어의 관계가 같도록 빈칸에 알맞은 단어를 쓰시오.

> courage – cowardice : novice – _____

02 다음 문장의 빈칸 (a)와 (b)에 들어갈 말이 바르게 짝지어진 것은?

> • Anger can be a good thing because it helps you ___(a)___ yourself when you are treated unfairly.
> • Teachers, journalists, and public civil servants cannot ___(b)___ expensive gifts.

① break down – accept
② get over – allow
③ stand up for – accept
④ stand up for – remove
⑤ get over – compete

[03~04] 다음 영영풀이에 해당하는 것을 고르시오.

03

> the person in a court who decides how criminals should be punished

① magician ② volunteer ③ manager
④ reporter ⑤ judge

04

> a large cylinder-shaped object that moves very fast and is used for space travel

① rocket ② permission ③ ability
④ figure ⑤ plane

05 빈칸에 들어갈 전치사를 〈영영풀이〉를 참고하여 쓰시오.

> A: Why are you disappointed?
> B: My parents won't let me join the dance club.
> A: I'm sorry to hear that. Why are they _____ it?
> B: They want me to study hard to be a lawyer. They're always worried about my grades.

> 〈영영풀이〉 disagreeing with a plan or activity

➡ _____

06 다음 밑줄 친 부분의 뜻이 잘못된 것은?

① I'm concerned about my low grades. (성적)
② The actors went to the audition for the movie. (관객)
③ Bibimbap is one of the most popular Korean dishes. (요리)
④ I'm worried about my presentation tomorrow. (발표)
⑤ They laughed at me when I made a mistake. (비웃었다)

Conversation

07 다음 대화에서 단어의 쓰임이 어색한 부분을 찾아 바르게 고치시오.

> B: I want to be a cooker, but everybody laughs at me. Do you think I should give up my dream?
> G: No, never give up. I think you're really good at cooking.

_____ ➡ _____

08 주어진 문장에 이어질 대화를 순서에 맞게 바르게 배열한 것은?

> G: Why are you disappointed?
> (A) Yes. It will help your classmates understand you better.
> (B) I didn't give a good presentation.
> (C) Do you think I should speak more slowly?
> (D) Take it easy. Your speech was a little fast, but I liked your presentation.

① (B) – (A) – (C) – (D)
② (B) – (D) – (C) – (A)
③ (C) – (B) – (D) – (A)
④ (D) – (A) – (C) – (B)
⑤ (D) – (B) – (A) – (C)

09 다음 짝지어진 대화 중 어색한 것은?

① A: Why are you disappointed?
　 B: I didn't give a good presentation.
② A: Why are you disappointed?
　 B: I failed the math exam.
③ A: Do you think I should learn more cooking tips?
　 B: Yes. I think they will help.
④ A: Do you think I should study harder for my future?
　 B: Yes. I think you should read many books.
⑤ A: Do you think I should have a role model for my future?
　 B: Yes. Making a model plane is not easy.

[10~12] 다음 대화를 읽고 물음에 답하시오.

> Jisu: Why are you so disappointed, Ryan?
> Ryan: My parents (a)won't let me enter Superstar 101, a singing competition.
> Jisu: I'm sorry to hear that. Why are they (b)for it?
> Ryan: They want me to study hard and be a doctor. They're always (c)worried about my grades.
> Jisu: Did you tell your parents you really want to be a singer?
> Ryan: (d)Not yet. Do you think I should talk with them about it?
> Jisu: Yes. Just show them how much you (e)love singing. Why don't you sing the songs you made in front of them?
> Ryan: Okay. I'll try. Thank you for your advice, Jisu.

10 위 대화의 밑줄 친 (a)~(e) 중 어휘의 쓰임이 어색한 것은?

① (a)　② (b)　③ (c)　④ (d)　⑤ (e)

11 위 대화의 제목으로 가장 적절한 것은?

① How to Enter a Singing Competition
② Disagreement Between Parents and Their Child
③ Difficulty in Making Songs
④ I Want to Be a Singer
⑤ Saying and Doing are Two Different Things

12 위 대화의 내용과 일치하지 않는 것을 고르시오.

① Ryan is disappointed because his parents won't let him enter Superstar 101.
② Ryan's parents aren't worried about his grade but they want him to be a doctor.
③ Jisu advises him to tell his parents about his dream.
④ Ryan wants to enter a singing competition.
⑤ Ryan thanks Jisu for her advice.

13 주어진 문장의 밑줄 친 what과 쓰임이 같은 것은?

> Q3 Are you happy with your job?
>
> A3 Yes, I am. It's a tough job, but I love what I do. I feel proud, seeing people enjoy my dishes.

① Not knowing what to do, I asked him for help.

② Judging from what he's wearing, he's probably a soldier.

③ Can you tell me what the main ingredients are in this dish?

④ I want to know what reason you are crying for.

⑤ I don't remember what color she likes.

14 다음 문장에서 어법상 어색한 부분을 찾아 바르게 고치시오.

> Leaving alone in the room, the baby began to cry.

➡ _____

15 다음 우리말을 바르게 영작한 것은?

> 비가 와서, 우리는 밖에서 축구를 하지 않았다.

① Raining, we didn't play soccer outside.

② It raining, we didn't play soccer outside.

③ As rained, we didn't play soccer outside.

④ As was raining, we didn't play soccer outside.

⑤ Raining it, we didn't play soccer outside.

16 다음 중 어법상 어색한 문장의 개수로 알맞은 것은?

> a. Walk along the street, I saw a big cat.
> b. Lives in America, he speaks English very well.
> c. When he saw me, he ran away
> d. They sat on the beach, looked at the rising sun.
> e. While I was walking the dog, I saw a UFO over the roof.
> f. As he was running down the stairs, he fell down.

① 1개　② 2개　③ 3개　④ 4개　⑤ 5개

17 다음 중 밑줄 친 부분의 쓰임이 나머지 넷과 다른 하나는?

① I can't believe what I saw.

② Baseball is what I like most.

③ I'm sorry, but this isn't what we ordered.

④ I don't know what your name is.

⑤ What I need is a new computer.

18 밑줄 친 부분에 유의하여, 바르게 해석하시오.

(1) David remembers what she said.

➡ _____

(2) That's what you should learn.

➡ _____

(3) What matters is that you tried your best.

➡ _____

19 다음 빈칸에 들어갈 말로 적절하지 않은 것을 고르시오.

> Tell me _____ you did yesterday.

① the things　② what

③ that　④ anything

⑤ the things that

Reading

[20~21] 다음 글을 읽고 물음에 답하시오.

Katherine Johnson was one of the three "hidden figures" in this movie. She worked hard and showed a talent in math, and her manager Al Harrison recognized her ability. One day, he got upset when Katherine was missing from her desk for too long. @<u>Al은 Katherine에게 어디에 갔었는지 물었고</u>, and she answered.

Katherine: The bathroom. There are no COLORED bathrooms in this building. I have to run half a mile away just to use the bathroom.

Hearing this, I felt really sorry for her. However, I was glad that she had courage to talk to the manager about the problem. This made Al Harrison break down the "Colored Ladies Room" sign.

20 위 글의 밑줄 친 @의 우리말에 맞게 주어진 어휘를 알맞게 배열하시오.

Katherine / asked / had / Al / been / where

➡ _____

21 According to the passage, which is NOT true?

① There were two more "hidden figures" except Katherine Johnson in the movie.

② Katherine Johnson worked hard and showed a talent in math.

③ Al Harrison was Katherine's manager and envied her ability.

④ There were no COLORED bathrooms in the building.

⑤ Al Harrison was a considerate man.

[22~24] 다음 글을 읽고 물음에 답하시오.

Mary Jackson was the character I liked the most of the three. She wanted to learn more about rocket science, but she wasn't allowed to go to a white school. So, she asked a judge to give her permission.

Mary: I can't change the color of my skin. So ... I have no choice but to be the first. Your Honor, of all the @<u>cases</u> you'll hear today, which one will matter in a hundred years? Which one will make you the "first?"

The judge was impressed by what she said and finally gave her permission. Mary stood up for herself and for other African-Americans. That was what impressed me most in the movie. Finally, she became the first African-American woman engineer at NASA.

22 위 글의 밑줄 친 @<u>cases</u>와 같은 의미로 쓰인 것을 고르시오.

① In some <u>cases</u> people have had to wait several weeks for an appointment.

② She has won many court <u>cases</u> until now.

③ The most serious <u>cases</u> were treated at the scene of the accident.

④ The museum was full of stuffed animals in glass <u>cases</u>.

⑤ In some <u>cases</u>, you can't really tell people the truth.

23 위 글의 제목으로 알맞은 것을 고르시오.

① My Favorite Character of the Three
② How to Learn More about Rocket Science
③ I Can't Change the Color of My Skin
④ A Woman Who Had No Choice but to Be the First
⑤ Which One Will Make You the "First?"

24 위 글의 내용과 일치하도록 다음 빈칸 (A)와 (B)에 알맞은 단어를 쓰시오.

> Mary Jackson was given (A)_____ _____ to go to a white school, where she learned more about rocket science, and she (B)_____ _____ for herself and for other African-Americans.

[25~27] 다음 글을 읽고 물음에 답하시오.

Dorothy: I'm not accepting the offer if I can't bring my ladies with me. We need a lot of people to program that machine. (A)I can't do it alone. My girls are ready.

_____ⓐ_____ Dorothy, her team members could become programmers. She wasn't afraid of change and used (B)it as a chance. That's what I need to learn from her.

Watching this movie, I could learn how to face challenges in life. I won't forget the tears and laughter of Katherine, Mary, and Dorothy.

25 위 글의 빈칸 ⓐ에 들어갈 알맞은 말을 고르시오.

① In spite of   ② Thanks to
③ Rather than   ④ In terms of
⑤ Instead of

26 위 글의 밑줄 친 (A)를 다음과 같이 바꿔 쓸 때 빈칸에 들어갈 알맞은 말을 두 단어로 쓰시오.

➡ I can't do it _____.

27 위 글의 밑줄 친 (B)it이 가리키는 것을 본문에서 찾아 쓰시오.

➡ _____

[28~29] 다음 글을 읽고 물음에 답하시오.

I had a good time with the baker. He told me about his job, ⓐdecorating some cupcakes. I will not forget ⓑwhat he said, "Make what your family will love."

28 위 글의 밑줄 친 ⓐdecorating some cupcakes를 부사절로 고치시오.

➡ _____

29 위 글의 밑줄 친 ⓑwhat과 문법적 쓰임이 같은 것을 모두 고르시오.

① What kind of music do you like?
② What you need is a good meal.
③ What is your name?
④ What a beautiful house!
⑤ She pointed to what looked like a bird.

단원별 예상문제

01 출제율 90%

다음 짝지어진 단어의 관계가 같도록 빈칸에 알맞은 말을 쓰시오.

> accept – acceptance : compete – _____

02 출제율 95%

다음 영영풀이에 해당하는 단어는?

> the series of jobs that you do during your working life

① figure   ② expert   ③ career
④ engineer   ⑤ courage

03 출제율 90%

다음 대화를 읽고 빈칸에 들어갈 말을 〈조건〉에 맞게 쓰시오.

┤ 조건 ├
• 슬픔, 불만족, 실망의 원인에 대해 물을 것.
• 'face'를 사용하여 4 단어로 쓸 것.

> B: _____
> G: I failed the audition for the Mapo Youth Band. Do you think I should keep trying?
> B: Sure. Don't give up. You'll do better next time.
> G: Thank you.

➡ _____

[04~05] 다음 대화를 읽고 물음에 답하시오.

> (A) Please come in. Are you interested in designing things?
> (B) I think that will help, but it's more important to practice drawing every day. Reading design magazines will also help you.

> (C) Yes, I want to be a product designer. Do you think I should go to design school?
> Boy: Thank you. I'll keep that in mind.

04 출제율 100%

위 대화의 (A)~(C)를 순서대로 배열하시오.

➡ _____

05 출제율 95%

위 대화를 읽고 다음 질문에 영어로 답하시오.

> Q: What should the boy do to be a product designer?

➡ _____

_____

06 출제율 100%

다음 대화의 빈칸에 들어갈 말로 알맞은 것은?

> W: You don't look happy. Why are you disappointed?
> B: I want to be a wonderful magician like you, but I failed the magic competition.
> _____
> W: No. Practice hard every day and you'll get better and better. It's important to keep trying.
> B: Okay, I'll try. Thank you for your advice.

① Do you like this trick?
② Do you think I should keep trying?
③ Do you think I should give up?
④ Do you think I should study harder?
⑤ Do you think I should practice harder?

07 아래 대화에서 다음 문장이 들어갈 위치로 알맞은 것은?

> How about getting useful tips from cooking shows online?

> G: Junsu, you look down today. Why are you disappointed? (①)
>
> B: I lost the cooking competition.
>
> G: I'm sorry to hear that. I know you tried hard. (②)
>
> B: Yeah, but maybe that wasn't enough. (③) Do you think I should learn more cooking tips? (④)
>
> G: Yes. I think they will help. (⑤)
>
> B: Okay. I'll try. Thank you for your advice, Mina.
>
> G: You're welcome. Just remember I'm a fan of your dishes.

①   ②   ③   ④   ⑤

08 다음 대화의 빈칸 (A)에 들어갈 말로 적절하지 않은 것은?

> B: You look down today, Minji. _____(A)_____
>
> G: We lost the soccer game because I made a mistake.
>
> B: Don't be so sad. It can happen to anyone.
>
> G: Do you think I should practice more?
>
> B: Well, yes. I can help you if you want. You know, I'm a good soccer player.
>
> G: Really? Thank you, Seho.

① Why are you disappointed?

② What's wrong?

③ Is there anything wrong?

④ Why don't you play soccer with us?

⑤ Why the long face?

09 빈칸에 들어갈 말로 알맞은 것은?

> B: You don't look happy. Why are you disappointed?
>
> G: We lost the basketball game because of my mistake.
>
> B: Come on. Everyone makes mistakes.
>
> G: _____
>
> B: Well, yes. You know, practice makes perfect.

① Why don't you practice dancing hard?

② Do you think I should practice more?

③ Why don't you perform in front of them?

④ Do you think I should give up?

⑤ Do you think I should go to design school?

10 밑줄 친 부분에 유의하여, 바르게 해석하시오.

> (1) <u>Having a cold</u>, he went to bed early.
>
> (2) <u>Arriving at the airport</u>, she called her parents.
>
> (3) <u>Drinking a lot of water</u>, you will be healthier.

➡ (1) _____

   (2) _____

   (3) _____

11 밑줄 친 부분과 바꾸어 쓸 수 없는 것은? (2개)

> <u>While I was walking</u> down the street, I saw my cat cross the street.

① While walking   ② Walking

③ While I walking   ④ While walked

⑤ As I was walking

12 잘못된 부분을 바르게 고쳐 문장을 다시 쓰시오.
출제율 90%

(1) Make the things what your family will love.

➡ _____

(2) Design that you dream of.

➡ _____

(3) I will not forget what he said it.

➡ _____

(4) She told me about her job, and drawing some product designs.

➡ _____
_____

(5) You can be which you act.

➡ _____

13 괄호 안에 주어진 표현을 사용하여 우리말로 된 대화를 영어로 완성하시오.
출제율 95%

(1) (That, what, want)
A: Do you like this book?
B: Yes. 그것이 내가 읽기를 원하는 것이야.

➡ _____

(2) (That, what, looking)
A: Here is your cap.
B: Thanks. 그것이 내가 찾고 있었던 것이야.

➡ _____

(3) (That, what, have, mind)
A: Is this doll what you want?
B: No. 그것은 내가 생각하는 것이 아니야.

➡ _____

[14~15] 다음 글을 읽고 물음에 답하시오.

I watched the movie *Hidden Figures* last weekend. It was a movie about three African-American women who worked at NASA. They began their ___ⓐ___ in the 1960s ⓑas "human computers." However, they dreamed of becoming space experts at NASA and tried hard to get over difficulties.

14 주어진 영영풀이를 참고하여 빈칸 ⓐ에 철자 c로 시작하는 단어를 쓰시오.
출제율 90%

the job or profession that someone does for a long period of their life

➡ _____

15 위 글의 밑줄 친 ⓑas와 같은 의미로 쓰인 것을 고르시오.
출제율 95%

① They did as I had asked.
② He runs as fast as you run.
③ I respect him as a doctor.
④ As you were out, I left a message.
⑤ Such flowers as the rose require special care.

[16~18] 다음 글을 읽고 물음에 답하시오.

Katherine Johnson was one of the three "hidden figures" in this movie. She worked hard and showed a talent in math, and her manager Al Harrison recognized her ability. ⓐOne day, he got upset when Katherine was missed from her desk for too long. Al asked where Katherine had been, and she answered.
Katherine: The bathroom. There are no COLORED bathrooms in this building. I have to run half a mile away just to use the bathroom.

Hearing this, I felt really sorry for her. However, I was glad that she had courage ⓑto talk to the manager about the problem. This made Al Harrison break down the "Colored Ladies Room" sign.

16 출제율 95%
위 글의 밑줄 친 ⓐ에서 어법상 틀린 부분을 찾아 고치시오.

_____ ➡ _____

17 출제율 90%
아래 〈보기〉에서 위 글의 밑줄 친 ⓑto talk와 to부정사의 용법이 같은 것의 개수를 고르시오.

┌─ 보기 ┐
① He grew up to be a movie director.
② She had the kindness to show me the way.
③ It is a lot of fun to play tennis.
④ He was the first man to land on the moon.
⑤ His dream is to start a business.
└─────────┘

① 1개   ② 2개   ③ 3개   ④ 4개   ⑤ 5개

18 출제율 95%
What made Al Harrison break down the "Colored Ladies Room" sign? Fill in the blank with a suitable word.

Katherine's _____ to his question got him to break down the "Colored Ladies Room" sign.

[19~21] 다음 글을 읽고 물음에 답하시오.

Mary Jackson was the character I liked the most of the three. She wanted to learn more about rocket science, but she wasn't allowed to go to a white school. So, she asked a judge to give her permission.

Mary: I can't change the color of my skin. So ... I have no choice but to be the first. Your Honor, of all the cases you'll hear today, which one will matter in a hundred years? Which one will make you the "first?"

(A)판사는 그녀가 말한 것에 감명을 받고 마침내 그녀에게 허락해 주었다. Mary stood up for herself and for other African-Americans. That was _____ ⓐ impressed me most in the movie. Finally, she became the first African-American woman engineer at NASA.

19 출제율 95%
위 글의 빈칸 ⓐ에 들어갈 알맞은 말을 고르시오.

① which   ② why   ③ how
④ that   ⑤ what

20 출제율 90%
위 글의 밑줄 친 (A)의 우리말에 맞게 주어진 어휘를 알맞게 배열하시오.

she / permission / finally / said / the judge / impressed / gave / what / and / by / her / was

➡ _____
_____

21 출제율 100%
According to the passage, which is NOT true?

① The writer liked Mary Jackson the most of the three.
② Mary Jackson asked a judge to give her permission to go to a white school.
③ Mary Jackson couldn't be the first.
④ Mary Jackson supported herself and other African-Americans.
⑤ There was no other African-American woman engineer at NASA before Mary Jackson.

01 다음 대화의 우리말에 맞게 주어진 단어를 알맞은 순서로 배열하시오.

> B: You don't look happy. Why are you disappointed?
> G: We lost the basketball game because of my mistake.
> B: Come on. Everyone makes mistakes.
> G: 내가 더 연습해야 한다고 생각하니? (do / I / practice / you / should / more / think / ?)
> B: Well, yes. You know, practice makes perfect.

➡ _____

02 다음 대화를 읽고 요약문을 완성하시오.

> Jisu: Why are you so disappointed, Ryan?
> Ryan: My parents won't let me enter Superstar 101, a singing competition.
> Jisu: I'm sorry to hear that. Why are they against it?
> Ryan: They want me to study hard and be a doctor. They're always worried about my grades.
> Jisu: Did you tell your parents you really want to be a singer?
> Ryan: Not yet. Do you think I should talk with them about it?
> Jisu: Yes. Just show them how much you love singing. Why don't you sing the songs you made in front of them?
> Ryan: Okay. I'll try. Thank you for your advice, Jisu.

> Ryan's _____ is to be a singer, so he wants to _____ a singing competition. But his parents are _____ it because they want him to be a _____. Ryan

is very _____. Jisu _____ him to tell his parents about his dream and to _____ them _____ _____ he loves singing. Ryan _____ Jisu for her _____.

03 다음 글에서 어법상 틀린 곳의 기호를 쓰고 바르게 고치시오.

> Q2 What is difficult about your job?
> A2 I have so many things ㉠doing other than cooking. I have to buy fresh meat and vegetables every day. I also wash the dishes and keep my kitchen ㉡clean.
> Q3 Are you happy ㉢with your job?
> A3 Yes, I am. It's a tough job, but I love ㉣which I do. I feel proud, ㉤see people enjoy my dishes.

(1) ____ → _____ (2) ____ → _____
(3) ____ → _____

04 〈보기〉의 문장을 참고하여 그림에 나타난 사람들을 설명하는 문장을 괄호 안에 주어진 단어를 사용하여 완성하시오

> ┌── 보기 ──┐
> Listening to music, Amy jumped rope.

(1) (sing, song), Jack danced wonderfully.
 ➡ _____
(2) (drink, milk), Sam walked his dog.
 ➡ _____
(3) Eating some cookies, (read, book).
 ➡ _____
(4) Holding some balloons, (kick, ball).
 ➡ _____

Mary Jackson was the character I liked the most of the three. She wanted to learn more about rocket science, but she wasn't allowed ____ⓐ____ to a white school. So, she asked a judge to give her permission.

Mary: I can't change the color of my skin. So ... I have no choice but to be the first. Your Honor, of all the cases you'll hear today, which one will matter in a hundred years? Which one will make you the "first?"

The judge was impressed by what she said and finally gave her permission. Mary stood up for herself and for other African-Americans. That was what impressed me most in the movie. Finally, she became the first African-American woman engineer at NASA.

05 위 글의 빈칸 ⓐ에 go를 알맞은 형태로 쓰시오.

➡ _____

06 다음 문장에서 위 글의 내용과 <u>다른</u> 부분을 찾아서 고치시오.

> Mary Jackson became the first woman engineer at NASA.

_____ ➡ _____

07 본문의 내용과 일치하도록 다음 빈칸 (A)와 (B)에 알맞은 단어를 쓰시오.

> Mary Jackson was a hidden figure who made the judge become the (A)_____ who permitted a black student to take classes with white students. She also (B)_____ African-Americans as well as herself.

Dorothy Vaughan was the last "hidden figure." ⓐ<u>When IBM computers installed at NASA in 1961, she was worried the "human computers" would lose their jobs.</u> She studied a new programming language, FORTRAN. She also taught it to her team members. Later, when she was asked to be the leader of a new IBM team, she made a suggestion.

Dorothy: I'm not accepting the offer if I can't bring my ladies with me. We need a lot of people to program that machine. I can't do it alone. My girls are ready.

Thanks to Dorothy, her team members could become programmers. ⓑ<u>그녀는 변화를 두려워하지 않고 그것을 기회로 이용했다.</u> That's what I need to learn from her.

ⓒ<u>Watching this movie,</u> I could learn how to face challenges in life. I won't forget the tears and laughter of Katherine, Mary, and Dorothy.

08 위 글의 밑줄 친 ⓐ에서 어법상 틀린 부분을 찾아 고치시오.

_____ ➡ _____

09 위 글의 밑줄 친 ⓑ의 우리말에 맞게 주어진 어휘를 알맞게 배열하시오.

> afraid / a chance / used / of / change / wasn't / and / it / as / she

➡ _____

10 위 글의 밑줄 친 ⓒWatching this movie를 부사절로 고치시오.

➡ _____

01 아래 표의 (A)의 고민과 어울리는 충고의 말을 (B)에서 골라 〈보기〉와 같이 대화를 완성하시오.

(A)	(B)
• lost the dance competition	• study harder
• got a bad grade	• practice harder
• fought with my friend	• talk to my friend about it

보기

A: Why are you disappointed?

B: I got a bad grade. Do you think I should study harder?

A: Yes, I think so.

02 다음 내용을 바탕으로 빈칸을 채워 직업에 대한 부스 체험 소감문을 완성하시오.

1. W: Please come in. Are you interested in designing things?

   B: Yes, I want to be a product designer. Do you think I should go to design school?

   W: I think that will help, but it's more important to design what you dream of. Reading design magazines will also help you.

   B: Thank you. I'll keep that in mind.

2. W: You don't look happy. Why are you disappointed?

   B: I want to be a wonderful magician like you, but I failed the magic competition. Do you think I should give up?

   W: No. Practice hard every day and you'll get better and better. It's important not to believe what you see.

   B: Okay, I'll try. Thank you for your advice.

1. I had a good time with the (A)_____. She told me about her job, drawing some product designs. I will not forget what she said, "Design (B)_____."

2. I had a good time with the (C)_____. She told me about her job, doing some magic tricks. I will not forget what she said, "Don't believe (D)_____."

단원별 모의고사

01 다음 단어에 대한 영어 설명이 <u>어색한</u> 것은?

① hidden: not easy to find
② figure: a well-known person
③ recognize: to know someone or something because you have experienced it before
④ courage: the skill or qualities that you need to do something
⑤ impress: to cause someone to feel admiration or respect

02 다음 짝지어진 단어의 관계가 같도록 빈칸에 알맞은 말을 쓰시오.

courage – bravery : veiled – _____

03 다음 영영풀이에 해당하는 단어를 고르시오.

to put a machine or a piece of equipment into position and to make it ready to use

① reach   ② accept   ③ install
④ fill   ⑤ throw

04 다음 중 짝지어진 대화가 <u>어색한</u> 것은?

① A: Do you like this book?
   B: Yes. That's what I want to read.
② A: Do you like this camera?
   B: Yes. That's what I want.
③ A: Here is your notebook.
   B: Thanks. That's what I was looking for.
④ A: Is this doll what you want?
   B: No. That's not what I have in mind.
⑤ A: Do you think I should take magic lessons?
   B: I want to be a magician like you.

05 대화의 흐름상 빈칸에 들어갈 문장을 〈조건〉에 맞게 쓰시오.

G: Junsu, you look down today. Why are you disappointed?
B: I lost the cooking competition.
G: I'm sorry to hear that. I know you tried hard.
B: Yeah, but maybe that wasn't enough. Do you think I should learn more cooking tips?
G: Yes. I think they will help. _____ from cooking shows online?
B: Okay. I'll try. Thank you for your advice, Mina.
G: You're welcome. Just remember I'm a fan of your dishes.

┤ 조건 ├
• How about을 이용하여 '~하는 게 어때?'라는 제안의 표현을 쓸 것.
• 'get useful tips'를 이용할 것.

➡ _____

06 다음 빈칸에 들어갈 말로 <u>어색한</u> 것은?

G: You look down today. _____
B: I want to take dance classes, but my father doesn't like that idea. He thinks that boys should play sports.
G: I'm sorry to hear that.

① What's the matter?
② Why are you disappointed?
③ What happened?
④ What makes you so sad?
⑤ What are you looking forward to?

07 대화의 흐름상 밑줄 친 ①~⑤ 중 어색한 것은?

> W: You don't ①look sad. Why are you disappointed?
> B: I want to ②be a wonderful magician like you, but I ③failed the magic competition. Do you think I should give up?
> W: No. Practice hard every day and you'll ④get better and better. It's important to keep trying.
> B: Okay, I'll try. ⑤Thank you for your advice.

① ② ③ ④ ⑤

08 다음 대화의 빈칸에 들어갈 말로 알맞은 것은?

> G: Why are you disappointed?
> B: I didn't give a good presentation.
> G: Take it easy. Your speech was a little fast, but I liked your presentation.
> B: _____
> G: Yes. It will help your classmates understand you better.

① Do you think I should talk with them about it?
② Do you think I should speak more slowly?
③ Do you think I should keep trying?
④ Do you think I should give up my dream?
⑤ Do you think I should practice more?

09 다음 주어진 문장에 이어질 대화 순서를 알맞게 배열하시오.

> A: Why are you disappointed?
> (A) I'm sorry to hear that.
> (B) Sure. You'll do better next time.
> (C) I failed the audition for the band.
> (D) Do you think I should keep trying?

➡ _____

[10~11] 다음 대화를 읽고 물음에 답하시오.

> W: Please come in. Are you interested in designing things? (①)
> B: Yes, I want to be a product designer. (②) Do you think I should go to design school? (③)
> W: I think that will help, but it's more important to practice drawing every day. (④)
> B: Thank you. (⑤) I'll __(A)__ that in mind.

10 위 대화의 (①)~(⑤) 중 주어진 문장이 들어갈 위치로 알맞은 곳은?

> Reading design magazines will also help you.

① ② ③ ④ ⑤

11 위 대화의 빈칸 (A)에 들어갈 단어를 쓰시오.

➡ _____

[12~14] 다음 대화를 읽고 물음에 답하시오.

Jisu: Why are you so disappointed, Ryan?

Ryan: My parents won't let me enter Superstar 101, a singing competition.

Jisu: I'm sorry to hear that. Why are they (a) against it?

Ryan: _____ (A) _____ They're always worried about my grades.

Jisu: Did you tell your parents you really want to be a singer?

Ryan: Not yet. Do you think I should talk with them about it?

Jisu: Yes. Just show them how much you love singing. Why don't you sing the songs you made in front of them?

Ryan: Okay. I'll try. Thank you for your advice, Jisu.

12 위 대화의 빈칸 (A)에 들어갈 말로 알맞은 것은?

① They want me to pursue my dream.

② They really want me to sing a song at Superstar 101.

③ They want me to be a singer.

④ They don't want to talk with me.

⑤ They want me to study hard and be a doctor.

13 위 대화를 읽고 다음 질문에 영어로 답하시오.

Q: Why is Ryan disappointed?

➡ _____

14 위 대화의 밑줄 친 (a)의 'against'와 같은 의미로 사용된 것은?

① I was standing, leaning against Mahatma Gandhi's statue.

② They took precautions against fire.

③ In 1959, Tibetan people rose up in a movement against the Chinese rule.

④ His red clothes stood out clearly against the snow.

⑤ You must weigh the benefits against the cost.

15 다음 중 어법상 어색한 문장을 모두 고르시오.

① This is the thing that she likes it.

② He gave me what I wanted.

③ He read a newspaper, drank coffee.

④ Feeling sick, I had to take the test.

⑤ He had breakfast, going to work.

16 다음 주어진 문장과 뜻이 가장 가까운 문장은?

Doing a lot of exercise, I'm still gaining weight.

① If I do a lot of exercise, I'm still gaining weight.

② As I do a lot of exercise, I'm still gaining weight.

③ Because I do a lot of exercise, I'm still gaining weight.

④ Though I do a lot of exercise, I'm still gaining weight.

⑤ After I do a lot of exercise, I'm still gaining weight.

17 다음 우리말을 영어로 바르게 옮긴 것은?

> 그는 손을 흔들며 작별인사를 했다.

① Saying good-bye, waving his hand.
② He said good-bye, waving his hand.
③ He saying good-bye, waved his hand.
④ As he said good-bye, waving his hand.
⑤ He said good-bye, waved his hand.

18 다음은 직업 체험에 대한 소감의 일부이다. 〈보기〉에 주어진 표현을 골라 분사구문을 사용하여 글을 완성하시오.

> ┤ 보기 ├
> • decorate some cupcakes
> • control robots
> • do some magic tricks
> • say one's famous lines
> • show ... one's news reports

(1) I had a good time with the baker, _____.

(2) I had a good time with the actor. He told me about his job, _____ _____.

(3) I had a good time with the magician. She told me about her job, _____ _____.

(4) I had a good time with the TV reporter. He told me about his job, _____.

(5) I had a good time with the robot scientist. She told me about her job, _____.

19 다음 주어진 우리말을 관계대명사 'what'을 사용하여 영어로 옮기시오.

> (1) 당신이 보는 것을 믿지 마세요.
> (2) 사실인 것을 보도하세요.
> (3) 로봇은 당신이 할 수 없는 것을 할 수 있습니다.

(1) Don't believe _____.
(2) Report _____.
(3) Robots can do _____.

[20~22] 다음 글을 읽고 물음에 답하시오.

Dorothy Vaughan was the last "hidden figure." When IBM computers were installed at NASA in 1961, she was worried the "human computers" would lose their jobs. She studied a new programming language, FORTRAN. She also taught it to her team members. Later, when she was asked to be the leader of a new IBM team, she made a suggestion.

Dorothy: I'm not accepting ⓐthe offer if I can't bring my ladies with me. We need a lot of people to program that machine. I can't do it alone. My girls are ready.

Thanks to Dorothy, her team members could become programmers. She wasn't afraid of change and used it as a chance. That's what I need to learn from her.

Watching this movie, I could learn how to ⓑface challenges in life. I won't forget the tears and laughter of Katherine, Mary, and Dorothy.

20 위 글의 밑줄 친 ⓐthe offer가 가리키는 내용을 우리말로 쓰시오.

➡ _____

21 위 글의 밑줄 친 ⓑface와 바꿔 쓸 수 없는 말을 고르시오.

① confront　　② cope with
③ tackle　　④ overlook
⑤ deal with

22 What was FORTRAN? Answer in English in a full sentence. (6 words)

➡ _____

[23~25] 다음 글을 읽고 물음에 답하시오.

Katherine Johnson was one of the three "hidden figures" in this movie. She worked hard and showed a talent in math, and her manager Al Harrison recognized her ability. One day, he got upset when Katherine was missing from her desk for too long. Al asked where Katherine had been, and she answered.

Katherine: The bathroom. There are no COLORED bathrooms in this building. I have to run half a mile away just to use the bathroom.

Hearing this, I felt really sorry for her. ⓐ , I was glad that ⓑshe had courage to talk to the manager about the problem. This made Al Harrison break down the "Colored Ladies Room" sign.

23 위 글의 빈칸 ⓐ에 들어갈 알맞은 말을 고르시오.

① Moreover　　② Thus
③ Similarly　　④ As a result
⑤ However

24 위 글의 밑줄 친 ⓑ를 다음과 같이 바꿔 쓸 때 빈칸에 공통으로 들어갈 알맞은 단어를 쓰시오.

➡ she was _____ enough to talk to the manager about the problem
= she was so _____ as to talk to the manager about the problem

25 위 글에서 알 수 있는 Al Harrison의 심경 변화로 가장 알맞은 것을 고르시오.

① upset　　→　disappointed
② nervous　　→　satisfied
③ unpleasant　→　sympathetic
④ bored　　→　upset
⑤ satisfied　　→　disappointed

[26~28] 다음 글을 읽고 물음에 답하시오.

Mary Jackson was the (A)character I liked the most of the three. (①) So, she asked a judge to give her permission. (②)

Mary: I can't change the color of my skin. (③) So ... I have no choice but to be the first. (④) Your Honor, of all the cases you'll hear today, which one will matter ⓐ a hundred years? (⑤) Which one will make you the "first?"

The judge was impressed by what she said and finally gave her permission. Mary stood up ⓑ herself and ⓑ other African-Americans. That was what impressed me most in the movie. Finally, she became the first African-American woman engineer at NASA.

26 위 글의 빈칸 ⓐ와 ⓑ에 들어갈 전치사가 바르게 짝지어진 것은?

	ⓐ	ⓑ			ⓐ	ⓑ
①	for	– to		②	in	– for
③	in	– to		④	for	– by
⑤	at	– for				

27 위 글의 흐름으로 보아, 주어진 문장이 들어가기에 가장 적절한 곳은?

> She wanted to learn more about rocket science, but she wasn't allowed to go to a white school.

①   ②   ③   ④   ⑤

28 위 글의 밑줄 친 (A)character와 같은 의미로 쓰인 것을 고르시오.

① She has a strong character.
② The modern hotels here have no real character.
③ Please write in a large character.
④ Who is the leading character in this drama?
⑤ He was a man of good character.

[29~30] 다음 글을 읽고 물음에 답하시오.

Dorothy Vaughan was the last "hidden figure." When IBM computers were installed at NASA in 1961, she was worried the "human computers" would lose their jobs. She studied a new programming language, FORTRAN. She also taught it to her team members. Later, when she was asked to be the leader of a new IBM team, she made a suggestion.

Dorothy: I'm not accepting the offer if I can't bring my ladies with me. We need a lot of people to program that machine. I can't do it alone. My girls are ready.

Thanks to Dorothy, her team members could become programmers. She wasn't afraid of change and used it as a chance. That's what I need to learn from her.

Watching this movie, I could learn how to face challenges in life. I won't forget the tears and laughter of Katherine, Mary, and Dorothy.

29 위 글의 제목으로 가장 알맞은 것을 고르시오.

① Who Was the Last Hidden Figure?
② What If the "Human Computers" Would Lose Their Jobs?
③ Don't Be Afraid of Change
④ Are You Afraid of Change?
⑤ What Do You Need to Learn from Her?

30 Which question CANNOT be answered after reading the passage?

① When were IBM computers installed at NASA?
② What was Dorothy worried about?
③ Did Dorothy lose her job when IBM computers were installed at NASA?
④ What did Dorothy suggest before accepting the offer?
⑤ How many team members could become programmers thanks to Dorothy?

Lesson

Special

The Frog Prince Continued

Words & Expressions

Key Words

- **anything** [éniθìŋ] 때 (부정문·의문문·조건문) 아무것도, 어떤 일도
- **believe** [bilí:v] 통 믿다
- **bright** [brait] 형 밝은, 눈부신
- **cart** [kɑ:rt] 명 수레
- **chance** [tʃæns] 명 기회
- **clothes** [klouz] 명 옷, 의복
- **delicious** [dilíʃəs] 형 맛있는
- **enough** [inʌ́f] 부 충분히
- **even** [í:vən] 부 ~조차도; 훨씬
- **ever** [évər] 부 언제나, 항상; (부정문, 의문문에 쓰여) 한 번도
- **fairy** [fɛ́əri] 명 요정
- **fat** [fæt] 형 통통한, 살찐
- **find** [faind] 통 찾다
- **fool** [fu:l] 명 바보, 멍청이
- **frog** [frɔ:g] 명 개구리
- **funny** [fʌ́ni] 형 웃긴
- **hit** [hit] 통 치다, 때리다
- **inside** [insáid] 부 안에, 안으로
- **instead** [instéd] 부 대신에
- **invite** [inváit] 통 초대하다
- **kill** [kil] 통 죽이다

- **lesson** [lésn] 명 교훈, 단원
- **matter** [mǽtər] 통 중요하다, 문제가 되다
- **mess** [mes] 명 엉망진창
- **monster** [mánstər] 명 괴물
- **oops** [ups] 감 아이쿠, 이런
- **people** [pí:pl] 명 백성, 국민, 사람들
- **pond** [pɑnd] 명 연못
- **princess** [prínsis] 명 공주
- **problem** [prábləm] 명 문제
- **rest** [rest] 명 (the ~) 나머지
- **save** [seiv] 통 구하다
- **serve** [sə:rv] 통 대접하다
- **shout** [ʃaut] 통 외치다
- **still** [stil] 부 여전히, 아직도
- **stuck** [stʌk] 형 꼼짝 못 하는, 움직일 수 없는
- **unhappily** [ʌnhǽpəli] 부 불행하게
- **water** [wɔ́:tər] 통 침이 고이다, 침을 흘리다
- **wave** [weiv] 통 (손을) 흔들다
- **wheel** [hwi:l] 명 바퀴
- **witch** [witʃ] 명 마녀
- **worry** [wɔ́:ri] 통 걱정하다

Key Expressions

- **be better off** 더 잘 살다
- **by the name of** ~라는 이름의
- **feel like -ing** ~하고 싶다
- **from now on** 지금부터 죽
- **give it a try** 한번 해 보다, 시도하다
- **hand in hand** 손에 손을 잡고
- **hundreds of** 수백 개의 ~
- **jump around** 뛰어다니다
- **keep one's fingers crossed** 행운을 빌다
- **let+목적어+동사원형** …가 ~하도록 허락하다
- **look forward to+명사[동명사]** ~을 고대하다
- **look like** ~처럼 보이다

- **not ~ anymore** 더 이상 ~ 않다
- **on one's way to** ~에 가는 길[도중]에
- **pick up** 줍다, 집어들다
- **run away** 도망가다, 달아나다
- **so (that)+주어+can** ~ 하기 위해
- **thank A for B** B에 대해 A에게 감사하다
- **these days** 요즘에
- **to oneself** 혼자
- **turn … into** ~ …을 ~로 바꾸다
- **What's wrong with you?** 무슨 문제가 있니?
- **wait a minute** 잠깐

Word Power

※ 서로 비슷한 뜻을 가진 어휘

☐ **save** : **rescue** (구하다)

☐ **matter** : **count** (중요하다)

☐ **delicious** : **tasty** (맛있는)

☐ **chance** : **opportunity** (기회)

☐ **hit** : **strike** (때리다)

☐ **mess** : **untidiness** (엉망진창)

☐ **shout** : **yell** (외치다)

☐ **stuck** : **fixed** (움직이지 않는)

※ 서로 반대의 뜻을 가진 어휘

☐ **funny** (웃긴) ↔ **serious** (진지한)

☐ **believe** (믿다) ↔ **disbelieve** (믿지 않다)

☐ **bright** (밝은) ↔ **dark** (어두운)

☐ **find** (찾다) ↔ **lose** (잃어버리다)

☐ **inside** (안에) ↔ **outside** (밖에)

☐ **thin** (마른) ↔ **fat** (통통한, 살찐)

☐ **wrong** (잘못된) ↔ **right** (옳은)

☐ **happily** (행복하게) ↔ **unhappily** (불행하게)

English Dictionary

☐ **cart** 수레
→ a vehicle with wheels that is pulled by an animal
동물이 끄는 바퀴가 달린 탈것

☐ **delicious** 맛있는
→ very good to eat or drink
먹거나 마시기에 매우 좋은

☐ **fairy** 요정
→ an imaginary creature like a small person with wings who has magic powers
마법의 힘을 가진 날개가 있는 작은 사람 같은 상상 속의 생명체

☐ **frog** 개구리
→ a small, green animal with long back legs for jumping, that lives in or near water
물속이나 물가에 사는, 점프하기 위한 긴 뒷다리를 가진 작은 녹색의 동물

☐ **hit** 치다, 때리다
→ to touch something or someone quickly and with force, usually hurting or damaging something
대개 무언가를 다치게 하거나 손상시키기 위해 물건이나 사람을 힘을 가해 빠르게 손을 대다

☐ **invite** 초대하다
→ to ask someone to come to your house, to a party, etc.
누군가에게 당신의 집이나 파티에 오라고 청하다

☐ **monster** 괴물
→ an imaginary creature that is large, ugly, and frightening
크고, 추하고, 무서운 상상 속의 생명체

☐ **princess** 공주
→ the daughter of a king or queen, or one of their close female relatives
왕이나 왕비의 딸, 또는 그들의 가까운 여성 친척 중 한 명

☐ **rest** 나머지
→ the part of something that remains
어떤 것의 남아 있는 일부

☐ **shout** 외치나
→ to say something very loudly
무언가를 매우 크게 말하다

☐ **stuck** 꼼짝 못하는
→ not able to move anywhere
아무데도 움직일 수 없는

☐ **wave** (손을) 흔들다
→ to put your hand up and move it from side to side in order to attract someone's attention or to say goodbye
누군가의 관심을 끌거나 작별 인사를 하기 위해 손을 위로 올리고 좌우로 움직이다

☐ **wheel** 바퀴
→ a circular object fixed under a vehicle so that it moves smoothly over the ground
지면 위로 차량이 부드럽게 움직이도록 차량 아래에 고정되어 있는 원형 물체

☐ **witch** 마녀
→ in stories, a woman who has magical powers
이야기에서 마법의 힘을 가진 여자

Reading

The Frog Prince Continued

Characters: Frog Prince, Princess, Witch 1, Witch 2, Fairy

Scene 1: In a room

(Prince comes in, jumping around.)
'뛰면서'의 뜻으로 동시동작을 나타내는 분사구문

Princess: Stop jumping around, honey.
stop+동명사: ~하기를 멈추다. stop+to부정사: ~하기 위해 멈추다

Prince: Well, I just can't stop.

Princess: You're not a frog anymore.

Prince: What's wrong with you? You don't go down to the pond these days.

Princess: I don't like it when you jump around in the room. Go out to
'when' 이하의 내용을 받는 것
kill monsters and save our people.

Prince: I don't want to go out and kill anything. I just feel like running away. *(Picking up a book)* Listen! "They lived happily ever after. The end." I'm living my life as the book says, but we're not happy.
'~하는 대로, ~하는 바와 같이'(접속사)
What's the problem?

Princess: What's the problem? There are hundreds of problems! Sometimes I think we were better off when you were still a frog.
'I think' 뒤에 접속사 'that'이 생략된 구문   '더 잘 살다, 더 부유하다'('be well off'의 비교급)

Prince: Still a frog .... Yes! That's it! *(Goes out)*

Scene 2: On the mountain

Prince: *(To himself)* I need to find the witch, who will turn me back into
재귀대명사   계속적 용법의 관계대명사
a frog.

(Shouting) Ms. Witch, Ms. Witch. Where are you? Please help me!

Witch 1: *(Coming out of the house)* Hi, Prince. How are you feeling?

Prince: I'm glad to meet you. I'm the Frog Prince. I hope you can turn me back into a frog so I can live happily ever after.

Witch 1: Frog Prince, you say? That's funny. You don't look like a frog. Well, it doesn't matter. If you're a prince, you're a prince. And I won't let you save Snow White. Here, eat the rest of this apple.
let+목적어+목적격보어(동사원형): 목적어가 ~하도록 내버려 두다

Prince: No, thank you. That's not what I want! *(Runs away)*
선행사를 포함한 관계대명사: ~하는 것

witch 마녀
fairy 요정
princess 공주
not ~ anymore 더 이상 ~ 않다
pond 연못
these days 요즘에
monster 괴물
save 구하다
feel like -ing ~하고 싶다
pick up 줍다, 집어들다
ever 언제나, 항상; (부정문, 의문문에 쓰여) 한 번도
problem 문제
hundreds of 수백 개의 ~
be better off 더 잘 살다
still 여전히, 아직도
to oneself 혼잣말로
turn … into ~ …을 ~로 바꾸다
look like ~처럼 보이다
matter 중요하다; 문제가 되다
rest 나머지
run away 도망가다, 달아나다

(Prince and Witch 2 come in.)

Prince: Ms. Witch, Ms. Witch. Where are you? Please help me! I'm the Frog ....

Witch 2: If you're a frog, I'm the King of France.

Prince: No, I'm not a frog. I'm the Frog Prince. But I need a witch to turn me back into a frog so I can live happily ever after. Can you do it?

to부정사의 형용사적 용법

Witch 2: Let's talk about it inside. I will serve you a delicious lunch. Come in.

'serve(수여동사)+간접목적어+직접목적어' 구문

Prince: Thank you for inviting me. Oh, this house is made of cookies and candies. Wait a minute. Do you know any children by the name of Hansel and Gretel?

'~으로 만들어지다'(수동태)

Witch 2: Yes, Prince, I do. *(With her mouth watering)* They are not fat enough yet, but you are ....

(Prince runs away and finds a fairy.)

Prince: I'm glad to meet you, Ms. Fairy. I am the Frog Prince. Could you turn me back into a frog so I can live happily ever after?

Fairy: Well, I'm on my way to see Cinderella, but I'll give it a try. It's my first time, you know. *(Fairy turns Prince into a wheel.)*

= so that I can: 내가 ~하도록

Fairy: Oops! Sorry, but don't worry. Everything will be okay.

Prince: *(To himself)* Oh, what a fool I've been! I want to be sitting at home with the Princess, living happily ever after. But instead, I'm stuck here under this cart and I'll live unhappily ever after.

'what'으로 시작하는 감탄문, 동사는 현재완료 시제로 쓰임
동시동작을 나타내는 분사구문: 앞으로는 행복하게 살면서
'stick'의 과거분사: (~에 빠져) 움직일 수 없는(형용사로 쓰임)

(The clock hits twelve, and the wheel turns into Prince.)

Prince: I can't believe this. Thank you for giving me a second chance. Now I know how I should live my life. *(Goes out)*

live의 동족목적어

Fairy: *(Waving her hand)* You learned a good lesson. I'll keep my fingers crossed.

동시동작의 분사구문

Scene 3: In the Frog Prince's house

(Prince runs in, smiling.)

Princess: Where have you been? I've been worried. Your clothes are a mess.

'have+과거분사'의 현재완료 시제

Prince: *(Looking at Princess)* You believed me when no one else in the world did. You loved me even when I was a frog. From now on, I will make you happier.

'세상의 어느 누구도 …하지 않았다'(부정의 뜻), 'did': 'believed'를 받는 대동사

Princess: I'm glad to hear that. I'll make you even happier.

Prince: Great! I'm looking forward to our bright future. Ha-ha ....

비교급을 강조하는 부사('훨씬') = much = still = far = a lot
look forward to+명사[동명사]: ~을 고대하다

(They run to the pond together, jumping hand in hand.)

동시동작을 나타내는 분사구문

inside 안에, 안으로

serve 대접하다

delicious 맛있는

wait a minute 잠깐

by the name of ~라는 이름의

water 침이 고이다, 침을 흘리다

fat 통통한, 살찐

on one's way to ~에 가는 길[도중]에

give it a try 한번 해 보다, 시도하다

fool 바보, 멍청이

instead 대신에

stuck 꼼짝 못 하는, 움직일 수 없는

cart 수레

wave (손을) 흔들다

lesson 교훈; 단원

keep one's fingers crossed 행운을 빌다

clothes 의복, 옷

mess 엉망진창

even ~조차도; 훨씬

from now on 지금부터 죽

hand in hand 손에 손을 잡고

● 우리말을 참고하여 빈칸에 알맞은 말을 쓰시오.

1 The _____ _____ Continued

2 _____: Frog Prince, Princess, Witch 1, Witch 2, Fairy

3 _____ 1: In a room

4 *(Prince comes in, _____ around.)*

5 Princess: _____ _____ around, honey.

6 Prince: Well, I just _____ _____.

7 Princess: You're not a frog _____.

8 Prince: _____ _____ _____ you? You don't go down to the pond these days.

9 Princess: _____ _____ _____ _____ _____ you jump around in the room. Go out to kill monsters and save our people.

10 Prince: I don't want to go out and kill anything. I just _____ _____ _____ away. *(Picking up a book)* Listen! "They lived happily ever after. The end." I'm living my life _____ the book says, but we're not happy. What's the problem?

11 Princess: What's the problem? There are _____ _____ problems! Sometimes I think we _____ _____ _____ when you were still a frog.

12 Prince: Still a frog .... Yes! _____ _____! *(Goes out)*

13 _____ 2: On the mountain

14 Prince: *(_____ _____)* I need to find the witch, who will turn me back _____ a frog. *(Shouting)* Ms. Witch, Ms. Witch. Where are you? Please help me!

15 Witch 1: *(Coming out of the house)* Hi, Prince. _____ are you feeling?

---

1 계속된 개구리 왕자

2 등장인물: 개구리 왕자, 공주, 마녀 1, 마녀 2, 요정

3 장면 1: 방 안에서

4 (왕자가 이리저리 뛰어다니며 등장한다.)

5 공주: 여보, 이리저리 뛰어다니지 마세요.

6 왕자: 저, 나는 단지 멈출 수 없을 뿐이에요.

7 공주: 당신은 이제 개구리가 아니에요.

8 왕자: 당신한테 무슨 문제가 있어요? 요즘 당신은 연못으로 내려가지도 않잖아요.

9 공주: 나는 당신이 방 안에서 이리저리 뛰어다니는 게 마음에 안 들어요. 나가서 괴물들을 죽이고 우리 백성을 구하세요.

10 왕자: 나는 밖에 나가서 아무것도 죽이고 싶지 않아요. 나는 단지 멀리 뛰어다니고 싶을 뿐이오. (책을 집어 들고) 들어 봐요! "그들은 그 후로 행복하게 살았다. 끝." 나는 책에서 말한 것처럼 내 인생을 살고 있지만, 우리는 행복하지 않아요. 뭐가 문제일까요?

11 공주: 뭐가 문제냐고요? 수백 가지 문제가 있어요! 가끔 나는 당신이 아직 개구리일 때 더 잘 살지 않았나 생각해요.

12 왕자: 아직 개구리라 …. 그래! 바로 그거요! (퇴장한다.)

13 장면 2: 산속에서

14 왕자: (혼잣말로) 나는 마녀를 찾아야 해. 그녀가 나를 다시 개구리로 바꿔 줄 거야. (소리치며) 마녀님, 마녀님. 어디 계세요? 저 좀 도와주세요!

15 마녀 1: (집 밖으로 나오며) 안녕, 왕자님. 기분이 어때요?

---

16 Prince: I'm glad to meet you. I'm the Frog Prince. I hope you can
_____ _____ _____ _____ a frog so I can live happily
_____ _____.

17 Witch 1: Frog Prince, you say? That's funny. You don't _____
_____ a frog. Well, it doesn't matter. If you're a prince, you're
a prince. And I won't _____ _____ _____ Snow White.
Here, eat the rest of this apple.

18 Prince: No, thank you. That's not what I _____! *(Runs away)*

19 *(Prince and Witch 2 _____ _____.)*

20 Prince: Ms. Witch, Ms. Witch. _____ are you? Please help me!
I'm the Frog ....

21 Witch 2: _____ you're a frog, I'm the King of France.

22 Prince: No, I'm not a frog. I'm the Frog Prince. But I need a witch
to _____ _____ _____ _____ a frog so I can _____
_____ ever after. Can you do it?

23 Witch 2: Let's talk about it inside. I will _____ you a delicious
lunch. Come in.

24 Prince: Thank you for inviting me. Oh, this house _____
_____ _____ _____ and candies. Wait a minute. Do you
know any children _____ _____ _____ _____ Hansel
and Gretel?

25 Witch 2: Yes, Prince, _____ _____. *(With her mouth
watering)* They are not fat enough yet, but you are ....

26 *(Prince _____ _____ and finds a fairy.)*

27 Prince: I'm glad to meet you, Ms. Fairy. I am the Frog Prince.
_____ _____ turn me back into a frog _____ I can live
happily ever after?

16 왕자: 당신을 만나서 기뻐요. 저는 개구리 왕자예요. 저는 당신이 저를 다시 개구리로 바꿔줘서 제가 앞으로 행복하게 살 수 있게 되기를 원해요.

17 마녀 1: 개구리 왕자라고 했어요? 그거 웃기는군요. 당신은 개구리처럼 보이지 않아요. 음, 그건 중요하지 않아요. 당신이 왕자라면 왕자인 거죠. 그리고 나는 당신이 백설공주를 구하도록 놔두지 않을 거예요. 여기, 이 사과의 나머지를 먹어요.

18 왕자: 고맙지만 됐어요. 그건 제가 원하는 게 아니에요! (도망간다)

19 (왕자와 마녀 2가 등장한다.)

20 왕자: 마녀님, 마녀님. 어디 계세요? 저 좀 도와주세요! 저는 개구리 ….

21 마녀 2: 당신이 개구리라면 나는 프랑스의 왕이에요.

22 왕자: 아니요, 저는 개구리가 아니에요. 저는 개구리 왕자예요. 하지만 저를 다시 개구리로 바꿔 줘서 제가 앞으로 행복하게 살 수 있게 해 줄 마녀가 필요해요. 그렇게 해 주실 수 있나요?

23 마녀 2: 안에서 그것에 관해 이야기해 봅시다. 내가 당신에게 맛있는 점심을 대접할게요. 들어와요.

24 왕자: 저를 초대해 주셔서 감사합니다. 오, 이 집은 과자와 사탕으로 만들어져 있네요. 잠깐만요. 당신은 헨젤과 그레텔이라는 이름의 아이들을 혹시 알아요?

25 마녀 2: 그래요, 왕자님, 알고 있어요. (그녀가 군침을 흘리면서) 그 애들은 아직 충분히 살이 찌지 않았지만, 당신은 ….

26 (왕자는 도망치다가 요정을 발견한다.)

27 왕자: 만나게 되어 기쁩니다, 요정님. 저는 개구리 왕자예요. 저를 다시 개구리로 바꿔 앞으로 행복하게 살 수 있게 해 주실 수 있나요?

28 Fairy: Well, I'm _____ _____ _____ to see Cinderella, but I'll _____ _____ _____ _____. It's my first time, you know. *(Fairy turns Prince into a wheel.)*

29 Fairy: Oops! Sorry, but don't worry. Everything _____ _____ _____.

30 Prince: *(To himself)* Oh, _____ _____ _____ I've been! I want to be sitting at home with the Princess, living happily ever after. But instead, I'm _____ here under this cart and I'll live _____ ever after.

31 *(The clock hits twelve, and the wheel _____ _____ Prince.)*

32 Prince: I can't believe this. Thank you for _____ _____ _____ _____ _____. Now I know _____ _____ _____ _____ my life. *(Goes out)*

33 Fairy: *(Waving her hand)* You learned a good lesson. I'll _____ _____ _____ _____.

34 **Scene 3:** In the Frog Prince's house

35 *(Prince runs in, _____.)*

36 Princess: Where _____ _____ _____? I've been worried. Your clothes are a mess.

37 Prince: *(Looking at Princess)* You believed me when no one _____ in the world _____. You loved me even when I was a frog. From now on, I will make you happier.

38 Princess: I'm glad to hear that. I'll make you _____ happier.

39 Prince: Great! I'm _____ _____ _____ our bright future. Ha-ha ....

40 *(They run to the pond together, jumping _____ _____.)*

---

28 요정: 음, 저는 신데렐라를 만나러 가는 길이지만, 한번 해 볼게요. 아시다시피 이건 제가 처음으로 해 보는 거예요. (요정이 왕자를 바퀴로 바꾼다.)

29 요정: 이런! 미안하지만 걱정하지 마세요. 모든 게 잘될 거예요.

30 왕자: (혼잣말로) 오, 내가 얼마나 바보였던가! 앞으로 행복하게 살면서 집에서 공주와 함께 앉아 있고 싶구나. 하지만 대신에 여기 이 수레 아래에 붙박여 있고 앞으로 불행하게 살게 되겠구나.

31 (시계가 12시를 치자 바퀴가 왕자로 바뀐다.)

32 왕자: 믿을 수가 없네. 두 번째 기회를 주셔서 감사합니다. 이제 나는 내 인생을 어떻게 살아야 할지 알겠어요. (퇴장한다)

33 요정: (손을 흔들며) 좋은 교훈을 배웠군요. 행운을 빌어요.

34 장면 3: 개구리 왕자의 집 안에서

35 (왕자가 미소를 지으며 뛰어 들어온다.)

36 공주: 어디 있었어요? 걱정했잖아요. 옷이 엉망진창이네요.

37 왕자: (공주를 바라보며) 당신은 세상 어느 누구도 나를 믿지 않을 때 나를 믿어 주었어요. 당신은 내가 개구리일 때조차도 나를 사랑해 주었죠. 이제부터는 내가 당신을 더 행복하게 해 주겠어요.

38 공주: 그 말을 들으니 기뻐요. 제가 당신을 훨씬 더 행복하게 해 줄게요.

39 왕자: 좋아요! 난 우리의 밝은 미래를 기대할게요. 하하 ….

40 (그들은 서로 손을 잡고 함께 연못으로 뛰어간다.)

● 우리말을 참고하여 본문을 영작하시오.

1 계속된 개구리 왕자

➡ _____

2 등장인물: 개구리 왕자, 공주, 마녀 1, 마녀 2, 요정

➡ _____

3 장면 1: 방 안에서

➡ _____

4 (왕자가 이리저리 뛰어다니며 등장한다.)

➡ _____

5 공주: 여보, 이리저리 뛰어다니지 마세요.

➡ _____

6 왕자: 저, 나는 단지 멈출 수 없을 뿐이에요.

➡ _____

7 공주: 당신은 이제 개구리가 아니에요.

➡ _____

8 왕자: 당신한테 무슨 문제가 있어요? 요즘 당신은 연못으로 내려가지도 않잖아요.

➡ _____

9 공주: 나는 당신이 방 안에서 이리저리 뛰어다니는 게 마음에 안 들어요. 나가서 괴물들을 죽이고 우리 백성을 구하세요.

➡ _____

_____

10 왕자: 나는 밖에 나가서 아무것도 죽이고 싶지 않아요. 나는 단지 멀리 뛰어다니고 싶을 뿐이오. (책을 집어 들고) 들어 봐요! "그들은 그 후로 행복하게 살았다. 끝." 니는 책에서 말한 것처럼 내 인생을 살고 있지만, 우리는 행복하지 않아요. 뭐가 문제일까요?

➡ _____

_____

11 공주: 뭐가 문제냐고요? 수백 가지 문제가 있어요! 가끔 나는 당신이 아직 개구리일 때 더 잘 살지 않았나 생각해요.

➡ _____

_____

12 왕자: 아직 개구리라 …. 그래! 바로 그거요! (퇴장한다.)

➡ _____

13 장면 2: 산속에서

➡ _____

14 왕자: (혼잣말로) 나는 마녀를 찾아야 해. 그녀가 나를 다시 개구리로 바꿔 줄 거야. (소리치며) 마녀님, 마녀님. 어디 계세요? 저 좀 도와주세요!

➡ _____

15 마녀 1: (집 밖으로 나오며) 안녕, 왕자님. 기분이 어때요?

➡ _____

16 왕자: 당신을 만나서 기뻐요. 저는 개구리 왕자예요. 저는 당신이 저를 다시 개구리로 바꿔줘서 제가 앞으로 행복하게 살 수 있게 되기를 원해요.

➡ _____
_____

17 마녀 1: 개구리 왕자라고 했어요? 그거 웃기는군요. 당신은 개구리처럼 보이지 않아요. 음, 그건 중요하지 않아요. 당신이 왕자라면 왕자인 거죠. 그리고 나는 당신이 백설공주를 구하도록 놔두지 않을 거예요. 여기, 이 사과의 나머지를 먹어요.

➡ _____
_____
_____

18 왕자: 고맙지만 됐어요. 그건 제가 원하는 게 아니에요! (도망간다)

➡ _____

19 (왕자와 마녀 2가 등장한다.)

➡ _____

20 왕자: 마녀님, 마녀님. 어디 계세요? 저 좀 도와주세요! 저는 개구리 ….

➡ _____

21 마녀 2: 당신이 개구리라면 나는 프랑스의 왕이에요.

➡ _____

22 왕자: 아니요, 저는 개구리가 아니에요. 저는 개구리 왕자예요. 하지만 저를 다시 개구리로 바꿔 줘서 제가 앞으로 행복하게 살 수 있게 해 줄 마녀가 필요해요. 그렇게 해 주실 수 있나요?

➡ _____
_____

23 마녀 2: 안에서 그것에 관해 이야기해 봅시다. 내가 당신에게 맛있는 점심을 대접할게요. 들어와요.

➡ _____

24 왕자: 저를 초대해 주셔서 감사합니다. 오, 이 집은 과자와 사탕으로 만들어져 있네요. 잠깐만요. 당신은 헨젤과 그레텔이라는 이름의 아이들을 혹시 알아요?

➡ _____

25 마녀 2: 그래요, 왕자님, 알고 있어요. (그녀가 군침을 흘리면서) 그 애들은 아직 충분히 살이 찌지 않았지만, 당신은 ….

➡ _____

26 (왕자는 도망치다가 요정을 발견한다.)

➡ _____

27 왕자: 만나게 되어 기쁩니다, 요정님. 저는 개구리 왕자예요. 저를 다시 개구리로 바꿔 앞으로 행복하게 살 수 있게 해 주실 수 있나요?

➡ _____

28 요정: 음, 저는 신데렐라를 만나러 가는 길이지만, 한번 해 볼게요. 아시다시피 이건 제가 처음으로 해 보는 거예요. (요정이 왕자를 바퀴로 바꾼다.)

➡ _____

29 요정: 이런! 미안하지만 걱정하지 마세요. 모든 게 잘될 거예요

➡ _____

30 왕자: (혼잣말로) 오, 내가 얼마나 바보였던가! 앞으로 행복하게 살면서 집에서 공주와 함께 앉아 있고 싶구나. 하지만 대신에 여기 이 수레 아래에 붙박여 있고 앞으로 불행하게 살게 되겠구나.

➡ _____

_____

31 (시계가 12시를 치자 바퀴가 왕자로 바뀐다.)

➡ _____

32 왕자: 믿을 수가 없네. 두 번째 기회를 주셔서 감사합니다. 이제 나는 내 인생을 어떻게 살아야 할지 알겠어요. (퇴장한다)

➡ _____

_____

33 요정: (손을 흔들며) 좋은 교훈을 배웠군요. 행운을 빌어요.

➡ _____

34 장면 3: 개구리 왕자의 집 안에서

➡ _____

35 (왕자가 미소를 지으며 뛰어 들어온다.)

➡ _____

36 공주: 어디 있었어요? 걱정했잖아요. 옷이 엉망진창이네요.

➡ _____

37 왕자: (공주를 바라보며) 당신은 세상 어느 누구도 나를 믿지 않을 때 나를 믿어 주었어요. 당신은 내가 개구리일 때조차도 나를 사랑해 주었죠. 이제부터는 내가 당신을 더 행복하게 해 주겠어요.

➡ _____

_____

38 공주: 그 말을 들으니 기뻐요. 제가 당신을 훨씬 더 행복하게 해 줄게요.

➡ _____

39 왕자: 좋아요! 난 우리의 밝은 미래를 기대할게요. 하하….

➡ _____

40 (그들은 서로 손을 잡고 함께 연못으로 뛰어간다.)

➡ _____

01 다음 문장에 공통으로 들어갈 말을 쓰시오.

> (1) On hot summer days, you often _____ eating ice cream.
> (2) It is so cold that I _____ we are in the North Pole!

02 영영풀이에 해당하는 단어를 〈보기〉에서 찾아 첫 번째 빈칸에 쓰고, 두 번째 빈칸에는 우리말 뜻을 쓰시오.

> ┌─── 보기 ───┐
> wheel   fairy   princess   frog
> └──────────┘

(1) _____ : a circular object fixed under a vehicle so that it moves smoothly over the ground: _____

(2) _____ : a small, green animal with long back legs for jumping, that lives in or near water : _____

(3) _____ : the daughter of a king or queen, or one of their close female relatives: _____

(4) _____ : an imaginary creature like a small person with wings who has magic powers : _____

03 다음 우리말에 맞게 빈칸에 알맞은 말을 쓰시오.

(1) 고르디아스 왕은 황소 수레를 갖고 있었다.
➡ King Gordias had an ox c_____.

(2) 가장 가까운 쉼터에서, 우리는 점심 시간 동안 음식을 대접했어.
➡ At the closest shelter, we s_____ food during lunch time.

(3) 대신에, 그녀는 그녀의 방에서 대략 하루 동안 혼자 기도했습니다.
➡ I_____, she prayed alone for about a day in her room.

04 다음 우리말을 주어진 어휘를 이용하여 영어로 옮기시오.

(1) 음악을 들으면서, 그녀는 창문을 닦았다. (listening, wiped)
➡ _____

(2) 그 소식을 들었을 때, 그녀는 울기 시작했다. (hearing, news, began)
➡ _____

(3) 지금 떠나면, 너는 지각하지 않을 거야. (leaving, won't, late)
➡ _____

05 다음 문장에서 어법상 어색한 부분을 찾아 바르게 고치시오.

> I couldn't understand which the teacher said.

_____ ➡ _____

[06~08] 다음 글을 읽고 물음에 답하시오.

Scene 1: In a room
(Prince comes in, jumping around.)
Princess: (A)Stop to jump around, honey.
Prince: Well, I just can't stop.
Princess: You're not a frog anymore.
Prince: What's wrong with you? You don't go down to the pond these days.
Princess: I don't like it when you jump around in the room. Go out to kill monsters and save our people.

Prince: I don't want to go out and kill anything. I just feel like ___ⓐ___ away. *(Picking up a book)* Listen! "They lived happily ever after. The end." I'm living my life as the book says, but we're not happy. What's the problem?

Princess: What's the problem? There are hundreds of problems! Sometimes I think we were better off when you were still a frog.

Prince: Still a frog .... Yes! That's it! *(Goes out)*

06 위 글의 빈칸 ⓐ에 run을 알맞은 형태로 쓰시오.

➡ _____

07 위 글의 밑줄 친 (A)에서 어법상 틀린 부분을 찾아 고치시오.

_____ ➡ _____

08 본문의 내용과 일치하도록 다음 빈칸 (A)와 (B)에 알맞은 단어를 쓰시오.

Princess doesn't like it when Prince (A)_____ _____ in the room, and tells Prince to go out to kill monsters and save the people, but Prince (B)_____ _____ to go out and kill anything.

Scene 2: On the mountain

Prince: *(To (A)[him / himself])* I need to find the witch, who will turn me back into a frog.

(Shouting) Ms. Witch, Ms. Witch. Where are you? Please help me!

Witch 1: *(Coming out of the house)* Hi, Prince. (B)[How / What] are you feeling?

Prince: I'm glad to meet you. I'm the Frog Prince. I hope you can turn me back into a frog so I can live happily ever after.

Witch 1: Frog Prince, you say? That's funny. You don't (C)[look / look like] a frog. Well, it doesn't matter. If you're a prince, you're a prince. ⓐAnd I won't let you save Snow White. Here, eat the rest of this apple.

Prince: No, thank you. That's not what I want! *(Runs away)*

09 위 글의 괄호 (A)~(C)에서 문맥이나 어법상 알맞은 낱말을 골라 쓰시오.

➡ (A) _____ (B) _____ (C) _____

10 위 글의 밑줄 친 ⓐ를 다음과 같이 바꿔 쓸 때 빈칸에 들어갈 알맞은 말을 두 단어로 쓰시오.

➡ And I won't allow you _____ _____ Snow White.

11 Why does Prince want Witch 1 to turn him back into a frog? Answer in English beginning with "Because".

➡ _____

_____

01 출제율 90%

다음 단어에 대한 영어 설명이 어색한 것은?

① stuck: not able to move anywhere

② dinosaur: an imaginary creature that is large, ugly, and frightening

③ witch: in stories, a woman who has magical powers

④ delicious: very good to eat or drink

⑤ wave: to put your hand up and move it from side to side in order to attract someone's attention or to say goodbye

02 출제율 95%

다음 짝지어진 단어의 관계가 같도록 빈칸에 알맞은 말을 쓰시오.

save : rescue – yell : _____

03 출제율 90%

다음 영영풀이에 해당하는 단어를 고르시오.

to touch something or someone quickly and with force, usually hurting or damaging something

① hit   ② wound
③ rest   ④ save
⑤ worry

04 출제율 95%

다음 문장에 공통으로 들어갈 단어를 쓰시오.

• The smells from the kitchen made our mouths _____.
• Rain is the result of the circulation of _____ in nature.   *circulation 순환

05 출제율 95%

다음 문장의 밑줄 친 어구와 의미가 같은 말을 5 단어로 쓰시오.

I am longing to watch this movie.

➡ _____

06 출제율 100%

다음 빈칸에 들어갈 말이 알맞게 짝지어진 것은?

• They run to the pond together, jumping hand _____ hand.
• Could you turn me back _____ a frog so I can live happily ever after?
• Do you know any children _____ the name of Hansel and Gretel?

① on – with – down
② into – of – up
③ by – of – up
④ in – into – by
⑤ by – of – down

07 출제율 95%

다음 중 짝지어진 단어의 관계가 다른 것은?

① funny : serious   ② bright : dark
③ win : lose   ④ shout : yell
⑤ wrong : right

08 출제율 95%

다음 문장의 빈칸에 공통으로 들어갈 말을 쓰시오.

• Taking a _____ helps you be more energetic and active.
• For the _____ of the break, we're going to Disneyland!

09 다음 빈칸에 들어갈 말을 〈보기〉에서 찾아 쓰시오. (필요하면 변형하여 쓰시오.)

┌─ 보기 ┐

run away   from now on   good off

(1) He is far _____ than he was three years ago.

(2) If a strange adult comes to you or call you, _____.

(3) _____, we will not sell any Japanese products.

10 〈보기〉의 밑줄 친 As[as]와 의미가 같은 것은?

┌─ 보기 ┐

<u>As</u> I told you before, I want some time to think by myself.

① <u>As</u> times goes by, you will understand everything.

② We were busy <u>as</u> we had a lot of guests.

③ The boys laughed <u>as</u> she passed by.

④ <u>As</u> I took a shower, someone knocked the door.

⑤ Please be prepared <u>as</u> you promised me.

11 다음 중 밑줄 친 단어의 쓰임이 <u>다른</u> 하나를 고르시오.

① It's too hot here. I feel like <u>drinking</u> iced coffee.

② I'm sorry about <u>breaking</u> your favorite plates.

③ Jenny's job is <u>writing</u> lyrics for pop music.

④ He got lost, <u>being</u> a stranger there.

⑤ I'm looking forward to <u>seeing</u> your family sometime.

12 주어진 〈보기〉를 참고하여 같은 의미의 문장을 쓰시오.

┌─ 보기 ┐

He sent me a birthday present, and it made me happy.

→ He sent me a birthday present, which made me happy.

(1) We went to the hospital, but it was closed because it was Sunday.

➡ We went to the hospital, _____

_____.

(2) Jake works for a bank, and it is located near my school.

➡ Jake works for a bank, _____

_____.

(3) Cathy likes a Chinese actor, and he is good at kung fu.

➡ Cathy likes a Chinese actor, _____

_____.

13 다음 주어진 문장과 의미가 같은 문장을 고르시오.

You did a really foolish thing.

① How foolish a thing is!

② How foolish thing you did!

③ What a foolish you did a thing!

④ What really foolish thing you did!

⑤ What a foolish thing you did!

14 다음 주어진 우리말에 맞게 괄호 안에서 필요한 단어만 골라 영어로 쓰시오.

아버지는 내가 밤을 새우는 것을 허락하지 않으실 거야.

(my, not, let, allow, dad, me, up, down, every, will, night, all, stay)

➡ _____

15 다음 빈칸에 들어갈 말이 순서대로 짝지어진 것은?

> • I have a stomachache. I should stop
> _____ .
> • A boy was looking for his toy, so I
> stopped _____ him.

① eat – help

② eating – helping

③ eating – to help

④ to eat – to help

⑤ to eat – helping

16 다음 중 어법상 어색한 문장을 고르시오.

① Ms. Lee, who lives in New York, wants to be a musical actress.

② I have a friend, who was born in France.

③ Jen is holding a poodle which has curly brown hair.

④ I want to see the robot that was made by Dr. Kim.

⑤ Can you be friends with Thomas, that you have never met before?

17 다음 중 어법상 어색한 문장을 고르시오.

① My shoes were covered with mud.

② Cheese is made from milk.

③ BTS is known to people from all over the world.

④ The library is filled with old books.

⑤ The house is made by candies and cookies.

18 밑줄 친 부분이 〈보기〉와 쓰임이 같은 것을 고르시오.

> ┤ 보기 ├
> He asked me to tell the truth and I did.

① I did the dishes at least once a week for my family.

② You should say what you did yesterday.

③ The wind moved slowly, so did the clouds.

④ When I was younger, I did my homework right after school.

⑤ All of the athletes did their best to win gold medals.

[19~21] 다음 글을 읽고 물음에 답하시오.

Scene 2: On the mountain

Prince: (To ①himself) I need to find the witch, who will turn me back into a frog. (Shouting) Ms. Witch, Ms. Witch. Where are ②you? Please help me!

Witch 1: (Coming out of the house) Hi, Prince. How are ③you feeling?

Prince: I'm glad to meet you. I'm the Frog Prince. I hope you can turn me back into a frog so ④I can live happily ever after.

Witch 1: Frog Prince, ⑤you say? That's funny. You don't look like a frog. Well, it doesn't matter. If you're a prince, you're a prince. And I won't let you save Snow White. Here, eat the rest of this apple.

Prince: No, thank you. That's not ___@___ I want! (Runs away)

19 위 글의 빈칸 @에 들어갈 알맞은 말을 고르시오.

① that ② whom

③ how ④ which

⑤ what

20 밑줄 친 ①~⑤ 중에서 가리키는 대상이 나머지 넷과 **다른** 것은?

①   ②   ③   ④   ⑤

21 Which question CANNOT be answered after reading the passage?

① Where is the setting of Scene 2?
② Whom does Prince want to meet?
③ What does Prince want Witch 1 to do?
④ What will Prince give Witch 1 as the price for turning him back into a frog?
⑤ Why does Witch 1 tell Prince "That's funny?"

[22~24] 다음 글을 읽고 물음에 답하시오.

Scene 1: In a room
(Prince comes in, jumping around.)

Princess: Stop jumping around, honey.

Prince: Well, I just can't stop.

Princess: You're not a frog anymore.

Prince: What's wrong with you? You don't go down to the pond these days.

Princess: I don't like it when you jump around in the room. Go out to kill monsters and save our people.

Prince: I don't want to go out and kill anything. I just feel like running away. *(Picking up a book)* Listen! "They lived happily ever after. The end." I'm living my life ⓐas the book says, but we're not happy. What's the problem?

Princess: What's the problem? There are hundreds of problems! Sometimes I think we were better off when you were still a frog.

Prince: Still a frog .... Yes! That's it! *(Goes out)*

22 위 글의 밑줄 친 ⓐas와 같은 의미로 쓰인 것을 고르시오.

① As you were out, I left a message.
② Treat me as a friend.
③ Susan is not as pretty as Jane.
④ As the poet says, a little learning is a dangerous thing.
⑤ He sat watching her as she got ready.

23 위 글의 종류로 알맞은 것을 고르시오.

① article   ② play
③ biography   ④ essay
⑤ review

24 According to the passage, which is NOT true?

① Princess tells Prince to stop jumping around.
② Prince just can't stop.
③ Prince doesn't go down to the pond these days.
④ Prince doesn't want to go out and kill anything.
⑤ Prince just feels inclined to run away.

[25~27] 다음 글을 읽고 물음에 답하시오.

(Prince and Witch 2 come in.)

Prince: Ms. Witch, Ms. Witch. Where are you? Please help me! I'm the Frog ....

Witch 2: (A)If you're a frog, I'm the King of France.

Prince: No, I'm not a frog. I'm the Frog Prince. But I need a witch to turn me back ⓐ a frog so I can live happily ever after. Can you do it?

단원별 예상문제 **131**

Witch 2: Let's talk about it inside. I will serve you a delicious lunch. Come in.

Prince: Thank you for inviting me. Oh, this house is made ___ⓑ___ cookies and candies. Wait a minute. (B)당신은 헨젤과 그레텔이라는 이름의 아이들을 알아요?

Witch 2: Yes, Prince, I do. *(With her mouth watering)* They are not fat enough yet, but you are ....

✏ 출제율 95%

25 위 글의 빈칸 ⓐ와 ⓑ에 들어갈 전치사가 바르게 짝지어진 것은?

	ⓐ	ⓑ		ⓐ	ⓑ
①	into	from	②	for	of
③	in	from	④	in	to
⑤	into	of			

✏ 출제율 95%

26 위 글의 밑줄 친 (A)에서 알 수 있는 'Witch 2'의 심경으로 가장 알맞은 것을 고르시오.

① excited   ② doubtful
③ bored   ④ depressed
⑤ satisfied

✏ 출제율 90%

27 위 글의 밑줄 친 (B)의 우리말에 맞게 주어진 어휘를 이용하여 12 단어로 영작하시오.

> any children, Hansel and Gretel

➡ _____

_____

[28~30] 다음 글을 읽고 물음에 답하시오.

Prince: *(To himself)* Oh, (A)what a fool I've been! I want to be sitting at home with the Princess, living happily ever after. But instead, I'm stuck here under this cart and I'll live unhappily ever after.

(The clock hits twelve, and the wheel turns into Prince.)

Prince: I can't believe this. Thank you for giving me ___ⓐ___ . Now I know how I should live my life. *(Goes out)*

Fairy: *(Waving her hand)* You learned a good lesson. I'll keep my fingers crossed.

✏ 출제율 95%

28 위 글의 빈칸 ⓐ에 들어갈 알맞은 말을 고르시오.

① all the challenges
② a handsome appearance
③ the popular identity
④ a second chance
⑤ an attractive personality

✏ 출제율 90%

29 위 글의 밑줄 친 (A)를 how를 사용하여 고치시오.

➡ _____

✏ 출제율 100%

30 According to the passage, which is NOT true?

① Prince wants to stay at home with the Princess.
② Prince wants to live happily with the Princess.
③ Fairy made Prince turn into a frog.
④ Fairy gave a good lesson to Prince.
⑤ When the clock hits twelve, the wheel turns into Prince.

Lesson 5

Pictures Speak a Thousand Words

🎙 의사소통 기능

- 궁금증 표현하기
  I'm curious about that balloon.

- 정의하기
  It means you must not enter.

🎙 언어 형식

- 가정법 과거
  I **would** be so happy **if** you **were** with me.

- 관계대명사 whose
  It was written in 1973 by a woman **whose** husband was far away.

교과서
Words & Expressions

Key Words

- **ad**(= **advertisement**)[æd] 명 광고
- **awesome**[ɔ́:səm] 형 근사한, 멋진, 엄청난, 어마어마한
- **backpack**[bǽkpæk] 명 배낭
- **balloon**[bəlú:n] 명 풍선
- **battery**[bǽtəri] 명 건전지
- **battle**[bǽtl] 명 전쟁, 전투
- **bee**[bi:] 명 벌
- **board**[bɔ:rd] 명 넓은 판, 판자
- **border**[bɔ́:rdər] 명 국경, 경계
- **Braille**[breil] 명 점자
- **cell phone** 휴대 전화
- **chimney**[tʃímni] 명 굴뚝
- **close**[klous] 부 가까이, 근접하여
- **cross**[krɔ:s] 동 건너다, 가로지르다
- **curious**[kjúəriəs] 형 호기심이 많은, 궁금한
- **dead**[ded] 형 죽은, 쓸모없는
- **discover**[diskʌ́vər] 동 발견하다
- **dot**[dɑt] 명 점
- **enemy**[énəmi] 명 적군, 적대자
- **exactly**[igzǽktli] 부 정확하게
- **expression**[ikspréʃən] 명 표현
- **foreign**[fɔ́:rən] 형 외국의
- **gesture**[dʒéstʃər] 명 몸짓, 몸동작
- **ground**[graund] 명 땅, 지면
- **hidden**[hídn] 형 숨은, 숨겨진
- **hire**[haiər] 동 고용하다
- **hug**[hʌg] 명 포옹 동 포옹하다
- **hunter**[hʌ́ntər] 명 사냥꾼
- **husband**[hʌ́zbənd] 명 남편
- **ill**[il] 형 아픈, 병든

- **knock**[nɑk] 동 치다, 두드리다
- **Latin**[lǽtən] 명 라틴어 형 라틴어의
- **letter**[létər] 명 글자, 문자
- **light**[lait] 동 불을 붙이다, 불을 밝히다
- **loudly**[láudli] 부 큰 소리로, 시끄럽게
- **mean**[mi:n] 동 의미하다
- **message**[mésidʒ] 명 메시지, 전갈, 전언
- **misunderstanding**[misəndərstǽndiŋ] 명 오해
- **oil**[ɔil] 명 기름
- **point**[pɔint] 동 가리키다, 지시하다
- **pond**[pɑnd] 명 연못
- **powerful**[páuərfəl] 형 강한, 강력한
- **prepare**[pripɛ́ər] 동 준비하다
- **product**[prɑ́dʌkt] 명 상품, 제품
- **pull**[pul] 동 끌다, 잡아당기다
- **rather**[rǽðər] 부 다소, 약간
- **reply**[riplái] 명 답장
- **ring**[riŋ] 명 반지
- **seat**[si:t] 명 좌석, 의석
- **seem**[si:m] 동 ~처럼 보이다
- **seriously**[síəriəsli] 부 진지하게, 심각하게
- **sign language** 수화
- **soldier**[sóuldʒər] 명 군인
- **son**[sʌn] 명 아들
- **system**[sístəm] 명 체계, 시스템
- **toward**[tɔ:rd] 전 ~을 향하여
- **traffic**[trǽfik] 명 교통
- **translate**[trænsléit] 동 번역하다, 해석하다
- **vote**[vout] 동 투표하다, 선출하다
- **whether**[hwéðər] 접 ~이든지 아니든지

Key Expressions

- **at a price of** ~의 가격으로
- **be careful with** ~에 조심하다
- **be covered with** ~로 덮이다
- **be curious about** ~에 대하여 궁금해 하다
- **except for** ~을 제외하고
- **get over** 이겨내다, 극복하다
- **in good health** 건강하여
- **instead of** ~ 대신에
- **Let's see.** (= **Let me see.**) 글쎄., 어디 보자.

- **look after** ~을 돌보다
- **pick up** 집어 올리다, 차에 태우다
- **right away** 즉시, 당장
- **step back** 물러서다
- **the rich** (= **rich people**) 부자들
- **turn off** ~을 끄다
- **vote for** ~에 (찬성하는) 투표를 하다
- **wait for** ~을 기다리다
- **win many seats** 많은 의석을 확보하다

Word Power

※ 서로 비슷한 뜻을 가진 어휘

- □ **ad** 광고 : **commercial** 광고
- □ **border** 국경, 경계 : **boundary** 경계
- □ **enemy** 적군, 적대자 : **foe** 적
- □ **hug** 포옹; 포옹하다 : **embrace** 끌어안다

- □ **battle** 전쟁, 전투 : **combat** 전투
- □ **curious** 궁금한 : **inquisitive** 탐구심이 많은
- □ **hire** 고용하다 : **employ** 고용하다
- □ **vote** 투표하다, 선출하다 : **elect** 선출하다

※ 서로 반대의 뜻을 가진 어휘

- □ **war** 전쟁 ↔ **peace** 평화
- □ **discover** 발견하다 ↔ **hide** 숨기다
- □ **hire** 고용하다 ↔ **fire** 해고하다

- □ **dead** 죽은, 쓸모없는 ↔ **alive** 살아 있는
- □ **enemy** 적군, 적대자 ↔ **friend** 친구
- □ **ill** 아픈, 병든 ↔ **healthy** 건강한

※ -ous = 형용사 어미

- □ **curious** 호기심이 많은
- □ **serious** 심각한
- □ **adventurous** 모험적인, 대담한

- □ **famous** 유명한
- □ **various** 다양한
- □ **dangerous** 위험한

- □ **delicious** 맛있는
- □ **nervous** 불안한

English Dictionary

- □ **dead** 죽은
  → no longer alive 더 이상 살아 있지 않은

- □ **discover** 발견하다
  → to find out something that you did not know before
  전에 알지 못했던 것을 찾아내다

- □ **foreign** 외국의
  → from another country 다른 나라로부터

- □ **ground** 땅, 지면
  → the surface of the Earth 지구의 표면

- □ **hire** 고용하다
  → to pay someone to work for you
  당신을 위해 일하도록 누군가에게 돈을 지급하다

- □ **hug** 포옹
  → the action of putting your arms around someone to show your love or friendship 당신의 애정이나 우정을 보여 주기 위하여 양팔로 다른 사람을 안는 행위

- □ **husband** 남편
  → the man that a woman is married to
  한 여자가 결혼한 남자

- □ **ill** 아픈, 병든
  → suffering from an illness or disease 질병으로 고통을 겪는

- □ **oil** 기름
  → a thick liquid made from plants or animals that is used in cooking
  요리를 위하여 사용되는 식물이나 동물로부터 만들어진 걸쭉한 액체

- □ **prepare** 준비하다
  → to make something ready for use
  어떤 것을 사용할 준비가 되도록 만들다

- □ **rather** 다소, 약간
  → in some degree 어느 정도로

- □ **reply** 답장
  → an answer to a letter 편지에 대한 답장

- □ **ring** 반지
  → a piece of jewelry in the form of a circle that you wear on a finger 손가락에 끼는 둥근 형태의 보석

- □ **seat** 의석
  → a position as a member of a committee, court, etc.
  위원회, 법정 등의 구성원으로서의 지위

- □ **son** 아들
  → someone's male child 누군가의 남자아이

- □ **toward** ~을 향하여
  → in the direction of ~ 방향으로

- □ **translate** 번역하다, 해석하다
  → to change spoken or written words into another language 구어 또는 문어를 다른 언어로 바꾸다

- □ **vote** 투표하다, 선출하다
  → to express one's preference for a candidate
  후보자에 대하여 선호를 표시하다

01 다음 문장의 빈칸에 〈영어 설명〉에 해당하는 단어를 주어진 철자로 시작하여 쓰시오.

> The child was very c_____ about the strange animal.
> <영어 설명> wanting to know or learn about something

02 다음 빈칸에 공통으로 들어갈 말로 가장 적절한 것은?

> • Traditional mail contains a special meaning because someone wrote a _____ by hand.
> • A long time ago, we didn't have our own _____s.

① border ② letter
③ gesture ④ product
⑤ reply

[03~04] 다음 설명에 해당하는 단어를 고르시오.

03

> to express one's preference for a candidate

① permit ② hug
③ hire ④ discover
⑤ vote

04

> the action of putting your arms around someone to show your love or friendship

① gesture ② prepare
③ pull ④ hug
⑤ hire

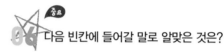

05 다음 우리말에 맞게 주어진 단어를 이용하여 쓰시오.

> 나무는 곧 푸른 잎으로 덮일 것입니다! (cover)

➡ Trees will _____ green leaves soon!

06 다음 빈칸에 들어갈 말로 알맞은 것은?

> (A) Niagara Falls is a truly _____ sight.
> (B) He showed his _____ talents as an actor.

① powerful – recognized
② curious – allowed
③ awesome – hidden
④ curious – hidden
⑤ awesome – allowed

07 다음 문장의 빈칸에 들어갈 단어를 〈보기〉에서 고르고, 각 단어의 첫 글자를 조합한 단어를 쓰시오.

> ┌── 보기 ──┐
> son lit except crossing oil

> 1. A woman was _____ the road toward me.
> 2. I _____ a candle.
> 3. You should put _____ at first in the frying pan to make a fried egg.
> 4. He has three daughters and two _____s.
> 5. I like to play every sport _____ for basketball.

➡ _____

01 〈보기〉에서 알맞은 단어를 찾아 빈칸을 완성하시오. (한 단어를 추가하고 필요하면 변형하여 쓰시오.)

┌─ 보기 ─────────────────┐
│ except   look   wait   lot │
└───────────────────────┘

(1) There are _____ great shoes in this store.

(2) We had to _____ him at the restaurant for twenty minutes.

(3) I am doing okay, and the weather is nice _____ the fine dust.

(4) My neighbor asked me to _____ her cat.

02 대화의 빈칸에 〈영영풀이〉에 해당하는 단어를 주어진 철자로 쓰시오.

┌───────────────────────────┐
│ G: What are these dots for? I'm curious │
│   about them. │
│ B: Oh, they are _____. They are for │
│   blind people. │
│ G: I see. Now I can guess what they mean. │
└───────────────────────────┘

┌───────────────────────────┐
│ <영영풀이> a system of printing for blind │
│ people, using raised patterns that they │
│ read by touching │
└───────────────────────────┘

➡ _____

03 다음 우리말과 같은 표현이 되도록 문장의 빈칸을 채우시오.

(1) 그들은 또한 감시를 위해 경비원을 고용할 수도 있다.
  ➡ They can also _____ a security guard to keep watch.

(2) 이건 나와 지나 사이에 오해가 있었기 때문이었어.
  ➡ This was because there was a _____ between Jina and me.

(3) 그는 다소 별나지만 그의 소설 속의 메시지는 우리에게 매우 친근하다.
  ➡ He is _____ strange, but his novels' messages are very familiar to us.

04 영영풀이에 해당하는 단어를 〈보기〉에서 찾아 첫 번째 빈칸에 쓰고, 두 번째 빈칸에는 우리말 뜻을 쓰시오.

┌───────────────────────────┐
│ oil   translate   ring   discover │
└───────────────────────────┘

(1) _____: a piece of jewelry in the form of a circle that you wear on a finger: _____

(2) _____: to find out something that you did not know before: _____

(3) _____: a thick liquid made from plants or animals that is used in cooking: _____

(4) _____: to change spoken or written words into another language: _____

05 다음 빈칸에 주어진 철자로 시작하는 알맞은 단어를 쓰시오.

(A) Koreans use more water than other f_____ countries with large populations.

(B) Human beings are the greatest h_____ and have always eaten meat.

(C) He must be a s_____ because he is wearing the uniform.

Conversation

① 궁금증 표현하기

• **I'm curious about that balloon.** 나는 저 풍선이 궁금해.

■ 궁금증을 표현할 때는 curious(궁금한, 호기심이 많은), wonder(궁금하다), want to know(알고 싶다) 등의 표현을 이용하여 'I'm curious about ~.(나는 ~이 궁금해.)', 'I wonder ~.(나는 ~이 궁금하다.)' 라고 말한다. 또한 궁금한 내용을 알고 싶다는 의미를 'I would like to know ~', 'I want to know ~.', 'I don't know why ~.'라고 표현할 수도 있다.

■ 궁금함을 나타내는 'I'm curious'와 명사구를 같이 쓸 때는 'I'm curious about+명사구'이고, 명사절과 함께 쓸 때는 'I'm curious if/whether ~.' 또는 'I'm curious 의문사 (주어)+동사 ~.'이다. 'I wonder ~.'를 사용할 때의 어순은 'I wonder+의문사+주어+동사 ~.', 'I wonder+if/whether+주어+동사 ~.'이고, 명사(구)와 함께 나타낼 때는 'I wonder about+명사(구)'이다.

■ 궁금한 점에 대하여 알고 싶을 때는 'Can you tell me about ~?(~에 대하여 이야기해 줄 수 있니?)', 'I'm interested to know ~.(나는 ~을 아는 것에 관심 있어.)'와 같이 표현할 수 있고, 'Can I ~?', 'Can/Could you ~?' 등과 같이 요구/요청을 나타내는 조동사 표현을 사용하여 'Can I ask you ~?' 또는 'Can you tell me ~?'와 같이 궁금한 점에 대하여 물어볼 수 있다. 그 외에 궁금증을 나타낼 때는 'Do you know ~?' 등을 사용할 수도 있다.

궁금증 표현하기

• I am curious about ~. 나는 ~이 궁금하다.
• I'm curious if/whether 주어+동사 ~. 나는 ~가 궁금하다.
• I'm wondering + if/whether/의문사 주어+동사 ~. 나는 ~인지 궁금하다.
• I would like/want to know ~. 나는 ~이 알고 싶다.
• I'd be very interested to know ~. 나는 ~이 알고 싶다.
• Can you tell me about ~? ~에 대해 말해 줄 수 있니?
• I want to know 명사구/명사절 ~. 나는 ~을 알고 싶다.

핵심 Check

1. 다음 밑줄 친 부분 대신 바꿔 쓰기에 적절하지 <u>않은</u> 것은?

G: <u>I'm curious about that robot.</u> Why is it standing there?

B: It's a kind of ad. It tells people their batteries are very powerful.

① I'm wondering about that robot.
② Can I tell you about that robot?
③ I would like to know about that robot.
④ Can you tell me about that robot?
⑤ I'd be very interested to know about that robot.

② 정의하기

- **It means you must not enter.** 그것은 네가 들어가지 말아야 한다는 것을 의미해.

■ 'I'm curious ~.' 등으로 상대방이 궁금증을 표현하거나 의미를 물어보면 'This/It means ~.(그것은 ~을 의미한다.)' 또는 'It is ~.(그것은 ~이다.)' 등의 표현을 사용하여 상대방이 궁금해 하거나, 알고 싶어 하는 것의 의미나 정의를 설명하게 된다.

■ 정의를 말할 때는 'X means ~.(X는 ~을 의미한다.)' 또는 'The meaning of X is ~.(X의 의미는 ~이다.)'를 사용하고, 'X stands for ~.(X는 ~을 나타낸다.)'도 어떤 말이나 문자, 기호, 신호, 상징 등의 의미를 설명할 때 사용한다.

■ 보통 의미를 설명하거나 정의를 나타내는 말은 상대방이 궁금증을 표현하거나 설명을 요청할 때 그 대답으로 쓰인다. 설명을 요청할 때 쓰는 표현은 'What is X (exactly)?(X가 (정확하게) 무엇이니?)', 'What does that mean?(그것이 무슨 뜻입니까?)', 'What do you mean by X?(X가 무슨 뜻이니?)' 등이다.

■ 상대방에게 설명을 요청할 때는 'Could you explain the meaning of it?', 'Could you tell me more about them?' 등의 표현을 사용하거나, Could 대신 Would, Can, Will 등을 사용하기도 한다. 또한 'Do you mind if I ask you to explain ~?'이라고 말할 수도 있다.

정의하기

- This means ~. 이것은 ~을 의미한다.
- X stands for ~. X는 ~을 나타낸다.
- The meaning of this is ~. 이것의 의미는 ~이다.

설명 요청하기

- What is X exactly? X가 정확하게 무엇이니?
- What do you mean by X? X가 무슨 뜻이니?
- What is the meaning of that exactly? 정확하게 그게 무슨 뜻입니까?
- Could you explain what it means? 그게 무엇을 의미하는지 설명 좀 해주시겠습니까?
- What does that mean? 그것이 무슨 뜻입니까?

핵심 Check

2. 주어진 어휘를 이용하여 밑줄 친 우리말에 해당하는 영어 문장을 쓰시오.

B: If there's no enemy, they don't smoke at all, do they?

G: Yes, they do. Smoke from one chimney means "No enemy."

B: Now smoke is rising from three chimneys. What does that mean?

G: <u>그것은 적이 국경선 근처에 접근하고 있다는 것을 의미해.</u> (come close, the border)

➡ _____

Step Up – Real-life Scene

B: This painting has some hidden secrets in it.

G: Really? ❶I'm curious about them. Where are the secrets?

B: Find one yourself.

G: ❷Let's see. ... Oh, I see some letters here.

B: You found one! ❸It means "Jan van Eyck was here. 1434." It's Latin.

G: That's awesome! Any other secrets?

B: Okay. This dog tells us the man here was very rich.

G: I don't understand.

B: They had to spend lots of money ❹to buy a dog of that kind at that time.

G: I see. Only ❺the rich could have that kind of dog, right?

B: Exactly. Pictures speak a thousand words, you know.

B: 이 그림은 그 안에 숨겨진 비밀이 몇 개 있어.

G: 정말? 난 그것들이 궁금해. 그 비밀들은 어디에 있니?

B: 너 스스로 하나 찾아봐.

G: 어디 보자. … 오, 여기 글자들이 몇 개 보여.

B: 너 하나 찾았구나! 그것은 "Jan van Eyck가 여기 있었다. 1434."를 의미해. 그것은 라틴어야.

G: 멋지다! 다른 비밀들은?

B: 좋아. 이 개는 여기 있는 이 남자가 매우 부자였다는 것을 우리에게 말해 주지.

G: 나는 이해가 안 돼.

B: 당시에 저런 종류의 개를 사려면 많은 돈을 써야 했어.

G: 알겠다. 단지 부자들만 저런 종류의 개를 살 수 있었어, 맞지?

B: 정확해. 알다시피, 그림이 천 마디 말을 하지.

❶ 궁금증을 나타내는 표현으로 '~가 궁금해'로 해석한다.

❷ '글쎄., 어디 보자.'의 의미로 'Let me see.'와 같은 의미로 사용된다.

❸ 상대방이 궁금증을 표현하거나 의미를 물어보면 'This/It means ~.(그것은 ~을 의미한다.)' 또는 'It is ~.(그것은 ~이다.)' 등의 표현을 사용해서 상대방이 궁금해 하거나 알고 싶어 하는 것의 의미나 정의를 설명하는 표현이다.

❹ 부정사의 부사적 용법 중 '목적'으로 '~하기 위해'로 해석한다.

❺ 'the+형용사'는 '복수명사'로 '~한 사람들'의 의미이다.

Check(√) True or False

(1) The girl found one secret in the painting.   T ☐ F ☐

(2) The man in the picture wasn't very rich.   T ☐ F ☐

Start Off – Listen & Talk A 1

B: What are the soldiers doing with the five chimneys on TV?

G: They are sending messages to the king ❶by using the chimneys.

B: Really? I'm curious about the system. Can you tell me more?

G: Well, do you see the two ❷smoking chimneys?

B: Yes. What do ❸they mean?

G: ❸They mean ❹they just saw an enemy.

B: TV에서 병사들이 5개의 굴뚝으로 무엇을 하고 있니?

G: 그들은 그 굴뚝을 이용하여 왕에게 메시지를 보내고 있어.

B: 정말? 난 그 체계가 궁금해. 좀 더 말해 줄 수 있어?

G: 음, 연기 나는 굴뚝 두 개가 보이지?

B: 그래. 그것들은 무엇을 의미하니?

G: 그것들은 그들이 방금 적을 봤다는 것을 의미해.

❶ 'by+-ing'는 '~함으로써'로 해석한다.

❷ 'smoking'은 현재분사로 '연기 나는'의 의미이다.

❸ 'the two smoking chimneys'를 가리킨다.

❹ 'the soldiers'를 가리키는 대명사다.

Check(√) True or False

(3) The soldiers are sending messages to the king by using the chimneys.   T ☐ F ☐

(4) The boy wants to know about the system.   T ☐ F ☐

Get Ready 2

(1) G: I'm curious about that robot. Why is it standing there?

B: It's a kind of ad. ❶It tells people their batteries are very powerful.

(2) G: What's this? I'm curious about it.

B: It's a traffic sign. ❷It means "Do not enter."

G: Oh, I see.

(3) G: ❸What are these dots for? I'm curious about them.

B: Oh, they are Braille. They are for blind people.

G: I see. Now I can guess what they mean.

(4) G: I'm curious about that balloon. Why is it hanging there?

B: Oh, that. It's an ad. ❹It says the product is very powerful.

❶ people 뒤에 목적어를 이끄는 접속사 that이 생략되어 있다.
❷ '그것은 ~을 의미하다'라는 뜻으로 정의를 나타내는 표현이다.
❸ 'What ~ for?'는 '~은 무엇을 위한 것이니?'라는 의미이다.
❹ says 뒤에 목적어를 이끄는 접속사 that이 생략되어 있다.

Start Off – Listen & Talk A 2

B: If there's no enemy, they don't smoke at all, ❶do they?

G: Yes, they do. ❷Smoke from one chimney means "No enemy."

B: Now smoke is rising from three chimneys. What does that mean?

G: It means an enemy is coming ❸close to the border.

❶ 앞 문장이 일반동사 부정문일 때 사용하는 부가의문문으로 '그렇지?'의 의미로 사용된다.
❷ 주어가 단수명사 'Smoke'이므로 동사는 단수 'means'이다.
❸ 이 문장에서 'close'는 부사로 '가까이'란 의미이다.

Start Off – Listen & Talk B

B: Now the enemy is crossing the border in the dark. What are the soldiers going to do ❶to send messages? I'm curious about that.

G: They will ❷light four chimneys.

B: ❸When they light all five of the chimneys, what does that mean?

G: ❹It means the battle has started.

❶ 부정사의 부사적 용법 중 '목적'으로 '메시지를 보내기 위해'라고 해석한다.
❷ 여기서 'light'는 동사로 '불을 붙이다'의 의미이다.
❸ 'when'이 이끄는 문장은 시간의 부사절로 '~할 때'로 해석한다.
❹ 동사 'means'와 주어 'the battle' 사이에는 목적어를 이끄는 접속사 'that'이 생략되어 있다.

Start Off – Speak Up

B: I'm curious about sign language.

G: ❶Are you? ❷Let me show you one expression. Look.

B: What does it mean?

G: It means "Hello."

❶ Are you curious about sign language?를 줄여 쓴 표현이다.
❷ 'let(사역동사)+목적어+동사원형' 형태로 'Let me show ~'는 '내가 …에게 ~을 보여줄게'로 해석한다.

Express Yourself A

1. W: What does this woman's gesture mean? I'm curious about it.

M: ❶I think it means "Jump into the pond."

W: Why do you think so?

M: The boy has lots of bees on his head. And the woman is pointing at the pond.

2. W: This woman doesn't want a dollar. So what does her gesture mean?

M: It means she wants a chicken.

W: Then the boy should bring a chicken ❷to get the fruit, right?

M: I think so.

3. W: What does this man's gesture mean? I'm curious about it.

M: It means "Turn it off."

W: Really? ❸What makes you think so?

M: ❹The other hunter there is coming close to an animal.

W: Oh, I see.

❶ 상대방이 궁금해 하는 것의 의미나 정의를 설명하는 표현이다.
❷ 부정사의 부사적 용법 중 '목적'으로 '과일을 얻기 위해'라고 해석한다.
❸ 여기서 make는 사역동사로 '목적어+목적보어(동사원형)' 형태를 취한다. 그리고 '왜 그렇게 생각하니?'의 뜻으로 'Why do you think so?'와 같은 표현이다.
❹ 'The other+단수명사' 형태로 '나머지 사냥꾼 한 명'을 나타낸다.

● 다음 우리말과 일치하도록 빈칸에 알맞은 말을 쓰시오.

Get Ready 2

(1) G: I'm _____ _____ that robot. Why _____ _____ standing there?

B: It's _____ _____ _____ ad. It _____ people their _____ are very _____.

(2) G: What's this? I'_____ _____ _____ it.

B: It's a _____ _____. It _____ "Do not _____."

G: Oh, I see.

(3) G: What are these _____ _____? I'_____ _____ _____ them.

B: Oh, they are _____. They are for _____ people.

G: I see. Now I can _____ what they _____.

(4) G: I'm _____ about that _____. Why is it _____ there?

B: Oh, that. It's an _____. It says the _____ is very _____.

Start Off – Listen & Talk A

1. B: What are the _____ doing with the five _____ on TV?

G: They are sending _____ to the king _____ _____ the _____.

B: Really? I'_____ _____ _____ the _____. Can you tell me more?

G: Well, do you see the two _____ _____?

B: Yes. _____ do they _____?

G: They mean they just saw an _____.

2. B: If there's no _____, they don't _____ _____, _____ they?

G: Yes, they do. _____ from one _____ means "No enemy."

B: Now smoke is _____ from three chimneys. _____ _____ that _____?

G: _____ _____ an enemy is coming _____ to the _____.

Start Off B

B: Now the enemy _____ _____ the _____ in the _____. What are the _____ _____ _____ _____ to send _____? I'm curious _____ that.

G: They will _____ four _____.

B: When they _____ all five of the _____, what does that mean?

G: _____ _____ the _____ has started.

(1) G: 나는 저 로봇에 대해 알고 싶어. 그건 왜 저기에 서 있는 거니?
B: 그건 일종의 광고야. 그것은 그들의 건전지가 매우 강력하다는 것을 사람들에게 말하고 있어.

(2) G: 이것은 뭐지? 난 그게 궁금해.
B: 그것은 교통 표지판이야. 그것은 "들어오지 마시오."를 의미해.
G: 오, 알겠어.

(3) G: 이 점들은 무엇을 위한 거니? 난 그것들에 대해 알고 싶어.
B: 오, 그것들은 점자야. 그것들은 시각장애인을 위한 것이야.
G: 알겠어. 이제 그것들이 무엇을 의미하는지 추측할 수 있어.

(4) G: 나는 저 풍선이 궁금해. 그건 왜 저기에 매달려 있니?
B: 오, 저것. 그건 광고야. 그것은 그 상품이 매우 강력하다는 것을 말하고 있어.

1. B: TV에서 병사들이 5개의 굴뚝으로 무엇을 하고 있니?
G: 그들은 그 굴뚝을 이용하여 왕에게 메시지를 보내고 있어.
B: 정말? 난 그 체계가 궁금해. 좀 더 말해 줄 수 있어?
G: 음, 연기 나는 굴뚝 두 개가 보이지?
B: 그래. 그것들은 무엇을 의미하니?
G: 그것들은 그들이 방금 적을 봤다는 것을 의미해.

2. B: 만약 적이 없다면, 그들은 연기를 전혀 피우지 않아, 그렇지?
G: 아니, 연기를 피워. 굴뚝 한 곳에서 연기가 나오면 "적이 없음"을 의미해.
B: 이제 연기가 굴뚝 세 개에서 올라가고 있어. 그것은 무엇을 의미하니?
G: 그것은 적이 국경 가까이 접근하고 있음을 의미해.

B: 이제 적이 어둠 속에서 국경을 침입하고 있어. 메시지를 보내기 위해서 병사들은 무슨 일을 할까? 나는 그것이 궁금해.
G: 그들은 굴뚝 4개에 불을 붙일 거야.
B: 그들이 5개 굴뚝 모두에 불을 붙였을 때, 그것은 무엇을 의미하니?
G: 그것은 전투가 시작되었음을 의미해.

Start Off – Speak Up

B: I'_____ _____ _____ sign _____.
G: Are you? _____ me _____ you one _____. Look.
B: _____ does it _____?
G: _____ _____ "Hello."

Step Up– Real-life Scene

B: This painting has some _____ _____ in it.
G: Really? I'm _____ _____ them. Where are the _____?
B: Find one _____.
G: _____ _____. ... Oh, I see some _____ here.
B: You found _____! It _____ "Jan van Eyck was here. 1434." It's _____.
G: That's _____! _____ _____ secrets?
B: Okay. This dog _____ us the man here was very _____.
G: I don't _____.
B: They had to _____ _____ _____ money _____ _____ a dog of that _____ at that time.
G: I see. Only _____ _____ could have _____ _____ of dog, right?
B: _____. Pictures _____ _____ _____ words, you know.

Express Yourself A

1. W: What does this woman's _____ mean? I'm _____ _____ it.
   M: I think _____ _____ "Jump into the _____."
   W: _____ do you _____ _____?
   M: The boy has _____ _____ bees on his head. And the woman is _____ at the _____.
2. W: This woman doesn't want a dollar. _____ what does her _____ _____?
   M: _____ _____ she wants a _____.
   W: Then the boy _____ _____ a chicken _____ _____ the fruit, _____?
   M: _____ _____ _____.
3. W: _____ does this man's _____ _____? I'm curious about it.
   M: It means "_____ _____ _____."
   W: Really? _____ _____ you think so?
   M: _____ _____ there is coming _____ to an animal.
   W: Oh, I _____.

B: 난 수화가 궁금해.
G: 그러니? 내가 표현 하나를 알려줄게. 봐.
B: 그것은 무엇을 의미하니?
G: 그것은 "안녕하세요."를 의미해.

B: 이 그림은 그 안에 숨겨진 비밀이 몇 개 있어.
G: 정말? 난 그것들이 궁금해. 그 비밀들은 어디에 있니?
B: 너 스스로 하나 찾아봐.
G: 어디 보자. … 오, 여기 글자들이 몇 개 보여.
B: 너 하나 찾았구나! 그것은 "Jan van Eyck가 여기 있었다. 1434."를 의미해. 그것은 라틴어야.
G: 멋지다! 다른 비밀들은?
B: 좋아. 이 개는 여기 있는 이 남자가 매우 부자였다는 것을 우리에게 말해 주지.
G: 나는 이해가 안 돼.
B: 당시에 저런 종류의 개를 사려면 많은 돈을 써야 했어.
G: 알겠다. 단지 부자들만 저런 종류의 개를 살 수 있었어, 맞지?
B: 정확해. 알다시피, 그림이 천 마디 말을 하지.

1. W: 이 여자의 몸짓은 무엇을 의미하니? 난 그것이 궁금해.
   M: 내 생각에 그것은 "연못으로 뛰어들어."를 의미해.
   W: 왜 그렇게 생각하니?
   M: 그 소년은 머리 위에 많은 벌이 있어. 그리고 그 여자는 연못을 가리키고 있어.
2. W: 이 여자는 1달러를 원하지 않아. 그렇다면 그녀의 몸짓은 무엇을 의미하니?
   M: 그것은 그녀가 닭 한 마리를 원한다는 것을 의미해.
   W: 그럼 그 소년은 과일을 얻기 위해 닭을 한 마리 가져와야 하는구나, 맞지?
   M: 난 그렇게 생각해.
3. W: 이 남자의 몸짓은 무엇을 의미하니? 난 그것이 궁금해.
   M: 그것은 "그것을 꺼."를 의미해.
   W: 정말? 왜 그렇게 생각하니?
   M: 거기 있는 나머지 다른 사냥꾼이 어떤 동물 가까이 접근하고 있어.
   W: 오, 알겠어.

01 우리말에 맞도록 주어진 단어를 활용하여 빈칸을 채우시오.

> 그것은 네가 들어가지 말아야 한다는 것을 의미해. (mean)

➡ _____ _____ you must _____ _____.

02 다음 대화의 빈칸에 들어갈 말로 <u>어색한</u> 것은?

> G: What are these dots for? _____
> B: Oh, they are Braille. They are for blind people.
> G: I see. Now I can guess what they mean.

① I'm curious about them.
② I would like to know about them.
③ I'd be very interested to know about them.
④ Let me show you one expression
⑤ Can you tell me about them?

03 다음 대화의 빈칸에 들어갈 말로 적절한 것은?

> A: What does your name mean? I'm curious about it.
> B: _____
> A: That's beautiful.

① I know whose name it is. It's Hyeja's.
② What does it mean?   ③ It means "bright girl."
④ What does this letter mean? ⑤ I don't care about it.

04 다음 대화의 밑줄 친 말의 의도로 알맞은 것은?

> G: <u>I'm curious about that balloon.</u> Why is it hanging there?
> B: Oh, that. It's an ad.

① 관심 표현하기   ② 충고 구하기
③ 가능성 묻기   ④ 유감 표현하기
⑤ 궁금증 표현하기

[01~02] 다음 대화를 읽고 물음에 답하시오.

W: What does this man's gesture (a)mean? I'm curious about (b)it.

M: It means "(c)Turn it off."

W: Really? _____(A)_____

M: (d)Other hunter there is coming (e)close to an animal.

W: Oh, I see.

01 위 대화의 빈칸 (A)에 들어갈 말로 알맞은 것을 <u>모두</u> 고르시오.

① How do you think so?

② What do you think about it?

③ What makes you think so?

④ Do you think I should turn it off?

⑤ Why do you think so?

서답형

02 위 대화의 (a)~(e)에서 어법상 <u>틀린</u> 곳을 찾아 바르게 고치시오. (1개)

➡ 틀린 것: _____

➡ 고치기: _____ ➡ _____

[03~04] 다음 대화를 읽고 물음에 답하시오.

B: Now the enemy is crossing the border in the dark. What are the soldiers going to do to send messages? _____(A)_____

G: They will light four chimneys.

B: When they light all five of the chimneys, _____(B)_____?

G: It means the battle has started.

03 위 대화의 빈칸 (A)에 들어갈 말로 알맞은 것은?

① I'm curious about who the soldiers are.

② Can you tell me how to light chimneys?

③ Do you think they should light chimneys?

④ I'm curious about that.

⑤ Can you tell me about the messages?

04 위 대화의 흐름상 빈칸 (B)에 들어갈 알맞은 표현은?

① why did you say so

② what does that mean

③ do you think so

④ why not

⑤ do you mean the battle has started

[05~06] 다음 대화를 읽고 물음에 답하시오.

B: What are the soldiers doing with the five chimneys on TV?

G: They are sending (a)messages to the king by using the chimneys.

B: Really? I'm (b)curious about the system. Can you tell me more?

G: Well, do you see the two (c)smoking chimneys?

B: Yes. What do they mean?

G: They mean they just (d)saw an enemy.

B: If there's no enemy, they don't smoke at all, do they?

G: (A)Yes, they do. Smoke from one chimney means "(e)An enemy."

B: Now smoke is rising from three chimneys. What does that mean?

G: It means an enemy is coming close to the border.

05 위 대화의 흐름상 어휘의 쓰임이 <u>어색한</u> 것은?

① (a)　② (b)　③ (c)　④ (d)　⑤ (e)

06 위 대화의 밑줄 친 (A)의 우리말을 바르게 옮긴 것은?

① 응, 적이 와.　　　② 아니, 적이 오지 않아.

③ 응, 연기를 피워.　④ 아니, 연기를 피워.

⑤ 응, 연기를 피우지 않아.

서답형

07 다음 대화의 빈칸에 들어갈 단어를 주어진 영영풀이를 보고 '복수형'으로 쓰시오.

> G: I'm curious about that robot. Why is it standing there?
> B: It's a kind of ad. It tells people their _____ are very powerful.

> <영영풀이> an object that provides electricity for things such as radios, toys, or cars

➡ _____

[08~09] 다음 대화를 읽고 물음에 답하시오.

> G: What are these dots ___(a)___ ?
> ___(A)___ them.
> B: Oh, they are Braille. They are ___(b)___ blind people.
> G: I see. Now I can guess what they mean.
>
> G: ___(A)___ that balloon. Why is it hanging there?
> B: Oh, that. It's an ad. It says the product is very powerful.

08 위 대화의 빈칸 (A)에 공통으로 들어갈 말로 어색한 것은?

① I'm curious about

② I'm surprised about

③ I'd like to know about

④ I wonder about

⑤ I want to know about

서답형

09 위 대화의 빈칸 (a)와 (b)에 공통으로 들어갈 단어를 쓰시오.

➡ _____

[10~11] 다음 대화를 읽고 물음에 답하시오.

> B: This painting has some hidden secrets in (a)it.
> G: Really? I'm curious about them. Where are the secrets?
> B: Find one yourself. (A)
> G: Let's see. ... Oh, I see some letters here.
> B: You found one! (B) It means "Jan van Eyck was here. 1434." It's Latin.
> G: That's awesome! Any other secrets?
> B: Okay. (C)
> G: I don't understand. (D)
> B: They had to spend lots of money to buy a dog of that kind at that time.
> G: I see. (E) Only the rich could have that kind of dog, right?
> B: Exactly. Pictures speak a thousand words, you know.

10 위 대화의 (A)~(E) 중 주어진 문장이 들어갈 위치로 알맞은 것은?

> This dog tells us the man here was very rich.

① (A)　② (B)　③ (C)　④ (D)　⑤ (E)

11 밑줄 친 (a)가 가리키는 것을 영어로 쓰시오.

➡ _____

[01~02] 다음 대화를 읽고 물음에 답하시오.

B: This painting has some hidden secrets in it.

G: Really? _____(A)_____ Where are the secrets?

B: Find one yourself.

G: Let's see. ... Oh, I see some letters here.

B: You found one! ____(B)____ "Jan van Eyck was here. 1434." It's Latin.

G: That's awesome! Any other secrets?

B: Okay. This dog tells us the man here was very rich.

G: I don't understand.

B: They had to spend lots of money to buy a dog of that kind at that time.

G: I see. Only the rich could have that kind of dog, right?

B: Exactly. Pictures speak a thousand words, you know.

01 위 대화를 읽고 다음 물음에 영어로 답하시오.

Q: What do the letters the girl found mean?

➡ _____

02 위 대화의 빈칸 (A)와 (B)에 들어갈 말을 〈조건〉에 맞게 영어로 쓰시오.

┤ 조건 ├

(A) • 궁금증을 표현하는 말을 쓸 것.
　　 • '대명사'와 'curious'를 사용할 것.

(B) • 상대방이 알고 싶어 하는 것의 의미나 정의를 표현하는 말을 2단어로 쓸 것.

➡ (A) _____
　 (B) _____

03 다음 대화의 밑줄 친 우리말 해석에 맞게 주어진 〈조건〉에 맞게 영어로 쓰시오.

W: What does this woman's gesture mean? I'm curious about it.

M: I think it means "Jump into the pond."

W: 왜 그렇게 생각하니?

M: The boy has lots of bees on his head. And the woman is pointing at the pond.

┤ 조건 ├

• 'make', 'think'를 이용할 것

➡ _____

[04~05] 다음 대화를 읽고 물음에 답하시오.

B: What are the soldiers doing with the five chimneys on TV?

G: (a)그들은 그 굴뚝을 이용하여 왕에게 메시지를 보내고 있어.

B: Really? I'm curious about the system. Can you tell me more?

G: Well, do you see the two smoking chimneys?

B: Yes. What do they mean?

G: _____(A)_____

04 위 대화의 흐름상 빈칸 (A)에 주어진 어구를 알맞은 순서로 배열하시오.

(saw / they / mean / just / an enemy / they)

➡ _____

05 위 대화의 (a)의 우리말을 주어진 〈조건〉에 맞게 영작하시오.

┤ 조건 ├

• '진행형'과 'by ~ing'를 이용할 것.

➡ _____
　 _____

교과서 Grammar

1 가정법 과거

> • I **would** be so happy if you **were** with me. 당신이 나와 함께 있다면 난 정말 행복할 거예요.

■ 형태: If+주어+동사 과거형, 주어+조동사 과거형(would/should/could/might)+동사원형
  의미: 만약 …한다면 ~할 텐데(현재 사실과 반대되는 상상이나 가정)

■ 가정법 문장이라는 표시로 과거 동사를 사용할 뿐 의미상 과거를 나타내지 않고, 현재 말하는 사람의 느낌이나 감정을 표현한다.

  • If I **had** a car, I **could** give you a ride home. 만일 내가 차가 있다면, 너를 집까지 태워 줄 텐데.

  = As I **don't have** a car, I **can't give** you a ride home.
  나는 차를 가지고 있지 않아서, 너를 집까지 태워줄 수 없다.

■ if절에 쓰이는 be동사의 과거형은 'were'를 사용하지만, 구어체에서는 주어가 'I' 또는 3인칭 단수인 경우 'was'를 쓰기도 한다.

  • If I **were[was]** rich, I **would** help all the children in need.
  내가 부자라면, 도움이 필요한 모든 어린이들을 도와줄 텐데.

■ 가정법 과거 문장을 현재시제의 직설법으로 바꿀 수 있다.

  • If he **knew** the answer, he **would** be very glad. 그가 정답을 안다면, 그는 매우 기쁠 텐데.

  = As he **doesn't know** the answer, he **is not** very glad. 그는 정답을 모르기 때문에, 그는 별로 기쁘지 않다.

■ if는 if절의 동사가 'were' 또는 'had'일 때 생략될 수 있으며, 이때는 주어와 동사가 도치된다.

  • If my family **were** at home, I **would** tell them everything about my school life.
  만일 가족들이 집에 있다면, 나는 그들에게 내 학교생활에 관한 모든 것을 말할 텐데.

  = **Were** my family at home, I **would** tell them everything about my school life.

  • If Tom **had** a sister, he **could** play with her all day long.
  만일 Tom이 여동생이 있다면, 그는 하루 종일 그녀와 놀 수 있을 텐데.

  = **Had** Tom a sister, he **could** play with her all day long

핵심 Check

1. 다음 괄호 안에서 알맞은 것을 고르시오.

  (1) If I (am / were) a fish, I would swim in the pond.

  (2) She (will / would) be very happy if she won the lottery.

② 관계대명사 whose

> • It was written in 1973 by a woman **whose** husband was far away.
> 그것은 남편이 멀리 떨어져 살았던 한 여자에 의해 1973년에 쓰여졌다.

- 형태: 선행사+whose+명사

  의미: ~인, ~의

- 소유격을 대신하고 두 문장을 이어주는 접속사 역할을 하는 관계대명사이다.

  - My brother has a girl friend. + He likes **her cat**.

    → My brother has a girl friend **whose cat** he likes.

      나의 남동생은 그녀의 고양이를 그가 좋아하는 여자 친구가 있다.

- 선행사가 사물인 경우 'of which'를 쓰기도 한다.

  - I have a bag. + **Its handle** is made of bamboo.

    → I have a bag **whose handle** is made of bamboo. 나는 손잡이가 대나무로 만들어진 가방을 가지고 있다.

  - I have a bag. + The handle **of it** is made of bamboo.

    → I have a bag the handle **of which** is made of bamboo.

    → I have a bag **of which** the handle is made of bamboo.

- 소유격 관계대명사 다음의 동사는 소유격 관계대명사가 갖고 있는 명사의 수를 따른다.

  - I know a small girl whose **parents are** tall. 나는 부모님이 키가 큰 작은 소녀를 알고 있다.

- 소유격과 한정사(a, an, the, this, that, some, any 등)는 함께 쓸 수 없으므로 소유격 관계사 다음에 한정사를 쓰지 않는다.

  - I have a dog whose the tail is long. (×)

    → I have a dog **whose** tail is long. 또는 I have a dog **of which** the tail is long.

핵심 Check

2. 다음 괄호 안에서 알맞은 것을 고르시오.

  (1) He has a sister (of which / whose) eyes are brown.

  (2) The house (of which / whose) windows are very big is my father's.

  (3) I have a friend whose brothers (enjoy / enjoys) skateboarding.

01 다음 우리말에 맞게 괄호 안에 주어진 단어를 이용하여 문장을 완성하시오.

(1) 내가 오리라면, 물속에서 수영할 수 있을 텐데. (if, be)

➡ _____, I could swim in the water.

(2) 날개를 가졌다면 너는 뭘 하겠니? (what, do)

➡ _____ if you had wings?

(3) Bubu는 그의 개가 인형을 가지고 다니는 소년이야. (be, carry)

➡ Bubu is the boy _____.

(4) Lala는 그녀의 개가 핫도그를 원하는 소녀야. (want, hot dog)

➡ Lala is the girl _____.

02 다음 문장에서 어법상 <u>어색한</u> 부분을 바르게 고쳐 쓰시오.

(1) If I had wings, I will fly in the sky.

➡ _____

(2) What would you do if you are a fish?

➡ _____

(3) Koko is the boy of which the bag is on a big cat.

➡ _____

(4) The girl who cat is dancing is Didi.

➡ _____

03 다음 〈보기〉의 문장을 참고하여 빈칸을 완성하시오.

┌─ 보기 ├─

As she doesn't know the result, she is not happy.
= If she knew the result, she would be happy.

(1) As I don't have a lot of money, I can't travel around the world.

= _____

(2) As I am not tall, I can't be a basketball player.

= _____

01 다음 두 문장을 한 문장으로 고칠 때 빈칸에 알맞은 말은?

> • The movie attracted 10 million viewers.
> • The director of the movie won the Academy award.
> → The movie _____ the director won the Academy award attracted 10 million viewers.

① who   ② whose   ③ which
④ of which   ⑤ what

02 중요 다음 빈칸에 들어갈 알맞은 것은?

> I have a ring _____ owner is unknown.

① whose   ② who   ③ that
④ of which   ⑤ whom

03 서답형 관계대명사를 이용하여 두 문장을 한 문장으로 바꿔 쓰시오.

> • There was a queen.
> • Her daughter was cursed by an evil fairy.

➡ _____
_____

04 다음 중 어법상 올바른 문장을 고르시오.

① If I were him, I would buy the bag.
② If I had a car, I could drove her home.
③ Were I rich, I can help all of you.
④ She would be very happy if she wins the prize.
⑤ If your mom knew you passed the test, she will be very surprised.

05 중요 다음 문장의 뜻이 나머지 넷과 <u>다른</u> 것은?

① If I were in good physical condition, I could work out with you.
② Were I in good physical condition, I could work out with you.
③ With good physical condition, I can work out with you.
④ As I am not in good physical condition, I can't work out with you.
⑤ Because I am not in good physical condition, I can't work out with you.

06 빈칸에 공통으로 들어갈 말은? (대 · 소문자 무시)

> • If I _____ you, I would save some money for the future.
> • _____ I you, I would save some money for the future.

① am   ② were   ③ had
④ had been   ⑤ weren't

07 서답형 다음 괄호 안에 주어진 단어들을 바르게 배열하여 문장을 완성하시오.

> Miso (a girl, jumping, dog, is, whose, rope, is).

➡ _____

08 서답형 다음 두 문장을 가정법을 이용하여 한 문장으로 쓰시오.

> • I don't have a lot of money.
> • I can't buy that car.

➡ _____
_____

09 다음 문장과 같은 뜻을 가진 문장을 <u>모두</u> 고르시오.

> As we don't have enough time, we can't stay longer.

① If we didn't have enough time, we couldn't stay longer.
② If we have enough time, we can stay longer.
③ If we had enough time, we could stay longer.
④ Without enough time, we could stay longer.
⑤ With enough time, we could stay longer.

서답형
10 다음 문장에서 어법상 <u>어색한</u> 것을 바르게 고쳐 다시 쓰시오.

(1) If I have a monkey, I could play with it.
 ➡ _____
 _____

(2) The boys whose mom is a lawyer lives next door.
 ➡ _____
 _____

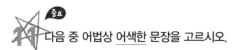
11 다음 중 어법상 <u>어색한</u> 문장을 고르시오.

① If he were here, he could help us.
② If I were a cheetah, I could run faster than you.
③ If I were not tired, I could go swimming.
④ If my brother were tall, he could play basketball better.
⑤ I lent it to you if I had the book.

서답형
12 다음 괄호 안에서 알맞은 말을 고르시오.

(1) If I were a millionaire, I (built / would build) a castle.
(2) I would call him if I (knew / had known) his phone number.
(3) I have a friend, (who / whose) family is from Germany.
(4) This is the student (who / whose) came from France.
(5) We need to help animals in Australia (which / whose) lives are in danger.

13 다음 우리말을 영어로 바르게 옮긴 것은?

> 내가 날개를 가졌다면, 내 친구를 만나러 부산으로 날아갈 텐데.

① If I have wings, I will fly to Busan to meet my friend.
② If I have wings, I would fly to Busan to meet my friend.
③ If I had wings, I will fly to Busan to meet my friend.
④ If I had wings, I would fly to Busan to meet my friend.
⑤ If I had had wings, I would fly to Busan to meet my friend.

서답형
14 주어진 어휘를 이용하여 다음 우리말을 영어로 쓰시오.

> 내가 새라면, 나는 산 너머로 날아갈 텐데. (a bird, fly, over)

 ➡ _____

15 다음 괄호 안에 주어진 단어들을 바르게 배열하여 문장을 완성하시오.

> The animal (begins, with z, whose, is, a zebra, name).

➡ _____

_____

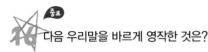 다음 우리말을 바르게 영작한 것은?

> 내 아들이 더 열심히 공부하면 나는 더 행복할 텐데.

① I will be happier if my son studied harder.

② I am happier if my son studied harder.

③ I would be happier if my son studies harder.

④ I would be happier if my son studied harder.

⑤ I would be happier if my son has studied harder.

17 다음 두 문장을 한 문장으로 바르게 옮긴 것은?

> • A girl is preparing for the audition.
> • Her dream is to be a movie star.

① A girl is preparing for the audition whose dream is to be a movie star.

② A girl is preparing for the audition who dream is to be a movie star.

③ A girl is preparing for the audition her dream is to be a movie star.

④ A girl whose dream is to be a movie star is preparing for the audition.

⑤ A girl of which the dream is to be a movie star is preparing for the audition.

18 빈칸에 들어갈 말을 순서대로 바르게 연결한 것은?

> • I like the candies _____ taste like apples.
> • I like the fresh baked bread _____ smell is so sweet.

① whose   –   whose

② whose   –   which

③ of which   –   which

④ which   –   of which

⑤ which   –   whose

19 주어진 어휘를 이용하여 다음 우리말을 영어로 쓰시오.

> 내가 대통령을 만난다면, 그와 악수를 할 텐데.
> (the President, shake)

➡ _____

_____

20 대화의 빈칸에 공통으로 들어갈 단어를 쓰시오.

(1) A: What _____ you do if you were a fish?

B: If I were a fish, I _____ swim in the pond.

(2) A: What would you do if you _____ a duck?

B: If I _____ a duck, I could swim in the water.

21 다음 두 문장이 같은 뜻이 되도록 빈칸에 알맞은 말을 쓰시오.

> If she worked with him, she would be very disappointed with him.
> = As _____,
> she _____.

01 관계대명사를 이용하여 두 문장을 한 문장으로 쓰시오.

(1) • I have a friend.
   • His brother enjoys skateboarding.

   ➡ _____

   _____

(2) • The boy is my brother.
   • He is dancing on the floor.

   ➡ _____

   _____

(3) • He wants to ride a bike.
   • I bought it yesterday.

   ➡ _____

   _____

(4) • Do you like the house?
   • Its roof looks like a hat.

   ➡ _____

   _____

(5) • The boy is Jeje.
   • His cat is spinning a hula hoop.

   ➡ _____

   _____

02 다음 우리말을 주어진 어휘를 이용하여 영어로 옮기시오.

(1) 내가 강한 팔을 가졌다면, 나는 나무에 오를 수 있을 텐데. (strong, climb)

   ➡ _____

   _____

(2) 내가 긴 코를 가졌다면, 나는 샤워하기 위해 그것을 쓸 수 있을 텐데. (nose, shower)

   ➡ _____

(3) 내가 아름다운 목소리를 가졌다면, 나는 나무에서 노래할 거야. (voice, on the tree)

   ➡ _____

   _____

03 주어진 문장을 가정법 문장으로 다시 쓰시오.

(1) As I am not an English teacher, I don't play word games every day.

   ➡ _____

   _____

(2) As I am not on the moon, I can't jump much higher.

   ➡ _____

   _____

04 잘못된 부분을 바르게 고쳐 문장을 다시 쓰시오.

(1) Did he rich, he could travel to Europe.

   ➡ _____

   _____

(2) The boy whose is talking to Mary is my cousin.

   ➡ _____

   _____

(3) He lent me the book of which I want to read.

   ➡ _____

   _____

(4) I stayed at the house which walls are white.

   ➡ _____

   _____

(5) If I were you, I took a swimming lesson.

   ➡ _____

   _____

05 다음 그림을 보고 빈칸에 알맞은 말을 써 넣으시오.

(1)

If I were the boy, I _____ the fruit to the monkey right away.

(2)

If I were the boy, I _____.

(3)

If I were the girl, I _____ out of the water right away.

06 다음 주어진 우리말에 맞게 빈칸에 들어갈 단어를 각각 쓰시오.

내가 만일 BTS 멤버라면, 나는 가난한 어린이들을 위해 춤추고 노래할 수 있을 텐데.
→ If I _____ a member of BTS, I _____ _____ _____ for poor children.

07 주어진 문장이 같은 뜻이 되도록 빈칸에 알맞은 말을 쓰시오.

(1) If he knew her, he would talk to her.
➡ As he doesn't know her, _____
_____.

(2) If he were at home, I would tell him the truth.
➡ _____, I would tell him the truth.

08 주어진 〈보기〉를 참고하여 두 문장을 하나의 문장으로 쓰시오.

┤ 보기 ├
The boy doesn't understand her gesture.
The woman doesn't want his money.
→ The boy whose money the woman doesn't want doesn't understand her gesture.

(1) The boy doesn't understand the man's gesture. His cell phone is ringing loudly.
➡ _____
_____

(2) The girl doesn't understand the man's gesture. Her feet are in the water.
➡ _____
_____

(3) The boy doesn't understand her gesture. The woman is pulling his hand.
➡ _____
_____

(4) The boy doesn't understand its gesture. The monkey is pulling his bag.
➡ _____
_____

Reading

A Picture Letter from a Mother of Three

<u>Speaking</u> to family members or friends in a foreign country is rather
동명사 주어
easy and simple today. But before the <u>days</u> of phones and the Internet,
시대
it was not that easy. People just sent a letter and waited for a reply for
= Speaking to family members or friends in a foreign country
weeks. And it was a <u>lot</u> harder if they couldn't read or write.
비교급을 강조하는 부사: a lot. much. far. still. even(훨씬)
This letter shows <u>how</u> people got over these difficulties. It was
관계부사 = the way. the way how(×)
written in 1973 by a woman <u>whose</u> husband was far away. She lived
소유격 관계대명사
in <u>Sicily, an Italian island</u>, while her husband worked in Germany. At
Sicily와 an Italian island는 동격
the time, <u>more than</u> 5% of the people in Italy could <u>not read or write</u>,
= over   illiterate: 글을 (읽거나 쓸 줄) 모르는, 문맹의
and she was one of them. <u>This letter was discovered by Sicilian writer</u>
→ 능동태: Sicilian writer Gesualdo Bufalino discovered this letter.
<u>Gesualdo Bufalino.</u>

Here's how he translated the pictures into words.
~가 여기 있다
My dear love, I miss you so much, and I <u>reach</u> my arms out toward
My dear love: 부부간의 호칭(여보, 당신)   reach ~ out: (손 등을) 내밀다, 뻗다
you, together with our three kids. We are all <u>in good health</u> except for
be in good health: 건강 상태가 좋다
the little <u>one</u>. He's a little sick, but <u>not seriously</u>.
= kid   = he's not seriously sick.

foreign 외국의
rather 다소, 약간
wait for ~을 기다리다
reply 답장
get over 이겨내다, 극복하다
husband 남편
discover 발견하다
translate 번역하다, 해석하다
toward ~을 향하여
in good health 건강하여
except for ~을 제외하고
seriously 진지하게, 심각하게

 확인문제

● 다음 문장이 본문의 내용과 일치하면 T, 일치하지 <u>않으면</u> F를 쓰시오.

1 It is rather easy and simple today to speak to family members or friends in a foreign country. ☐

2 Before the days of phones and the Internet, people just sent a letter and waited for a reply for a few days. ☐

3 Speaking to family members or friends in a foreign country was a lot harder if people couldn't read or write. ☐

4 In 1973, more than 5% of the people in the world could not read or write ☐

5 Gesualdo Bufalino was a Sicilian writer. ☐

6 Gesualdo Bufalino translated words into the pictures. ☐

I already sent you a letter, but there was no reply, so I am sad about it.
there was no reply(편지를 보냈는데 답장이 없는 것)

If I got a letter from you, I would be very happy. Your mother fell ill,
가정법 과거 → 직설법: As I don't get a letter from you. I'm not very happy.　　　　*= became ill*

and I'm going to visit her in the hospital with some money and food. I'll

go there with our middle son while the oldest looks after the youngest.
while: ~하는 동안에(접속사)　*– the oldest kid*　　*– the youngest kid*

I had two workers prepare our field and plant seeds for 150,000
사역동사 had로 목적어 다음에 동사원형(prepare. plant)을 쓴다.　　　*~의 비용으로*

lire. I voted for the DC. The PCI lost so many seats that it almost
너무 …해서 ~하다

seems dead. But whether one or the other wins, it's the same. Nothing
seem+형용사: ~해 보인다　*whether ~ or: ~이든지 아니든지*

changes for us poor people. We worked yesterday, and we will work

again tomorrow.

We picked lots of olives from our olive trees this year. I hired a man

whose sons are good workers. He knocked the olives down, and his
소유격 관계대명사　　　*knock ~ down: ~을 두드려 떨어뜨리다*

two sons helped him, picking them up from the ground. I paid him
'주우면서'라는 의미로 동시 동작을 표현

27,000 lire for the work. I spent 12,000 more for the olive press. I got
pay A B for C: A에게 C에 대한 대가로 B를 지불하다

enough oil to fill a large pot and a small one. I can sell it at a price of
enough … to ~: ~할 만큼 충분한 …　　　*= pot*　　*~의 가격으로*

1,300 lire a liter.
~당, ~에

My love, my heart thinks of you as Christmas is coming. I would be

so happy if you were with me. We all miss you so much. I'm sending
가정법 과거, → 직설법: As you are not with me. I'm not so happy.

you a big hug from me and our three little kids. Goodbye, dear love.

My heart is yours, joined to you as our two rings are.
과거분사(분사구문)　　*as: ~하듯이, ~하는 것처럼*　*are 뒤에 'joined'가 생략되었음.*

Glossary (right column):

ill 아픈, 병든
look after ~을 돌보다
prepare 준비하다
vote 투표하다, 선출하다
seat 의석
seem ~처럼 보이다
dead 죽은, 쓸모없는
whether ~이든지 아니든지
lots of 많은
hire 고용하다
knock 치다, 두드리다
ground 땅, 지면
oil 기름
at a price of ~의 가격으로
hug 포옹; 포옹하다
ring 반지

📎 확인문제

● 다음 문장이 본문의 내용과 일치하면 T, 일치하지 <u>않으면</u> F를 쓰시오.

1 The writer already sent her husband a letter, but there was no reply. ☐

2 The writer visited her mother-in-law in the hospital with some money and food. ☐

3 The writer got two workers to prepare their field and to plant seeds for 150,000 lire. ☐

4 The writer spent 27,000 lire for the olive press. ☐

5 The writer would be so happy if her husband were with her. ☐

6 The writer's husband is sending the writer and his three little kids a big hug. ☐

● 우리말을 참고하여 빈칸에 알맞은 말을 쓰시오.

1 _____ _____ _____ from a Mother of Three

2 _____ to family members or friends in a foreign country _____ _____ easy and simple today.

3 But before the days of phones and the Internet, it was not _____ _____.

4 People just sent a letter and _____ _____ a reply _____ _____.

5 And it was a lot harder if they _____ _____ _____ _____.

6 This letter shows how people _____ _____ these difficulties.

7 It was written in 1973 by a woman _____ husband was _____ _____.

8 She lived in Sicily, an Italian island, while her husband worked _____ _____.

9 At the time, _____ _____ _____ of the people in Italy could not read or write, and she was _____ _____.

10 This letter _____ _____ _____ Sicilian writer Gesualdo Bufalino.

11 Here's how he _____ the pictures _____ words.

12 My dear love, I miss you so much, and I _____ my arms _____ toward you, together with our three kids.

13 We are _____ _____ _____ _____ except for the little _____.

14 He's a little sick, but _____ _____.

15 I already sent you a letter, but _____ _____ _____ _____, so I am sad about it.

16 If I _____ a letter from you, I _____ _____ very happy.

1	세 아이의 엄마가 보낸 그림 편지
2	오늘날 외국에 있는 가족이나 친구와 대화하는 것은 다소 쉽고 간단하다.
3	하지만 전화와 인터넷 시대 이전에는 그것이 그렇게 쉽지 않았다.
4	사람들은 단지 편지를 보내고 답장을 몇 주 동안 기다렸다.
5	그리고 그들이 읽거나 쓸 수 없었다면 그건 훨씬 더 힘들었다.
6	이 편지는 사람들이 이런 어려움을 어떻게 극복했는지 보여 준다.
7	그것은 남편이 멀리 떨어져 살았던 한 여자에 의해 1973년에 쓰여졌다.
8	그녀의 남편은 독일에서 일한 반면, 그녀는 이탈리아의 섬인 시실리에서 살았다.
9	그 당시에는 5% 이상의 이탈리아 사람들이 읽거나 쓸 수 없었고, 그녀도 그들 중 한 명이었다.
10	이 편지는 시실리의 작가 Gesualdo Bufalino가 발견하였다.
11	그가 그림들을 어떻게 글로 번역했는지는 다음과 같다.
12	사랑하는 여보. 난 당신이 정말 그립고, 우리 세 아이와 함께 당신을 향해 내 팔을 쭉 뻗고 있어요.
13	막내를 제외하고는 우리 모두 건강해요.
14	그 아이는 약간 아프지만 심각하진 않아요.
15	난 당신에게 이미 편지를 보냈지만, 답장이 없어서 그것 때문에 나는 슬퍼요.
16	당신에게서 편지를 받는다면, 나는 정말 행복할 거예요.

17 Your mother _____ _____, and I'm going to visit her in the hospital with some money and food.

18 I'll go there with our middle son _____ the oldest _____ _____ the youngest.

19 I _____ two workers _____ our field and _____ seeds for 150,000 lire.

20 I _____ _____ the DC.

21 The PCI lost _____ many seats _____ it almost seems dead.

22 But _____ _____ _____ _____ _____ wins, it's the same.

23 _____ _____ for us poor people.

24 We worked yesterday, and we _____ _____ _____ tomorrow.

25 We _____ lots of olives _____ our olive trees this year.

26 I _____ a man _____ sons are good workers.

27 He _____ the olives _____, and his two sons helped him, _____ them _____ from the ground.

28 I _____ him 27,000 lire _____ the work.

29 I _____ 12,000 more _____ the olive press.

30 I got _____ oil _____ _____ a large pot and a small _____.

31 I can sell it _____ _____ _____ _____ 1,300 lire a liter.

32 My love, my heart thinks of you _____ Christmas is coming.

33 I _____ _____ so happy if you _____ with me.

34 We all _____ you so much.

35 I'm sending you _____ _____ _____ from me and our three little kids.

36 Goodbye, _____ _____.

37 My heart is yours, _____ to you _____ our two rings are.

---

17 당신의 어머니께서는 병이 드셨고, 나는 약간의 돈과 음식을 가지고 병원에 있는 어머니를 방문할 예정이에요.

18 큰애가 막내를 돌보는 동안 둘째와 함께 그곳에 갈 거예요.

19 나는 150,000리라에 두 일꾼을 시켜 우리 밭을 준비하고 씨앗을 심게 했어요.

20 나는 DC에 투표했어요.

21 PCI는 매우 많은 의석을 잃어서 거의 죽은 것처럼 보여요.

22 하지만 이쪽이 이기건 저쪽이 이기건, 상황은 똑같아요.

23 우리 가난한 사람들에게는 아무것도 바뀌지 않지요.

24 우리는 어제도 일했고, 내일도 다시 일할 거예요.

25 우리는 올해 올리브나무에서 올리브를 많이 땄어요.

26 나는 아들들이 훌륭한 일꾼인 한 남자를 고용했어요.

27 그가 올리브를 쳐서 떨어뜨리면 그의 두 아들이 땅에서 올리브를 주우면서 그를 도왔어요.

28 나는 그 일을 위해 그에게 27,000리라를 지급했어요.

29 올리브 압착을 위해 12,000리라를 더 썼어요.

30 나는 큰 항아리 하나와 작은 항아리 하나를 채울 만큼 충분한 기름을 얻었어요.

31 리터당 1,300리라의 가격으로 팔 수 있을 것 같아요.

32 여보, 크리스마스가 다가오면서 내 마음은 당신을 떠올려요.

33 당신이 나와 함께 있다면 난 정말 행복할 거예요.

34 우리는 모두 당신을 매우 많이 그리워해요.

35 나와 우리 세 아이의 큰 포옹을 보내요.

36 잘 있어요, 여보.

37 내 마음은 당신의 것이에요, 우리들의 두 반지처럼 당신과 연결된 채로요.

● 우리말을 참고하여 본문을 영작하시오.

1 세 아이의 엄마가 보낸 그림 편지

➡ _____

2 오늘날 외국에 있는 가족이나 친구와 대화하는 것은 다소 쉽고 간단하다.

➡ _____

3 하지만 전화와 인터넷 시대 이전에는 그것이 그렇게 쉽지 않았다.

➡ _____

4 사람들은 단지 편지를 보내고 답장을 몇 주 동안 기다렸다.

➡ _____

5 그리고 그들이 읽거나 쓸 수 없었다면 그건 훨씬 더 힘들었다.

➡ _____

6 이 편지는 사람들이 이런 어려움을 어떻게 극복했는지 보여 준다.

➡ _____

7 그것은 남편이 멀리 떨어져 살았던 한 여자에 의해 1973년에 쓰여졌다.

➡ _____

8 그녀의 남편은 독일에서 일한 반면, 그녀는 이탈리아의 섬인 시실리에서 살았다.

➡ _____

9 그 당시에는 5% 이상의 이탈리아 사람들이 읽거나 쓸 수 없었고, 그녀도 그들 중 한 명이었다.

➡ _____

10 이 편지는 시실리의 작가 Gesualdo Bufalino가 발견하였다.

➡ _____

11 그가 그림들을 어떻게 글로 번역했는지는 다음과 같다.

➡ _____

12 사랑하는 여보, 난 당신이 정말 그립고, 우리 세 아이와 함께 당신을 향해 내 팔을 쭉 뻗고 있어요.

➡ _____

13 막내를 제외하고는 우리 모두 건강해요.

➡ _____

14 그 아이는 약간 아프지만 심각하진 않아요.

➡ _____

15 난 당신에게 이미 편지를 보냈지만, 답장이 없어서 그것 때문에 나는 슬퍼요.

➡ _____

16 당신에게서 편지를 받는다면, 나는 정말 행복할 거예요.

➡ _____

17 당신의 어머니께서는 병이 드셨고, 나는 약간의 돈과 음식을 가지고 병원에 있는 어머니를 방문할 예정이에요.

➡ _____

18 큰애가 막내를 돌보는 동안 둘째와 함께 그곳에 갈 거예요.
➡ _____

19 나는 150,000리라에 두 일꾼을 시켜 우리 밭을 준비하고 씨앗을 심게 했어요.
➡ _____

20 나는 DC에 투표했어요.
➡ _____

21 PCI는 매우 많은 의석을 잃어서 거의 죽은 것처럼 보여요.
➡ _____

22 하지만 이쪽이 이기건 저쪽이 이기건, 상황은 똑같아요.
➡ _____

23 우리 가난한 사람들에게는 아무 것도 바뀌지 않지요.
➡ _____

24 우리는 어제도 일했고, 내일도 다시 일할 거예요.
➡ _____

25 우리는 올해 올리브나무에서 올리브를 많이 땄어요.
➡ _____

26 나는 아들들이 훌륭한 일꾼인 한 남자를 고용했어요.
➡ _____

27 그가 올리브를 쳐서 떨어뜨리면 그의 두 아들이 땅에서 올리브를 주우면서 그를 도왔어요.
➡ _____

28 나는 그 일을 위해 그에게 27,000리라를 지급했어요.
➡ _____

29 올리브 압착을 위해 12,000리라를 더 썼어요.
➡ _____

30 나는 큰 항아리 하나와 작은 항아리 하나를 채울 만큼 충분한 기름을 얻었어요.
➡ _____

31 리터딩 1,300리라의 가격으로 팔 수 있을 것 같아요.
➡ _____

32 여보, 크리스마스가 다가오면서 내 마음은 당신을 떠올려요.
➡ _____

33 당신이 나와 함께 있다면 난 정말 행복할 거예요.
➡ _____

34 우리는 모두 당신을 매우 많이 그리워해요.
➡ _____

35 나와 우리 세 아이의 큰 포옹을 보내요.
➡ _____

36 잘 있어요, 여보.
➡ _____

37 내 마음은 당신의 것이에요, 우리들의 두 반지처럼 당신과 연결된 채로요.
➡ _____

[01~03] 다음 글을 읽고 물음에 답하시오.

ⓐSpeaking to family members or friends in a foreign country is rather easy and simple today. But before the days of phones and the Internet, it was not that easy. People just sent a letter and waited for a reply for weeks. And it was a lot harder if they couldn't read or write.

01 위 글의 밑줄 친 ⓐSpeaking과 문법적 쓰임이 같은 것을 모두 고르시오.

① They were speaking in low voices.
② He went out without speaking to me.
③ Generally speaking, the more you pay, the more you get.
④ He is good at speaking English.
⑤ Be quiet! He hasn't finished speaking.

02 위 글의 제목으로 알맞은 것을 고르시오.

① How to Communicate with Family Members Who Couldn't Read or Write
② The Advantage of Phones and the Internet
③ The Development of the International Mail Service
④ The Difficulty of Speaking to People Abroad in Old Days
⑤ The Hard Lives of People Who Couldn't Read or Write

03 Which question CANNOT be answered after reading the passage?

① Today, is it difficult to speak to family members or friends in a foreign country?

② Before the days of phones and the Internet, was it easy to speak to family members or friends in a foreign country?
③ Before the days of phones and the Internet, how did people speak to people in a foreign country?
④ How long did it take to receive a reply after sending a letter to people in a foreign country?
⑤ How did people who couldn't read or write speak to people in a foreign country?

[04~06] 다음 글을 읽고 물음에 답하시오.

We picked lots of olives from our olive trees this year. I ____ⓐ____ a man whose sons are good workers. He knocked the olives down, and his two sons helped him, picking them up from the ground. I paid him 27,000 lire for ⓑthe work. I spent 12,000 more for the olive press. I got enough oil to fill a large pot and a small one. I can sell it at a price of 1,300 lire ⓒa liter.

서답형

04 주어진 영영풀이를 참고하여 빈칸 ⓐ에 철자 h로 시작하는 단어를 쓰시오.

employed

➡ _____

서답형

05 위 글의 밑줄 친 ⓑthe work가 가리키는 것을 우리말로 쓰시오.

➡ _____

_____

162 Lesson 5. Pictures Speak a Thousand Words

서답형

06 위 글의 밑줄 친 ⓒa와 바꿔 쓸 수 있는 말을 쓰시오.

➡ _____

[07~09] 다음 글을 읽고 물음에 답하시오.

This letter shows how people got over these difficulties. (①) She lived in Sicily, an Italian island, while her husband worked in Germany. (②) At the time, more than 5% of the people in Italy could not read or write, and she was one of them. (③) This letter was discovered ___ⓐ___ Sicilian writer Gesualdo Bufalino. (④)

Here's how he translated the pictures ___ⓑ___ words. (⑤)

07 위 글의 빈칸 ⓐ와 ⓑ에 들어갈 전치사가 바르게 짝지어진 것은?

	ⓐ	ⓑ			ⓐ	ⓑ
①	for – to			②	by – into
③	in – to			④	for – into
⑤	by – on				

08 위 글의 흐름으로 보아, 주어진 문장이 들어가기에 가장 적절한 곳은?

> It was written in 1973 by a woman whose husband was far away.

① ② ③ ④ ⑤

중요

09 According to the passage, which is NOT true?

① A woman whose husband worked in Germany wrote this letter in 1973.

② She lived in Sicily, an Italian island, and she was illiterate.

③ At the time, over 5% of the Italians could not read or write.

④ Sicilian writer Gesualdo Bufalino discovered this letter.

⑤ Gesualdo Bufalino translated her words into pictures.

[10~12] 다음 글을 읽고 물음에 답하시오.

I had two workers ___ⓐ___ our field and plant seeds for (A)150,000 lire. I voted for the DC. (B)The PCI lost ___ⓑ___ many seats ___ⓒ___ it almost seems dead. But whether one or the other wins, it's the same. Nothing changes for us poor people. We worked yesterday, and we will work again tomorrow.

10 위 글의 빈칸 ⓐ에 들어갈 알맞은 말을 고르시오.

① prepare   ② to prepare

③ prepared   ④ to have prepared

⑤ had prepared

서답형

11 문장 (B)가 다음과 같은 뜻이 되도록, 빈칸 ⓑ와 ⓒ에 들어갈 알맞은 말을 쓰시오.

> The PCI lost so many seats as to seem almost dead.

➡ ⓑ _____ ⓒ _____

서답형

12 위 글의 밑줄 친 (A)150,000을 영어로 읽는 법을 쓰시오.

➡ _____

[13~14] 다음 글을 읽고 물음에 답하시오.

My dear love, I miss you so much, and I reach my arms out toward you, together with our three kids. We are all in good health except for the little one. He's a little sick, but not seriously.

13 다음 중 위 글의 내용을 나타내는 그림 편지를 고르시오.

① ② ③ ④ ⑤

14 위 글의 내용을 다음과 같이 정리하고자 한다. 빈칸 (A)와 (B)에 들어갈 알맞은 단어를 쓰시오.

> A woman (A)_____ her husband who was far away and wrote a letter showing how she and their (B)_____ _____ were getting along.

[15~17] 다음 글을 읽고 물음에 답하시오.

> I'm sending you a big hug from me and our three little kids. Goodbye, dear love. My heart is yours, ___ⓐ___ to you as our two rings (A)are.

서답형

15 위 글의 빈칸 ⓐ에 join을 알맞은 형태로 쓰시오.

➡ _____

16 다음 중 위 글의 내용을 나타내는 그림 편지를 고르시오.

① ② ③ ④ ⑤

서답형

17 위 글의 밑줄 친 (A)are 뒤에 생략된 말을 쓰시오.

➡ _____

[18~20] 다음 글을 읽고 물음에 답하시오.

> I already sent you a letter, but there was no reply, so I am sad about it. ⓐIf I got a letter from you, I would be very happy. Your mother fell ill, and I'm going to visit her in the hospital with some money and food. I'll go there with our middle son while the oldest ⓑlooks after the youngest.

서답형

18 위 글의 밑줄 친 ⓐ를 직설법 문장으로 고치시오.

➡ _____

또는 _____

19 위 글의 밑줄 친 ⓑlooks after와 바꿔 쓸 수 있는 말을 모두 고르시오.

① takes care of
② takes after
③ cares for
④ looks for
⑤ asks after

서답형

20 Why does the writer say that it is the same whether the DC or the PCI wins? Fill in the blanks (A)~(C) with suitable words.

> Because (A)_____ changes for poor people and they (B)_____ yesterday, and they (C)_____ _____ again tomorrow.

[21~23] 다음 글을 읽고 물음에 답하시오.

My dear love, I ⓐmiss you so much, and I reach my arms out toward you, together with our three kids. We are all in good health except for the little one. He's a little sick, but not seriously.

I already sent you a letter, but there was no reply, so I am sad about ⓑit. ⓒ당신에게서 편지를 받는다면, 나는 정말 행복할 거예요. Your mother fell ill, and I'm going to visit her in the hospital with some money and food. I'll go there with our middle son while the oldest looks after the youngest.

21 위 글의 밑줄 친 ⓐmiss와 같은 의미로 쓰인 것을 고르시오.

① The bullet did miss her by about six inches.
② I will miss her when she leaves.
③ You must not miss meals when you're training.
④ The sale prices were too good to miss.
⑤ She didn't want to miss a good party last night.

서답형

22 위 글의 밑줄 친 ⓑit이 가리키는 것을 본문에서 찾아 쓰시오.

➡ _____

서답형

23 위 글의 밑줄 친 ⓒ의 우리말에 맞게 주어진 어휘를 이용하여 12 단어로 영작하시오.

got, from, very happy

➡ _____

[24~26] 다음 글을 읽고 물음에 답하시오.

We picked lots of olives from our olive trees this year. I hired a man whose sons are good workers. He knocked the olives down, and his two sons helped him, picking them up from the ground. I paid him 27,000 lire ____ⓐ____ the work. I spent 12,000 more for the olive press. I got enough oil to fill a large pot and a small one. I can sell it ____ⓑ____ a price of 1,300 lire ⓒa liter.

24 위 글의 빈칸 ⓐ와 ⓑ에 들어갈 전치사가 바르게 짝지어진 것은?

	ⓐ	ⓑ		ⓐ	ⓑ
①	for	to	②	in	by
③	in	at	④	for	at
⑤	on	by			

25 위 글의 밑줄 친 ⓒa와 같은 의미로 쓰인 것을 모두 고르시오.

① There's a Mrs. Green to see you.
② They cost 7 dollars a kilo.
③ A lion is a dangerous animal.
④ I can type 50 words a minute.
⑤ There's a visitor for you.

26 위 글을 읽고 알 수 없는 것을 고르시오.

① Did they pick lots of olives from their olive trees this year?
② Whom did the writer hire?
③ How much did the writer pay the worker?
④ How much oil did the writer get?
⑤ How much did the writer earn by selling the olive oil?

[01~03] 다음 글을 읽고 물음에 답하시오.

ⓐ이 편지는 사람들이 이런 어려움을 어떻게 극복했는지 보여 준다. It was written in 1973 by a woman whose husband was far away. She lived in Sicily, an Italian island, while her husband worked in Germany. At the time, more than 5% of the people in Italy could not read or write, and she was one of them. ⓑThis letter was discovered by Sicilian writer Gesualdo Bufalino.

Here's how he translated the pictures into words.

01 위 글의 밑줄 친 ⓐ의 우리말에 맞게 주어진 어휘를 알맞게 배열하시오.

these difficulties / people / how / this letter / shows / got over

➡ _____

_____

02 위 글의 밑줄 친 ⓑ를 능동태로 고치시오.

➡ _____

_____

03 To whom did the woman write the letter? Fill in the blanks (A) and (B) with suitable words.

She wrote it to (A)_____ _____
who worked (B)_____ _____.

[04~06] 다음 글을 읽고 물음에 답하시오.

My dear love, I miss you so much, and I ⓐreach my arms out toward you, together with our three kids. ⓑ우리 모두 건강해요 except for the little ⓒone. He's a little sick, but not seriously.

04 위 글의 밑줄 친 ⓐ와 바꿔 쓸 수 있는 단어를 철자 s로 시작하여 쓰시오.

➡ _____

05 위 글의 밑줄 친 ⓑ의 우리말에 맞게 6단어로 영작하시오.

➡ _____

06 위 글의 밑줄 친 ⓒone이 가리키는 것을 본문에서 찾아 쓰시오.

➡ _____

[07~09] 다음 글을 읽고 물음에 답하시오.

We picked lots of olives from our olive trees this year. I hired a man whose sons are good workers. He knocked the olives down, and his two sons helped him, picking ⓐthem up from the ground. I paid him ___(A)___ lire for the work. I spent ___(B)___ more for the olive press. I got enough oil to fill a large pot and a small one. I can sell it at a price of ___(C)___ lire a liter.

07 다음 그림을 참조하여 위 글의 빈칸 (A)~(C)에 들어갈 알맞은 숫자를 쓰시오.

➡ (A) _____ (B) _____ (C) _____

08 위 글의 밑줄 친 ⓐthem이 가리키는 것을 본문에서 찾아 쓰시오.

➡ _____

09 How much did the writer spend picking the olives and pressing them? Answer in English in a full sentence. (4 words)

➡ _____

[10~12] 다음 글을 읽고 물음에 답하시오.

> ⓐI already sent you a letter, but there was no reply, so I am sad about it. ⓑIf I got a letter from you, I will be very happy. Your mother fell ill, and I'm going to visit her in the hospital with some money and food. I'll go there with our middle son while the oldest looks after the youngest.

10 위 글의 밑줄 친 ⓐ를 3형식 문장으로 고치시오.

➡ _____

11 위 글의 밑줄 친 ⓑ에서 어법상 틀린 부분을 찾아 고치시오.

_____ ➡ _____

12 Why is she going to the hospital and with what will she go there? Fill in the blanks (A) and (B) with suitable words.

> Because her mother-in-law (A)_____ _____ and is in the hospital, she is going to the hospital with (B)_____ _____ _____ _____.

[13~14] 다음 글을 읽고 물음에 답하시오.

> (A)I had two workers prepare our field and plant seeds ⓐ 150,000 lire. I voted ⓑ the DC. The PCI lost so many seats that it almost seems dead. But whether one or the other wins, it's the same. Nothing changes for us poor people. We worked yesterday, and we will work again tomorrow.

13 위 글의 빈칸 ⓐ와 ⓑ에 공통으로 들어갈 알맞은 전치사를 쓰시오.

➡ _____

14 위 글의 밑줄 친 (A)를 got을 사용하여 고칠 때, 빈칸에 들어갈 알맞은 말을 쓰시오.

➡ I got two workers _____ our field

[15~16] 다음 글을 읽고 물음에 답하시오.

> My love, my heart thinks of you ⓐ Christmas is coming. (A)I would be so happy if you were with me. We all miss you so much.
> I'm sending you a big hug from me and our three little kids. Goodbye, dear love. My heart is yours, joined to you ⓑ our two rings are.

15 위 글의 빈칸 ⓐ와 ⓑ에 공통으로 들어갈 알맞은 말을 쓰시오.

➡ _____

16 위 글의 밑줄 친 (A)를 직설법 문장으로 고치시오.

➡ _____
또는 _____

해석

Express Yourself C1

The boy <u>whose</u> head is covered with bees <u>doesn't</u> understand the woman's
소유격 관계대명사   don't(×)

gesture. I think <u>it</u> means "Jump into the pond." If I <u>were</u> the boy, I would jump
= the woman's gesture   = Were I

into the pond <u>right away</u>.
= right now = at once = immediately

구문해설 • be covered with: ~로 덮이다 • gesture: 몸짓 • right away: 즉시, 당장

머리가 벌로 덮인 소년은 그 여자의 몸짓을 이해하지 못합니다. 제 생각에 그것은 "연못으로 뛰어들어."를 의미합니다. 제가 그 소년이라면, 저는 당장 연못으로 뛰어들겠습니다.

Project Do it Yourself

"Climb up the mountain."

If <u>I had</u> soldiers to lead, I <u>would use</u> kites to send my messages. For example,
가정법 과거형으로 if절에 과거동사를, 주절에는 '조동사 과거형+동사원형'을 사용한다.

I would fly a kite <u>whose</u> face <u>looks like</u> a mountain to <u>make the soldiers climb</u>
소유격 관계대명사   look like+명사: ~처럼 보이다   사역동사+목적어+동사원형

up the mountain.

구문해설 • kite: 연

"산 위로 올라가라"

내가 병사를 지휘한다면, 나는 나의 메시지를 보내기 위해 연을 사용하겠다. 예를 들어, 나는 병사들이 산 위로 올라가게 하려고 앞면이 산처럼 보이는 연을 날리겠다.

Link to the World

Hangeul <u>was created</u> by King Sejong. At first, many people didn't want to
수동태

use this new writing system. However, King Sejong tried hard <u>to help people</u>
~하기 위해서

use Hangeul. Thanks to him, we can express anything with Hangeul now. If
목적보어(= to use)

we <u>didn't know</u> Hangeul, we <u>could not express</u> <u>ourselves</u> easily.
가정법 과거   조동사의 과거+동사원형   재귀대명사(주어 = 목적어)

구문해설 • writing system: 문자 체계 • thanks to: ~ 덕택에
• express ourselves: 자기 자신을 표현하다

한글은 세종대왕에 의해 창제되었다. 처음에는 많은 사람이 이 새로운 문자 체계를 사용하는 것을 원하지 않았다. 하지만, 세종대왕은 사람들이 한글을 사용하도록 돕기 위해 열심히 노력했다. 그분 덕택에, 우리는 지금 한글로 무엇이든 표현할 수 있다. 우리가 한글을 모른다면, 우리 자신을 쉽게 표현할 수 없을 것이다.

영역별 핵심문제

01 다음 주어진 두 단어의 관계가 같도록 빈칸에 알맞은 단어를 쓰시오.

> hire – employ : embrace – _____

02 다음 문장의 빈칸 (a)와 (b)에 들어갈 단어가 바르게 짝지어진 것은?

> • Do you have your own way to ___(a)___ the cold?
> • This is why it is important to ___(b)___ respectable politicians.

① break down – reject
② get over – vote for
③ stand up for – accept
④ pick up – vote for
⑤ get over – compete

[03~04] 다음 영영풀이에 해당하는 것을 고르시오.

03
> the man that a woman is married to

① son   ② hunter
③ manager   ④ reporter
⑤ husband

04
> a position as a member of a committee, court, etc.

① seat   ② permission
③ reply   ④ figure
⑤ vote

05 다음 대화의 빈칸에 들어갈 말을 〈영영풀이〉를 참고하여 주어진 철자로 시작하여 쓰시오.

> B: I'm curious about sign language.
> G: Are you? Let me show you one e_____. Look.
> B: What does it mean?
> G: It means "Hello."

> <영영풀이> a group of words that has a special meaning

➡ _____

06 다음 밑줄 친 부분의 뜻이 잘못된 것은?

① The little boy seemed very hungry. (~하게 보였다)
② The woman was so surprised to see the dead insects by the window. (죽은)
③ Whether or not you come to the party, you must call him. (~인지 아닌지)
④ I was asked to prepare a report for our next meeting. (준비하다)
⑤ He knocked me on the head. (쳤다)

07 다음 대화의 흐름상 단어의 쓰임이 어색한 부분을 찾아 바르게 고치시오. (1개)

> B: Now the enemy is crossing the (a)board in the dark. What are the soldiers going to do to send (b)messages? I'm curious about that.
> G: They will (c)light four chimneys.
> B: When they light all five of the (d)chimneys, what does that mean?
> G: It means the (e)battle has started.

_____ ➡ _____

[08~09] 다음 대화를 읽고 물음에 답하시오.

B: This painting has some hidden secrets in it.

G: Really? I'm curious about them. Where are the secrets?

B: Find one yourself.

G: Let's see. ... Oh, I see some letters here.

B: You found one! It means "Jan van Eyck was here. 1434." It's Latin.

G: That's awesome! Any other secrets?

B: Okay. This dog tells us the man here was very rich.

G: I don't understand.

B: They had to spend lots of money to buy a dog of that kind at that time.

G: I see. Only the rich could have that kind of dog, right?

B: Exactly. Pictures speak a thousand words, you know.

08 위 대화를 읽고 답할 수 <u>없는</u> 질문은?

① What does the painting have?

② What do the letters the girl found mean?

③ Are the letters the girl found English?

④ What kind of a dog did people at that time like to raise?

⑤ What makes people think the man in the picture was very rich?

09 위 대화의 제목으로 가장 적절한 것은?

① How to Hide the Secrets in the Painting

② Can You Read Jan van Eyck's Painting?

③ Different Hobbies in Different Times

④ Can You Appreciate the Painting Correctly?

⑤ Jan van Eyck's Genius for Drawing the Painting

10 다음 대화를 순서에 맞게 바르게 배열한 것은?

(A) I see. Now I can guess what they mean.

(B) Oh, they are Braille. They are for blind people.

(C) What are these dots for? I'm curious about them.

① (A) – (B) – (C)

② (B) – (A) – (C)

③ (C) – (B) – (A)

④ (A) – (C) – (B)

⑤ (C) – (A) – (B)

11 다음 짝지어진 대화 중 <u>어색한</u> 것은?

① A: What does his gesture mean? I'm curious about it.

B: It means "Step back from the pond."

② A: What would you do if you were a fish?

B: If I were a fish, I would swim in the pond.

③ A: What would you do if you had a beautiful voice?

B: If I had a beautiful voice, I would sing on the tree.

④ A: This woman doesn't want a dollar. So what does her gesture mean?

B: It means she wants a chicken.

⑤ A: I'm curious about sign language.

B: Let me show you one expression. What is sign language?

Grammar

12 주어진 문장과 같은 뜻이 되도록 바꾼 것 중 올바르지 <u>않은</u> 것을 고르시오.

① As the bag is expensive, I can't buy it.
= If the bag were cheap, I could buy it.

② As I don't have a car, I can't give you a ride to school.
= If I had a car, I could give you a ride to school.

③ As he doesn't know how to open the door, he can't enter the house.
= If he knew how to open the door, he could enter the house.

④ If I had a bike, I would ride it to school.
= As I have no bike, I don't ride it to school.

⑤ If he were good at dancing, he could take part in the contest.
= As he is not poor at dancing, he can't take part in the contest.

13 다음 주어진 문장과 같은 의미의 문장을 가정법을 이용하여 쓰시오.

(1) As I know the singer, I can shake hands with him.
= If _____
_____.

(2) As he is not smart, he doesn't prepare for the game in advance.
= If _____
_____.

14 다음 빈칸에 들어길 말이 <u>다른</u> 하나를 고르시오.

① I have speakers _____ sound loud.

② The girl _____ shirt is red is Emma's sister.

③ That is the shop _____ owner is not kind.

④ I know a boy _____ parents are both teachers.

⑤ My partner is the man _____ mother used to be an announcer.

15 다음 ⓐ~ⓔ 중 어법상 <u>어색한</u> 것을 찾아 바르게 고치시오.

Hangeul ⓐwas created by King Sejong. At first, many people didn't want ⓑto use this new writing system. However, King Sejong tried hard ⓒto help people use Hangeul. Thanks to him, we can express anything with Hangeul now. If we ⓓdon't know Hangeul, we could not express ⓔourselves easily.

_____ ➡ _____

16 다음 중 밑줄 친 부분의 쓰임이 나머지 넷과 <u>다른</u> 것은?

① Look at the car <u>whose</u> color is gold.

② I climbed the mountain <u>whose</u> top was covered with snow.

③ I'm not sure <u>whose</u> bag this is.

④ This is the backpack <u>whose</u> owner is unknown.

⑤ The girl <u>whose</u> dog has died is crying.

17 다음 중 어법상 <u>어색한</u> 문장의 개수로 알맞은 것은?

a. If I felt better, I could go shopping.
b. Were she you, she would never do that.
c. If I have more time, I could do it better.
d. If I were you, I won't go there.
e. If I knew her, I will introduce her to you.

① 1개   ② 2개   ③ 3개   ④ 4개   ⑤ 5개

18 우리말과 같은 뜻이 되도록 빈칸에 알맞은 말을 쓰시오.

> 그 소년이 키가 더 크다면, 그 장면을 볼 수 있을 텐데.
> → The boy _____ the scene if he _____ .

19 다음 우리말을 주어진 어휘를 이용하여 영어로 옮기시오.

(1) 내가 병사들을 지휘한다면, 나는 나의 메시지를 보내기 위해 연을 사용하겠다.
➡ If I had soldiers to lead, I _____
_____ . (kites, messages)

(2) 나는 앞면이 산처럼 보이는 연을 날리겠다.
➡ I would fly a kite _____
_____ . (face, look like)

(3) 가방이 과일로 가득한 소년은 원숭이를 보는 중이다.
➡ The boy _____ is looking at the monkey. (full of, fruit)

Reading

[20~22] 다음 글을 읽고 물음에 답하시오.

This letter shows how people ①got over these difficulties. It was written in 1973 by a woman ②whose husband was far away. She lived in Sicily, an Italian island, while her husband worked in Germany. At the time, ③ more than 5% of ④the people in Italy could not read or write, and she was one of ⓐthem. This letter was discovered by Sicilian writer Gesualdo Bufalino.

Here's ⑤how he translated the pictures into words.

20 위 글의 밑줄 친 ①~⑤와 바꿔 쓸 수 있는 말로 옳지 <u>않은</u> 것을 고르시오.

① overcame ② of which
③ over ④ the Italians
⑤ the way

21 위 글의 밑줄 친 ⓐthem이 가리키는 것을 영어로 쓰시오.

➡ _____
_____

22 위 글의 뒤에 올 내용으로 가장 알맞은 것을 고르시오.

① Gesualdo Bufalino가 시실리 여인의 그림 편지를 발견한 상황
② 이탈리아 사람들의 높은 문맹율
③ Gesualdo Bufalino가 그림 편지들을 글로 번역한 내용
④ 여인의 남편이 보낸 답장의 내용
⑤ Gesualdo Bufalino가 시실리 여인의 말을 그림 편지로 옮겨준 내용

[23~25] 다음 글을 읽고 물음에 답하시오.

My dear love, I miss you so much, and I reach my arms out toward you, together with our three kids. We are all in good health except for the little ⓐone. He's a little sick, but not seriously.

I already sent you a letter, but there was no reply, so I am sad about it. If I got a ⓑletter from you, I would be very happy. Your mother fell ill, and I'm going to visit her in the hospital with some money and food. I'll go there with our middle son while the oldest looks after the youngest.

23 위 글의 밑줄 친 ⓐone과 문법적 쓰임이 같은 것을 고르시오.

① Do you want <u>one</u> biscuit or two?
② I saw her <u>one</u> afternoon last week.
③ They all went off in <u>one</u> direction.
④ <u>One</u> must observe the rules.
⑤ I have many bags, and this <u>one</u> is my favorite.

24 위 글의 밑줄 친 ⓑletter와 바꿔 쓸 수 있는 말을 본문에서 찾아 쓰시오.

➡ _____

25 According to the passage, which is NOT true?

① The writer misses her husband so much.
② The writer's little kid is a little sick.
③ The writer is sending a letter to her husband for the first time.
④ The writer's mother-in-law fell ill and is in the hospital now.
⑤ The writer's oldest kid will look after the youngest while their mom goes to visit their grandmother in the hospital.

[26~27] 다음 글을 읽고 물음에 답하시오.

We picked lots of olives from our olive trees this year. (①) He knocked the olives down, and his two sons helped him, ⓐ땅에서 그것들을 주우면서. (②) I paid him 27,000 lire for the work. (③) I spent 12,000 more for the olive press. (④) I got enough oil to fill a large pot and a small one. (⑤) I can sell it at a price of 1,300 lire a liter.

26 위 글의 흐름으로 보아, 주어진 문장이 들어가기에 가장 적절한 곳은?

> I hired a man whose sons are good workers.

① ② ③ ④ ⑤

27 위 글의 밑줄 친 ⓐ의 우리말에 맞게 주어진 어휘를 이용하여 6 단어로 영작하시오.

> picking, ground

➡ _____

[28~29] 다음 글을 읽고 물음에 답하시오.

The boy whose backpack the monkey is pulling doesn't understand its gesture. I think (A)<u>it</u> means "Give the fruit to me." If I ___ⓐ___ the boy, I would give the fruit to the monkey right away.

28 위 글의 빈칸 ⓐ에 be를 알맞은 형태로 쓰시오.

➡ _____

29 위 글의 밑줄 친 (A)<u>it</u>이 가리키는 것을 본문에서 찾아 쓰시오.

➡ _____

출제율 90%

01 다음 짝지어진 단어의 관계가 같도록 주어진 철자로 시작하는 단어를 쓰시오.

> ill – healthy : dead – a_____

출제율 95%

02 다음 영영풀이에 해당하는 단어는?

> to make something ready for use

① prefer   ② prepare
③ vote   ④ translate
⑤ encourage

출제율 90%

03 다음 대화를 읽고 빈칸에 들어갈 말을 〈조건〉에 맞게 쓰시오.

┌─ 조건 ─┐
• 'It means'와 enter를 사용
  하여 정의를 나타내는 표현
  을 쓸 것.

> G: What's this? I'm curious about it.
> B: It's a traffic sign. _____
> G: Oh, I see.

➡ _____

_____

[04~05] 다음 대화를 읽고 물음에 답하시오.

> B: What are the soldiers doing with the five chimneys on TV?
>
> (A) Really? I'm curious about the system. Can you tell me more?
> (B) Well, do you see the two smoking chimneys?
> (C) They are sending messages to the king by using the chimneys.

(D) Yes. What do they mean?

G: They mean they just saw an enemy.

출제율 100%

04 위 대화의 (A)~(D)를 순서대로 배열하시오.

➡ _____

출제율 95%

05 위 대화를 읽고 다음 질문에 영어로 답하시오. (be for를 이용하시오)

> Q: What do you think the chimneys are for?

➡ _____

출제율 90%

06 다음 대화의 빈칸 (A)에 들어갈 말로 알맞은 것은?

> B: If there's no enemy, they don't smoke at all, do they?
> G: _____(A)_____ Smoke from one chimney means "No enemy."
> B: Now smoke is rising from three chimneys. What does that mean?
> G: It means an enemy is coming close to the border.

① No, they don't.
② Yes, they don't.
③ Yes, they do.
④ No, they do.
⑤ Yes, they are.

07 다음 대화에서 주어진 문장이 들어갈 위치로 알맞은 것은?

B: This painting has some hidden secrets in it.

G: Really? I'm curious about them. Where are the secrets?

B: Find one yourself. (A)

G: Let's see. ... Oh, I see some letters here.

B: You found one! (B) It's Latin.

G: That's awesome! (C) Any other secrets?

B: Okay. This dog tells us the man here was very rich.

G: (D) I don't understand.

B: They had to spend lots of money to buy a dog of that kind at that time.

G: I see. (E) Only the rich could have that kind of dog, right?

B: Exactly. Pictures speak a thousand words, you know.

It means "Jan van Eyck was here. 1434."

---

① (A)　② (B)　③ (C)　④ (D)　⑤ (E)

08 다음 대화의 빈칸 (A)에 들어갈 말로 알맞은 것은?

W: What does this woman's gesture mean? I'm curious about it.

M: _____ (A)

W: Why do you think so?

M: The boy has lots of bees on his head. And the woman is pointing at the pond.

① It means "You're welcome."

② It means "History repeats itself."

③ It means she wants a chicken.

④ I think it means "Jump into the pond."

⑤ It means "Turn it off."

09 다음 짝지어진 대화 중 어색한 것은?

① A: What does its gesture mean? I'm curious about it.

　B: It means "Give the fruit to me."

② A: What would you do if you had strong arms?

　B: If I had strong arms, I could climb trees.

③ A: Do you know what this means?

　B: Sure.

④ A: Do you know what this means?

　B: No, I don't. What does it mean?

⑤ A: This house is famous for having thousands of secrets in it.

　B: Really? It means you must find the secrets.

10 다음 대화의 빈칸에 들어갈 말로 알맞은 것은?

W: This woman doesn't want a dollar. So what does her gesture mean?

M: _____

W: Then the boy should bring a chicken to get the fruit, right?

M: I think so.

① It means you must not ride a bike here.

② It means you must be careful with the animals.

③ It means she wants a chicken.

④ It means you must drive slowly here.

⑤ It means the battle has started.

11 다음 ①~⑤ 중 어법상 어색한 것은?

The house ①which doors ②are painted ③red ④is ⑤my grandfather's.

12 'whose'를 사용하여 〈보기〉와 같이 두 문장을 한 문장으로 연결하시오.

> ┌ 보기 ┐
> Tom easily found the store.
> + Its address was on the Internet.
> → Tom easily found the store whose address was on the Internet.

(1) Is there any student?
+ His name was not called.

➡ _____

_____

(2) Mike is the boy.
+ His hair is very short.

➡ _____

_____

(3) The house is my uncle's.
+ Its windows are very big.

➡ _____

_____

(4) My sister is the girl.
+ Her cat is eating a fish.

➡ _____

_____

(5) Do you know the old man?
+ His shoes are red and blue.

➡ _____

_____

13 잘못된 부분을 바르게 고쳐 문장을 다시 쓰시오.

(1) I know a boy who mother grows bananas.

➡ _____

(2) The boy of which dog is barking is my cousin.

➡ _____

(3) The girl whose hat is covered with flowers are a great dancer.

➡ _____

_____

(4) You were with me, I could show you my painting.

➡ _____

_____

(5) If I were a fish, I can swim in the water.

➡ _____

[14~16] 다음 글을 읽고 물음에 답하시오.

> Speaking to family members or friends in a foreign country is rather easy and simple today. But before the days of phones and the Internet, ⓐit was not ⓑthat easy. People just sent a letter and waited for a reply for weeks. And ⓒit was ⓓa lot harder if they couldn't read or write.

14 위 글의 밑줄 친 ⓐit과 ⓒit이 공통으로 가리키는 것을 본문에서 찾아 쓰시오.

➡ _____

_____

15 아래 〈보기〉에서 위 글의 밑줄 친 ⓑthat과 문법적 쓰임이 같은 것의 개수를 고르시오.

> ┌ 보기 ┐
> ① I can't walk that far.
> ② Can you see that dog?
> ③ I know that you are busy.
> ④ This book is mine and that one is yours.
> ⑤ Are you sure she's that young?

① 1개　② 2개　③ 3개　④ 4개　⑤ 5개

16 위 글의 밑줄 친 ⓓa lot과 바꿔 쓸 수 없는 말을 고르시오.

① much   ② even   ③ still

④ rather   ⑤ far

[17~19] 다음 글을 읽고 물음에 답하시오.

My dear love, I miss you so much, and ⓐI reach my arms out toward you, together with our three kids. (①) He's a little sick, but not seriously. (②)

I already sent you a letter, but there was no reply, so I am sad about it. (③) If I got a letter from you, I would be very happy. (④) Your mother fell ill, and I'm going to visit her in the hospital with some money and food. (⑤) I'll go there with our middle son while the oldest looks after the youngest.

17 위 글의 흐름으로 보아, 주어진 문장이 들어가기에 가장 적절한 곳은?

> We are all in good health except for the little one.

①   ②   ③   ④   ⑤

18 위 글의 밑줄 친 ⓐ를 다음과 같이 바꿔 쓸 때 빈칸에 들어갈 알맞은 단어를 쓰시오.

➡ I reach _____ my arms toward you

19 위 글을 읽고 알 수 없는 것을 고르시오.

① How many kids were there in the writer's family?

② Was the oldest kid sick?

③ Why was there no reply from her husband?

④ With whom will the writer visit the hospital?

⑤ Who will look after her youngest son while she goes to the hospital?

[20~21] 다음 글을 읽고 물음에 답하시오.

ⓐThe boy whose head is covered with bees don't understand the woman's gesture. I think it means "Jump into the pond." If I were the boy, I would jump into the pond ⓑright away.

20 위 글의 밑줄 친 ⓐ에서 어법상 틀린 부분을 찾아 고치시오.

_____ ➡ _____

21 위 글의 밑줄 친 ⓑright away와 바꿔 쓸 수 있는 말을 모두 고르시오.

① hesitatingly   ② right now

③ at once   ④ gradually

⑤ immediately

01 다음 대화의 우리말에 맞게 주어진 단어를 알맞은 순서로 배열하시오.

> G: I'm curious about that robot. Why is it standing there?
>
> B: It's a kind of ad. <u>그것은 그들의 건전지가 매우 강력하다는 것을 사람들에게 말하고 있어.</u>

(their / it / people / tells / batteries / powerful / are / very)

➡ _____

[02~03] 다음 대화를 읽고 물음에 답하시오.

> B: This painting has some hidden secrets in it.
>
> G: Really? I'm curious about them. Where are the secrets?
>
> B: Find one yourself.
>
> G: Let's see. ... Oh, I see some letters here.
>
> B: You found one! It means "Jan van Eyck was here. 1434." It's Latin.
>
> G: That's awesome! Any other secrets?
>
> B: Okay. This dog tells us the man here was very rich.
>
> G: I don't understand.
>
> B: They had to spend lots of money to buy a dog of that kind at that time.
>
> G: I see. Only the rich could have that kind of dog, right?
>
> B: Exactly. _____, you know.

02 위 대화의 흐름상 빈칸은 글의 주제문에 해당한다. 〈조건〉에 맞게 쓰시오.

> ┤ 조건 ├
> • 'pictures'와 'a thousand'를 이용하시오.

➡ _____

03 위 대화를 읽고 요약문을 완성하시오.

> The boy and the girl are talking about the _____ of Jan van Eyck's painting. The girl finds some _____ letters. It _____ "Jan van Eyck was here. 1434." The boy tells her about the dog. Only _____ could have that kind of dog at that time, so the man in the picture was very _____.

04 다음 글에서 어법상 틀린 곳의 기호를 쓰고 바르게 고치시오.

> Hangeul ㉠created by King Sejong. At first, many people didn't want to use this new writing system. However, King Sejong tried hard to help people ㉡using Hangeul. ㉢Thanks to him, we can express ㉣anything with Hangeul now. If we didn't know Hangeul, we ㉤can't express ourselves easily.

➡ (1) _____ (2) _____
　 (3) _____

05 다음 문장을 가정법을 이용하여 같은 의미의 문장으로 바꾸어 쓰시오.

(1) As I have some money, I can buy the new shoes.

➡ _____

(2) As Suji is not here, I can't tell her the story.

➡ _____

06 괄호 안에 주어진 표현을 사용하여 밑줄 친 우리말을 영어로 완성하시오.

(1) (the alarm clock)

A: I was late for school again today. I don't want to be late anymore.

B: 내가 너라면, 자명종을 맞춰 놓겠어.

➡ _____

(2) (by hand)

A: I can't finish my report. My computer is broken.

B: 내가 너라면, 그것을 손으로 쓰겠어.

➡ _____

(3) (search)

A: The music in the movie is so touching. I want to know the name of the song.

B: 내가 너라면, 인터넷에서 그것을 검색해 볼 텐데.

➡ _____

[07~08] 다음 글을 읽고 물음에 답하시오.

We picked lots of olives from our olive trees this year. I hired a man whose sons are good workers. ⓐHe knocked the olives down, and his two sons helped him, picking up them from the ground. I paid him 27,000 lire for the work. I spent 12,000 more for the olive press. I got enough oil to fill a large pot and a small one. I can sell ⓑit at a price of 1,300 lire a liter.

07 위 글의 밑줄 친 ⓐ에서 어법상 틀린 부분을 찾아 고치시오.

_____ ➡ _____

08 위 글의 밑줄 친 ⓑit이 가리키는 것을 영어로 쓰시오.

➡ _____

[09~11] 다음 글을 읽고 물음에 답하시오.

Speaking to family members or friends in a foreign country (A)[is / are] rather easy and simple today. But before the days of phones and the Internet, it was not that easy. People just sent a letter and waited for a reply for weeks. And (a)그들이 읽거나 쓸 수 없었다면 그건 훨씬 더 힘들었다.

This letter shows how people got over these difficulties. It was written in 1973 by a woman ___ⓐ___ husband was far away. She lived in Sicily, an Italian island, (B)[during / while] her husband worked in Germany. At the time, more than 5% of the people in Italy could not read or write, and she was one of them. This letter was discovered by Sicilian writer Gesualdo Bufalino.

Here's (C)[how / what] he translated the pictures into words.

09 Fill in the blank ⓐ with a suitable word.

➡ _____

10 위 글의 괄호 (A)~(C)에서 어법상 알맞은 낱말을 골라 쓰시오.

➡ (A) _____ (B) _____ (C) _____

11 위 글의 밑줄 친 (a)의 우리말에 맞게 주어진 어휘를 이용하여 11 단어로 영작하시오.

a lot

➡ _____

창의사고력 서술형 문제

01 주어진 〈보기〉와 같이 표지판에 관한 의미를 묻고 답을 하시오.

be careful with the animals

SPEED 30
drive slowly here

not ride a bike here

보기
A: What does this sign mean?
B: It means you must be careful with the animals.

(1) _____

(2) _____

02 가정법 과거를 이용하여, 친구에게 충고하는 말을 써 보시오.

(1) If I were you, _____ .

(2) Were I you, _____ .

(3) If I were in your position, _____ .

(4) If I were in your shoes, _____ .

03 다음 내용과 대화를 바탕으로 기자의 방송 내용을 완성하시오.

The girl's bag is in the pond. The girl is trying to pick up her bag, but she seems to be in danger.
A: What does the man's gesture mean? I'm curious about it.
B: It means "Step back from the pond."

The girl whose bag is (A)_____ doesn't understand the man's (B)_____. I think it means "(C)_____." If I were the girl, I would step back from the pond.

180 Lesson 5. Pictures Speak a Thousand Words

단원별 모의고사

01 다음 단어에 대한 영어 설명이 <u>어색한</u> 것은?

① hidden: not easy to find
② reply: an answer to a letter
③ rather: in some degree
④ ill: in a way that is bad or dangerous enough to make you worried
⑤ toward: in the direction of

02 다음 짝지어진 단어의 관계가 같도록 빈칸에 알맞은 말을 쓰시오.

curious – inquisitive : boundary – _____

03 다음 영영풀이에 해당하는 단어를 고르시오.

the surface of the Earth

① disease   ② hospital   ③ climate
④ ground   ⑤ health

04 다음 중 짝지어진 대화가 <u>어색한</u> 것은?

① A: What does that mean?
   B: It means an enemy is coming close to the border.
② A: What does this man's gesture mean? I'm curious about it.
   B: It means "Turn it off."
③ A: I'm curious about sign language.
   B: Are you? Let me show you one expression. Look.
④ A: What does her name mean? I'm curious about it.
   B: It means "bright girl."
⑤ A: What does this letter mean?
   B: This letter was written in blue ink.

05 대화의 빈칸에 들어갈 말로 알맞은 것은?

B: Now the enemy is crossing the border in the dark. What are the soldiers going to do to send messages? I'm curious about that.
G: _____
B: When they light all five of the chimneys, what does that mean?
G: It means the battle has started.

① Can you tell me more?
② They will light four chimneys.
③ They're curious about that, too.
④ They mean they just saw an enemy.
⑤ It means you must not enter.

06 대화의 흐름상 빈칸에 들어갈 말을 본문에서 찾아 쓰시오. (2 단어)

B: If there's no enemy, they don't smoke at all, do they?
G: Yes, they do. Smoke from one chimney means "_____."
B: Now smoke is rising from three chimneys. What does that mean?
G: It means an enemy is coming close to the border.

➡ _____

07 다음 대화의 빈칸에 들어갈 말로 알맞은 것은?

G: What are these dots for? I'm curious _____ them.
B: Oh, they are Braille. They are for blind people.

① about   ② from   ③ with
④ for   ⑤ to

[08~09] 다음 대화를 읽고 물음에 답하시오.

B: This painting has _____(A)_____ in it.

G: Really? I'm curious about them. Where are the secrets?

B: Find one yourself.

G: Let's see. ... Oh, I see some letters here.

B: You found one! It means "Jan van Eyck was here. 1434." It's Latin.

G: That's awesome! Any other secrets?

B: Okay. This dog tells us the man here was very rich.

G: I don't understand.

B: They had to spend lots of money to buy a dog of that kind at that time.

G: I see. Only the rich could have that kind of dog, right?

B: Exactly. Pictures speak a thousand words, you know.

08 위 대화의 빈칸 (A)에 들어갈 말로 알맞은 것은?

① some values

② several disappointing facts

③ some hidden secrets

④ wide gap between the rich and poor

⑤ some obvious facts

09 Why do people think the man in the picture was very rich?

➡ _____

_____

10 봉수대 신호에 관한 다음 대화의 빈칸 (A)~(C)에 들어갈 말을 〈보기〉에서 찾아 쓰시오.

B: What are the soldiers doing with the five chimneys on TV?

G: They are sending messages to the king by using the chimneys.

B: Really? I'm curious about the system. Can you tell me more?

G: Well, do you see the two smoking chimneys?

B: Yes. What do they mean?

G: _____(A)_____

B: If there's no enemy, they don't smoke at all, do they?

G: Yes, they do. Smoke from one chimney means "No enemy."

B: Now smoke is rising from three chimneys. What does that mean?

G: It means an enemy is coming close to the border.

B: _____(B)_____ What are the soldiers going to do to send messages? I'm curious about that.

G: They will light four chimneys.

B: When they light all five of the chimneys, what does that mean?

G: _____(C)_____

┤ 보기 ├

• It means the battle has started.

• They mean they just saw an enemy.

• Now the enemy is crossing the border in the dark.

➡ (A) _____

(B) _____

(C) _____

11 빈칸 (A)에 들어갈 말로 알맞은 것은?

W: What does this man's gesture mean?
_____(A)_____

M: It means "Turn it off."

W: Really? What makes you think so?

M: The other hunter there is coming close to an animal.

W: Oh, I see.

① It means " History repeats itself."

② I'm curious about it.

③ I'm curious about sign language.

④ I'm curious about the system.

⑤ I'm curious about that balloon.

12 다음 중 빈칸에 들어갈 단어가 다른 것은?

① If she _____ in Seoul now, she could see the parade.

② If it _____ not for your beautiful voice, people wouldn't listen to your song.

③ If you _____ on a desert island, what would you do first?

④ We couldn't live for a day if there _____ no water in the world.

⑤ I would fight bad guys if I _____ super powers.

13 다음 두 문장을 한 문장으로 바르게 옮긴 것은?

• The man is good at playing soccer.
• His son is a world-famous soccer player.

① The man is good at playing soccer whose son is a world-famous soccer player.

② The man whose son is a world-famous soccer player is good at playing soccer.

③ The man whose son is good at playing soccer is a world-famous soccer player.

④ The man his son is a world-famous soccer player is good at playing soccer.

⑤ The man is good at playing soccer his son is a world-famous soccer player.

14 다음 우리말을 영어로 바르게 옮긴 것은?

네가 좋아하는 아이돌이 너와 사랑에 빠지면, 너는 어떻게 하겠니?

① If your favorite idol star falls in love with you, what would you do?

② If your favorite idol star fell in love with you, what would you do?

③ If your favorite idol star fell in love with you, what will you do?

④ If your favorite idol star fell in love with you, what you would do?

⑤ If your favorite idol star were fallen in love with you, what would you do?

15 다음 우리말과 일치하도록 주어진 단어를 알맞게 배열하시오.

나는 직업이 소방관인 오빠가 있다.
(have, job, is, a, I, brother, a, fire fighter, whose)

➡ _____

16 다음 문장에서 밑줄 친 우리말을 영어로 옮기시오.

(1) 내가 신이라면, I would help poor children.

➡ _____

(2) 내가 과거로 여행한다면, I would tell people to protect our environment more.

➡ _____

[17~19] 다음 글을 읽고 물음에 답하시오.

Speaking to family members or friends in a foreign country is rather easy and simple today. But before the days of phones and the Internet, it was not that easy. People just sent a letter and waited for a reply for weeks. And it was a lot harder if they couldn't read or write.

This letter shows how people got over ⓐ these difficulties. It was written in 1973 by a woman whose husband was far away. She lived in Sicily, an Italian island, while her husband worked in Germany. At the time, more than 5% of the people in Italy could not read or write, and she was one of them. This letter was discovered by Sicilian writer Gesualdo Bufalino.

ⓑHere's the way how he translated the pictures into words.

17 위 글의 주제로 알맞은 것을 고르시오.

① the easy way to speak to people in a foreign country
② the difficulties that illiterate people experienced in the past
③ the high illiteracy rate of Italy in the past
④ a picture letter from a woman who couldn't read or write to her husband in a foreign country
⑤ the letter from Gesualdo Bufalino to a Sicilian woman

18 What do the underlined ⓐthese difficulties mean? Fill in the blanks (A) and (B) with suitable words.

They mean the difficulties that people, especially the illiterate, experienced while trying to speak to family members or friends in (A)_____ _____ _____ before the days of (B)_____ _____ _____ _____.

19 위 글의 밑줄 친 ⓑ에서 어법상 틀린 부분을 찾아 고치시오.

_____ ➡ _____

[20~22] 다음 글을 읽고 물음에 답하시오.

We picked lots of olives from our olive trees this year. I hired a man whose sons are good workers. He knocked the olives down, and his two sons helped him, ⓐpicking them up from the ground. I paid him ⓑ27,000 lire for the work. I spent ⓒ12,000 more for the olive press. I got enough oil to fill a large pot and a small one. I can sell it at a price of ⓓ1,300 lire a liter.

20 아래 〈보기〉에서 위 글의 밑줄 친 ⓐpicking과 문법적 쓰임이 다른 것의 개수를 고르시오.

┤ 보기 ├
① I like to study, listening to pop music.
② They supported him, saying that he was right.
③ I punished him for being dishonest.
④ He extended his hand, smiling brightly.
⑤ My dream is traveling in Europe.

① 1개   ② 2개   ③ 3개   ④ 4개   ⑤ 5개

21 위 글의 밑줄 친 ⓑ27,000, ⓒ12,000, ⓓ1,300을 영어로 읽는 법을 쓰시오.

➡ ⓑ _____
   ⓒ _____
   ⓓ _____

22 According to the passage, which is NOT true?

① The writer employed a man whose sons are good workers.
② The worker's two sons helped him pick the olives up from the ground.

③ The writer paid the worker 27,000 lire for the work.

④ The writer spent 12,000 lire for the olive press.

⑤ The writer can sell the olive oil at a price of 1,300 lire a liter.

[23~25] 다음 글을 읽고 물음에 답하시오.

My dear love, I miss you so much, and I reach my arms out toward you, together with our three kids. We are all ____ⓐ____ good health except for the little one. He's a little sick, but not seriously.

I already sent you (A)_____ _____, but there was no reply, so I am sad about it. If I got a letter from you, I would be very happy. Your mother fell ill, and I'm going to visit her in (B)_____ _____ with some money and food. I'll go there with our middle son while the oldest looks ____ⓑ____ the youngest.

23 위 글의 빈칸 ⓐ와 ⓑ에 들어갈 전치사가 바르게 짝지어진 것은?

	ⓐ	ⓑ		ⓐ	ⓑ
①	on	– for	②	in	– for
③	in	– after	④	on	– to
⑤	for	– after			

24 다음 그림을 참조하여 위 글의 빈칸 (A)와 (B)에 들어갈 알맞은 말을 쓰시오.

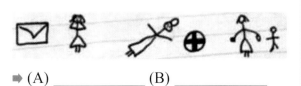

➡ (A) _____ (B) _____

25 다음 문장에서 위 글의 내용과 <u>다른</u> 부분을 찾아서 고치시오.

> The writer will visit her husband's mother with her oldest son.

_____ ➡ _____

[26~27] 다음 글을 읽고 물음에 답하시오.

We picked lots of olives from our olive trees this year. I hired a man whose sons are good workers. He knocked the olives down, and his two sons helped him, picking them up from the ground. I paid him 27,000 lire for the work. I spent 12,000 more for the olive press. I got enough oil ⓐ<u>to fill</u> a large pot and a small ⓑ<u>one</u>. I can sell it at a price of 1,300 lire a liter.

26 아래 <보기>에서 위 글의 밑줄 친 ⓐ<u>to fill</u>과 to부정사의 용법이 같은 것의 개수를 고르시오.

┤ 보기 ├
① It's time for you <u>to go</u> to bed.
② He went to the library <u>to borrow</u> books.
③ I have a pet <u>to play</u> with.
④ She has a special way <u>to cook</u> rice.
⑤ It is very good <u>to get up</u> early in the morning.

① 1개 ② 2개 ③ 3개 ④ 4개 ⑤ 5개

27 위 글의 밑줄 친 ⓑone이 가리키는 것을 본문에서 찾아 쓰시오.

➡ _____

MEMO

INSIGHT
on the textbook
교과서 파헤치기

※ 다음 영어를 우리말로 쓰시오.

01 brave

02 discovery

03 university

04 backward

05 bomb

06 float

07 mistake

08 honor

09 imaginative

10 maybe

11 award

12 opening

13 invention

14 laughable

15 ceremony

16 store

17 worth

18 accept

19 magnet

20 eager

21 repeatedly

22 cheer

23 tradition

24 perform

25 actually

26 economics

27 navy

28 present

29 interest

30 research

31 sailor

32 useful

33 trillion

34 unusual

35 instead of

36 keep -ing

37 succeed in

38 laugh out loud

39 take part in

40 keep A from -ing

41 be eager to

42 get out of

43 keep one's fingers crossed

※ 다음 우리말을 영어로 쓰시오.

01 받아들이다 _____

02 개막 _____

03 뒤로 _____

04 발견 _____

05 열렬한, 간절히 바라는 _____

06 반복적으로 _____

07 공연하다 _____

08 경제학 _____

09 뜨다 _____

10 평화 _____

11 존중하다; 명예 _____

12 폭탄 _____

13 용감한 _____

14 수여하다; 상 _____

15 의식, 식 _____

16 발명, 발명품 _____

17 ~하는 동안, ~인 반면에 _____

18 웃기는 _____

19 실제로, 사실은 _____

20 드문, 득이한 _____

21 해군 _____

22 자석 _____

23 아마도 _____

24 실수 _____

25 선원 _____

26 전통 _____

27 연구, 조사; 조사하다 _____

28 1조 _____

29 유용한 _____

30 가치; ~의 가치가 있는 _____

31 창의적인, 상상력이 풍부한 _____

32 관심 _____

33 대학, 대학교 _____

34 받다 _____

35 ~ 이하, ~보다 적은 _____

36 ~ 대신에 _____

37 ~에 성공하다 _____

38 ~에 참여하다 _____

39 큰 소리로 웃다 _____

40 계속 ~하다 _____

41 ~에서 떠나다, 나가다 _____

42 ~을 (열렬히) 하고 싶어 하다 _____

43 A가 ~하지 못하게 하다 _____

※ 다음 영영풀이에 알맞은 단어를 <보기>에서 골라 쓴 후, 우리말 뜻을 쓰시오.

1 _____ : not dead: _____

2 _____ : to give a prize: _____

3 _____ : someone who works on a ship: _____

4 _____ : the number 1,000,000,000,000: _____

5 _____ : to take something offered: _____

6 _____ : a piece of metal that attracts other iron: _____

7 _____ : a military force made up of boats and ships: _____

8 _____ : looking or facing in the direction that is behind you: _____

9 _____ : the act of finding something for the first time: _____

10 _____ : to be on a liquid and not sink: _____

11 _____ : the study of something to discover new facts: _____

12 _____ : to make, design, or think of a new type of thing: _____

13 _____ : wanting very much to do or have something: _____

14 _____ : • something you are proud to do: _____
              • to show great respect for someone, esp. in public: _____

15 _____ : having or showing new and exciting ideas: _____

16 _____ : an educational institution at the highest level, where you study for a
              degree: _____

honor	float	live	sailor
backward	invent	accept	navy
university	award	imaginative	trillion
eager	research	magnet	discovery

※ 다음 우리말과 일치하도록 빈칸에 알맞은 말을 쓰시오.

Get Ready 2

(1) **G:** You _____ _____ _____ _____ problems in class.
_____ _____ you'll _____ the Class Brain _____.
   B: Do you really _____ _____?
   G: Of course. I'll _____ my fingers _____ for you, Sangjun!

(2) **B:** The _____ of the Oh So Sweet _____ will get some candies.
   G: Oh, I want _____ _____ the _____.
   B: _____ _____ you'll _____ the _____ this time.
_____ _____, Jiu!

(3) **B:** I'm _____ _____ _____ the Best Joker award this time.
   G: Ha-ha. You always _____ us _____ _____ _____. So
you'll _____ _____ _____, Yunki. Good luck.
   B: Thank you.

(4) **B:** Minji, you're a happy girl. I think you'll _____ the Ms.
Cheerful _____. I'll _____ _____ _____ _____!
   G: Oh, thank you, Jiho.

Start Off – Listen & Talk A

1. **G:** Mom, I _____ _____ _____ the sports day.
   W: _____ are you _____ _____ _____ on that day, Minji?
   G: I'm going to play basketball for my class. We've _____ hard
_____ _____ _____ _____.
   W: Oh, I'm _____ _____ _____ your game.
   G: _____, I'm _____ _____ _____ _____. I'm _____ I'll
_____ a _____.
   W: _____ _____. You'll _____ a good _____. I'll keep
_____ _____ _____!

2. **W:** Soyun, are you going to _____ _____ _____ any races
on the sports day?
   G: Sure. I'_____ _____ _____ a 100 meter race at
the _____ of the day.
   W: Wow, I'm _____ _____ to _____ you at the race.
   G: But, Mom, I'm not _____ I'll _____ the race.
   W: Just _____ _____ _____. I'll _____ _____
_____ _____!

해석

(1) **G:** 너는 수업 중 많은 문제를 해결했
잖아. 나는 네가 'Class Brain'상
을 탈 거라고 확신해.
   B: 정말 그렇게 생각하니?
   G: 물론이야. 행운을 빌게, 상순아!
(2) **B:** 'Oh So Sweet'상 수상자는 사탕
을 받을 거야.
   G: 오, 그 상을 받고 싶다.
   B: 네가 이번에는 그 상을 탈 거라고
확신해. 행운을 빌어, 지우야!
(3) **B:** 난 이번에 'Best Joker'상을 받기
를 기대해.
   G: 하하. 너는 항상 우리를 웃게 하잖
아. 그러니 네가 그 상을 탈 거야,
윤기야. 행운을 빌어.
   B: 고마워.
(4) **B:** 민지야, 너는 쾌활한 아이야. 나는
네가 'Ms. Cheerful'상을 탈 거라
고 생각해. 행운을 빌게!
   G: 오, 고마워, 지호야.

1. **G:** 엄마, 체육 대회가 정말 기다려져
요.
   W: 민지야, 너는 그날 무엇을 할 거
니?
   G: 저는 학급을 대표해서 농구를 할
거예요. 우리는 몇 주간 열심히 연
습해 왔어요.
   W: 오, 너의 경기가 기대되는구나.
   G: 사실은, 전 조금 걱정이 돼요. 제
가 실수를 할까봐 겁나요.
   W: 걱정하지 마. 넌 잘할 거야. 행운
을 빌어줄게!

2. **W:** 소윤아, 넌 체육 대회에서 경주에
참가하니?
   G: 물론이죠. 전 그날 마지막에 있는
100 미터 달리기를 뛸 거예요.
   W: 와, 네가 경주에서 달리는 모습을
보는 것이 기대되는구나.
   G: 하지만 엄마, 전 경주에서 이길지
잘 모르겠어요.
   W: 그냥 최선을 다하렴. 행운을 빌어
줄게!

G: Mom, _____ _____ _____ to the sports day?

W: Sure. I'm _____ _____ _____ the game Kick a Shoe. This will be the first time _____ _____ _____ _____ it.

G: Don't worry. I'm _____ you'll _____ _____ . I'll _____ my _____ _____ for you!

W: Thank you. I'm also _____ _____ _____ a funny dance with some _____ _____ .

G: That _____ _____ . I'm _____ _____ to _____ you on the _____ .

A: I'm _____ _____ _____ the _____ airplane contest tomorrow. Are you _____ ?

B: Well, I think _____ , but I'm _____ .

A: You will _____ _____ . I'll _____ _____ _____ _____ _____ !

Miso: We're going on a _____ _____ next Tuesday. What are you going to do in the _____ _____ , Jimin?

Jimin: I'm _____ _____ talk _____ our teachers _____ _____ _____ and tell some _____ .

Miso: Wow! I'm really _____ _____ _____ _____ .

Jimin: Will everyone like my _____ ? I'm not _____ .

Miso: Don't _____ . I'm sure you'll _____ _____ . I'll _____ _____ _____ _____ !

Jimin: Thank you, Miso. _____ _____ _____ you one part of my _____ . _____ who? "Goood Jooob!"

Miso: Ha-ha, you _____ _____ our English teacher.

Jimin: Do I? I'm _____ _____ _____ you more at the show.

Miso: Great! You always _____ us _____ _____ _____ .

G: 엄마, 체육 대회에 오실 거예요?

W: 물론이지. 나는 'Kick a Shoe' 게임에 참가할 거야. 이번에 처음 해 보는 거야.

G: 걱정하지 마세요. 엄마는 잘하실 거예요. 행운을 빌어 드릴게요!

W: 고맙다. 나는 다른 엄마들과 코믹 댄스도 할 거야.

G: 재밌겠네요. 무대에 선 엄마 모습을 보는 것이 기대돼요.

B: 나는 내일 모형 비행기 대회가 기대돼. 너는 준비됐니?

G: 음, 그런 것 같아. 하지만 긴장돼.

B: 너는 잘할 거야. 내가 행운을 빌어 줄게!

미소: 다음 주 화요일에 수학여행을 갈 거야. 지민아, 너는 장기 자랑에서 뭘 할 거니?

지민: 나는 수업 시간에 선생님들이 말하는 것을 흉내 내고 농담도 할 거야.

미소: 와! 정말 기대되는데.

지민: 모든 사람이 나의 쇼를 좋아할까? 잘 모르겠어.

미소: 걱정하지 마. 나는 네가 잘할 거라고 확신해. 행운을 빌어 줄게!

지민: 고마워, 미소야. 내가 나의 연기의 한 부분을 보여 줄게. 누군지 맞힐 수 있겠니? "잘~ 했어~요!"

미소: 하하. 우리 영어 선생님처럼 들리는데.

지민: 그래? 장기 자랑에서 더 많이 보여 줄게.

미소: 멋지다! 너는 항상 우리를 웃게 만들어.

Fun Time

A: I'_____ _____ _____ _____ to Jejudo next week.

B: Wow! That _____ _____.

A: Yeah, I'_____ _____ _____ _____ _____ it.

A: I'm _____ _____ _____ the dance contest next week, but I'_____ _____ _____ it.

B: _____ _____. You'll do great. I'll _____ _____ _____ _____.

A: Thank you.

A: 나는 다음 주에 제주도를 여행할 거야.

B: 와! 멋지다.

A: 응, 난 그것이 정말 기대돼.

A: 난 다음 주에 춤 대회에 나갈 건데, 걱정이 된다.

B: 걱정하지 마. 넌 잘할 거야. 행운을 빌어 줄게.

A: 고마워.

Express Yourself A

1. **G:** _____ _____ _____ _____ something about your _____?

   B: They are _____ _____ _____ _____ shoes. You can also _____ the _____ with them.

   G: Great! I'm sure you'll _____ _____ _____. I'll _____ my fingers _____!

2. **B:** This _____ _____. Is this a _____ _____ or a bird _____?

   G: It is _____ _____ a cutting _____ _____ _____ a bird _____. You can do two things _____ _____ _____ _____.

   B: That's a great _____!

   G: Do you _____ _____ _____?

   B: Yes. I'm really _____ _____ to _____ it.

1. **G:** 너의 발명품에 관해 이야기를 좀 해 줄래?

   B: 그것은 특별한 신발이야. 너는 그것으로 바닥을 청소할 수도 있어.

   G: 멋지다! 네가 상을 탈 거라고 확신해. 행운을 빌게!

2. **B:** 이것은 흥미로워 보여. 도마니, 아니면 새 모이통이니?

   G: 그것은 도마일 뿐만 아니라 새 모이통이기도 해. 너는 동시에 두 가지를 할 수 있어.

   B: 멋진 아이디어야!

   G: 정말 그렇게 생각하니?

   B: 응. 난 그것을 사용해 보는 게 정말 기대가 되는 걸.

※ 다음 우리말에 맞도록 대화를 영어로 쓰시오.

Get Ready 2

(1) G: _____

_____

B: _____

G: _____

(2) B: _____

G: _____

B: _____

(3) B: _____

G: _____

B: _____

(4) B: _____

_____

G: _____

Start Off – Listen & Talk A

1. G: _____

W: _____

G: _____

W: _____

G: _____

W: _____

2. W: _____

G: _____

W: _____

G: _____

W: _____

 해석

(1) G: 너는 수업 중 많은 문제를 해결했잖아. 나는 네가 'Class Brain'상을 탈 거라고 확신해.
   B: 정말 그렇게 생각하니?
   G: 물론이야. 행운을 빌게, 상준아!
(2) B: 'Oh So Sweet'상 수상자는 사탕을 받을 거야.
   G: 오, 그 상을 받고 싶다.
   B: 네가 이번에는 그 상을 탈 거라고 확신해. 행운을 빌어, 지우야!
(3) B: 난 이번에 'Best Joker'상을 받기를 기대해.
   G: 하하. 너는 항상 우리를 웃게 하잖아. 그러니 네가 그 상을 탈 거야, 윤기야. 행운을 빌어.
   B: 고마워.
(4) B: 민지야, 너는 쾌활한 아이야. 나는 네가 'Ms. Cheerful'상을 탈 거라고 생각해. 행운을 빌게!
   G: 오, 고마워, 지호야.

1. G: 엄마, 체육 대회가 정말 기다려져요.
   W: 민지야, 너는 그날 무엇을 할 거니?
   G: 저는 학급을 대표해서 농구를 할 거예요. 우리는 몇 주간 열심히 연습해 왔어요.
   W: 오, 너의 경기가 기대되는구나.
   G: 사실은, 전 조금 걱정이 돼요. 제가 실수를 할까봐 겁나요.
   W: 걱정하지 마. 넌 잘할 거야. 행운을 빌어줄게!

2. W: 소윤아, 넌 체육 대회에서 경주에 참가하니?
   G: 물론이죠. 전 그날 마지막에 있는 100 미터 달리기를 뛸 거예요.
   W: 와, 네가 경주에서 달리는 모습을 보는 것이 기대되는구나.
   G: 하지만 엄마, 전 경주에서 이길지 잘 모르겠어요.
   W: 그냥 최선을 다하렴. 행운을 빌어줄게!

Start Off – Listen & Talk B

G: _____

W: _____

_____

G: _____

W: _____

G: _____

G: 엄마, 체육 대회에 오실 거예요?

W: 물론이지. 나는 'Kick a Shoe' 게임에 참가할 거야. 이번에 처음 해 보는 거야.

G: 걱정하지 마세요. 엄마는 잘하실 거예요. 행운을 빌어 드릴게요!

W: 고맙다. 나는 다른 엄마들과 쿠미 댄스도 할 거야.

G: 재밌겠네요. 무대에 선 엄마 모습을 보는 것이 기대돼요.

Start Off – Speak Up

A: _____

B: _____

A: _____

B: 나는 내일 모형 비행기 대회가 기대돼. 너는 준비됐니?

G: 음, 그런 것 같아. 하지만 긴장돼.

B: 너는 잘할 거야. 내가 행운을 빌어 줄게!

Step Up – Real-life Scene

Miso: _____

_____

Jimin: _____

Miso: _____

Jimin: _____

Miso: _____

Jimin: _____

Miso: _____

Jimin: _____

Miso: _____

미소: 다음 주 화요일에 수학여행을 갈 거야. 지민아, 너는 장기 자랑에서 뭘 할 거니?

지민: 나는 수업 시간에 선생님들이 말하는 것을 흉내 내고 농담도 할 거야.

미소: 와! 정말 기대되는데.

지민: 모든 사람이 나의 쇼를 좋아할까? 잘 모르겠어.

미소: 걱정하지 마. 나는 네가 잘할 거라고 확신해. 행운을 빌어 줄게!

지민: 고마워, 미소야. 내가 나의 연기의 한 부분을 보여 줄게. 누군지 맞힐 수 있겠니? "잘~ 했어~요!"

미소: 하하. 우리 영어 선생님처럼 들리는데.

지민: 그래? 장기 자랑에서 더 많이 보여 줄게.

미소: 멋지다! 너는 항상 우리를 웃게 만들어.

Fun Time

A: _____

B: _____

A: _____

A: _____

B: _____

A: _____

A: 나는 다음 주에 제주도를 여행할 거야.

B: 와! 멋지다.

A: 응, 난 그것이 정말 기대돼.

A: 난 다음 주에 춤 대회에 나갈 건데, 걱정이 된다.

B: 걱정하지 마. 넌 잘할 거야. 행운을 빌어 줄게.

A: 고마워.

Express Yourself A

1. G: _____

   B: _____

   G: _____

2. B: _____

   G: _____

   _____

   B: _____

   G: _____

   B: _____

1. G: 너의 발명품에 관해 이야기를 좀 해 줄래?

   B: 그것은 특별한 신발이야. 너는 그것으로 바닥을 청소할 수도 있어.

   G: 멋지다! 네가 상을 탈 거라고 확신해. 행운을 빌게!

2. B: 이것은 흥미로워 보여. 도마니, 아니면 새 모이통이니?

   G: 그것은 도마일 뿐만 아니라 새 모이통이기도 해. 너는 동시에 두 가지를 할 수 있어.

   B: 멋진 아이디어야!

   G: 정말 그렇게 생각하니?

   B: 응. 난 그것을 사용해 보는 게 정말 기대가 되는 걸.

※ 다음 우리말과 일치하도록 빈칸에 알맞은 것을 골라 쓰시오.

1 The _____ _____ _____
A. Prize   B. Nobel   C. Ig

2 "What _____ when you walk _____ _____ you are _____ a cup of coffee?"
A. backward   B. happens   C. carrying   D. while

3 Han Jiwon, a Korean high school student, _____ _____ _____ this _____ in 2015.
A. research   B. on   C. did   D. topic

4 Is this _____ project good _____ _____ _____ a Nobel Prize?
A. win   B. research   C. enough   D. to

5 _____ _____.
A. not   B. maybe

6 But _____ _____ an Ig Nobel Prize?
A. about   B. how

7 He _____ one in 2017 for this _____ _____.
A. fun   B. won   C. research

8 The Ig Nobel Prizes are _____ _____ discoveries that "first make one _____ and then _____."
A. awarded   B. laugh   C. for   D. think

9 They were started in 1991 by *AIR* magazine to increase people's _____ in science by _____ the _____ and the _____.
A. interest   B. imaginative   C. honoring   D. unusual

10 The prizes _____ _____ _____ real Nobel _____ in Sanders Theater at Harvard University.
A. winners   B. are   C. by   D. presented

1 이그노벨상

2 "당신이 커피 한 잔을 들고 가면서 뒤로 걸을 때 무슨 일이 일어날까?"

3 한국의 한 고등학생인 한지원은 2015년에 이 주제에 관해 연구했다.

4 이 연구 과제는 노벨상을 받을 정도로 훌륭할까?

5 아마도 아닐 것이다.

6 하지만 이그노벨상은 어떤가?

7 그는 이 재미있는 연구로 2017년에 상을 탔다.

8 이그노벨상은 '먼저 웃고 나서 다음에 생각하게 하는' 발견에 수여된다.

9 그것은 특이하고 창의적인 사람들을 높이 평가함으로써 과학에 대한 사람들의 흥미를 늘리기 위해 AIR 잡지에 의해 1991년에 시작되었다.

10 그 상들은 하버드 대학의 Sanders 극장에서 진짜 노벨상 수상자들에 의해 수여된다.

11 The room is usually _____ _____ people who are eager to _____ for the brave scientists with their "_____" research.

    A. cheer   B. with   C. laughable   D. filled

12 The U.K. Navy _____ the Ig Nobel Prize _____ Peace _____ 2000.

    A. for   B. won   C. in

13 _____ _____ money, the Navy made its sailors shout, "Bang!" _____ _____ using real bombs.

    A. of   B. save   C. to   D. instead

14 Is that funny _____ for you to _____ _____ _____?

    A. laugh   B. loud   C. enough   D. out

15 Andre Geim _____ _____ an _____ that year.

    A. award   B. also   C. won

16 He _____ _____ _____ a live frog in the air by _____ magnets.

    A. using   B. succeeded   C. floating   D. in

17 "In my experience, if people don't have a _____ of _____, they are usually not very good scientists," he said when he _____ his _____.

    A. humor   B. accepted   C. sense   D. award

18 If that still does not _____ a smile _____ your _____, _____ about this?

    A. to   B. bring   C. how   D. face

19 In 2005, Gauri Nanda won the Ig Nobel Prize _____ Economics _____ _____ an _____ clock.

    A. for   B. alarm   C. inventing   D. in

20 It _____ _____ _____ until the sleeper finally gets _____ of bed.

    A. away   B. out   C. running   D. keeps

11 그 방은 대개 '웃기는' 연구를 한 용감한 과학자들을 열렬히 격려하고자 하는 사람들로 가득 찬다.

12 영국 해군은 2000년에 이그노벨 평화상을 탔다.

13 돈을 아끼기 위해, 해군에서는 선원들에게 진짜 폭탄을 사용하는 대신에 "쾅!"이라고 소리치게 했다.

14 그것이 당신이 큰 소리로 웃을 정도로 우스운가?

15 Andre Geim도 그해에 상을 탔다.

16 그는 자석을 이용해서 살아 있는 개구리를 공중에 띄우는 데 성공했다.

17 그는 상을 받을 때, "내 경험상, 사람들이 유머 감각이 없다면, 그들은 대개 별로 훌륭한 과학자가 아니다."라고 말했다.

18 그것이 아직도 당신의 얼굴에 미소를 띠게 하지 않는다면, 이것은 어떤가?

19 2005년에 Gauri Nanda는 자명종을 발명해서 이그노벨 경제학상을 받았다.

20 그것은 잠자는 사람이 결국 침대 밖으로 나올 때까지 계속 도망을 다닌다.

21 _____ _____ the winners' fun studies _____ also the ceremony for the Ig Nobel Prizes _____ people laugh.

A. but   B. only   C. makes   D. not

22 There are a _____ of interesting things that _____ people _____ getting _____.

A. from   B. number   C. bored   D. keep

23 The _____ and _____ speeches are just two _____ : "Welcome. Welcome." and "Goodbye. Goodbye."

A. each   B. closing   C. words   D. opening

24 If someone talks for too long, an eight-year-old girl _____ Miss Sweetie Poo _____ _____ , "Please stop! I'm _____."

A. called   B. bored   C. repeatedly   D. shouts

25 Each winner receives ten _____ Zimbabwean dollars, _____ is _____ _____ than one U.S. dollar.

A. less   B. trillion   C. worth   D. which

26 _____ paper planes _____ _____ fun _____ .

A. is   B. throwing   C. tradition   D. another

27 The Ig Nobel Prize ceremony _____ _____ the words, "If you didn't _____ a prize — and if you _____ — better luck next year!"

A. with   B. did   C. win   D. ends

28 The _____ do not _____ _____ _____ money.

A. receive   B. lots   C. winners   D. of

29 And the _____ are not _____ _____ _____ the Nobel Prizes.

A. honors   B. awards   C. like   D. great

30 But the Ig Nobel Prizes make science _____ _____ _____ !

A. fun   B. a   C. more   D. lot

21 수상자들의 재미있는 연구뿐만 아니라 이그노벨상 시상식도 또한 사람들을 웃게 만든다.

22 사람들이 지루해하지 않도록 하는 재미있는 것들이 많이 있다.

23 개회사와 폐회사는 단지 두 마디이다: "환영합니다. 환영합니다."와 "안녕. 안녕."

24 만일 누군가가 너무 오랫동안 말을 하면, Miss Sweetie Poo 라고 하는 여덟 살짜리 여자아이가 "제발 멈춰요! 지루해요." 라고 계속 외친다.

25 각 수상자는 10조의 짐바브웨 달러를 받는데, 그것은 미국의 1 달러보다 가치가 낮다.

26 종이비행기를 날리는 것은 또 다른 재미있는 전통이다.

27 이그노벨상 시상식은 "만일 당신이 상을 타지 못했다면 – 그리고 만일 탔다면 – 내년에는 좀 더 많은 행운이 있기를!"이라는 말로 끝이 난다.

28 수상자들은 많은 상금을 받지 않는다.

29 그리고 그 상은 노벨상같이 훌륭한 영광은 아니다.

30 하지만 이그노벨상은 과학을 훨씬 더 재미있게 만든다!

※ 다음 우리말과 일치하도록 빈칸에 알맞은 말을 쓰시오.

1 The _____ _____ _____

2 "What _____ when you walk _____ _____ you are _____ a cup of coffee?"

3 Han Jiwon, a Korean high school student, _____ _____ on this _____ in 2015.

4 Is this research project _____ _____ _____ _____ a Nobel Prize?

5 _____ not.

6 But _____ _____ an Ig Nobel Prize?

7 He _____ _____ in 2017 for this _____ _____.

8 The Ig Nobel Prizes _____ _____ _____ _____ that "first make one _____ and then _____."

9 They were started in 1991 by *AIR* magazine _____ _____ people's _____ in science _____ _____ _____ and _____ _____.

10 The prizes _____ _____ _____ _____ _____ _____ _____ in Sanders Theater at Harvard University.

---

1 이그노벨상

2 "당신이 커피 한 잔을 들고 가면서 뒤로 걸을 때 무슨 일이 일어날까?"

3 한국의 한 고등학생인 한지원은 2015년에 이 주제에 관해 연구했다.

4 이 연구 과제는 노벨상을 받을 정도로 훌륭할까?

5 아마도 아닐 것이다.

6 하지만 이그노벨상은 어떤가?

7 그는 이 재미있는 연구로 2017년에 상을 탔다.

8 이그노벨상은 '먼저 웃기고 나서 다음에 생각하게 하는' 발견에 수여된다.

9 그것은 특이하고 창의적인 사람들을 높이 평가함으로써 과학에 대한 사람들의 흥미를 늘리기 위해 AIR 잡지에 의해 1991년에 시작되었다.

10 그 상들은 하버드 대학의 Sanders 극장에서 진짜 노벨상 수상자들에 의해 수여된다.

11 The room _____ usually _____ _____ people who are _____ _____ _____ for the brave scientists with their "_____" research.

12 The U.K. Navy _____ the Ig Nobel Prize _____ Peace in 2000.

13 _____ _____ money, the Navy _____ its sailors _____, "Bang!" _____ _____ _____ real bombs.

14 Is that _____ _____ for you to _____ _____ _____?

15 Andre Geim also _____ _____ _____ that year.

16 He _____ _____ _____ a live frog in the air _____ _____ _____.

17 "In my experience, if people don't have _____ _____ _____ _____, they are usually not very good scientists," he said _____ he _____ his _____.

18 If that still does not _____ a smile _____ your face, _____ _____ this?

19 In 2005, Gauri Nanda won the Ig Nobel Prize _____ Economics _____ _____ an alarm clock.

20 It _____ _____ _____ until the sleeper finally _____ _____ _____ bed.

11 그 방은 대개 '웃기는' 연구를 한 용감한 과학자들을 열렬히 격려하고자 하는 사람들로 가득 찬다.

12 영국 해군은 2000년에 이그노벨 평화상을 탔다.

13 돈을 아끼기 위해, 해군에서는 선원들에게 진짜 폭탄을 사용하는 대신에 "쾅!"이라고 소리치게 했다.

14 그것이 당신이 큰 소리로 웃을 정도로 우스운가?

15 Andre Geim도 그해에 상을 탔다.

16 그는 자석을 이용해서 살아 있는 개구리를 공중에 띄우는 데 성공했다.

17 그는 상을 받을 때, "내 경험상, 사람들이 유머 감각이 없다면, 그들은 대개 별로 훌륭한 과학자가 아니다."라고 말했다.

18 그것이 아직도 당신의 얼굴에 미소를 띠게 하지 않는다면, 이것은 어떤가?

19 2005년에 Gauri Nanda는 자명종을 발명해서 이그노벨 경제학상을 받았다.

20 그것은 잠자는 사람이 결국 침대 밖으로 나올 때까지 계속 도망을 다닌다.

21 _____ _____ the winners' fun studies _____ _____ the ceremony for the Ig Nobel Prizes _____ people _____.

22 There are _____ _____ _____ interesting things that _____ people _____ _____ _____.

23 The _____ and _____ _____ are just _____ _____ _____: "Welcome. Welcome." and "Goodbye. Goodbye."

24 If someone talks for too long, _____ _____ _____ _____ Miss Sweetie Poo shouts _____, "Please stop! I'm bored."

25 Each winner receives _____ _____ Zimbabwean dollars, _____ is _____ _____ _____ one U.S. dollar.

26 _____ paper planes _____ another fun _____.

27 The Ig Nobel Prize ceremony _____ _____ the words, "If you didn't _____ a _____ — and if you _____ — better luck next year!"

28 The winners _____ _____ _____ lots of money.

29 And the awards are not _____ _____ _____ the Nobel Prizes.

30 But the Ig Nobel Prizes make science _____ _____ _____!

21 수상자들의 재미있는 연구뿐만 아니라 이그노벨상 시상식도 또한 사람들을 웃게 만든다.

22 사람들이 지루해하지 않도록 하는 재미있는 것들이 많이 있다.

23 개회사와 폐회사는 단지 두 마디이다: "환영합니다. 환영합니다."와 "안녕. 안녕."

24 만일 누군가가 너무 오랫동안 말을 하면, Miss Sweetie Poo 라고 하는 여덟 살짜리 여자아이가 "제발 멈춰요! 지루해요." 라고 계속 외친다.

25 각 수상자는 10조의 짐바브웨 달러를 받는데, 그것은 미국의 1 달러보다 가치가 낮다.

26 종이비행기를 날리는 것은 또 다른 재미있는 전통이다.

27 이그노벨상 시상식은 "만일 당신이 상을 타지 못했다면 – 그리고 만일 탔다면 – 내년에는 좀 더 많은 행운이 있기를!"이라는 말로 끝이 난다.

28 수상자들은 많은 상금을 받지 않는다.

29 그리고 그 상은 노벨상같이 훌륭한 영광은 아니다.

30 하지만 이그노벨상은 과학을 훨씬 더 재미있게 만든다!

※ 다음 문장을 우리말로 쓰시오.

1 The Ig Nobel Prize

➡ _____

2 "What happens when you walk backward while you are carrying a cup of coffee?"

➡ _____

3 Han Jiwon, a Korean high school student, did research on this topic in 2015.

➡ _____

4 Is this research project good enough to win a Nobel Prize?

➡ _____

5 Maybe not.

➡ _____

6 But how about an Ig Nobel Prize?

➡ _____

7 He won one in 2017 for this fun research.

➡ _____

8 The Ig Nobel Prizes are awarded for discoveries that "first make one laugh and then think."

➡ _____

9 They were started in 1991 by AIR magazine to increase people's interest in science by honoring the unusual and the imaginative.

➡ _____

_____

10 The prizes are presented by real Nobel winners in Sanders Theater at Harvard University.

➡ _____

11 The room is usually filled with people who are eager to cheer for the brave scientists with their "laughable" research.

➡ _____

12 The U.K. Navy won the Ig Nobel Prize for Peace in 2000.

➡ _____

13 To save money, the Navy made its sailors shout, "Bang!" instead of using real bombs.

➡ _____

14 Is that funny enough for you to laugh out loud?

➡ _____

15 Andre Geim also won an award that year.

➡ _____

16 ▸ He succeeded in floating a live frog in the air by using magnets.

➡ _____

17 ▸ "In my experience, if people don't have a sense of humor, they are usually not very good scientists," he said when he accepted his award.

➡ _____

18 ▸ If that still does not bring a smile to your face, how about this?

➡ _____

19 ▸ In 2005, Gauri Nanda won the Ig Nobel Prize in Economics for inventing an alarm clock.

➡ _____

20 ▸ It keeps running away until the sleeper finally gets out of bed.

➡ _____

21 ▸ Not only the winners' fun studies but also the ceremony for the Ig Nobel Prizes makes people laugh.

➡ _____

22 ▸ There are a number of interesting things that keep people from getting bored.

➡ _____

23 ▸ The opening and closing speeches are just two words each: "Welcome. Welcome." and "Goodbye. Goodbye."

➡ _____

24 ▸ If someone talks for too long, an eight-year-old girl called Miss Sweetie Poo shouts repeatedly, "Please stop! I'm bored."

➡ _____
_____

25 ▸ Each winner receives ten trillion Zimbabwean dollars, which is worth less than one U.S. dollar.

➡ _____

26 ▸ Throwing paper planes is another fun tradition.

➡ _____

27 ▸ The Ig Nobel Prize ceremony ends with the words, "If you didn't win a prize — and if you did — better luck next year!"

➡ _____
_____

28 ▸ The winners do not receive lots of money.

➡ _____

29 ▸ And the awards are not great honors like the Nobel Prizes.

➡ _____

30 ▸ But the Ig Nobel Prizes make science a lot more fun!

➡ _____

※ 다음 괄호 안의 단어들을 우리말에 맞도록 바르게 배열하시오.

1 (Ig / The / Prize / Nobel)

➡ _____

2 (happens / "what / you / when / backward / walk / you / while / carrying / are / cup / a / of / coffee?")

➡ _____
_____

3 (Jiwon, / Han / Korean / a / school / high / student, / research / did / this / on / topic / 2015. / in)

➡ _____
_____

4 (this / is / project / research / enough / good / win / to / a / Prize? / Nobel)

➡ _____

5 (not. / maybe)

➡ _____

6 (how / but / an / about / Nobel / Ig / Prize?)

➡ _____

7 (won / he / in / one / 2017 / this / for / research. / fun)

➡ _____

8 (Ig / The / Prizes / Nobel / awarded / are / discoveries / for / "first / that / one / make / laugh / then / and / think.")

➡ _____
_____

9 (were / they / in / started / 1991 / *AIR* / by / to / magazine / interest / people's / increase / in / by / science / the / honoring / unusual / and / imaginative. / the)

➡ _____
_____

10 (prizes / the / presented / are / real / by / winners / Nobel / Sanders / in / Theater / Harvard / at / University.)

➡ _____
_____

---

1 이그노벨상

2 "당신이 커피 한 잔을 들고 가면서 뒤로 걸을 때 무슨 일이 일어날까?"

3 한국의 한 고등학생인 한지원은 2015년에 이 주제에 관해 연구했다.

4 이 연구 과제는 노벨상을 받을 정도로 훌륭할까?

5 아마도 아닐 것이다.

6 하지만 이그노벨상은 어떤가?

7 그는 이 재미있는 연구로 2017년에 상을 탔다.

8 이그노벨상은 '먼저 웃기고 니서 다음에 생각하게 하는' 발견에 수여된다.

9 그것은 특이하고 창의적인 사람들을 높이 평가함으로써 과학에 대한 사람들의 흥미를 늘리기 위해 AIR 잡지에 의해 1991년에 시작되었다.

10 그 상들은 하버드 대학의 Sanders 극장에서 진짜 노벨상 수상자들에 의해 수여된다.

11 (room / the / usually / is / with / filled / who / people / eager / are / to / for / cheer / the / scientists / brave / their / with / research. / "laughable")

➡ _____

_____

12 (U.K. / the / won / Navy / Ig / the / Prize / Nobel / Peace / in / 2000. / for)

➡ _____

13 (save / to / money, / Navy / the / its / made / sailors / "Bang!" / shout, / of / instead / using / of / bombs. / real)

➡ _____

_____

14 (that / is / enough / funny / you / for / laugh / to / loud? / out)

➡ _____

15 (Geim / Andre / won / also / award / an / year. / that)

➡ _____

16 (succeeded / he / floating / in / live / a / in / frog / the / by / air / magnets. / using)

➡ _____

17 (my / "in / experience, / people / if / have / don't / sense / a / of / they / humor, / are / not / usually / very / scientists," / good / said / he / he / when / his / award. / accepted)

➡ _____

_____

18 (that / if / does / still / bring / not / smile / a / your / to / face, / about / this? / how)

➡ _____

19 (2005, / in / Nanda / Gauri / the / won / Nobel / Ig / in / Prize / for / Economics / inventing / alarm / an / clock.)

➡ _____

20 (keeps / it / away / running / the / until / finally / sleeper / out / gets / bed. / of)

➡ _____

21 (only / not / winners' / the / studies / fun / also / but / ceremony / the / the / for / Ig / Prizes / Nobel / people / laugh. / makes)

➡ _____

22 (are / there / number / a / interesting / of / that / things / people / keep / from / bored. / getting)

➡ _____

23 (opening / the / and / speeches / closing / just / are / words / two / each: / "welcome. / goodbye." / welcome." / and / "goodbye.)

➡ _____
_____

24 (someone / if / for / talks / long, / too / eight-year-old / an / called / girl / Sweetie / Miss / shouts / Poo / repeatedly, / stop! / "please / bored." / I'm)

➡ _____
_____

25 (winner / each / ten / receives / trillion / dollars, / Zimbabwean / is / which / less / worth / one / than / dollar. / U.S.)

➡ _____
_____

26 (paper / throwing / planes / another / is / tradition. / fun)

➡ _____

27 (Ig / The / Prize / ceremony / with / ends / words, / the / you / "if / win / didn't / prize / a / — / if / and / did / you / — / luck / year!" / better / next)

➡ _____
_____

28 (winners / the / not / do / lots / receive / money. / of)

➡ _____

29 (the / and / are / awards / great / not / like / honors / the / Prizes. / Nobel)

➡ _____

30 (the / but / Nobel / Ig / make / Prizes / a / science / more / lot / fun!)

➡ _____

21 수상자들의 재미있는 연구뿐만 아니라 이그노벨상 시상식도 또한 사람들을 웃게 만든다.

22 사람들이 지루해하지 않도록 하는 재미있는 것들이 많이 있다.

23 개회사와 폐회사는 단지 두 마디이다: "환영합니다. 환영합니다."와 "안녕. 안녕."

24 만일 누군가가 너무 오랫동안 말을 하면, Miss Sweetie Poo 라고 하는 여덟 살짜리 여자아이가 "제발 멈춰요! 지루해요." 라고 계속 외친다.

25 각 수상자는 10조의 짐바브웨 달러를 받는데, 그것은 미국의 1 달러보다 가치가 낮다.

26 종이비행기를 날리는 것은 또 다른 재미있는 전통이다.

27 이그노벨상 시상식은 "만일 당신이 상을 타지 못했다면 – 그리고 만일 탔다면 – 내년에는 좀 더 많은 행운이 있기를!"이라는 말로 끝이 난다.

28 수상자들은 많은 상금을 받지 않는다.

29 그리고 그 상은 노벨상같이 훌륭한 영광은 아니다.

30 하지만 이그노벨상은 과학을 훨씬 더 재미있게 만든다!

※ 다음 우리말을 영어로 쓰시오.

1 이그노벨상

➡ _____

2 "당신이 커피 한 잔을 들고 가면서 뒤로 걸을 때 무슨 일이 일어날까?"

➡ _____

3 한국의 한 고등학생인 한지원은 2015년에 이 주제에 관해 연구했다.

➡ _____

4 이 연구 과제는 노벨상을 받을 정도로 훌륭할까?

➡ _____

5 아마도 아닐 것이다.

➡ _____

6 하지만 이그노벨상은 어떤가?

➡ _____

7 그는 이 재미있는 연구로 2017년에 상을 탔다.

➡ _____

8 이그노벨상은 '먼저 웃기고 나서 다음에 생각하게 하는' 발견에 수여된다.

➡ _____

9 그것은 특이하고 창의적인 사람들을 높이 평가함으로써 과학에 대한 사람들의 흥미를 늘리기 위해 AIR 잡지에 의해 1991년에 시작되었다.

➡ _____

_____

10 그 상들은 하버드 대학의 Sanders 극장에서 진짜 노벨상 수상자들에 의해 수여된다.

➡ _____

11 그 방은 대개 '웃기는' 연구를 한 용감한 과학자들을 열렬히 격려하고자 하는 사람들로 가득 찬다.

➡ _____

_____

12 영국 해군은 2000년에 이그노벨 평화상을 탔다.

➡ _____

13 돈을 아끼기 위해, 해군에서는 선원들에게 진짜 폭탄을 사용하는 대신에 "쾅!"이라고 소리치게 했다.

➡ _____

14 그것이 당신이 큰 소리로 웃을 정도로 우스운가?

➡ _____

15 Andre Geim도 그해에 상을 탔다.

➡ _____

16 그는 자석을 이용해서 살아 있는 개구리를 공중에 띄우는 데 성공했다.

➡ _____

17 그는 상을 받을 때, "내 경험상, 사람들이 유머 감각이 없다면, 그들은 대개 별로 훌륭한 과학자기 이니다."라고 **말했디.**

➡ _____
_____

18 그것이 아직도 당신의 얼굴에 미소를 띠게 하지 않는다면, 이것은 어떤가?

➡ _____

19 2005년에 Gauri Nanda는 자명종을 발명해서 이그노벨 경제학상을 받았다.

➡ _____

20 그것은 잠자는 사람이 결국 침대 밖으로 나올 때까지 계속 도망을 다닌다.

➡ _____

21 수상자들의 재미있는 연구뿐만 아니라 이그노벨상 시상식도 또한 사람들을 웃게 만든다.

➡ _____

22 사람들이 지루해하지 않도록 하는 재미있는 것들이 많이 있다.

➡ _____

23 개회사와 폐회사는 단지 두 마디이다: "환영합니다. 환영합니다."와 "안녕. 안녕."

➡ _____

24 만일 누군가가 너무 오랫동안 말을 하면, Miss Sweetie Poo라고 하는 여덟 살짜리 여자아이가 "제발 멈춰요! 지루해요."라고 계속 외친다.

➡ _____
_____

25 각 수상자는 10조의 짐바브웨 달러를 받는데, 그것은 미국의 1달러보다 가치가 낮다.

➡ _____

26 종이비행기를 날리는 것은 또 다른 재미있는 전통이다.

➡ _____

27 이그노벨상 시상식은 "만일 당신이 상을 타지 못했다면 – 그리고 만일 탔다면 – 내년에는 좀 더 많은 행운이 있기를!"이라는 말로 끝이 난다.

➡ _____
_____

28 수상자들은 많은 상금을 받지 않는다.

➡ _____

29 그리고 그 상은 노벨상같이 훌륭한 영광은 아니다.

➡ _____

30 하지만 이그노벨상은 과학을 훨씬 더 재미있게 만든다!

➡ _____

※ 다음 우리말과 일치하도록 빈칸에 알맞은 말을 쓰시오.

Self-study Guide

1. New _____ again!

2. He _____ great _____ _____ _____ new things.

3. Oh, I _____ the _____ of "-ness."

4. Now I know _____ _____ the meaning of "eager" _____ _____ the meaning of "eagerness."

1. 또 새 단어네!
2. 그는 새로운 것들을 배우고자 하는 열정을 보여주었다.
3. 오, 나는 '-ness'의 의미를 알았어.
4. 이제 나는 'eager'의 뜻뿐만 아니라 'eagerness'의 뜻도 알아.

Express Yourself C

1. Magic _____

2. _____ are _____ Stairs.

3. You can use them _____ _____ for _____ up and down _____ _____ for _____ things.

4. This invention is _____ _____ _____ _____ your life _____ _____.

1. 마법의 계단
2. 이것은 '마법의 계단'입니다.
3. 당신은 그것을 올라가고 내려가기 위해서 뿐만 아니라 물건을 보관하기 위해서도 사용할 수 있습니다.
4. 이 발명품은 당신의 삶을 훨씬 더 편안하게 할 정도로 충분히 유용합니다.

Link to the World

1. The _____ _____

2. The Nobel Prize was _____ _____ Alfred Nobel, a _____ _____.

3. It _____ _____ _____ people _____ have done _____ _____ for the world.

4. Of _____ _____ _____, Malala Yousafzai is _____ _____.

5. She won the Nobel Prize _____ _____ _____ _____ 17 because she _____ _____ for women's and _____ _____.

6. The Curie family _____ the Nobel Prize _____ _____.

7. _____ _____ Marie Curie _____ _____ her daughter _____ _____ the Nobel Prize.

1. 노벨상
2. 노벨상은 스웨덴 과학자인, Alfred Nobel의 이름을 따서 지었다.
3. 그 상은 세계를 위해 위대한 일을 행한 사람들에게 수여된다.
4. 모든 수상자들 중에서, Malala Yousafzai가 최연소이다.
5. 그녀는 여성과 어린이의 권리를 위해서 싸웠기 때문에 17세의 나이에 노벨상을 수상했다.
6. Curie 가족은 노벨상을 3번 수상했다.
7. Marie Curie뿐만 아니라 그녀의 딸도 노벨상을 수상했다.

※ 다음 우리말을 영어로 쓰시오.

Self-study Guide

1. 또 새 단어네!

➡ _____

2. 그는 새로운 것들을 배우고자 하는 열정을 보여주었다.

➡ _____

3. 오, 나는 '-ness'의 의미를 알았어.

➡ _____

4. 이제 나는 'eager'의 뜻뿐만 아니라 'eagerness'의 뜻도 알아.

➡ _____

Express Yourself C

1. 마법의 계단

➡ _____

2. 이것은 '마법의 계단'입니다.

➡ _____

3. 당신은 그것을 올라가고 내려가기 위해서 뿐만 아니라 물건을 보관하기 위해서도 사용할 수 있습니다.

➡ _____

4. 이 발명품은 당신의 삶을 훨씬 더 편안하게 할 정도로 충분히 유용합니다.

➡ _____

Link to the World

1. 노벨상

➡ _____

2. 노벨상은 스웨덴 과학자인, Alfred Nobel의 이름을 따서 지었다.

➡ _____

3. 그 상은 세계를 위해 위대한 일을 행한 사람들에게 수여된다.

➡ _____

4. 모든 수상자들 중에서, Malala Yousafzai가 최연소이다.

➡ _____

5. 그녀는 여성과 어린이의 권리를 위해서 싸웠기 때문에 17세의 나이에 노벨상을 수상했다.

➡ _____

6. Curie 가족은 노벨상을 3번 수상했다.

➡ _____

7. Marie Curie뿐만 아니라 그녀의 딸도 노벨상을 수상했다.

➡ _____

※ 다음 영어를 우리말로 쓰시오.

01 recognize _____

02 career _____

03 competition _____

04 hidden _____

05 ability _____

06 impress _____

07 case _____

08 face _____

09 judge _____

10 magician _____

11 expert _____

12 permission _____

13 control _____

14 figure _____

15 laughter _____

16 match _____

17 line _____

18 presentation _____

19 useful _____

20 accept _____

21 matter _____

22 courage _____

23 record _____

24 colored _____

25 manager _____

26 offer _____

27 decorate _____

28 character _____

29 hanger _____

30 disappointed _____

31 install _____

32 against _____

33 allow _____

34 later _____

35 get upset _____

36 stand up for _____

37 give up _____

38 break down _____

39 get over _____

40 thanks to _____

41 prepare for _____

42 laugh at _____

43 have no choice but to _____

※ 다음 우리말을 영어로 쓰시오.

01	능력	
02	숨겨진, 비밀의	
03	감명을 주다, 깊은 인상을 주다	
04	용기	
05	받아들이다	
06	장식하다	
07	색깔이 있는, 유색 인종의	
08	직업, 직장 생활	
09	~에 반대하여, ~에 맞서	
10	등장인물	
11	실망한	
12	발표	
13	소송 사건	
14	기록	
15	마술사	
16	(중요한) 인물, 거물, 숫자	
17	허락	
18	알아보다, 인정하다	
19	조종하다	
20	설치하다	
21	판사	
22	나중에, 후에	
23	중요하다, 문제가 되다	
24	제의, 제안	
25	지다, 패배하다	
26	전문가	
27	(상황에) 직면하다	
28	시합, 경기	
29	(연극, 영화 등의) 대사	
30	대회, 시합	
31	유용한	
32	연설, 말	
33	관리자, 경영자	
34	웃음(소리)	
35	포기하다	
36	~ 덕분에	
37	~을 옹호하다, 지지하다	
38	우울해 보이다	
39	~을 명심하다	
40	~을 극복하다	
41	계속 ~하다	
42	~을 비웃다	
43	~을 부수다	

※ 다음 영영풀이에 알맞은 단어를 <보기>에서 골라 쓴 후, 우리말 뜻을 쓰시오.

1 _____ : of a race other than white: _____

2 _____ : not easy to find: _____

3 _____ : a well-known person: _____

4 _____ : someone who bakes bread, cakes, etc.: _____

5 _____ : to deal with a difficult situation: _____

6 _____ : to let someone do something: _____

7 _____ : the act or sound of laughing: _____

8 _____ : the series of jobs that you do during your working life: _____

9 _____ : a person who designs, builds, or maintains machines: _____

10 _____ : the ability to control your fear in a dangerous or difficult situation:
_____

11 _____ : the action of allowing someone to do something: _____

12 _____ : a person with a high level of knowledge or skill in a particular area:
_____

13 _____ : the person in a court who decides how criminals should be punished:
_____

14 _____ : a person who is responsible for controlling an organization: _____

15 _____ : the region beyond the Earth's atmosphere or beyond the solar system:
_____

16 _____ : a written account of something that is kept so that it can be looked at and
used in the future: _____

보기			
figure	judge	allow	laughter
space	permission	hidden	colored
engineer	manager	career	face
courage	expert	record	baker

※ 다음 우리말과 일치하도록 빈칸에 알맞은 말을 쓰시오.

Get Ready 2

(1) **G:** You _____ _____ today. What's _____ _____?
　　B: I want _____ _____ _____ _____, but my father doesn't like _____ _____. He thinks _____ boys _____ play sports.
　　G: I'm _____ _____ _____ _____.

(2) **G:** Why are you _____?
　　B: I'm _____ _____ the ski jumping _____, but my _____ is not good. _____ should I do?
　　G: I think you should _____ _____ more. I'm _____ you'll _____ _____ _____ _____.

(3) **B:** I want _____ _____ a _____, but everybody _____ _____ me. Do you think I should _____ _____ my dream?
　　G: No, _____ _____ _____. I think you're really _____ _____ _____. You'll be a great _____!
　　B: Thank you.

Start Off – Listen & Talk A

1. **B:** You don't _____ happy. _____ are you _____?
　　G: We _____ the basketball game _____ _____ my _____.
　　B: Come on. Everyone _____ _____.
　　G: Do you think I _____ _____ _____ _____?
　　B: Well, yes. You know, _____ _____ _____.

2. **G:** Why _____ _____ _____?
　　B: I didn't _____ a good _____.
　　G: _____ it _____. Your _____ was _____ _____ fast, but I liked your _____.
　　B: Do you think I should speak _____ _____?
　　G: Yes. It will _____ your classmates _____ you _____.

Start Off – Listen & Talk B

G: Junsu, you _____ _____ today. Why are you _____?
B: I _____ the _____ _____.
G: I'm _____ _____ _____ _____ _____. I know you _____ _____.
B: Yeah, but _____ that wasn't _____. Do you think I should _____ _____ _____ _____ _____?
G: Yes. I think they will help. _____ _____ _____ _____ tips _____ cooking shows _____?
B: Okay. I'll _____. Thank you _____ your _____, Mina.
G: You're _____. Just _____ I'm a fan of your _____.

Start Off – Speak Up

B: _____ are you _____?
G: I _____ the _____ for the Mapo Youth Band. Do you think I should _____ _____?
B: Sure. _____ _____ _____. You'll do _____ next time.
G: Thank you.

Start Up – Real-life Scene

Jisu: Why are you so _____, Ryan?
Ryan: My parents _____ _____ me _____ Superstar 101, a _____ _____.
Jisu: I'm _____ _____ _____ that. Why are they _____ it?
Ryan: They want me _____ _____ _____ and be a doctor. They're always _____ _____ _____ _____.
Jisu: Did you tell your _____ you really want _____ _____ a singer?
Ryan: _____ _____. Do you think I should _____ _____ them about it?
Jisu: Yes. Just show them _____ _____ you love singing. _____ _____ _____ _____ the songs you made _____ _____ _____ them?
Ryan: Okay. I'll try. _____ _____ your advice, Jisu.

Express Yourself A

1. W: You don't _____ _____. Why are you _____?
   B: I want to be a wonderful _____ _____ you, but I _____ the magic _____. Do you think I should _____ _____?
   W: No. _____ _____ every day and you'll _____ _____ and _____. _____ important _____ _____ _____.
   B: Okay, I'll try. Thank you for _____ _____.
2. W: Please _____ _____. _____ you _____ _____ _____?
   B: Yes, I want to be a _____. Do you think I should go to _____ school?
   W: I think that will help, but _____ more important _____ _____ _____ every day. _____ design _____ _____ _____ _____ you.
   B: Thank you. I'll _____ _____ _____ _____.

Learning Diary– Listen & Speak 1

B: You _____ _____ today, Minji. _____ _____ _____?
G: We _____ the soccer game _____ I _____ a _____.
B: _____ _____ so sad. It can _____ to _____.
G: Do you think I should _____ _____?
B: Well, yes. I can help you _____ you want. _____, I'm a good soccer player.
G: Really? Thank you, Seho.

B: 너는 왜 실망하고 있니?
G: 나는 마포 청소년 밴드 오디션에서 떨어졌어. 너는 내가 계속 노력해야 한다고 생각하니?
B: 물론이지. 포기하지 마. 너는 다음번에 더 잘할 거야.
G: 고마워.

지수: 너는 왜 그렇게 실망하고 있니, Ryan?
Ryan: 부모님은 내가 노래 경연 대회인 슈퍼스타 101에 참가하는 걸 허락하지 않으실 거야.
지수: 그 말을 들으니 유감이구나. 왜 부모님은 그것에 반대하시니?
Ryan: 부모님은 내가 열심히 공부해서 의사가 되기를 원하셔. 항상 내 성적을 걱정하시지.
지수: 부모님께 네가 정말로 가수가 되고 싶다고 말씀드렸니?
Ryan: 아니 아직. 너는 내가 부모님께 그것에 대해 말씀드려야 한다고 생각하니?
지수: 응. 그냥 부모님께 네가 얼마나 노래 부르는 것을 좋아하는지 보여 드려. 부모님 앞에서 네가 만든 노래를 부르는 건 어때?
Ryan: 알았어. 시도해 볼게. 조언해 줘서 고마워, 지수야.

1. W: 기분이 안 좋아 보이네요. 왜 실망하고 있나요?
   B: 저는 당신처럼 멋진 마술사가 되고 싶은데, 마술 대회에서 떨어졌어요. 제가 포기해야 한다고 생각하나요?
   W: 아뇨. 매일 열심히 연습하면 점점 더 나아질 거예요. 계속 노력하는 것이 중요해요.
   B: 네, 노력해 볼게요. 조언해 주셔서 감사합니다.
2. W: 어서 들어오세요. 물건을 디자인하는 것에 관심이 있나요?
   B: 네, 저는 상품 디자이너가 되고 싶어요. 제가 디자인 학교에 가야 한다고 생각하나요?
   W: 그것이 도움이 될 거라고 생각해요. 하지만 매일 그림을 연습하는 것이 더 중요해요. 디자인 잡지를 읽는 것도 도움이될 거예요.
   B: 감사합니다. 그 점을 명심할게요.

B: 오늘 우울해 보이는구나, 민지야. 왜 실망하고 있니?
G: 내가 실수를 해서 우리가 축구 시합에서 졌거든.
B: 너무 슬퍼하지 마. 그런 일은 누구에게나 일어날 수 있어.
G: 넌 내가 더 연습해야 한다고 생각하니?
B: 음, 그래. 네가 원한다면 내가 너를 도와줄 수 있어. 너도 알다시피, 내가 축구를 잘하잖아.
G: 정말이니? 고마워, 세호야.

※ 다음 우리말에 맞도록 대화를 영어로 쓰시오.

Get Ready 2

(1) G: _____

　　 B: _____

　　 _____

　　 G: _____

(2) G: _____

　　 B: _____

　　 G: _____

(3) B: _____

　　 G: _____

　　 B: _____

Start Off – Listen & Talk A

1. B: _____

　 G: _____

　 B: _____

　 G: _____

　 B: _____

2. G: _____

　 B: _____

　 G: _____

　 B: _____

　 G: _____

Start Off – Listen & Talk B

G: _____

B: _____

G: _____

B: _____

G: _____

B: _____

G: _____

해석

(1) G: 너는 오늘 우울해 보이는구나. 무슨 일이니?
　　B: 나는 춤 수업을 듣고 싶은데, 아버지는 그 생각을 마음에 들어하지 않으셔. 아버지는 남자아이들은 운동을 해야 한다고 생각하셔.
　　G: 그것 참 안됐구나.

(2) G: 너는 왜 실망하고 있니?
　　B: 스키 점프 대회를 준비하고 있는데, 내 기록이 좋지 않아. 내가 무엇을 해야 할까?
　　G: 네가 계속 더 많이 연습해야 한다고 생각해. 난 네가 점점 더 나아질 거라고 확신해.

(3) B: 나는 요리사가 되고 싶은데, 모두 나를 비웃어. 너는 내가 꿈을 포기해야 한다고 생각하니?
　　G: 아니, 절대 포기하지 마. 나는 네가 정말 요리를 잘한다고 생각해. 너는 훌륭한 요리사가 될 거야!
　　B: 고마워.

1. B: 너는 기분이 좋아 보이지 않는구나. 왜 실망하고 있니?
　 G: 내 실수 때문에 우리가 농구 시합에서 졌어.
　 B: 괜찮아. 모든 사람은 실수하기 마련이야.
　 G: 내가 더 연습해야 한다고 생각하니?
　 B: 음, 그래. 너도 알다시피, 연습이 완벽을 만들잖아.

2. G: 너는 왜 실망하고 있니?
　 B: 나는 발표를 잘하지 못했어.
　 G: 괜찮아. 너의 발표는 약간 빨랐지만, 나는 너의 발표가 마음에 들었어.
　 B: 너는 내가 더 천천히 말해야 한다고 생각하니?
　 G: 응. 그러면 너의 학급 친구들이 네 말을 더 잘 이해하게 될 거야.

G: 준수야, 너 오늘 우울해 보이는구나. 왜 실망하고 있니?
B: 요리 대회에서 떨어졌어.
G: 그것 참 안됐구나. 네가 열심히 노력했다는 걸 알아.
B: 응, 하지만 아마 그게 충분하지는 않았나 봐. 너는 내가 더 많은 요리 요령들을 배워야 한다고 생각하니?
G: 응. 나는 그것이 도움이 될 거라고 생각해. 온라인 요리 영상에서 유용한 조언들을 얻는 게 어때?
B: 알았어. 시도해 볼게. 조언해 줘서 고마워, 미나야.
G: 천만에. 내가 네 요리의 팬이라는 것만 기억해.

Start Off – Speak Up

B: _____

G: _____

_____

B: _____

G: _____

Start Up – Real-life Scene

Jisu: _____

Ryan: _____

Jisu: _____

Ryan: _____

_____

Jisu: _____

Ryan: _____

Jisu: _____

_____

Ryan: _____

Express Yourself A

1. W: _____

   B: _____

   W: _____

   _____

   B: _____

2. W: _____

   B: _____

   W: _____

   _____

   B: _____

Learning Diary– Listen & Speak 1

B: _____

G: _____

B: _____

G: _____

B: _____

G: _____

B: 너는 왜 실망하고 있니?

G: 나는 마포 청소년 밴드 오디션에서 떨어졌어. 너는 내가 계속 노력해야 한다고 생각하니?

B: 물론이지. 포기하지 마. 너는 다음번에 더 잘할 거야.

G: 고마워.

지수: 너는 왜 그렇게 실망하고 있니, Ryan?

Ryan: 부모님은 내가 노래 경연 대회인 슈퍼스타 101에 참가하는 걸 허락하지 않으실 거야.

지수: 그 말을 들으니 유감이구나. 왜 부모님은 그것에 반대하시니?

Ryan: 부모님은 내가 열심히 공부해서 의사가 되기를 원하셔. 항상 내 성적을 걱정하시지.

지수: 부모님께 네가 정말로 가수가 되고 싶다고 말씀드렸니?

Ryan: 아니 아직. 너는 내가 부모님께 그것에 대해 말씀드려야 한다고 생각하니?

지수: 응. 그냥 부모님께 네가 얼마나 노래 부르는 것을 좋아하는지 보여 드려. 부모님 앞에서 네가 만든 노래를 부르는 건 어때?

Ryan: 알았어. 시도해 볼게. 조언해 줘서 고마워, 지수야.

1. W: 기분이 안 좋아 보이네요. 왜 실망하고 있나요?

   B: 저는 당신처럼 멋진 마술사가 되고 싶은데, 마술 대회에서 떨어졌어요. 제가 포기해야 한다고 생각하나요?

   W: 아뇨. 매일 열심히 연습하면 점점 더 나아질 거예요. 계속 노력하는 것이 중요해요.

   B: 네, 노력해 볼게요. 조언해 주셔서 감사합니다.

2. W: 어서 들어오세요. 물건을 디자인하는 것에 관심이 있나요?

   B: 네, 저는 상품 디자이너가 되고 싶어요. 제가 디자인 학교에 가야 한다고 생각하나요?

   W: 그것이 도움이 될 거라고 생각해요. 하지만 매일 그림을 연습하는 것이 더 중요해요. 디자인 잡지를 읽는 것도 도움이될 거예요.

   B: 감사합니다. 그 점을 명심할게요.

B: 오늘 우울해 보이는구나, 민지야. 왜 실망하고 있니?

G: 내가 실수를 해서 우리가 축구 시합에서 졌거든.

B: 너무 슬퍼하지 마. 그런 일은 누구에게나 일어날 수 있어.

G: 넌 내가 더 연습해야 한다고 생각하니?

B: 음, 그래. 네가 원한다면 내가 너를 도와줄 수 있어. 너도 알다시피, 내가 축구를 잘하잖아.

G: 정말이니? 고마워, 세호야.

※ 다음 우리말과 일치하도록 빈칸에 알맞은 것을 골라 쓰시오.

1 The _____ _____ of _____
A. Figures　　　B. Hidden　　　C. NASA

2 I _____ the _____ *Hidden Figures* _____ _____.
A. last　　　B. movie　　　C. watched　　　D. weekend

3 It was a movie about three _____ _____ _____ _____ at NASA.
A. worked　　　B. women　　　C. African-American　　　D. who

4 They began their _____ _____ the 1960s _____ " _____ computers."
A. human　　　B. career　　　C. as　　　D. in

5 However, they dreamed of becoming space _____ at NASA and tried hard to _____ _____ _____.
A. over　　　B. experts　　　C. get　　　D. difficulties

6 **Katherine Johnson** was _____ of the three " _____ " in this _____.
A. one　　　B. hidden　　　C. figures　　　D. movie

7 She worked _____ and showed a _____ in math, and her manager Al Harrison _____ her _____.
A. ability　　　B. talent　　　C. hard　　　D. recognized

8 One day, he _____ _____ when Katherine was _____ from her desk _____ too long.
A. missing　　　B. upset　　　C. got　　　D. for

9 Al asked _____ _____ _____ _____, and she answered.
A. been　　　B. where　　　C. had　　　D. Katherine

10 Katherine: _____ _____.
A. bathroom　　　B. the

11 _____ _____ no _____ _____ in this building.
A. are　　　B. bathrooms　　　C. COLORED　　　D. there

12 I _____ to run _____ a mile _____ just to _____ the bathroom.
A. use　　　B. half　　　C. away　　　D. have

13 _____ this, I _____ really _____ for her.
A. sorry　　　B. felt　　　C. hearing

1 NASA의 숨겨진 인물들

2 나는 지난 주말에 〈히든 피겨스〉라는 영화를 보았다.

3 그것은 NASA에서 일했던 세 명의 아프리카계 미국인 여성들에 대한 영화였다.

4 그들은 1960년대에 '인간 컴퓨터(계산원)'로 일을 시작했다.

5 하지만 그들은 NASA에서 우주 전문가가 되기를 꿈꾸었고 어려움을 극복하기 위해 열심히 노력했다.

6 Katherine Johnson은 이 영화에서 세 명의 '숨겨진 인물들' 중 한 명이었다.

7 그녀는 열심히 일했고 수학에서 재능을 보였으며, 그녀의 상사인 Al Harrison은 그녀의 능력을 알아차렸다.

8 어느 날, 그는 Katherine이 너무 오래 자리를 비웠을 때 화가 났다.

9 Al은 Katherine에게 어디에 갔었는지 물었고 그녀는 대답했다.

10 Katherine: 화장실요.

11 이 건물에는 유색 인종 전용 화장실이 없어요.

12 저는 단지 화장실을 사용하기 위해 반 마일을 달려가야 해요.

13 이 말을 듣고서, 나는 그녀가 정말로 안됐다고 느꼈다.

14 However, I was glad that she _____ _____ _____ _____ to the manager about the problem.

    A. to   B. had   C. talk   D. courage

15 This _____ Al Harrison _____ _____ the "Colored Ladies Room" _____.

    A. sign   B. break   C. down   D. made

16 Mary Jackson was the _____ I liked the _____ of the _____.

    A. most   B. character   C. three

17 She wanted to _____ more about rocket science, but she _____ _____ _____ go to a white school.

    A. allowed   B. learn   C. to   D. wasn't

18 So, she asked a _____ to _____ _____ _____.

    A. permission   B. judge   C. her   D. give

19 Mary: I _____ _____ the _____ of my _____.

    A. color   B. can't   C. skin   D. change

20 So ... I have _____ _____ _____ _____ be the first.

    A. but   B. no   C. to   D. choice

21 Your Honor, of all the _____ you'll hear today, _____ one will _____ in a hundred _____?

    A. matter   B. cases   C. years   D. which

22 _____ _____ will _____ you the "first?"

    A. one   B. which   C. make

23 The judge was _____ by _____ she said and _____ gave her _____.

    A. what   B. permission   C. impressed   D. finally

24 Mary _____ _____ for _____ and for _____ African-Americans.

    A. other   B. stood   C. herself   D. up

25 That was _____ _____ _____ in the movie.

    A. most   B. what   C. me   D. impressed

26 Finally, she became the _____ _____ _____ _____ at NASA.

    A. engineer   B. first   C. woman   D. African-American

---

14 그러나 나는 그 문제에 대해 상사에게 말한 그녀의 용기를 보고 기뻤다.

15 이것은 Al Harrison으로 하여금 '유색 여성 화장실' 표지판을 부수게 만들었다.

16 Mary Jackson은 셋 중에 가장 나의 마음에 드는 인물이었다.

17 그녀는 로켓 공학에 대해 더 많이 배우고 싶었지만 백인 학교에 다니는 것이 허락되지 않았다.

18 그래서 그녀는 판사에게 허락해 달라고 요청했다.

19 Mary: 저는 제 피부색을 바꿀 수 없어요.

20 그래서… 저는 '최초'가 되는 것 이외에는 선택이 없어요.

21 판사님, 당신이 오늘 들을 모든 사건 중에서, 백 년 뒤에 어느 것이 중요할까요?

22 어느 것이 판사님을 '최초'로 만들까요?

23 판사는 그녀가 말한 것에 감명을 받고 마침내 그녀에게 허락해 주었다.

24 Mary는 그녀 자신과 다른 아프리카계 미국인들의 편에 섰다.

25 그것은 영화에서 나를 가장 감동하게 한 점이었다.

26 마침내 그녀는 NASA에서 최초의 아프리카계 미국인 여성 공학자가 되었다.

27 **Dorothy Vaughan** was _____ _____ "_____ _____."
A. last   B. the   C. figure   D. hidden

28 When IBM computers were _____ at NASA in 1961, she was _____ the "human computers" _____ _____ their jobs.
A. installed   B. lose   C. would   D. worried

29 She studied a _____ _____ _____, FORTRAN.
A. programming   B. new   C. language

30 She also _____ _____ to her team _____.
A. members   B. taught   C. it

31 Later, when she was _____ _____ be the leader of a new IBM team, she _____ a _____.
A. suggestion   B. asked   C. made   D. to

32 **Dorothy:** I'm not _____ the _____ if I can't _____ my ladies _____ me.
A. bring   B. accepting   C. offer   D. with

33 We _____ a _____ of people _____ _____ that machine.
A. lot   B. program   C. need   D. to

34 I _____ _____ it _____.
A. do   B. can't   C. alone

35 My girls _____ _____.
A. ready   B. are

36 _____ _____ Dorothy, her team members could _____ _____.
A. to   B. become   C. thanks   D. programmers

37 She wasn't _____ _____ change and used it _____ a _____.
A. chance   B. afraid   C. as   D. of

38 That's _____ I _____ _____ _____ from her.
A. need   B. what   C. learn   D. to

39 Watching this movie, I could learn _____ _____ _____ _____ in life.
A. to   B. challenges   C. face   D. how

40 I _____ _____ the _____ and _____ of Katherine, Mary, and Dorothy.
A. tears   B. won't   C. laughter   D. forget

27 Dorothy Vaughan은 마지막 '히든 피겨(숨은 인물)'였다.

28 1961년 NASA에 IBM 컴퓨터가 설치되었을 때, 그녀는 '인간 컴퓨터(계산원)'들이 직업을 잃을까봐 걱정했다.

29 그녀는 새로운 프로그래밍 언어인 포트란을 공부했다.

30 그녀는 또한 그것을 그녀의 팀원들에게 가르쳤다.

31 나중에 그녀가 새 IBM 팀의 리더가 되도록 요청받았을 때, 그녀는 제안했다.

32 Dorothy: 저는 저의 여성 팀원들을 데려올 수 없다면 그 제안을 받아들이지 않겠습니다.

33 그 기계의 프로그램을 짜기 위해서는 많은 사람이 필요합니다.

34 저는 그것을 혼자 할 수 없습니다.

35 제 여성 팀원들은 준비가 되어 있습니다.

36 Dorothy 덕분에, 그녀의 팀원들은 프로그래머가 될 수 있었다.

37 그녀는 변화를 두려워하지 않고 그것을 기회로 이용했다.

38 그것이 내가 그녀에게서 배울 필요가 있는 점이다.

39 이 영화를 보면서, 나는 삶에서 어떻게 도전에 직면해야 하는지 배울 수 있었다.

40 나는 Katherine, Mary, 그리고 Dorothy의 눈물과 웃음을 잊지 않을 것이다.

※ 다음 우리말과 일치하도록 빈칸에 알맞은 말을 쓰시오.

1 The _____ _____ of NASA

2 I _____ the movie *Hidden Figures* _____ _____.

3 It was a movie about three _____ _____ who _____ _____ NASA.

4 They began their career _____ _____ _____ "human computers."

5 However, they dreamed _____ _____ _____ _____ _____ at NASA and tried hard _____ _____ _____ _____.

6 **Katherine Johnson** was one of the _____ " _____ " in this movie.

7 She worked hard and _____ _____ _____ _____ math, and her manager Al Harrison _____ _____ _____.

8 One day, he _____ _____ when Katherine _____ _____ from her desk for too long.

9 Al asked _____ _____ _____ _____, and she answered.

10 **Katherine:** The _____.

11 _____ are no _____ _____ in this building.

12 I have to run _____ _____ away _____ _____ _____ the bathroom.

13 _____ _____, I _____ really _____ for her.

14 _____, I was glad that she _____ _____ _____ _____ to the manager about the problem.

15 This made Al Harrison _____ _____ the "Colored Ladies Room" sign.

16 **Mary Jackson** was the _____ I liked the most of the three.

17 She wanted to learn more about rocket science, but she _____ _____ _____ go to a _____.

18 So, she asked a judge _____ _____ _____ _____.

19 **Mary:** I _____ _____ the color of my _____.

---

1 NASA의 숨겨진 인물들

2 나는 지난 주말에 〈히든 피겨스〉라는 영화를 보았다.

3 그것은 NASA에서 일했던 세 명의 아프리카계 미국인 여성들에 대한 영화였다.

4 그들은 1960년대에 '인간 컴퓨터(계산원)'로 일을 시작했다.

5 하지만 그들은 NASA에서 우주 전문가가 되기를 꿈꾸었고 어려움을 극복하기 위해 열심히 노력했다.

6 Katherine Johnson은 이 영화에서 세 명의 '숨겨진 인물들' 중 한 명이었다.

7 그녀는 열심히 일했고 수학에서 재능을 보였으며, 그녀의 상사인 Al Harrison은 그녀의 능력을 알아차렸다.

8 어느 날, 그는 Katherine이 너무 오래 자리를 비웠을 때 화가 났다.

9 Al은 Katherine에게 어디에 갔었는지 물었고 그녀는 대답했다.

10 Katherine: 화장실요.

11 이 건물에는 유색 인종 전용 화장실이 없어요.

12 저는 단지 화장실을 사용하기 위해 반 마일을 달려가야 해요.

13 이 말을 듣고서, 나는 그녀가 정말로 안됐다고 느꼈다.

14 그러나 나는 그 문제에 대해 상사에게 말한 그녀의 용기를 보고 기뻤다.

15 이것은 Al Harrison으로 하여금 '유색 여성 화장실' 표지판을 부수게 만들었다.

16 Mary Jackson은 셋 중에 가장 나의 마음에 드는 인물이었다.

17 그녀는 로켓 공학에 대해 더 많이 배우고 싶었지만 백인 학교에 다니는 것이 허락되지 않았다.

18 그래서 그녀는 판사에게 허락해 달라고 요청했다.

19 Mary: 저는 제 피부색을 바꿀 수 없어요.

20 So ... I _____ _____ _____ _____ _____ be the first.

21 Your Honor, of all the _____ you'll hear today, which one will matter _____ _____ _____ _____?

22 _____ _____ will make you the "first?"

23 The judge was _____ by _____ she said and _____ _____ her _____.

24 Mary _____ _____ _____ _____ and for _____ African-Americans.

25 That was _____ _____ _____ _____ in the movie.

26 Finally, she became the _____ _____ _____ _____ at NASA.

27 Dorothy Vaughan was _____ _____ "hidden figure."

28 When IBM computers _____ _____ at NASA in 1961, she was worried the "human computers" _____ _____ their jobs.

29 She studied a _____ _____ _____, FORTRAN.

30 She also _____ _____ to her team members.

31 Later, when she _____ _____ _____ be the leader of a new IBM team, she _____ a _____.

32 Dorothy: _____ _____ _____ _____ the _____ if I can't bring my ladies with me.

33 We need a _____ of people _____ _____ that machine.

34 I can't do it _____.

35 My girls _____ _____.

36 _____ _____ Dorothy, her team members could become programmers.

37 She _____ _____ _____ change and used it _____ _____ _____.

38 That's _____ _____ _____ _____ _____ from her.

39 _____ this movie, I could learn _____ _____ _____ _____ in life.

40 I won't forget the _____ _____ _____ of Katherine, Mary, and Dorothy.

20 그래서… 저는 '최초'가 되는 것 이외에는 선택이 없어요.

21 판사님, 당신이 오늘 들을 모든 사건 중에서, 백 년 뒤에 어느 것이 중요할까요?

22 어느 것이 판사님을 '최초'로 만들까요?

23 판사는 그녀가 말한 것에 감명을 받고 마침내 그녀에게 허락해 주었다.

24 Mary는 그녀 자신과 다른 아프리카계 미국인들의 편에 섰다.

25 그것은 영화에서 나를 가장 감동하게 한 점이었다.

26 마침내 그녀는 NASA에서 최초의 아프리카계 미국인 여성 공학자가 되었다.

27 Dorothy Vaughan은 마지막 '히든 피겨(숨은 인물)'였다.

28 1961년 NASA에 IBM 컴퓨터가 설치되었을 때, 그녀는 '인간 컴퓨터(계산원)'들이 직업을 잃을까봐 걱정했다.

29 그녀는 새로운 프로그래밍 언어인 포트란을 공부했다.

30 그녀는 또한 그것을 그녀의 팀원들에게 가르쳤다.

31 나중에 그녀가 새 IBM 팀의 리더가 되도록 요청받았을 때, 그녀는 제안했다.

32 Dorothy: 저는 저의 여성 팀원들을 데려올 수 없다면 그 제안을 받아들이지 않겠습니다.

33 그 기계의 프로그램을 짜기 위해서는 많은 사람이 필요합니다.

34 저는 그것을 혼자 할 수 없습니다.

35 제 여성 팀원들은 준비가 되어 있습니다.

36 Dorothy 덕분에, 그녀의 팀원들은 프로그래머가 될 수 있었다.

37 그녀는 변화를 두려워하지 않고 그것을 기회로 이용했다.

38 그것이 내가 그녀에게서 배울 필요가 있는 점이다.

39 이 영화를 보면서, 나는 삶에서 어떻게 도전에 직면해야 하는지 배울 수 있었다.

40 나는 Katherine, Mary, 그리고 Dorothy의 눈물과 웃음을 잊지 않을 것이다.

※ 다음 문장을 우리말로 쓰시오.

1 The Hidden Figures of NASA
➡ _____

2 I watched the movie *Hidden Figures* last weekend.
➡ _____

3 It was a movie about three African-American women who worked at NASA.
➡ _____

4 They began their career in the 1960s as "human computers."
➡ _____

5 However, they dreamed of becoming space experts at NASA and tried hard to get over difficulties.
➡ _____

6 Katherine Johnson was one of the three "hidden figures" in this movie.
➡ _____

7 She worked hard and showed a talent in math, and her manager Al Harrison recognized her ability.
➡ _____

8 One day, he got upset when Katherine was missing from her desk for too long.
➡ _____

9 Al asked where Katherine had been, and she answered.
➡ _____

10 Katherine: The bathroom.
➡ _____

11 There are no COLORED bathrooms in this building.
➡ _____

12 I have to run half a mile away just to use the bathroom.
➡ _____

13 Hearing this, I felt really sorry for her.
➡ _____

14 However, I was glad that she had courage to talk to the manager about the problem.
➡ _____

15 This made Al Harrison break down the "Colored Ladies Room" sign.
➡ _____

16 Mary Jackson was the character I liked the most of the three.
➡ _____

17 She wanted to learn more about rocket science, but she wasn't allowed to go to a white school.
➡ _____

18 So, she asked a judge to give her permission.
➡ _____

19 Mary: I can't change the color of my skin.
➡ _____

20 So ... I have no choice but to be the first.
➡ _____

21 Your Honor, of all the cases you'll hear today, which one will matter in a hundred years?
➡ _____

22 Which one will make you the "first?"
➡ _____

23 The judge was impressed by what she said and finally gave her permission.
➡ _____

24 Mary stood up for herself and for other African-Americans.
➡ _____

25 That was what impressed me most in the movie.
➡ _____

26 Finally, she became the first African-American woman engineer at NASA.
➡ _____

27 Dorothy Vaughan was the last "hidden figure."
➡ _____

28 When IBM computers were installed at NASA in 1961, she was worried the "human computers" would lose their jobs.
➡ _____

29 She studied a new programming language, FORTRAN.
➡ _____

30 She also taught it to her team members.
➡ _____

31 Later, when she was asked to be the leader of a new IBM team, she made a suggestion.
➡ _____

32 Dorothy: I'm not accepting the offer if I can't bring my ladies with me.
➡ _____

33 We need a lot of people to program that machine.
➡ _____

34 I can't do it alone.
➡ _____

35 My girls are ready.
➡ _____

36 Thanks to Dorothy, her team members could become programmers.
➡ _____

37 She wasn't afraid of change and used it as a chance.
➡ _____

38 That's what I need to learn from her.
➡ _____

39 Watching this movie, I could learn how to face challenges in life.
➡ _____

40 I won't forget the tears and laughter of Katherine, Mary, and Dorothy.
➡ _____

※ 다음 괄호 안의 단어들을 우리말에 맞도록 바르게 배열하시오.

1 (Hidden / The / Figures / NASA / of)

➡ _____

2 (watched / I / movie / the / *Figures* / *Hidden* / weekend. / last)

➡ _____

3 (was / it / movie / a / three / about / women / African-American / worked / who / NASA. / at)

➡ _____

4 (began / they / career / their / the / in / 1960s / computers." / as / "human)

➡ _____

5 (they / however, / dreamed / becoming / of / experts / space / NASA / at / tried / and / to / hard / get / difficulties. / over)

➡ _____

_____

6 (Johnson / Katherine / one / was / of / three / the / figures" / "hidden / this / in / movie.)

➡ _____

7 (worked / she / hard / showed / and / talent / a / math, / in / her / and / AI / manager / recognized / Harrison / ability. / her)

➡ _____

_____

8 (day, / one / got / he / when / upset / Katherine / missing / was / her / from / desk / too / for / long.)

➡ _____

_____

9 (asked / AI / Katherine / where / been, / had / she / and / answered.)

➡ _____

10 (Katherine: / bathroom. / the)

➡ _____

11 (are / there / COLORED / no / bathrooms / this / in / building.)

➡ _____

12 (have / I / run / to / a / half / away / mile / to / just / the / use / bathroom.)

➡ _____

13 (this, / hearing / felt / I / sorry / really / her. / for)

➡ _____

1 NASA의 숨겨진 인물들

2 나는 지난 주말에 〈히든 피겨스〉라는 영화를 보았다.

3 그것은 NASA에서 일했던 세 명의 아프리카계 미국인 여성들에 대한 영화였다.

4 그들은 1960년대에 '인간 컴퓨터(계산원)'로 일을 시작했다.

5 하지만 그들은 NASA에서 우주 전문가가 되기를 꿈꾸었고 어려움을 극복하기 위해 열심히 노력했다.

6 Katherine Johnson은 이 영화에서 세 명의 '숨겨진 인물들' 중 한 명이었다.

7 그녀는 열심히 일했고 수학에서 재능을 보였으며, 그녀의 상사인 AI Harrison은 그녀의 능력을 알아차렸다.

8 어느 날, 그는 Katherine이 너무 오래 자리를 비웠을 때 화가 났다.

9 AI은 Katherine에게 어디에 갔었는지 물었고 그녀는 대답했다.

10 Katherine: 화장실요.

11 이 건물에는 유색 인종 전용 화장실이 없어요.

12 저는 단지 화장실을 사용하기 위해 반 마일을 달려가야 해요.

13 이 말을 듣고서, 나는 그녀가 정말로 안됐다고 느꼈다.

14 (I / however, / was / that / glad / had / she / to / courage / talk / to / the / about / manager / problem. / the)

➡ _____

_____

15 (made / this / Harrison / AI / down / break / the / Ladies / "Colored / sign. / Room")

➡ _____

16 (Jackson / Mary / the / was / character / liked / I / most / the / of / three. / the)

➡ _____

17 (wanted / she / learn / to / about / more / science, / rocket / she / but / allowed / wasn't / go / to / a / to / school. / white)

➡ _____

18 (she / so, / a / asked / to / judge / give / permission. / her)

➡ _____

19 (Mary: / can't / I / the / change / color / my / of / skin.)

➡ _____

20 (I / ... / so / no / have / but / choice / be / to / first. / the)

➡ _____

21 (Honor, / Your / all / of / cases / the / hear / you'll / today, / one / which / matter / will / a / in / years? / hundred)

➡ _____

_____

22 (one / which / make / will / the / you / "first?")

➡ _____

23 (judge / the / impressed / was / what / by / said / she / and / gave / finally / permission. / her)

➡ _____

24 (stood / Mary / for / up / and / herself / other / for / African-Americans.)

➡ _____

25 (was / that / impressed / what / most / me / the / in / movie.)

➡ _____

26 (she / finally, / the / became / first / woman / African-American / at / engineer / NASA.)

➡ _____

14 그러나 나는 그 문제에 대해 상사에게 말한 그녀의 용기를 보고 기뻤다.

15 이것은 AI Harrison으로 하여금 '유색 여성 화장실' 표지판을 부수게 만들었다.

16 Mary Jackson은 셋 중에 가장 나의 마음에 드는 인물이었다.

17 그녀는 로켓 공학에 대해 더 많이 배우고 싶었지만 백인 학교에 다니는 것이 허락되지 않았다.

18 그래서 그녀는 판사에게 허락해 달라고 요청했다.

19 Mary: 저는 제 피부색을 바꿀 수 없어요.

20 그래서… 저는 '최초'가 되는 것 이외에는 선택이 없어요.

21 판사님, 당신이 오늘 들을 모든 사건 중에서, 백 년 뒤에 어느 것이 중요할까요?

22 어느 것이 판사님을 '최초'로 만들까요?

23 판사는 그녀가 말한 것에 감명을 받고 마침내 그녀에게 허락해 주었다.

24 Mary는 그녀 자신과 다른 아프리카계 미국인들의 편에 섰다.

25 그것은 영화에서 나를 가장 감동하게 한 점이었다.

26 마침내 그녀는 NASA에서 최초의 아프리카계 미국인 여성 공학자가 되었다.

27 (Vaughan / Dorothy / the / was / last / figure." / "hidden)

➡ _____

28 (IBM / when / were / computers / at / installed / NASA / 1961, / in / was / she / the / worried / computers" / "human / lose / would / jobs. / their)

➡ _____

_____

29 (studied / she / a / new / language, / programming / FORTRAN.)

➡ _____

30 (also / she / it / taught / her / to / members. / team)

➡ _____

31 (when / later, / was / she / to / asked / be / leader / the / a / of / IBM / new / team, / made / she / suggestion. / a)

➡ _____

_____

32 (Dorothy: / not / I'm / accepting / offer / the / I / if / bring / can't / ladies / my / me. / with)

➡ _____

33 (need / we / lot / a / of / to / people / program / machine. / that)

➡ _____

34 (can't / I / it / do / alone.)

➡ _____

35 (girls / my / ready. / are)

➡ _____

36 (to / thanks / Dorothy, / team / her / could / members / programmers. / become)

➡ _____

37 (wasn't / she / of / afraid / and / change / used / as / it / chance. / a)

➡ _____

38 (what / that's / need / I / learn / to / her. / from)

➡ _____

39 (this / watchinig / movie, / could / I / how / learn / to / challenges / in / face / life.)

➡ _____

40 (won't / I / the / forget / tears / and / of / laughter / Katherine, / and / Mary, / Dorothy.)

➡ _____

27 Dorothy Vaughan은 마지막 '히든 피겨(숨은 인물)'였다.

28 1961년 NASA에 IBM 컴퓨터가 설치되었을 때, 그녀는 '인간 컴퓨터(계산원)'들이 직업을 잃을까봐 걱정했다.

29 그녀는 새로운 프로그래밍 언어인 포트란을 공부했다.

30 그녀는 또한 그것을 그녀의 팀원들에게 가르쳤다.

31 나중에 그녀가 새 IBM 팀의 리더가 되도록 요청받았을 때, 그녀는 제안했다.

32 Dorothy: 저는 저의 여성 팀원들을 데려올 수 없다면 그 제안을 받아들이지 않겠습니다.

33 그 기계의 프로그램을 짜기 위해서는 많은 사람이 필요합니다.

34 저는 그것을 혼자 할 수 없습니다.

35 제 여성 팀원들은 준비가 되어 있습니다.

36 Dorothy 덕분에, 그녀의 팀원들은 프로그래머가 될 수 있었다.

37 그녀는 변화를 두려워하지 않고 그것을 기회로 이용했다.

38 그것이 내가 그녀에게서 배울 필요가 있는 점이다.

39 이 영화를 보면서, 나는 삶에서 어떻게 도전에 직면해야 하는지 배울 수 있었다.

40 나는 Katherine, Mary, 그리고 Dorothy의 눈물과 웃음을 잊지 않을 것이다.

※ 다음 우리말을 영어로 쓰시오.

1 NASA의 숨겨진 인물들
➡ _____

2 나는 지난 주말에 〈히든 피겨스〉라는 영화를 보았다.
➡ _____

3 그것은 NASA에서 일했던 세 명의 아프리카계 미국인 여성들에 대한 영화였다.
➡ _____

4 그들은 1960년대에 '인간 컴퓨터(계산원)'로 일을 시작했다.
➡ _____

5 하지만 그들은 NASA에서 우주 전문가가 되기를 꿈꾸었고 어려움을 극복하기 위해 열심히 노력했다.
➡ _____

6 Katherine Johnson은 이 영화에서 세 명의 '숨겨진 인물들' 중 한 명이었다.
➡ _____

7 그녀는 열심히 일했고 수학에서 재능을 보였으며, 그녀의 상사인 Al Harrison은 그녀의 능력을 알아차렸다.
➡ _____

8 어느 날, 그는 Katherine이 너무 오래 자리를 비웠을 때 화가 났다.
➡ _____

9 Al은 Katherine에게 어디에 갔었는지 물었고 그녀는 대답했다.
➡ _____

10 Katherine: 화장실요.
➡ _____

11 이 건물에는 유색 인종 전용 화장실이 없어요.
➡ _____

12 저는 단지 화장실을 사용하기 위해 반 마일을 달려가야 해요.
➡ _____

13 이 말을 듣고서, 나는 그녀가 정말로 안됐다고 느꼈다.
➡ _____

14 그러나 나는 그 문제에 대해 상사에게 말한 그녀의 용기를 보고 기뻤다.
➡ _____

15 이것은 Al Harrison으로 하여금 '유색 여성 화장실' 표지판을 부수게 만들었다.
➡ _____

16 Mary Jackson은 셋 중에 가장 나의 마음에 드는 인물이었다.
➡ _____

17 그녀는 로켓 공학에 대해 더 많이 배우고 싶었지만 백인 학교에 다니는 것이 허락되지 않았다.
➡ _____

18 그래서 그녀는 판사에게 허락해 달라고 요청했다.
➡ _____

19 Mary: 저는 제 피부색을 바꿀 수 없어요.
➡ _____

20 그래서… 저는 '최초'가 되는 것 이외에는 선택이 없어요.
➡ _____

21 판사님, 당신이 오늘 들을 모든 사건 중에서, 백 년 뒤에 어느 것이 중요할까요?
➡ _____

22 어느 것이 판사님을 '최초'로 만들까요?
➡ _____

23 판사는 그녀가 말한 것에 감명을 받고 마침내 그녀에게 허락해 주었다.
➡ _____

24 Mary는 그녀 자신과 다른 아프리카계 미국인들의 편에 섰다.
➡ _____

25 그것은 영화에서 나를 가장 감동하게 한 점이었다.
➡ _____

26 마침내 그녀는 NASA에서 최초의 아프리카계 미국인 여성 공학자가 되었다.
➡ _____

27 Dorothy Vaughan은 마지막 '히든 피겨(숨은 인물)'였다.
➡ _____

28 1961년 NASA에 IBM 컴퓨터가 설치되었을 때, 그녀는 '인간 컴퓨터(계산원)'들이 직업을 잃을까 봐 걱정했다.
➡ _____

29 그녀는 새로운 프로그래밍 언어인 포트란을 공부했다.
➡ _____

30 그녀는 또한 그것을 그녀의 팀원들에게 가르쳤다.
➡ _____

31 나중에 그녀가 새 IBM 팀의 리더가 되도록 요청받았을 때, 그녀는 제안했다.
➡ _____

32 Dorothy: 저는 저의 여성 팀원들을 데려올 수 없다면 그 제안을 받아들이지 않겠습니다.
➡ _____

33 그 기계의 프로그램을 짜기 위해서는 많은 사람이 필요합니다.
➡ _____

34 저는 그것을 혼자 할 수 없습니다.
➡ _____

35 제 여성 팀원들은 준비가 되어 있습니다.
➡ _____

36 Dorothy 덕분에, 그녀의 팀원들은 프로그래머가 될 수 있었다.
➡ _____

37 그녀는 변화를 두려워하지 않고 그것을 기회로 이용했다.
➡ _____

38 그것이 내가 그녀에게서 배울 필요가 있는 점이다.
➡ _____

39 이 영화를 보면서, 나는 삶에서 어떻게 도전에 직면해야 하는지 배울 수 있었다.
➡ _____

40 나는 Katherine, Mary, 그리고 Dorothy의 눈물과 웃음을 잊지 않을 것이다.
➡ _____

※ 다음 우리말과 일치하도록 빈칸에 알맞은 말을 쓰시오.

Express Yourself C

1. 1. I _____ _____ _____ _____ the baker.

2. He _____ _____ about his job, _____ some cupcakes.

3. I will not forget _____ _____ _____, "Make _____
   _____ _____ _____."

4. 2. I _____ _____ _____ _____ _____ the actor.

5. He _____ _____ _____ his job, _____ _____ _____
   _____ .

6. I will not forget _____ _____ _____, "You can be _____
   _____ _____."

After You Read A

1. **Katherine Johnson:** I _____ _____ _____ _____ _____
   the "Colored Ladies Room" _____ .

2. **Mary Jackson:** I _____ _____ _____ _____ _____
   me _____ _____ at a white school.

3. **Dorothy Vaughan:** I studied a new programming language _____
   _____ _____ _____ .

Link to the World

1. Q1 _____ do you do _____ _____ _____ ?

2. A1 I _____ _____ _____ _____ and desserts.

3. Q2 What _____ _____ about _____ _____ ?

4. A2 I have so _____ _____ _____ _____ _____ than
   cooking.

5. I _____ _____ _____ _____ _____ and vegetables
   _____ _____ .

6. I also _____ _____ _____ and _____ _____ _____
   _____ .

7. Q3 _____ you _____ _____ your job?

8. A3 Yes, I am. It's a _____ _____ , but I love _____ _____
   _____ .

9. I _____ _____ , _____ _____ _____ my dishes.

---

1. 1. 저는 제빵사와 즐거운 시간을 보냈습니다.
2. 그는 컵케이크에 장식하며 그의 직업에 대해 말해 주었습니다,
3. 저는 그가 말한 것을 잊지 않을 것입니다. "가족이 좋아하게 될 것을 만드세요."
4. 2. 저는 배우와 즐거운 시간을 보냈습니다.
5. 그는 자신의 유명한 대사를 말하면서 그의 직업에 대해 말해 주었습니다.
6. 저는 그가 말한 것을 잊지 않을 것입니다. "당신은 자신이 연기하는 것이 될 수 있습니다."

1. Katherine Johnson: 나는 나의 상사로 하여금 '유색 여성 화장실' 표지판을 부수게 만들었다.
2. Mary Jackson: 나는 판사에게 백인 학교에서 공부하도록 허락해 달라고 요청했다.
3. Dorothy Vaughan: 나는 변화에 대비해 준비하기 위하여 새로운 프로그래밍 언어를 공부했다.

1. Q1. 당신은 이 식당에서 무엇을 합니까?
2. A1. 저는 다양한 이탈리아 요리와 후식을 만듭니다.
3. Q2. 당신 직업의 어려운 점은 무엇입니까?
4. A2. 저는 요리 외에도 할 일이 많습니다.
5. 저는 매일 신선한 고기와 채소를 사야 합니다.
6. 또한 설거지하고 주방을 깨끗이 유지합니다.
7. Q3. 당신은 당신의 직업에 만족합니까?
8. A3. 네, 그렇습니다. 힘든 직업이지만, 저는 제가 하는 일을 좋아합니다.
9. 저는 사람들이 제 요리를 즐기는 것을 보면서 자부심을 느낍니다.

※ 다음 우리말을 영어로 쓰시오.

Express Yourself C

1. 1. 저는 제빵사와 즐거운 시간을 보냈습니다.
   ➡ _____

2. 그는 컵케이크에 장식하며 그의 직업에 대해 말해 주었습니다.
   ➡ _____

3. 저는 그가 말한 것을 잊지 않을 것입니다. "가족이 좋아하게 될 것을 만드세요."
   ➡ _____

4. 2. 저는 배우와 즐거운 시간을 보냈습니다.
   ➡ _____

5. 그는 자신의 유명한 대사를 말하면서 그의 직업에 대해 말해 주었습니다.
   ➡ _____

6. 저는 그가 말한 것을 잊지 않을 것입니다. "당신은 자신이 연기하는 것이 될 수 있습니다."
   ➡ _____

After You Read A

1. Katherine Johnson: 나는 나의 상사로 하여금 '유색 여성 화장실' 표지판을 부수게 만들었다.
   ➡ _____

2. Mary Jackson: 나는 판사에게 백인 학교에서 공부하도록 허락해 달라고 요청했다.
   ➡ _____

3. Dorothy Vaughan: 나는 변화에 대비해 준비하기 위하여 새로운 프로그래밍 언어를 공부했다.
   ➡ _____

Link to the World

1. Q1. 당신은 이 식당에서 무엇을 합니까?
   ➡ _____

2. A1. 저는 다양한 이탈리아 요리와 후식을 만듭니다.
   ➡ _____

3. Q2. 당신 직업의 어려운 점은 무엇입니까?
   ➡ _____

4. A2. 저는 요리 외에도 할 일이 많습니다.
   ➡ _____

5. 저는 매일 신선한 고기와 채소를 사야 합니다.
   ➡ _____

6. 또한 설거지하고 주방을 깨끗이 유지합니다.
   ➡ _____

7. Q3. 당신은 당신의 직업에 만족합니까?
   ➡ _____

8. A3. 네, 그렇습니다. 힘든 직업이지만, 저는 제가 하는 일을 좋아합니다.
   ➡ _____

9. 저는 사람들이 제 요리를 즐기는 것을 보면서 자부심을 느낍니다.
   ➡ _____

※ 다음 영어를 우리말로 쓰시오.

01 anything _____

02 believe _____

03 cart _____

04 wave _____

05 delicious _____

06 enough _____

07 fairy _____

08 fat _____

09 people _____

10 bright _____

11 find _____

12 fool _____

13 chance _____

14 monster _____

15 water _____

16 clothes _____

17 hit _____

18 inside _____

19 instead _____

20 save _____

21 kill _____

22 lesson _____

23 matter _____

24 wheel _____

25 serve _____

26 witch _____

27 mess _____

28 princess _____

29 frog _____

30 rest _____

31 shout _____

32 stuck _____

33 unhappily _____

34 worry _____

35 from now on _____

36 hand in hand _____

37 to oneself _____

38 pick up _____

39 run away _____

40 on one's way to _____

41 be better off _____

42 by the name of _____

43 give it a try _____

※ 다음 우리말을 영어로 쓰시오.

01 수레	22 (손을) 흔들다
02 괴물	23 중요하다, 문제되다
03 맛있는	24 기회
04 충분히	25 ~조차도; 훨씬
05 믿다	26 나머지
06 요정	27 외치다
07 통통한, 살찐	28 연못
08 마녀	29 불행하게
09 엉망진창	30 침이 고이다, 침을 흘리다
10 구하다	31 교훈, 단원
11 꼼짝 못 하는, 움직일 수 없는	32 공주
12 밝은, 눈부신	33 걱정하다
13 바보, 멍청이	34 웃긴
14 백성, 국민	35 손에 손을 잡고
15 대접하다	36 더 이상 ~ 않다
16 치다, 때리다	37 ~에 가는 길(도중)에
17 안에, 안으로	38 더 잘 살다
18 여전히, 아직도	39 수백 개의 ~
19 대신에	40 지금부터 죽
20 옷, 의복	41 도망가다, 달아나다
21 죽이다	42 뛰어다니다
	43 혼자

※ 다음 영영풀이에 알맞은 단어를 <보기>에서 골라 쓴 후, 우리말 뜻을 쓰시오.

1 _____ : the part of something that remains: _____

2 _____ : to say something very loudly: _____

3 _____ : very good to eat or drink: _____

4 _____ : not able to move anywhere: _____

5 _____ : learned through experience: _____

6 _____ : in stories, a woman who has magical powers: _____

7 _____ : a vehicle with wheels that is pulled by an animal: _____

8 _____ : to ask someone to come to your house, to a party, etc.: _____

9 _____ : an imaginary creature that is large, ugly, and frightening: _____

10 _____ : an area of water that is surrounded by land and that is smaller than a
          lake: _____

11 _____ : the daughter of a king or queen, or one of their close female relatives:

          _____

12 _____ : a small, green animal with long back legs for jumping, that lives in or
          near water: _____

13 _____ : a circular object fixed under a vehicle so that it moves smoothly over the
          ground: _____

14 _____ : an imaginary creature like a small person with wings who has magic
          powers: _____

15 _____ : to put your hand up and move it from side to side in order to attract
          someone's attention or to say goodbye: _____

16 _____ : to touch something or someone quickly and with force, usually hurting
          or damaging something: _____

frog	wheel	cart	rest
hit	fairy	delicious	monster
princess	pond	invite	stuck
wave	lesson	shout	witch

※ 다음 우리말과 일치하도록 빈칸에 알맞은 것을 골라 쓰시오.

1 The _____ _____ _____
 A. Frog   B. Continued   C. Prince

2 _____ : Frog Prince, _____ , Witch 1, Witch 2, _____
 A. Fairy   B. Princess   C. Characters

3 _____ **1:** _____ a _____
 A. in   B. Scene   C. room

4 *(Prince comes* _____ , _____ _____ .)
 A. in   B. around   C. jumping

5 **Princess:** _____ _____ _____ , honey.
 A. jumping   B. stop   C. around

6 **Prince:** Well, I _____ _____ _____ .
 A. can't   B. just   C. stop

7 **Princess:** You're not _____ _____ _____ .
 A. anymore   B. frog   C. a

8 **Prince:** What's _____ with you? You don't go _____ to the _____ _____ days.
 A. wrong   B. these   C. down   D. pond

9 **Princess:** I don't like it when you jump _____ in the room. Go out to _____ _____ and _____ our people.
 A. save   B. around   C. monsters   D. kill

10 **Prince:** I don't want to go out and kill anything. I just _____ like running _____ . *(Picking up a book)* Listen! "They lived happily ever _____ . The end." I'm living my life _____ the book says, but we're not happy. What's the problem?
 A. away   B. as   C. after   D. feel

11 **Princess:** What's the problem? There are _____ _____ problems! Sometimes I think we were _____ _____ when you were still a frog.
 A. better   B. hundreds   C. off   D. of

12 **Prince:** _____ a frog .... Yes! That's _____ ! *(Goes _____)*
 A. out   B. still   C. it

13 _____ **2:** _____ the _____
 A. mountain   B. Scene   C. on

14 **Prince:** *(To* _____ *)* I need to find the _____ , who will _____ me _____ into a frog. *(Shouting)* Ms. Witch, Ms. Witch. Where are you? Please help me!
 A. back   B. himself   C. turn   D. witch

15 **Witch 1:** *(Coming* _____ _____ *the house)* Hi, Prince. _____ are you _____ ?
 A. of   B. how   C. out   D. feeling

1 계속된 개구리 왕자

2 등장인물: 개구리 왕자, 공주, 마녀 1, 마녀 2, 요정

3 장면 1: 방 안에서

4 (왕자가 이리저리 뛰어다니며 등장한다.)

5 공주: 여보, 이리저리 뛰어다니지 마세요.

6 왕자: 저, 나는 단지 멈출 수 없을 뿐이에요.

7 공주: 당신은 이제 개구리가 아니에요.

8 왕자: 당신한테 무슨 문제가 있어요? 요즘 당신은 연못으로 내려가지도 않잖아요.

9 공주: 나는 당신이 방 안에서 이리저리 뛰어다니는 게 마음에 안 들어요. 나가서 괴물들을 죽이고 우리 백성을 구하세요.

10 왕자: 나는 밖에 나가서 아무것도 죽이고 싶지 않아요. 나는 단지 멀리 뛰어다니고 싶을 뿐이오. (책을 집어 들고) 들어 봐요! "그들은 그 후로 행복하게 살았다. 끝." 나는 책에서 말한 것처럼 내 인생을 살고 있지만, 우리는 행복하지 않아요. 뭐가 문제일까요?

11 공주: 뭐가 문제냐고요? 수백 가지 문제가 있어요! 가끔 나는 당신이 아직 개구리일 때 더 잘 살지 않았나 생각해요.

12 왕자: 아직 개구리라 …. 그래! 바로 그거요! (퇴장한다.)

13 장면 2: 산속에서

14 왕자: (혼잣말로) 나는 마녀를 찾아야 해. 그녀가 나를 다시 개구리로 바꿔 줄 거야. (소리치며) 마녀님, 마녀님. 어디 계세요? 저 좀 도와주세요!

15 마녀 1: (집 밖으로 나오며) 안녕, 왕자님. 기분이 어때요?

16 **Prince:** I'm glad to _____ you. I'm the Frog Prince. I hope you can turn me back _____ a frog so I can live happily _____ _____.

A. ever   B. into   C. meet   D. after

17 **Witch 1:** Frog Prince, you say? That's funny. You don't look _____ a frog. Well, it doesn't _____. If you're a prince, you're a prince. And I won't _____ you _____ Snow White. Here, eat the rest of this apple.

A. matter   B. like   C. save   D. let

18 **Prince:** No, thank you. That's not _____ I _____! *(Runs _____)*

A. away   B. what   C. want

19 *(Prince and Witch 2 _____ _____.)*

A. in   B. come

20 **Prince:** Ms. Witch, Ms. Witch. _____ are you? _____ _____ me! I'm the Frog ....

A. help   B. where   C. please

21 **Witch 2:** _____ you're a _____, I'm the King of _____.

A. frog   B. if   C. France

22 **Prince:** No, I'm not a frog. I'm the Frog Prince. But I need a witch to _____ me _____ into a frog so I can _____ _____ ever after. Can you do it?

A. happily   B. turn   C. live   D. back

23 **Witch 2:** _____ talk about it _____. I will _____ you a _____ lunch. Come in.

A. serve   B. inside   C. delicious   D. let's

24 **Prince:** Thank you for inviting me. Oh, this house is _____ _____ cookies and candies. Wait a minute. Do you know any children _____ the _____ of Hansel and Gretel?

A. by   B. made   C. of   D. name

25 **Witch 2:** Yes, Prince, I do. *(_____ her mouth _____)* They are not _____ _____ yet, but you are ....

A. enough   B. watering   C. with   D. fat

26 *(Prince _____ _____ and _____ a fairy.)*

A. finds   B. runs   C. away

27 **Prince:** I'm glad to meet you, Ms. Fairy. I am the Frog Prince. _____ you _____ me back into a frog _____ I can live happily ever _____?

A. so   B. could   C. after   D. turn

16 왕자: 당신을 만나서 기뻐요. 저는 개구리 왕자예요. 저는 당신이 저를 다시 개구리로 바꿔줘서 제가 앞으로 행복하게 살 수 있게 되기를 원해요.

17 마녀 1: 개구리 왕자라고 했어요? 그거 웃기는군요. 당신은 개구리처럼 보이지 않아요. 음, 그건 중요하지 않아요. 당신이 왕자라면 왕자인 거죠. 그리고 나는 당신이 백설공주를 구하도록 놔두지 않을 거예요. 여기, 이 사과의 나머지를 먹어요.

18 왕자: 고맙지만 됐어요. 그건 제가 원하는 게 아니에요! (도망간다)

19 (왕자와 마녀 2가 등장한다.)

20 왕자: 마녀님, 마녀님. 어디 계세요? 저 좀 도와주세요! 저는 개구리 ….

21 마녀 2: 당신이 개구리라면 나는 프랑스의 왕이에요.

22 왕자: 아니요, 저는 개구리가 아니에요. 저는 개구리 왕자예요. 하지만 저를 다시 개구리로 바꿔 줘서 제가 앞으로 행복하게 살 수 있게 해 줄 마녀가 필요해요. 그렇게 해 주실 수 있나요?

23 마녀 2: 안에서 그것에 관해 이야기해 봅시다. 내가 당신에게 맛있는 점심을 대접할게요. 들어와요.

24 왕자: 저를 초대해 주셔서 감사합니다. 오, 이 집은 과자와 사탕으로 만들어져 있네요. 잠깐만요. 당신은 헨젤과 그레텔이라는 이름의 아이들을 혹시 알아요?

25 마녀 2: 그래요, 왕자님, 알고 있어요. (그녀가 군침을 흘리면서) 그 애들은 아직 충분히 살이 찌지 않았지만, 당신은 ….

26 (왕자는 도망치다가 요정을 발견한다.)

27 왕자: 만나게 되어 기쁩니다, 요정님. 저는 개구리 왕자예요. 저를 다시 개구리로 바꿔 앞으로 행복하게 살 수 있게 해 주실 수 있나요?

28 **Fairy:** Well, I'm _____ my _____ to see Cinderella, but I'll give it a _____. It's my first time, you know. *(Fairy turns Prince _____ a wheel.)*

    A. try   B. into   C. way   D. on

29 **Fairy:** Oops! Sorry, but don't _____. Everything _____ _____ _____.

    A. worry   B. okay   C. be   D. will

30 **Prince:** *(To himself)* Oh, _____ a _____ I've been! I want to be sitting at home with the Princess, living happily ever after. But instead, I'm _____ here under this cart and I'll live _____ ever after.

    A. stuck   B. unhappily   C. fool   D. what

31 *(The clock _____ twelve, and the wheel _____ _____ Prince.)*

    A. into   B. turns   C. hits

32 **Prince:** I can't believe this. Thank you for giving me a second _____. Now I know _____ I _____ _____ my life. *(Goes out)*

    A. chance   B. should   C. how   D. live

33 **Fairy:** *(_____ her hand)* You learned a good _____. I'll _____ my fingers _____.

    A. lesson   B. crossed   C. keep   D. waving

34 **Scene 3:** _____ the Frog _____ _____

    A. in   B. house   C. Prince's

35 *(Prince _____ _____, _____.)*

    A. in   B. runs   C. smiling

36 **Princess:** Where have you _____? I've been _____. Your _____ are a _____.

    A. been   B. mess   C. worried   D. clothes

37 **Prince:** *(Looking at Princess)* You _____ me when no one _____ in the world _____. You loved me even when I was a frog. From now _____, I will make you happier.

    A. else   B. on   C. believed   D. did

38 **Princess:** I'm _____ to _____ that. I'll _____ you _____ happier.

    A. hear   B. even   C. make   D. glad

39 **Prince:** Great! I'm _____ to our _____ _____. Ha-ha ....

    A. bright   B. looking   C. future   D. forward

40 *(They run _____ the pond together, _____ hand _____ _____.)*

    A. hand   B. to   C. in   D. jumping

---

28 요정: 음, 저는 신데렐라를 만나러 가는 길이지만, 한번 해 볼게요. 아시다시피 이건 제가 처음으로 해 보는 거예요. (요정이 왕자를 바퀴로 바꾼다.)

29 요정: 이런! 미안하지만 걱정하지 마세요. 모든 게 잘될 거예요.

30 왕자: (혼잣말로) 오, 내가 얼마나 바보였던가! 앞으로 행복하게 살면서 집에서 공주와 함께 앉아 있고 싶구나. 하지만 대신에 여기 이 수레 아래에 붙박여 있고 앞으로 불행하게 살게 되겠구나.

31 (시계가 12시를 치자 바퀴가 왕자로 바뀐다.)

32 왕자: 믿을 수가 없네. 두 번째 기회를 주셔서 감사합니다. 이제 나는 내 인생을 어떻게 살아야 할지 알겠어요. (퇴장한다)

33 요정: (손을 흔들며) 좋은 교훈을 배웠군요. 행운을 빌어요.

34 장면 3: 개구리 왕자의 집 안에서

35 (왕자가 미소를 지으며 뛰어 들어온다.)

36 공주: 어디 있었어요? 걱정했잖아요. 옷이 엉망진창이네요.

37 왕자: (공주를 바라보며) 당신은 세상 어느 누구도 나를 믿지 않을 때 나를 믿어 주었어요. 당신은 내가 개구리일 때조차도 나를 사랑해 주었죠. 이제부터는 내가 당신을 더 행복하게 해 주겠어요.

38 공주: 그 말을 들으니 기뻐요. 제가 당신을 훨씬 더 행복하게 해 줄게요.

39 왕자: 좋아요! 난 우리의 밝은 미래를 기대할게요. 하하 ….

40 (그들은 서로 손을 잡고 함께 연못으로 뛰어간다.)

※ 다음 우리말과 일치하도록 빈칸에 알맞은 것을 골라 쓰시오.

1 The _____ _____ _____

2 _____ : Frog Prince, _____ , Witch 1, Witch 2, _____

3 _____ 1: _____ a room

4 *(Prince comes in, _____ _____ .)*

5 Princess: _____ _____ around, honey.

6 Prince: Well, I just _____ _____ .

7 Princess: You're not a frog _____ .

8 Prince: _____ _____ _____ you? You don't go down to the pond _____ _____ .

9 Princess: _____ _____ _____ _____ _____ you jump around in the room. Go out to _____ _____ and _____ our people.

10 Prince: I don't want to go out and kill anything. I just _____ _____ _____ _____ . *(_____ _____ a book)* Listen! "They lived happily ever after. The end." I'm living my life _____ the book says, but we're not happy. What's the problem?

11 Princess: What's the problem? There are _____ problems! Sometimes I think we _____ _____ _____ you _____ _____ a frog.

12 Prince: Still a frog .... Yes! _____ _____ ! *(Goes out)*

13 _____ 2: _____ the mountain

14 Prince: *(_____ _____)* I need to find the witch, who will _____ me back _____ a frog. *(Shouting)* Ms. Witch, Ms. Witch. Where are you? Please help me!

15 Witch 1: *(Coming _____ the house)* Hi, Prince. _____ are you feeling?

1 계속된 개구리 왕자

2 등장인물: 개구리 왕자, 공주, 마녀 1, 마녀 2, 요정

3 장면 1: 방 안에서

4 (왕자가 이리저리 뛰어다니며 등장한다.)

5 공주: 여보, 이리저리 뛰어다니지 마세요.

6 왕자: 저, 나는 단지 멈출 수 없을 뿐이에요.

7 공주: 당신은 이제 개구리가 아니에요.

8 왕자: 당신한테 무슨 문제가 있어요? 요즘 당신은 연못으로 내려가지도 않잖아요.

9 공주: 나는 당신이 방 안에서 이리저리 뛰어다니는 게 마음에 안 들어요. 나가서 괴물들을 죽이고 우리 백성을 구하세요.

10 왕자: 나는 밖에 나가서 아무것도 죽이고 싶지 않아요. 나는 단지 멀리 뛰어다니고 싶을 뿐이오. (책을 집어 들고) 들어 봐요! "그들은 그 후로 행복하게 살았다. 끝." 나는 책에서 말한 것처럼 내 인생을 살고 있지만, 우리는 행복하지 않아요. 뭐가 문제일까요?

11 공주: 뭐가 문제냐고요? 수백 가지 문제가 있어요! 가끔 나는 당신이 아직 개구리일 때 더 잘 살지 않았나 생각해요.

12 왕자: 아직 개구리라 …. 그래! 바로 그거요! (퇴장한다.)

13 장면 2: 산속에서

14 왕자: (혼잣말로) 나는 마녀를 찾아야 해. 그녀가 나를 다시 개구리로 바꿔 줄 거야. (소리치며) 마녀님, 마녀님. 어디 계세요? 저 좀 도와주세요!

15 마녀 1: (집 밖으로 나오며) 안녕, 왕자님. 기분이 어때요?

16 Prince: I'm glad to meet you. I'm the Frog Prince. I hope you can _____ _____ _____ _____ a frog _____ I can _____ _____ _____ _____.

17 Witch 1: Frog Prince, you say? That's funny. You don't _____ _____ a frog. Well, it _____ _____. If you're a prince, you're a prince. And I won't _____ _____ _____ Snow White. Here, eat the _____ of this apple.

18 Prince: No, thank you. That's not what I _____! *(Runs away)*

19 *(Prince and Witch 2 _____ _____.)*

20 Prince: Ms. Witch, Ms. Witch. _____ are you? Please help me! I'm the Frog ....

21 Witch 2: _____ you're a frog, I'm the King of France.

22 Prince: No, I'm not a frog. I'm the Frog Prince. But I need a witch to _____ _____ _____ _____ a frog so I can _____ _____ ever after. Can you do it?

23 Witch 2: _____ talk about it inside. I will _____ you a _____ lunch. Come in.

24 Prince: Thank you _____ _____ me. Oh, this house _____ _____ _____ _____ and candies. Wait a minute. Do you know any children _____ _____ _____ _____ Hansel and Gretel?

25 Witch 2: Yes, Prince, _____ _____. *(With her mouth watering)* They are not _____ _____ yet, but you are ....

26 *(Prince _____ _____ and finds a fairy.)*

27 Prince: I'm glad to meet you, Ms. Fairy. I am the Frog Prince. _____ _____ turn me back into a frog _____ I can live happily ever after?

---

16 왕자: 당신을 만나서 기뻐요. 저는 개구리 왕자예요. 저는 당신이 저를 다시 개구리로 바꿔줘서 제가 앞으로 행복하게 살 수 있게 되기를 원해요.

17 마녀 1: 개구리 왕자라고 했어요? 그거 웃기는군요. 당신은 개구리처럼 보이지 않아요. 음, 그건 중요하지 않아요. 당신이 왕자라면 왕자인 거죠. 그리고 나는 당신이 백설공주를 구하도록 놔두지 않을 거예요. 여기, 이 사과의 나머지를 먹어요.

18 왕자: 고맙지만 됐어요. 그건 제가 원하는 게 아니에요! (도망간다)

19 (왕자와 마녀 2가 등장한다.)

20 왕자: 마녀님, 마녀님. 어디 계세요? 저 좀 도와주세요! 저는 개구리 ….

21 마녀 2: 당신이 개구리리면 니는 프랑스의 왕이에요.

22 왕자: 아니요, 저는 개구리가 아니에요. 저는 개구리 왕자예요. 하지만 저를 다시 개구리로 바꿔 줘서 제가 앞으로 행복하게 살 수 있게 해 줄 마녀가 필요해요. 그렇게 해 주실 수 있나요?

23 마녀 2: 안에서 그것에 관해 이야기해 봅시다. 내가 당신에게 맛있는 점심을 대접할게요. 들어와요.

24 왕자: 저를 초대해 주셔서 감사합니다. 오, 이 집은 과자와 사탕으로 만들어져 있네요. 잠깐만요. 당신은 헨젤과 그레텔이라는 이름의 아이들을 혹시 알아요?

25 마녀 2: 그래요, 왕자님. 알고 있어요. (그녀가 군침을 흘리면서) 그 애들은 아직 충분히 살이 찌지 않았지만, 당신은 ….

26 (왕자는 도망치다가 요정을 발견한다.)

27 왕자: 만나게 되어 기쁩니다, 요정님. 저는 개구리 왕자예요. 저를 다시 개구리로 바꿔 앞으로 행복하게 살 수 있게 해 주실 수 있나요?

28 Fairy: Well, I'm _____ _____ _____ to see Cinderella, but I'll _____ _____ _____ _____. It's my first time, you know. *(Fairy _____ Prince _____ a wheel.)*

29 Fairy: Oops! Sorry, but _____ _____. Everything _____ _____ _____.

30 Prince: *(To himself)* Oh, _____ _____ _____ I've been! I want to be sitting at home with the Princess, _____ _____ ever after. But instead, I'm _____ here under this cart and I'll live _____ ever after.

31 *(The clock hits twelve, and the wheel _____ _____ Prince.)*

32 Prince: I can't believe this. Thank you for _____ _____ _____ _____ _____. Now I know _____ _____ _____ _____ my life. *(Goes out)*

33 Fairy: *(_____ her hand)* You learned a good _____. I'll _____ _____ _____ _____.

34 **Scene 3:** In the Frog _____ _____

35 *(Prince runs in, _____.)*

36 Princess: Where _____ _____ _____? I've been worried. Your _____ are a _____.

37 Prince: *(Looking at Princess)* You believed me when no one _____ in the world _____. You loved me even when I was a frog. _____ _____ _____, I will make you happier.

38 Princess: I'm glad to hear that. I'll make you _____ happier.

39 Prince: Great! I'm _____ _____ _____ our _____ _____. Ha-ha ....

40 *(They run to the pond together; _____ _____ _____.)*

본문 Test **55**

※ 다음 문장을 우리말로 쓰시오.

1 The Frog Prince Continued

➡ _____

2 Characters: Frog Prince, Princess, Witch 1, Witch 2, Fairy

➡ _____

3 Scene 1: In a room

➡ _____

4 (*Prince comes in, jumping around.*)

➡ _____

5 Princess: Stop jumping around, honey.

➡ _____

6 Prince: Well, I just can't stop.

➡ _____

7 Princess: You're not a frog anymore.

➡ _____

8 Prince: What's wrong with you? You don't go down to the pond these days.

➡ _____

9 Princess: I don't like it when you jump around in the room. Go out to kill monsters and save our people.

➡ _____

10 Prince: I don't want to go out and kill anything. I just feel like running away. (*Picking up a book*) Listen! "They lived happily ever after. The end." I'm living my life as the book says, but we're not happy. What's the problem?

➡ _____

_____

_____

11 Princess: What's the problem? There are hundreds of problems! Sometimes I think we were better off when you were still a frog.

➡ _____

12 Prince: Still a frog .... Yes! That's it! (*Goes out*)

➡ _____

13 Scene 2: On the mountain

➡ _____

14 Prince: (*To himself*) I need to find the witch, who will turn me back into a frog. (*Shouting*)
Ms. Witch, Ms. Witch. Where are you? Please help me!

➡ _____

15 Witch 1: (Coming out of the house) Hi, Prince. How are you feeling?

➡ _____

16 Prince: I'm glad to meet you. I'm the Frog Prince. I hope you can turn me back into a frog
so I can live happily ever after.

➡ _____

17 Witch 1: Frog Prince, you say? That's funny. You don't look like a frog. Well, it doesn't matter.
If you're a prince, you're a prince. And I won't let you save Snow White. Here, eat the rest
of this apple.

➡ _____

_____

18 Prince: No, thank you. That's not what I want! (*Runs away*)

➡ _____

19 (*Prince and Witch 2 come in.*)

➡ _____

20 Prince: Ms. Witch, Ms. Witch. Where are you? Please help me! I'm the Frog ....

➡ _____

21 Witch 2: If you're a frog, I'm the King of France.

➡ _____

22 Prince: No, I'm not a frog. I'm the Frog Prince. But I need a witch to turn me back into a frog
so I can live happily ever after. Can you do it?

➡ _____

_____

23 Witch 2: Let's talk about it inside. I will serve you a delicious lunch. Come in

➡ _____

24 Prince: Thank you for inviting me. Oh, this house is made of cookies and candies.
Wait a minute. Do you know any children by the name of Hansel and Gretel?

➡ _____

25 Witch 2: Yes, Prince, I do. (*With her mouth watering*) They are not fat enough yet, but you are ....

➡ _____

26 (*Prince runs away and finds a fairy.*)

➡ _____

27 Prince: I'm glad to meet you, Ms. Fairy. I am the Frog Prince. Could you turn me back into a frog so I can live happily ever after?

➡ _____

_____

28 Fairy: Well, I'm on my way to see Cinderella, but I'll give it a try. It's my first time, you know. (*Fairy turns Prince into a wheel.*)

➡ _____

_____

29 Fairy: Oops! Sorry, but don't worry. Everything will be okay.

➡ _____

30 Prince: (*To himself*) Oh, what a fool I've been! I want to be sitting at home with the Princess, living happily ever after. But instead, I'm stuck here under this cart and I'll live unhappily ever after.

➡ _____

31 (*The clock hits twelve, and the wheel turns into Prince.*)

➡ _____

32 Prince: I can't believe this. Thank you for giving me a second chance. Now I know how I should live my life. (*Goes out*)

➡ _____

33 Fairy: (*Waving her hand*) You learned a good lesson. I'll keep my fingers crossed.

➡ _____

34 Scene 3: In the Frog Prince's house

➡ _____

35 (*Prince runs in, smiling.*)

➡ _____

36 Princess: Where have you been? I've been worried. Your clothes are a mess.

➡ _____

37 Prince: (*Looking at Princess*) You believed me when no one else in the world did. You loved me even when I was a frog. From now on, I will make you happier.

➡ _____

_____

38 Princess: I'm glad to hear that. I'll make you even happier.

➡ _____

39 Prince: Great! I'm looking forward to our bright future. Ha-ha ....

➡ _____

40 (*They run to the pond together, jumping hand in hand.*)

➡ _____

※ 다음 괄호 안의 단어들을 우리말에 맞도록 바르게 배열하시오.

1 (Frog / The / Continued / Prince)
➡ _____

2 (Characters: / Prince, / Frog / Witch 1, / Princess, / Fairy / Witch 2,)
➡ _____

3 (Scene 1: / a / room / in)
➡ _____

4 (comes / (Prince / in, / around.) / jumping)
➡ _____

5 (Princess: / jumping / stop / honey. / around,)
➡ _____

6 (Prince: / I / well, / stop. / can't / just)
➡ _____

7 (Princess: / not / you're / a / anymore. / frog)
➡ _____

8 (Prince: / wrong / what's / you? / with // don't / you / down / go / the / to / these / pond / days.)
➡ _____

9 (Princess: / don't / I / it / like / you / when / jump / in / around / room. / the // out / go / kill / to / and / monsters / save / people. / our)
➡ _____

10 (Prince: / don't / I / to / want / out / go / and / anything. / kill // just / I / like / feel / away. / running // up / (picking / book) / a // listen! // lived / "they / ever / happily / after. // end." / the // living / I'm / life / my / the / as / says, / book / but / not / we're / happy. // the / what's / problem?)
➡ _____

11 (Princess: / the / what's / problem? // are / there / of / hundreds / problems! / I / sometimes / we / think / better / were / off / you / when / still / were / frog. / a)
➡ _____

12 (Prince: / a / still / .... / frog // yes! // it! / that's // out) (goes)
➡ _____

13 (Scene 2: / the / on / mountain)
➡ _____

14 (Prince: / himself) (to // need / I / find / to / witch, / the / will / who / me / turn / back / a / frog. / into) // (shouting) // Witch, / Ms. / Witch. / Ms. // are / you? / where // help / me! / please)
➡ _____

15 (Witch 1: / out / (coming / the / of / house) // Prince. / hi, // are / how / feeling? / you)
➡ _____

1 계속된 개구리 왕자

2 등장인물: 개구리 왕자, 공주, 마녀 1, 마녀 2, 요성

3 장면 1: 방 안에서

4 (왕자가 이리저리 뛰어다니며 등장한다.)

5 공주: 여보, 이리저리 뛰어다니지 마세요.

6 왕자: 저, 나는 단지 멈출 수 없을 뿐이에요.

7 공주: 당신은 이제 개구리가 아니에요.

8 왕자: 당신한테 무슨 문제가 있어요? 요즘 당신은 연못으로 내려가지도 않잖아요.

9 공주: 나는 당신이 방 안에서 이리저리 뛰어다니는 게 마음에 안 들어요. 나가서 괴물들을 죽이고 우리 백성을 구하세요.

10 왕자: 나는 밖에 나가서 아무것도 죽이고 싶지 않아요. 나는 단지 멀리 뛰어다니고 싶을 뿐이오. (책을 집어 들고) 들어 봐요! "그들은 그 후로 행복하게 살았다. 끝." 나는 책에서 말한 것처럼 내 인생을 살고 있지만, 우리는 행복하지 않아요. 뭐가 문제일까요?

11 공주: 뭐가 문제냐고요? 수백 가지 문제가 있어요! 가끔 나는 당신이 아직 개구리일 때 더 잘 살지 않았나 생각해요.

12 왕자: 아직 개구리라 …. 그래! 바로 그거요! (퇴장한다.)

13 장면 2: 산속에서

14 왕자: (혼잣말로) 나는 마녀를 찾아야 해. 그녀가 나를 다시 개구리로 바꿔 줄 거야. (소리치며) 마녀님, 마녀님. 어디 계세요? 저 좀 도와주세요!

15 마녀 1: (집 밖으로 나오며) 안녕, 왕자님. 기분이 어때요?

16 (Prince: / glad / I'm / meet / to / you. // the / I'm / Prince. / Frog // hope / I / can / you / me / turn / into / back / so / a / frog / can / I / happily / live / after. / ever)

➡ _____

_____

17 (Witch 1: / Prince, / Frog / say? / you // funny. / that's // don't / you / like / look / frog. / a / it / well, / matter. / doesn't // you're / if / prince, / a / a / you're / prince. // I / and / let / won't / save / you / White. / Snow // eat / here, / rest / of / the / apple. / this)

➡ _____

_____

18 (Prince: / thank / no, / you. // not / that's / I / what / want! // away) / (runs)

➡ _____

19 (and / (Prince / come / Witch 2 / in.))

➡ _____

20 (Prince: / Witch, / Ms. / Witch. / Ms. // are / were / you? // help / please / me! // the / I'm / .... / Frog)

➡ _____

_____

21 (Witch 2: / you're / if / frog, / a / the / I'm / of / King / France.)

➡ _____

22 (Prince: / I'm / no, / a / not / frog. // the / I'm / Prince. / Frog // I / but / a / need / to / witch / me / turn / into / back / frog / a / I / so / live / can / ever / happily / after. / you / can / it? / do)

➡ _____

_____

23 (Witch 2: / talk / let's / it / about / inside. // will / I / you / serve / a / delicious / lunch. // in. / come)

➡ _____

_____

24 (Prince: / you / thank / inviting / for / me. // this / oh, / is / house / made / of / and / cookies / candies. // a / wait / minute. // you / do / know / children / any / the / by / name / of / and / Gretel? / Hansel)

➡ _____

_____

25 (Witch 2: / Prince, / yes, / do. / I // her / (with / watering) / mouth // are / they / fat / not / yet, / enough / you / but / .... / are)

➡ _____

26 (runs / (Prince / and / away / a / finds / fairy.))

➡ _____

27 (Prince: / glad / I'm / meet / to / you, / Fairy. / Ms. // am / I / Prince. / the / Frog // you / could / me / turn / back / into / frog / a / so / can / I / live / ever / happily / after?)

➡ _____

_____

16 왕자: 당신을 만나서 기뻐요. 저는 개구리 왕자예요. 저는 당신이 저를 다시 개구리로 바꿔줘서 제가 앞으로 행복하게 살 수 있게 되기를 원해요.

17 마녀 1: 개구리 왕자라고 했어요? 그거 웃기는군요. 당신은 개구리처럼 보이지 않아요. 음, 그건 중요하지 않아요. 당신이 왕자라면 왕자인 거죠. 그리고 나는 당신이 백설공주를 구하도록 놔두지 않을 거예요. 여기, 이 사과의 나머지를 먹어요.

18 왕자: 고맙지만 됐어요. 그건 제가 원하는 게 아니에요! (도망간다)

19 (왕자와 마녀 2가 등장한다.)

20 왕자: 마녀님, 마녀님. 어디 계세요? 저 좀 도와주세요! 저는 개구리 ….

21 마녀 2: 당신이 개구리라면 나는 프랑스의 왕이에요.

22 왕자: 아니요, 저는 개구리가 아니에요. 저는 개구리 왕자예요. 하지만 저를 다시 개구리로 바꿔 줘서 제가 앞으로 행복하게 살 수 있게 해 줄 마녀가 필요해요. 그렇게 해 주실 수 있나요?

23 마녀 2: 안에서 그것에 관해 이야기해 봅시다. 내가 당신에게 맛있는 점심을 대접할게요. 들어와요.

24 왕자: 저를 초대해 주셔서 감사합니다. 오, 이 집은 과자와 사탕으로 만들어져 있네요. 잠깐만요. 당신은 헨젤과 그레텔이라는 이름의 아이들을 혹시 알아요?

25 마녀 2: 그래요, 왕자님, 알고 있어요. (그녀가 군침을 흘리면서) 그 애들은 아직 충분히 살이 찌지 않았지만, 당신은 ….

26 (왕자는 도망치다가 요정을 발견한다.)

27 왕자: 만나게 되어 기쁩니다, 요정님. 저는 개구리 왕자예요. 저를 다시 개구리로 바꿔 앞으로 행복하게 살 수 있게 해 주실 수 있나요?

28 (Fairy: / I'm / well, / my / on / see / to / way / but / Cinderella, / give / I'll / a / it / try. // my / first / it's / time, / know. / you // turns / (Fairy / into / Prince / wheel.) / a)
➡ _____

29 (Fairy: / oops! // but / sorry, / worry. / don't // will / everything / be / okay.)
➡ _____

30 (Prince: / himself) / (to // what / oh, / fool / a / been! / I've // want / I / to / be / sitting / home / at / the / with / Princess, / happily / living / after. / ever // instead, / but / stuck / I'm / under / here / cart / this / and / live / I'll / ever / unhappily / after.)
➡ _____

31 (clock / (the / twelve, / hits // the / and / turns / wheel / Prince.) / into)
➡ _____

32 (Prince: / can't / I / this. / believe // you / thank / for / me / giving / a / chance. / second // I / now / how / know / should / I / my / live / life. // out) / (goes)
➡ _____

33 (Fairy: / her / (waving / hand) // learned / you / good / a / lesson. // keep / I'll / fingers / my / crossed.)
➡ _____

34 (Scene 3: / the / in / Prince's / Frog / house)
➡ _____

35 (runs / (Prince / smiling.) / in,)
➡ _____

36 (Princess: / have / where / been? / you // been / I've / worried. // clothes / your / a / are / mess.)
➡ _____

37 (Prince: / at / (looking / Princess) // belived / you / when / me / one / no / in / else / the / did. / world // loved / you / even / me / I / when / a / was / frog. // now / from / on, / will / I / you / happier. / make)
➡ _____

38 (Princess: / glad / I'm / to / that. / hear // make / I'll / even / you / happier.)
➡ _____

39 (Prince: / great! / looking / I'm / to / forward / our / future. / bright // .... / ha-ha)
➡ _____

40 (run / (they / the / to / together, / pond / hand / jumping / hand. / in)
➡ _____

28 요정: 음, 저는 신데렐라를 만나러 가는 길이지만, 한번 해 볼게요, 아시다시피 이거 제가 처음으로 해 보는 거예요. (요정이 왕자를 바퀴로 바꾼다.)

29 요정: 이런! 미안하지만 걱정하지 마세요. 모든 게 잘될 거예요.

30 왕자: (혼잣말로) 오, 내가 얼마나 바보였던가! 앞으로 행복하게 살면서 집에서 공주와 함께 앉아 있고 싶구나. 하지만 대신에 여기 이 수레 아래에 붙박여 있고 앞으로 불행하게 살게 되겠구나.

31 (시계가 12시를 치자 바퀴가 왕자로 바뀐다.)

32 왕자: 믿을 수가 없네. 두 번째 기회를 주셔서 감사합니다. 이제 나는 내 인생을 어떻게 살아야 할지 알겠어요. (퇴장한다)

33 요정: (손을 흔들며) 좋은 교훈을 배웠군요. 행운을 빌어요.

34 장면 3: 개구리 왕자의 집 안에서

35 (왕자가 미소를 지으며 뛰어 들어온다.)

36 공주: 어디 있었어요? 걱정했잖아요. 옷이 엉망진창이네요.

37 왕자: (공주를 바라보며) 당신은 세상 어느 누구도 나를 믿지 않을 때 나를 믿어 주었어요. 당신은 내가 개구리일 때조차도 나를 사랑해 주었죠. 이제부터는 내가 당신을 더 행복하게 해 주겠어요.

38 공주: 그 말을 들으니 기뻐요. 제가 당신을 훨씬 더 행복하게 해 줄게요.

39 왕자: 좋아요! 난 우리의 밝은 미래를 기대할게요. 하하 ….

40 (그들은 서로 손을 잡고 함께 연못으로 뛰어간다.)

※ 다음 우리말을 영어로 쓰시오.

1 계속된 개구리 왕자
➡ _____

2 등장인물: 개구리 왕자, 공주, 마녀 1, 마녀 2, 요정
➡ _____

3 장면 1: 방 안에서
➡ _____

4 (왕자가 이리저리 뛰어다니며 등장한다.)
➡ _____

5 공주: 여보, 이리저리 뛰어다니지 마세요.
➡ _____

6 왕자: 저, 나는 단지 멈출 수 없을 뿐이에요.
➡ _____

7 공주: 당신은 이제 개구리가 아니에요.
➡ _____

8 왕자: 당신한테 무슨 문제가 있어요? 요즘 당신은 연못으로 내려가지도 않잖아요.
➡ _____

9 공주: 나는 당신이 방 안에서 이리저리 뛰어다니는 게 마음에 안 들어요. 나가서 괴물들을 죽이고 우리 백성을 구하세요.
➡ _____

10 왕자: 나는 밖에 나가서 아무것도 죽이고 싶지 않아요. 나는 단지 멀리 뛰어다니고 싶을 뿐이오. (책을 집어 들고) 들어 봐요! "그들은 그 후로 행복하게 살았다. 끝." 나는 책에서 말한 것처럼 내 인생을 살고 있지만, 우리는 행복하지 않아요. 뭐가 문제일까요?
➡ _____
_____

11 공주: 뭐가 문제냐고요? 수백 가지 문제가 있어요! 가끔 나는 당신이 아직 개구리일 때 더 잘 살지 않았나 생각해요.
➡ _____
_____

12 왕자: 아직 개구리라 …. 그래! 바로 그거요! (퇴장한다.)
➡ _____

13 장면 2: 산속에서
➡ _____

14 왕자: (혼잣말로) 나는 마녀를 찾아야 해. 그녀가 나를 다시 개구리로 바꿔 줄 거야.
(소리치며) 마녀님, 마녀님. 어디 계세요? 저 좀 도와주세요!

➡ _____

_____

15 마녀 1: (집 밖으로 나오며) 안녕, 왕자님. 기분이 어때요?

➡ _____

16 왕자: 당신을 만나서 기뻐요. 저는 개구리 왕자예요. 저는 당신이 저를 다시 개구리로 바꿔줘서
제가 앞으로 행복하게 살 수 있게 되기를 원해요.

➡ _____

_____

17 마녀 1: 개구리 왕자라고 했어요? 그거 웃기는군요. 당신은 개구리처럼 보이지 않아요. 음, 그건
중요하지 않아요. 당신이 왕자라면 왕자인 거죠. 그리고 나는 당신이 백설공주를 구히도록 뇌두지
않을 거예요. 여기, 이 사과의 나머지를 먹어요.

➡ _____

_____

_____

18 왕자: 고맙지만 됐어요. 그건 제가 원하는 게 아니에요! (도망간다)

➡ _____

19 (왕자와 마녀 2가 등장한다.)

➡ _____

20 왕자: 마녀님, 마녀님. 어디 계세요? 저 좀 도와주세요! 저는 개구리 ….

➡ _____

21 마녀 2: 당신이 개구리라면 나는 프랑스의 왕이에요.

➡ _____

22 왕자: 아니요, 저는 개구리가 아니에요. 저는 개구리 왕자예요. 하지만 저를 다시 개구리로 바꿔
줘서 제가 앞으로 행복하게 살 수 있게 해 줄 마녀가 필요해요. 그렇게 해 주실 수 있나요?

➡ _____

_____

23 마녀 2: 안에서 그것에 관해 이야기해 봅시다. 내가 당신에게 맛있는 점심을 대접할게요. 들어와요.

➡ _____

24 왕자: 저를 초대해 주셔서 감사합니다. 오, 이 집은 과자와 사탕으로 만들어져 있네요. 잠깐만요.
당신은 헨젤과 그레텔이라는 이름의 아이들을 혹시 알아요?

➡ _____

_____

25 마녀 2: 그래요, 왕자님, 알고 있어요. (그녀가 군침을 흘리면서) 그 애들은 아직 충분히 살이
찌지 않았지만, 당신은 ….

➡ _____

26 (왕자는 도망치다가 요정을 발견한다.)

➡ _____

27 왕자: 만나게 되어 기쁩니다, 요정님. 저는 개구리 왕자예요. 저를 다시 개구리로 바꿔 앞으로 행복하게 살 수 있게 해 주실 수 있나요?

➡ _____

28 요정: 음, 저는 신데렐라를 만나러 가는 길이지만, 한번 해 볼게요. 아시다시피 이건 제가 처음으로 해 보는 거예요. (요정이 왕자를 바퀴로 바꾼다.)

➡ _____

_____

29 요정: 이런! 미안하지만 걱정하지 마세요. 모든 게 잘될 거예요

➡ _____

30 왕자: (혼잣말로) 오, 내가 얼마나 바보였던가! 앞으로 행복하게 살면서 집에서 공주와 함께 앉아 있고 싶구나. 하지만 대신에 여기 이 수레 아래에 붙박여 있고 앞으로 불행하게 살게 되겠구나.

➡ _____

_____

31 (시계가 12시를 치자 바퀴가 왕자로 바뀐다.)

➡ _____

32 왕사: 믿을 수가 없네. 두 번째 기회를 주셔서 감사합니다. 이세 나는 내 인생을 어떻게 살아야 할지 알겠어요. (퇴장한다)

➡ _____

_____

33 요정: (손을 흔들며) 좋은 교훈을 배웠군요. 행운을 빌어요.

➡ _____

34 장면 3: 개구리 왕자의 집 안에서

➡ _____

35 (왕자가 미소를 지으며 뛰어 들어온다.)

➡ _____

36 공주: 어디 있었어요? 걱정했잖아요. 옷이 엉망진창이네요.

➡ _____

37 왕자: (공주를 바라보며) 당신은 세상 어느 누구도 나를 믿지 않을 때 나를 믿어 주었어요. 당신은 내가 개구리일 때조차도 나를 사랑해 주었죠. 이제부터는 내가 당신을 더 행복하게 해 주겠어요.

➡ _____

_____

38 공주: 그 말을 들으니 기뻐요. 제가 당신을 훨씬 더 행복하게 해 줄게요.

➡ _____

39 왕자: 좋아요! 난 우리의 밝은 미래를 기대할게요. 하하….

➡ _____

40 (그들은 서로 손을 잡고 함께 연못으로 뛰어간다.)

➡ _____

※ 다음 영어를 우리말로 쓰시오.

01	awesome		22	seriously
02	battle		23	loudly
03	ground		24	seem
04	toward		25	enemy
05	traffic		26	seat
06	chimney		27	soldier
07	ad(= advertisement)		28	exactly
08	powerful		29	vote
09	close		30	border
10	translate		31	Braille
11	prepare		32	expression
12	curious		33	hire
13	rather		34	product
14	reply		35	get over
15	husband		36	look after
16	dead		37	be covered with
17	knock		38	at a price of
18	discover		39	except for
19	hidden		40	vote for
20	hug		41	be careful with
21	misunderstanding		42	right away
			43	instead of

※ 다음 우리말을 영어로 쓰시오.

01 교통 _____

02 근사한, 멋진,
   엄청난, 어마어마한 _____

03 글자, 문자 _____

04 전쟁, 전투 _____

05 번역하다, 해석하다 _____

06 죽은, 쓸모없는 _____

07 적군, 적대자 _____

08 발견하다 _____

09 불을 붙이다, 불을 밝히다 _____

10 큰 소리로, 시끄럽게 _____

11 정확하게 _____

12 호기심이 많은, 궁금한 _____

13 표현 _____

14 남편 _____

15 ~을 향하여 _____

16 굴뚝 _____

17 진지하게, 심각하게 _____

18 다소, 약간 _____

19 준비하다 _____

20 숨은, 숨겨진 _____

21 군인 _____

22 국경, 경계 _____

23 상품, 제품 _____

24 수화 _____

25 고용하다 _____

26 오해 _____

27 포옹; 포옹하다 _____

28 치다, 두드리다 _____

29 좌석, 의석 _____

30 연못 _____

31 외국의 _____

32 몸짓, 몸동작 _____

33 끌다, 잡아당기다 _____

34 투표하다, 선출하다 _____

35 ~ 대신에 _____

36 ~을 제외하고 _____

37 ~을 돌보다 _____

38 ~에 조심하다 _____

39 물러서다 _____

40 즉시, 당장 _____

41 ~로 덮이다 _____

42 ~의 가격으로 _____

43 이겨내다, 극복하다 _____

※ 다음 영영풀이에 알맞은 단어를 <보기>에서 골라 쓴 후, 우리말 뜻을 쓰시오.

1 _____ : no longer alive: _____

2 _____ : in the direction of: _____

3 _____ : an answer to a letter: _____

4 _____ : from another country: _____

5 _____ : the surface of the Earth: _____

6 _____ : to pay someone to work for you: _____

7 _____ : the man that a woman is married to: _____

8 _____ : suffering from an illness or disease:: _____

9 _____ : to make something ready for use: _____

10 _____ : a position as a member of a committee, court, etc.: _____

11 _____ : to express one's preference for a candidate: _____

12 _____ : a thick liquid made from plants or animals that is used in cooking: _____

13 _____ : a piece of jewelry in the form of a circle that you wear on a finger: _____

14 _____ : to change spoken or written words into another language: _____

15 _____ : to find out something that you did not know before: _____

16 _____ : the action of putting your arms around someone to show your love or friendship: _____

보기			
oil	vote	hire	foreign
hug	translate	dead	ill
seat	prepare	toward	reply
discover	ring	husband	ground

※ 다음 우리말과 일치하도록 빈칸에 알맞은 말을 쓰시오.

Get Ready 2

(1) G: I'm _____ _____ that robot. Why _____ _____ _____ there?

B: It's _____ _____ _____ ad. It _____ people their _____ are very _____.

(2) G: What's this? I' _____ _____ _____ it.

B: It's a _____ _____. It _____ "Do not _____."

G: Oh, I see.

(3) G: What are these _____ _____? I' _____ _____ _____ them.

B: Oh, they are _____. They are for _____ people.

G: I see. Now I can _____ _____ they _____.

(4) G: I'm _____ about that _____. Why is it _____ there?

B: Oh, that. It's an _____. It says the _____ is very _____.

Start Off – Listen & Talk A

1. B: What are the _____ doing _____ the five _____ on TV?

G: They are sending _____ to the king _____ _____ the _____.

B: Really? I' _____ _____ _____ the _____. Can you tell me more?

G: Well, do you see the two _____ _____?

B: Yes. _____ do they _____?

G: They mean they just _____ an _____.

2. B: If there's no _____, they don't _____ _____ _____, _____ they?

G: Yes, they do. _____ from one _____ means "No _____."

B: Now smoke is _____ from three chimneys. _____ that _____?

G: _____ _____ an enemy is coming _____ to the _____.

Start Off B

B: Now the enemy _____ _____ _____ the _____ in the _____. What are the _____ _____ _____ _____ to send _____? I'm _____ _____ that.

G: They will _____ four _____.

B: When they _____ all five of the _____, what does that mean?

G: _____ _____ the _____ has _____.

해석

(1) G: 나는 저 로봇에 대해 알고 싶어. 그건 왜 저기에 서 있는 거니?

B: 그건 일종의 광고야. 그것은 그들의 건전지가 매우 강력하다는 것을 사람들에게 말하고 있어.

(2) G: 이것은 뭐지? 난 그게 궁금해.

B: 그것은 교통 표지판이야. 그것은 "들어오지 마시오."를 의미해.

G: 오, 알겠어.

(3) G: 이 점들은 무엇을 위한 거니? 난 그것들에 대해 알고 싶어.

B: 오, 그것들은 점자야. 그것들은 시각장애인을 위한 것이야.

G: 알겠어. 이제 그것들이 무엇을 의미하는지 추측할 수 있어.

(4) G: 나는 저 풍선이 궁금해. 그건 왜 저기에 매달려 있니?

B: 오, 저것. 그건 광고야. 그것은 그 상품이 매우 강력하다는 것을 말하고 있어.

1. B: TV에서 병사들이 5개의 굴뚝으로 무엇을 하고 있니?

G: 그들은 그 굴뚝을 이용하여 왕에게 메시지를 보내고 있어.

B: 정말? 난 그 체계가 궁금해. 좀 더 말해 줄 수 있어?

G: 음, 연기 나는 굴뚝 두 개가 보이지?

B: 그래. 그것들은 무엇을 의미하니?

G: 그것들은 그들이 방금 적을 봤다는 것을 의미해.

2. B: 만약 적이 없다면, 그들은 연기를 전혀 피우지 않아, 그렇지?

G: 아니, 연기를 피워. 굴뚝 한 곳에서 연기가 나오면 "적이 없음"을 의미해.

B: 이제 연기가 굴뚝 세 개에서 올라가고 있어. 그것은 무엇을 의미하니?

G: 그것은 적이 국경 가까이 접근하고 있음을 의미해.

B: 이제 적이 어둠 속에서 국경을 침입하고 있어. 메시지를 보내기 위해서 병사들은 무슨 일을 할까? 나는 그것이 궁금해.

G: 그들은 굴뚝 4개에 불을 붙일 거야.

B: 그들이 5개 굴뚝 모두에 불을 붙였을 때, 그것은 무엇을 의미하니?

G: 그것은 전투가 시작되었음을 의미해.

Start Off – Speak Up

B: I'_____ _____ _____ sign _____.

G: Are you? _____ me _____ you one _____. Look.

B: _____ does it _____?

G: _____ _____ "Hello."

B: 난 수화가 궁금해.
G: 그러니? 내가 표현 하나를 알려줄게. 봐.
B: 그것은 무엇을 의미하니?
G: 그것은 "안녕하세요."를 의미해.

Step Up – Real-life Scene

B: This painting has some _____ _____ in it.

G: Really? I'm _____ _____ them. Where are the _____?

B: _____ one _____.

G: _____ _____. ... Oh, I see some _____ here.

B: You found _____! It _____ "Jan van Eyck was here. 1434." It's _____.

G: That's _____! _____ _____ _____?

B: Okay. This dog _____ us the man here was very _____.

G: I don't _____.

B: They had to _____ _____ _____ money _____ _____ a dog of that _____ _____ _____ _____.

G: I see. Only _____ _____ could have _____ _____ of dog, _____?

B: _____. Pictures _____ _____ _____ words, you know.

B: 이 그림은 그 안에 숨겨진 비밀이 몇 개 있어.
G: 정말? 난 그것들이 궁금해. 그 비밀들은 어디에 있니?
B: 너 스스로 하나 찾아봐.
G: 어디 보자. … 오, 여기 글자들이 몇 개 보여.
B: 너 하나 찾았구나! 그것은 "Jan van Eyck가 여기 있었다. 1434."를 의미해. 그것은 라틴어야.
G: 멋지다! 다른 비밀들은?
B: 좋아. 이 개는 여기 있는 이 남자가 매우 부자였다는 것을 우리에게 말해 주지.
G: 나는 이해가 안 돼.
B: 당시에 저런 종류의 개를 사려면 많은 돈을 써야 했어.
G: 알겠다. 단지 부자들만 저런 종류의 개를 살 수 있었어, 맞지?
B: 정확해. 알다시피, 그림이 천 마디 말을 하지.

Express Yourself A

1. W: What does this woman's _____ mean? I'm _____ _____ it.

   M: I think _____ _____ "Jump _____ the _____."

   W: _____ do you _____ _____?

   M: The boy has _____ _____ _____ on his head. And the woman is _____ at the _____.

2. W: This woman doesn't want a dollar. _____ what does her _____ _____?

   M: _____ _____ she wants a _____.

   W: Then the boy _____ _____ a chicken _____ _____ the fruit, _____?

   M: _____ _____ _____.

3. W: _____ does this man's _____ _____? I'm _____ _____ it.

   M: It means "_____ _____ _____."

   W: Really? _____ _____ you think _____?

   M: _____ _____ _____ there is coming _____ to an animal.

   W: Oh, I _____.

1. W: 이 여자의 몸짓은 무엇을 의미하니? 난 그것이 궁금해.
   M: 내 생각에 그것은 "연못으로 뛰어들이."를 의미해.
   W: 왜 그렇게 생각하니?
   M: 그 소년은 머리 위에 많은 벌이 있어. 그리고 그 여자는 연못을 가리키고 있어.
2. W: 이 여자는 1달러를 원하지 않아. 그렇다면 그녀의 몸짓은 무엇을 의미하니?
   M: 그것은 그녀가 닭 한 마리를 원한다는 것을 의미해.
   W: 그럼 그 소년은 과일을 얻기 위해 닭을 한 마리 가져와야 하는구나, 맞지?
   M: 난 그렇게 생각해.
3. W: 이 남자의 몸짓은 무엇을 의미하니? 난 그것이 궁금해.
   M: 그것은 "그것을 꺼."를 의미해.
   W: 정말? 왜 그렇게 생각하니?
   M: 거기 있는 나머지 다른 사냥꾼이 어떤 동물 가까이 접근하고 있어.
   W: 오, 알겠어.

※ 다음 우리말에 맞도록 대화를 영어로 쓰시오.

Get Ready 2

(1) G: _____

　　B: _____

(2) G: _____

　　B: _____

　　G: _____

(3) G: _____

　　B: _____

　　G: _____

(4) G: _____

　　B: _____

Start Off – Listen & Talk A

1. B: _____

　　G: _____

　　B: _____

　　G: _____

　　B: _____

　　G: _____

2. B: _____

　　G: _____

　　B: _____

　　G: _____

Start Off B

B: _____

　_____

G: _____

B: _____

G: _____

(1) G: 나는 저 로봇에 대해 알고 싶어. 그건 왜 저기에 서 있는 거니?

　B: 그건 일종의 광고야. 그것은 그들의 건전지가 매우 강력하다는 것을 사람들에게 말하고 있어.

(2) G: 이것은 뭐지? 난 그게 궁금해.

　B: 그것은 교통 표지판이야. 그것은 "들어오지 마시오."를 의미해.

　G: 오, 알겠어.

(3) G: 이 점들은 무엇을 위한 거니? 난 그것들에 대해 알고 싶어.

　B: 오, 그것들은 점자야. 그것들은 시각장애인을 위한 것이야.

　G: 알겠어. 이제 그것들이 무엇을 의미하는지 추측할 수 있어.

(4) G: 나는 저 풍선이 궁금해. 그건 왜 저기에 매달려 있니?

　B: 오, 저것. 그건 광고야. 그것은 그 상품이 매우 강력하다는 것을 말하고 있어.

1. B: TV에서 병사들이 5개의 굴뚝으로 무엇을 하고 있니?

　G: 그들은 그 굴뚝을 이용하여 왕에게 메시지를 보내고 있어.

　B: 정말? 난 그 체계가 궁금해. 좀 더 말해 줄 수 있어?

　G: 음, 연기 나는 굴뚝 두 개가 보이지?

　B: 그래. 그것들은 무엇을 의미하니?

　G: 그것들은 그들이 방금 적을 봤다는 것을 의미해.

2. B: 만약 적이 없다면, 그들은 연기를 전혀 피우지 않아, 그렇지?

　G: 아니, 연기를 피워. 굴뚝 한 곳에서 연기가 나오면 "적이 없음"을 의미해.

　B: 이제 연기가 굴뚝 세 개에서 올라가고 있어. 그것은 무엇을 의미하니?

　G: 그것은 적이 국경 가까이 접근하고 있음을 의미해.

B: 이제 적이 어둠 속에서 국경을 침입하고 있어. 메시지를 보내기 위해서 병사들은 무슨 일을 할까? 나는 그것이 궁금해.

G: 그들은 굴뚝 4개에 불을 붙일 거야.

B: 그들이 5개 굴뚝 모두에 불을 붙였을 때, 그것은 무엇을 의미하니?

G: 그것은 전투가 시작되었음을 의미해.

Start Off – Speak Up

B: _____

G: _____

B: _____

G: _____

Step Up – Real-life Scene

B: _____

G: _____

B: _____

G: _____

B: _____

G: _____

B: _____

G: _____

B: _____

G: _____

B: _____

Express Yourself A

1. W: _____

   M: _____

   W: _____

   M: _____

2. W: _____

   M: _____

   W: _____

   M: _____

3. W: _____

   M: _____

   W: _____

   M: _____

   W: _____

B: 난 수화가 궁금해.

G: 그러니? 내가 표현 하나를 알려줄게. 봐.

B: 그것은 무엇을 의미하니?

G: 그것은 "안녕하세요."를 의미해.

B: 이 그림은 그 안에 숨겨진 비밀이 몇 개 있어.

G: 정말? 난 그것들이 궁금해. 그 비밀들은 어디에 있니?

B: 너 스스로 하나 찾아봐.

G: 어디 보자. … 오, 여기 글자들이 몇 개 보여.

B: 너 하나 찾았구나! 그것은 "Jan van Eyck가 여기 있었다. 1434."를 의미해. 그것은 라틴어야.

G: 멋지다! 다른 비밀들은?

B: 좋아. 이 개는 여기 있는 이 남자가 매우 부자였다는 것을 우리에게 말해주지.

G: 나는 이해가 안 돼.

B: 당시에 저런 종류의 개를 사려면 많은 돈을 써야 했어.

G: 알겠다. 단지 부자들만 저런 종류의 개를 살 수 있었어, 맞지?

B: 정확해. 알다시피, 그림이 천 마디 말을 하지.

1. W: 이 여자의 몸짓은 무엇을 의미하니? 난 그것이 궁금해.

   M: 내 생각에 그것은 "연못으로 뛰어들어."를 의미해.

   W: 왜 그렇게 생각하니?

   M: 그 소년은 머리 위에 많은 벌이 있어. 그리고 그 여자는 연못을 가리키고 있어.

2. W: 이 여자는 1달러를 원하지 않아. 그렇다면 그녀의 몸짓은 무엇을 의미하니?

   M: 그것은 그녀가 닭 한 마리를 원한다는 것을 의미해.

   W: 그럼 그 소년은 과일을 얻기 위해 닭을 한 마리 가져와야 하는구나, 맞지?

   M: 난 그렇게 생각해.

3. W: 이 남자의 몸짓은 무엇을 의미하니? 난 그것이 궁금해.

   M: 그것은 "그것을 꺼."를 의미해.

   W: 정말? 왜 그렇게 생각하니?

   M: 거기 있는 나머지 다른 사냥꾼이 어떤 동물 가까이 접근하고 있어.

   W: 오, 알겠어.

※ 다음 우리말과 일치하도록 빈칸에 알맞은 것을 골라 쓰시오.

1 A _____ _____ _____ a Mother _____ Three
    A. from   B. Picture   C. Letter   D. of

2 _____ to family members or friends in a _____ country is _____ easy and _____ today.
    A. rather   B. speaking   C. simple   D. foreign

3 But _____ the _____ of phones and the Internet, it was not _____ _____.
    A. easy   B. before   C. that   D. days

4 People just _____ a letter and _____ _____ a _____ for weeks.
    A. reply   B. for   C. sent   D. waited

5 And it was a _____ _____ if they _____ read or _____.
    A. harder   B. write   C. lot   D. couldn't

6 This letter shows _____ people _____ _____ these _____.
    A. difficulties   B. got   C. how   D. over

7 It was written in 1973 _____ a woman _____ husband was _____ _____.
    A. away   B. by   C. whose   D. far

8 She lived in Sicily, an Italian _____, _____ her husband _____ _____ Germany.
    A. while   B. in   C. island   D. worked

9 At the time, _____ _____ 5% of the people in Italy could not read or write, and she was _____ _____ them.
    A. than   B. one   C. more   D. of

10 This letter _____ _____ _____ Sicilian _____ Gesualdo Bufalino.
    A. by   B. discovered   C. was   D. writer

11 Here's _____ he _____ the pictures _____ _____.
    A. into   B. how   C. translated   D. words

12 My dear love, I _____ you so much, and I _____ my arms _____ you, together with our three kids.
    A. toward   B. out   C. reach   D. miss

13 We are all _____ good health _____ _____ the _____ one.
    A. for   B. little   C. except   D. in

14 He's a _____ _____, but _____ _____ _____.
    A. little   B. seriously   C. not   D. sick

15 I already _____ you a letter, but _____ was no _____, _____ I am sad about it.
    A. reply   B. sent   C. there   D. so

16 If I _____ a letter _____ you, I _____ _____ very happy.
    A. be   B. got   C. would   D. from

---

1 세 아이의 엄마가 보낸 그림 편지

2 오늘날 외국에 있는 가족이나 친구와 대화하는 것은 다소 쉽고 간단하다.

3 하지만 전화와 인터넷 시대 이전에는 그것이 그렇게 쉽지 않았다.

4 사람들은 단지 편지를 보내고 답장을 몇 주 동안 기다렸다.

5 그리고 그들이 읽거나 쓸 수 없었다면 그건 훨씬 더 힘들었다.

6 이 편지는 사람들이 이런 어려움을 어떻게 극복했는지 보여준다.

7 그것은 남편이 멀리 떨어져 살았던 한 여자에 의해 1973년에 쓰여졌다.

8 그녀의 남편은 독일에서 일한 반면, 그녀는 이탈리아의 섬인 시실리에서 살았다.

9 그 당시에는 5% 이상의 이탈리아 사람들이 읽거나 쓸 수 없었고, 그녀도 그들 중 한 명이었다.

10 이 편지는 시실리의 작가 Gesualdo Bufalino가 발견하였다.

11 그가 그림들을 어떻게 글로 번역했는지는 다음과 같다.

12 사랑하는 여보, 난 당신이 정말 그립고, 우리 세 아이와 함께 당신을 향해 내 팔을 쭉 뻗고 있어요.

13 막내를 제외하고는 우리 모두 건강해요.

14 그 아이는 약간 아프지만 심각하진 않아요.

15 난 당신에게 이미 편지를 보냈지만, 답장이 없어서 그것 때문에 나는 슬퍼요.

16 당신에게서 편지를 받는다면, 나는 정말 행복할 거예요.

17 Your mother _____ _____, and I'm _____ to visit her in the hospital _____ some money and food.
A. ill   B. with   C. fell   D. going

18 I'll go there _____ our middle son _____ the oldest _____ after the _____.
A. looks   B. while   C. with   D. youngest

19 I _____ two workers _____ our field and _____ for 150,000 lire.
A. plant   B. had   C. seeds   D. prepare

20 I _____ _____ the DC.
A. for   B. voted

21 The PCI lost _____ many seats _____ it _____ dead.
A. that   B. seems   C. almost   D. so

22 But _____ one or the _____, it's the _____.
A. other   B. whether   C. same   D. wins

23 _____ for us _____ people.
A. changes   B. poor   C. nothing

24 We _____ yesterday, and we _____ _____ tomorrow.
A. will   B. again   C. worked   D. work

25 We _____ _____ of olives _____ our olive trees _____ year.
A. this   B. lots   C. from   D. picked

26 I _____ a man _____ sons are good _____.
A. workers   B. whose   C. hired

27 He _____ the olives _____, and his two sons helped him, _____ them _____ from the ground.
A. up   B. down   C. picking   D. knocked

28 I _____ him 27,000 lire _____ the _____.
A. for   B. paid   C. work

29 I _____ 12,000 more _____ the olive _____.
A. for   B. press   C. spent

30 I got _____ oil _____ a large _____ and a small one.
A. fill   B. enough   C. to   D. pot

31 I can _____ it _____ a _____ of 1,300 _____ a liter.
A. lire   B. sell   C. at   D. price

32 My love, my _____ thinks _____ you _____ Christmas is _____.
A. as   B. heart   C. coming   D. of

33 I _____ so happy _____ you _____ with me.
A. if   B. be   C. were   D. would

34 We _____ you _____ much.
A. miss   B. all   C. so

35 I'm _____ you a _____ _____ from me and our three _____ kids.
A. hug   B. sending   C. little   D. big

36 Goodbye, _____.
A. love   B. dear

37 My _____ is _____, _____ to you _____ our two rings are.
A. as   B. yours   C. joined   D. heart

---

17 당신의 어머니께서는 병이 드셨고, 나는 약간의 돈과 음식을 가지고 병원에 있는 어머니를 방문할 예정이에요.

18 큰애가 막내를 돌보는 동안 둘째와 함께 그곳에 갈 거예요.

19 나는 150,000리라에 두 일꾼을 시켜 우리 밭을 준비하고 씨앗을 심게 했어요.

20 나는 DC에 투표했어요.

21 PCI는 매우 많은 의석을 잃어서 거의 죽은 것처럼 보여요.

22 하지만 이쪽이 이기건 서쪽이 이기건, 상황은 똑같아요.

23 우리 가난한 사람들에게는 아무것도 바뀌지 않지요.

24 우리는 어제도 일했고, 내일도 다시 일할 거예요.

25 우리는 올해 올리브나무에서 올리브를 많이 땄어요.

26 나는 아들들이 훌륭한 일꾼인 한 남자를 고용했어요.

27 그가 올리브를 쳐서 떨어뜨리면 그의 두 아들이 땅에서 올리브를 주우면서 그를 도왔어요.

28 나는 그 일을 위해 그에게 27,000리라를 지급했어요.

29 올리브 압착을 위해 12,000리라를 더 썼어요.

30 나는 큰 항아리 하나와 작은 항아리 하나를 채울 만큼 충분한 기름을 얻었어요.

31 리터당 1,300리라의 가격으로 팔 수 있을 것 같아요.

32 여보, 크리스마스가 다가오면서 내 마음은 당신을 떠올려요.

33 당신이 나와 함께 있다면 난 정말 행복할 거예요.

34 우리는 모두 당신을 매우 많이 그리워해요.

35 나와 우리 세 아이의 큰 포옹을 보내요.

36 잘 있어요, 여보.

37 내 마음은 당신의 것이에요, 우리들의 두 반지처럼 당신과 연결된 채로요.

※ 다음 우리말과 일치하도록 빈칸에 알맞은 것을 골라 쓰시오.

1 _____ _____ _____ from a Mother of Three

2 _____ to family members or friends in a _____ _____ _____ _____ easy and _____ today.

3 But _____ the days of phones and the Internet, it was not _____ _____.

4 People just _____ a letter and _____ _____ a reply _____ _____.

5 And it was _____ _____ _____ if they _____ _____ _____ _____.

6 This letter shows how people _____ _____ these difficulties.

7 It _____ _____ _____ 1973 by a woman _____ husband was _____ _____.

8 She lived in Sicily, an Italian island, _____ her husband _____ _____ _____.

9 At the time, _____ _____ _____ of the people in Italy could not read or write, and she was _____ _____ _____.

10 This letter _____ _____ _____ Sicilian _____ Gesualdo Bufalino.

11 Here's _____ he _____ the pictures _____ words.

12 My dear love, I _____ you so much, and I _____ my arms _____ _____ you, together with our three kids.

13 We are _____ _____ _____ _____ _____ _____ the little _____.

14 He's _____ _____ sick, but _____ _____.

15 I _____ sent you a letter, but _____ _____ _____ _____, so I am sad about it.

16 If I _____ a letter from you, I _____ _____ very happy.

1 세 아이의 엄마가 보낸 그림 편지

2 오늘날 외국에 있는 가족이나 친구와 대화하는 것은 다소 쉽고 간단하다.

3 하지만 전화와 인터넷 시대 이전에는 그것이 그렇게 쉽지 않았다.

4 사람들은 단지 편지를 보내고 답장을 몇 주 동안 기다렸다.

5 그리고 그들이 읽거나 쓸 수 없었다면 그건 훨씬 더 힘들었다.

6 이 편지는 사람들이 이런 어려움을 어떻게 극복했는지 보여준다.

7 그것은 남편이 멀리 떨어져 살았던 한 여자에 의해 1973년에 쓰여졌다.

8 그녀의 남편은 독일에서 일한 반면, 그녀는 이탈리아의 섬인 시실리에서 살았다.

9 그 당시에는 5% 이상의 이탈리아 사람들이 읽거나 쓸 수 없었고, 그녀도 그들 중 한 명이었다.

10 이 편지는 시실리의 작가 Gesualdo Bufalino가 발견하였다.

11 그가 그림들을 어떻게 글로 번역했는지는 다음과 같다.

12 사랑하는 여보, 난 당신이 정말 그립고, 우리 세 아이와 함께 당신을 향해 내 팔을 쭉 뻗고 있어요.

13 막내를 제외하고는 우리 모두 건강해요.

14 그 아이는 약간 아프지만 심각하진 않아요.

15 난 당신에게 이미 편지를 보냈지만, 답장이 없어서 그것 때문에 나는 슬퍼요.

16 당신에게서 편지를 받는다면, 나는 정말 행복할 거예요.

17 Your mother _____ _____, and I'm going to visit her in the hospital _____ some money and food.

18 I'll go there with our middle son _____ the oldest _____ _____ the _____.

19 I _____ two workers _____ our field and _____ _____ for 150,000 lire.

20 I _____ _____ the DC.

21 The PCI lost _____ many seats _____ it almost seems dead.

22 But _____ _____ _____ _____ _____ wins, it's _____ _____.

23 _____ _____ for us poor people.

24 We worked yesterday, and we _____ _____ _____ tomorrow.

25 We _____ lots of olives _____ our olive trees this year.

26 I _____ a man _____ sons are good _____.

27 He _____ the olives _____, and his two sons helped him, _____ them _____ _____ the ground.

28 I _____ him 27,000 lire _____ the work.

29 I _____ 12,000 more _____ the olive _____.

30 I got _____ oil _____ _____ a large pot and a small _____.

31 I can sell it _____ _____ _____ _____ 1,300 lire a liter.

32 My love, my heart thinks of you _____ Christmas is coming.

33 I _____ _____ so happy if you _____ _____ me.

34 We all _____ you so much.

35 I'm sending you _____ _____ _____ from me and our three _____ _____.

36 Goodbye, _____ _____.

37 My heart is yours, _____ to you _____ our two rings are.

17 당신의 어머니께서는 병이 드셨고, 나는 약간의 돈과 음식을 가지고 병원에 있는 어머니를 방문할 예정이에요.

18 큰애가 막내를 돌보는 동안 둘째와 함께 그곳에 갈 거예요.

19 나는 150,000리라에 두 일꾼을 시켜 우리 밭을 준비하고 씨앗을 심게 했어요.

20 나는 DC에 투표했어요.

21 PCI는 매우 많은 의석을 잃어서 거의 죽은 것처럼 보여요.

22 하지만 이쪽이 이기건 저쪽이 이기건, 상황은 똑같아요.

23 우리 가난한 사람들에게는 아무것도 바뀌지 않지요.

24 우리는 어제도 일했고, 내일도 다시 일할 거예요.

25 우리는 올해 올리브나무에서 올리브를 많이 땄어요.

26 나는 아들들이 훌륭한 일꾼인 한 남자를 고용했어요.

27 그가 올리브를 쳐서 떨어뜨리면 그의 두 아들이 땅에서 올리브를 주우면서 그를 도왔어요.

28 나는 그 일을 위해 그에게 27,000리라를 지급했어요.

29 올리브 압착을 위해 12,000리라를 더 썼어요.

30 나는 큰 항아리 하나와 작은 항아리 하나를 채울 만큼 충분한 기름을 얻었어요.

31 리터당 1,300리라의 가격으로 팔 수 있을 것 같아요.

32 여보, 크리스마스가 다가오면서 내 마음은 당신을 떠올려요.

33 당신이 나와 함께 있다면 난 정말 행복할 거예요.

34 우리는 모두 당신을 매우 많이 그리워해요.

35 나와 우리 세 아이의 큰 포옹을 보내요.

36 잘 있어요, 여보.

37 내 마음은 당신의 것이에요, 우리들의 두 반지처럼 당신과 연결된 채로요.

※ 다음 문장을 우리말로 쓰시오.

1 A Picture Letter from a Mother of Three

➡ _____

2 Speaking to family members or friends in a foreign country is rather easy and simple today.

➡ _____

3 But before the days of phones and the Internet, it was not that easy.

➡ _____

4 People just sent a letter and waited for a reply for weeks.

➡ _____

5 And it was a lot harder if they couldn't read or write.

➡ _____

6 This letter shows how people got over these difficulties.

➡ _____

7 It was written in 1973 by a woman whose husband was far away.

➡ _____

8 She lived in Sicily, an Italian island, while her husband worked in Germany.

➡ _____

9 At the time, more than 5% of the people in Italy could not read or write, and she was one of them.

➡ _____

10 This letter was discovered by Sicilian writer Gesualdo Bufalino.

➡ _____

11 Here's how he translated the pictures into words.

➡ _____

12 My dear love, I miss you so much, and I reach my arms out toward you, together with our three kids.

➡ _____

13 We are all in good health except for the little one.

➡ _____

14 He's a little sick, but not seriously.

➡ _____

15 I already sent you a letter, but there was no reply, so I am sad about it.

➡ _____

16 If I got a letter from you, I would be very happy.

➡ _____

17 Your mother fell ill, and I'm going to visit her in the hospital with some money and food.

➡ _____

18 I'll go there with our middle son while the oldest looks after the youngest.
➡ _____

19 I had two workers prepare our field and plant seeds for 150,000 lire.
➡ _____

20 I voted for the DC.
➡ _____

21 The PCI lost so many seats that it almost seems dead.
➡ _____

22 But whether one or the other wins, it's the same.
➡ _____

23 Nothing changes for us poor people.
➡ _____

24 We worked yesterday, and we will work again tomorrow.
➡ _____

25 We picked lots of olives from our olive trees this year.
➡ _____

26 I hired a man whose sons are good workers.
➡ _____

27 He knocked the olives down, and his two sons helped him, picking them up from the ground.
➡ _____

28 I paid him 27,000 lire for the work.
➡ _____

29 I spent 12,000 more for the olive press.
➡ _____

30 I got enough oil to fill a large pot and a small one.
➡ _____

31 I can sell it at a price of 1,300 lire a liter.
➡ _____

32 My love, my heart thinks of you as Christmas is coming.
➡ _____

33 I would be so happy if you were with me.
➡ _____

34 We all miss you so much.
➡ _____

35 I'm sending you a big hug from me and our three little kids.
➡ _____

36 Goodbye, dear love.
➡ _____

37 My heart is yours, joined to you as our two rings are.
➡ _____

※ 다음 괄호 안의 단어들을 우리말에 맞도록 바르게 배열하시오.

1 (Picture / A / from / Letter / a / Three / of / Mother)
➡ _____

2 (to / speaking / members / family / or / in / friends / a / country / foreign / easy / is / rather / and / today. / simple)
➡ _____

3 (before / but / days / the / phones / of / and / Internet, / the / was / it / that / not / easy.)
➡ _____

4 (just / people / sent / letter / a / and / for / waited / reply / a / weeks. / for)
➡ _____

5 (it / and / was / lot / a / harder / they / if / read / couldn't / write. / or)
➡ _____

6 (letter / this / shows / people / how / over / got / difficulties. / these)
➡ _____

7 (was / it / in / written / 1973 / a / by / whose / woman / was / husband / away. / far)
➡ _____

8 (lived / she / Sicily, / in / Italian / an / island, / her / while / worked / husband / Germany. / in)
➡ _____

9 (the / at / time, / than / more / 5% / the / of / people / Italy / in / not / could / write, / or / read / and / was / she / of / one / them.)
➡ _____

10 (letter / this / discovered / was / Sicilian / by / writer / Bufalino. / Gesualdo)
➡ _____

11 (how / here's / translated / he / pictures / the / words. / into)
➡ _____

12 (dear / my / love, / miss / I / so / you / much, / and / reach / I / arms / my / toward / out / you, / with / together / three / our / kids.)
➡ _____

13 (are / we / in / all / health / good / for / except / little / the / one.)
➡ _____

14 (a / he's / little / sick, / not / but / seriously.)
➡ _____

15 (already / I / sent / a / you / letter, / there / but / no / was / reply, / I / so / am / about / sad / it.)
➡ _____

16 (I / if / got / letter / a / you, / from / would / I / very / be / happy.)
➡ _____

17 (mother / your / ill, / fell / and / going / I'm / visit / to / in / her / hospital / the / with / money / some / food. / and)
➡ _____

18 (go / I'll / with / there / our / son / middle / the / while / looks / oldest / the / after / youngest.)
➡ _____

1 세 아이의 엄마가 보낸 그림 편지

2 오늘날 외국에 있는 가족이나 친구와 대화하는 것은 다소 쉽고 간단하다.

3 하지만 전화와 인터넷 시대 이전에는 그것이 그렇게 쉽지 않았다.

4 사람들은 단지 편지를 보내고 답장을 몇 주 동안 기다렸다.

5 그리고 그들이 읽거나 쓸 수 없었다면 그건 훨씬 더 힘들었다.

6 이 편지는 사람들이 이런 어려움을 어떻게 극복했는지 보여준다.

7 그것은 남편이 멀리 떨어져 살았던 한 여자에 의해 1973년에 쓰여졌다.

8 그녀의 남편은 독일에서 일한 반면, 그녀는 이탈리아의 섬인 시실리에서 살았다.

9 그 당시에는 5% 이상의 이탈리아 사람들이 읽거나 쓸 수 없었고, 그녀도 그들 중 한 명이었다.

10 이 편지는 시실리의 작가 Gesualdo Bufalino가 발견하였다.

11 그가 그림들을 어떻게 글로 번역했는지는 다음과 같다.

12 사랑하는 여보, 난 당신이 정말 그립고, 우리 세 아이와 함께 당신을 향해 내 팔을 쭉 뻗고 있어요.

13 막내를 제외하고는 우리 모두 건강해요.

14 그 아이는 약간 아프지만 심각하진 않아요.

15 난 당신에게 이미 편지를 보냈지만, 답장이 없어서 그것 때문에 나는 슬퍼요.

16 당신에게서 편지를 받는다면, 나는 정말 행복할 거예요.

17 당신의 어머니께서는 병이 드셨고, 나는 약간의 돈과 음식을 가지고 병원에 있는 어머니를 방문할 예정이에요.

18 큰애가 막내를 돌보는 동안 둘째와 함께 그곳에 갈 거예요.

19 (had / I / two / prepare / workers / field / our / and / seeds / plant / for / lire. / 150,000)

➡ _____

20 (voted / I / the / for / DC.)

➡ _____

21 (PCI / the / so / lost / seats / many / that / almost / it / dead. / seems)

➡ _____

22 (whether / but / or / one / other / the / wins, / the / it's / same.)

➡ _____

23 (changes / nothing / us / for / people. / poor)

➡ _____

24 (worked / we / yesterday, / we / and / will / again / work / tomorrow.)

➡ _____

25 (picked / we / of / lots / olives / our / from / olive / this / trees / year.)

➡ _____

26 (hired / I / man / a / whose / are / sons / workers. / good)

➡ _____

27 (knocked / he / olives / the / down, / and / two / his / helped / sons / him, / them / picking / up / the / from / ground.)

➡ _____

➡ _____

28 (paid / I / him / lire / 27,000 / for / work. / the)

➡ _____

29 (spent / I / 12,000 / for / more / olive / the / press.)

➡ _____

30 (got / I / enough / to / oil / fill / large / a / pot / and / a / one. / small)

➡ _____

31 (can / I / sell / at / it / price / a / of / lire / 1,300 / liter. / a)

➡ _____

32 (love, / my / heart / my / thinks / of / as / you / is / Christmas / coming.)

➡ _____

33 (would / I / so / be / happy / you / if / with / were / me.)

➡ _____

34 (all / we / you / miss / much. / so)

➡ _____

35 (sending / I'm / a / you / big / from / hug / and / me / our / little / three / kids.)

➡ _____

36 (dear / goodbye, / love.)

➡ _____

37 (heart / my / yours, / is / to / joined / you / our / as / rings / two / are.)

➡ _____

---

19 나는 150,000리라에 두 일꾼을 시켜 우리 밭을 준비하고 씨앗을 심게 했어요.

20 나는 DC에 투표했어요.

21 PCI는 매우 많은 의석을 잃어서 거의 죽은 것처럼 보여요.

22 하지만 이쪽이 이기건 저쪽이 이기건, 상황은 똑같아요.

23 우리 가난한 사람들에게는 아무것도 바뀌지 않지요.

24 우리는 어제도 일했고, 내일도 다시 일할 거예요.

25 우리는 올해 올리브나무에서 올리브를 많이 땄어요.

26 나는 아들들이 훌륭한 일꾼인 한 남자를 고용했어요.

27 그가 올리브를 쳐서 떨어뜨리면 그의 두 아들이 땅에서 올리브를 주우면서 그를 도왔어요.

28 나는 그 일을 위해 그에게 27,000리라를 지급했어요.

29 올리브 압착을 위해 12,000리라를 더 썼어요.

30 나는 큰 항아리 하나와 작은 항아리 하나를 채울 만큼 충분한 기름을 얻었어요.

31 리터당 1,300리라의 가격으로 팔 수 있을 것 같아요.

32 여보, 크리스마스가 다가오면서 내 마음은 당신을 떠올려요.

33 당신이 나와 함께 있다면 난 정말 행복할 거예요.

34 우리는 모두 당신을 매우 많이 그리워해요.

35 나와 우리 세 아이의 큰 포옹을 보내요.

36 잘 있어요, 여보.

37 내 마음은 당신의 것이에요, 우리들의 두 반지처럼 당신과 연결된 채로요.

※ 다음 우리말을 영어로 쓰시오.

1 세 아이의 엄마가 보낸 그림 편지

➡ _____

2 오늘날 외국에 있는 가족이나 친구와 대화하는 것은 다소 쉽고 간단하다.

➡ _____

3 하지만 전화와 인터넷 시대 이전에는 그것이 그렇게 쉽지 않았다.

➡ _____

4 사람들은 단지 편지를 보내고 답장을 몇 주 동안 기다렸다.

➡ _____

5 그리고 그들이 읽거나 쓸 수 없었다면 그건 훨씬 더 힘들었다.

➡ _____

6 이 편지는 사람들이 이런 어려움을 어떻게 극복했는지 보여 준다.

➡ _____

7 그것은 남편이 멀리 떨어져 살았던 한 여자에 의해 1973년에 쓰여졌다.

➡ _____

8 그녀의 남편은 독일에서 일한 반면, 그녀는 이탈리아의 섬인 시실리에서 살았다.

➡ _____

9 그 당시에는 5% 이상의 이탈리아 사람들이 읽거나 쓸 수 없었고, 그녀도 그들 중 한 명이었다.

➡ _____

10 이 편지는 시실리의 작가 Gesualdo Bufalino가 발견하였다.

➡ _____

11 그가 그림들을 어떻게 글로 번역했는지는 다음과 같다.

➡ _____

12 사랑하는 여보, 난 당신이 정말 그립고, 우리 세 아이와 함께 당신을 향해 내 팔을 쭉 뻗고 있어요.

➡ _____

13 막내를 제외하고는 우리 모두 건강해요.

➡ _____

14 그 아이는 약간 아프지만 심각하진 않아요.

➡ _____

15 난 당신에게 이미 편지를 보냈지만, 답장이 없어서 그것 때문에 나는 슬퍼요.

➡ _____

16 당신에게서 편지를 받는다면, 나는 정말 행복할 거예요.

➡ _____

17 당신의 어머니께서는 병이 드셨고, 나는 약간의 돈과 음식을 가지고 병원에 있는 어머니를 방문할 예정이에요.

➡ _____

18 큰애가 막내를 돌보는 동안 둘째와 함께 그곳에 갈 거예요.
➡ _____

19 나는 150,000리라에 두 일꾼을 시켜 우리 밭을 준비하고 씨앗을 심게 했어요.
➡ _____

20 나는 DC에 투표했어요.
➡ _____

21 PCI는 매우 많은 의석을 잃어서 거의 죽은 것처럼 보여요.
➡ _____

22 하지만 이쪽이 이기건 저쪽이 이기건, 상황은 똑같아요.
➡ _____

23 우리 가난한 사람들에게는 아무 것도 바뀌지 않지요.
➡ _____

24 우리는 어제도 일했고, 내일도 다시 일할 거예요.
➡ _____

25 우리는 올해 올리브나무에서 올리브를 많이 땄어요.
➡ _____

26 나는 아들들이 훌륭한 일꾼인 한 남자를 고용했어요.
➡ _____

27 그가 올리브를 쳐서 떨어뜨리면 그의 두 아들이 땅에서 올리브를 주우면서 그를 도왔어요.
➡ _____

28 나는 그 일을 위해 그에게 27,000리라를 지급했어요.
➡ _____

29 올리브 압착을 위해 12,000리라를 더 썼어요.
➡ _____

30 나는 큰 항아리 하나와 작은 항아리 하나를 채울 만큼 충분한 기름을 얻었어요.
➡ _____

31 리터당 1,300리라의 가격으로 팔 수 있을 것 같아요.
➡ _____

32 여보, 크리스마스가 다가오면서 내 마음은 당신을 떠올려요.
➡ _____

33 당신이 나와 함께 있다면 난 정말 행복할 거예요.
➡ _____

34 우리는 모두 당신을 매우 많이 그리워해요.
➡ _____

35 나와 우리 세 아이의 큰 포옹을 보내요.
➡ _____

36 잘 있어요, 여보.
➡ _____

37 내 마음은 당신의 것이에요, 우리들의 두 반지처럼 당신과 연결된 채로요.
➡ _____

※ 다음 우리말과 일치하도록 빈칸에 알맞은 말을 쓰시오.

Express Yourself C1

1. The boy _____ head _____ _____ _____ bees _____
   _____ the woman's gesture.

2. I think it _____ "_____ _____ the pond."

3. If I _____ the boy, I _____ _____ _____ the pond
   _____ _____.

1. 머리가 벌로 덮인 소년은 그 여자의 몸짓을 이해하지 못합니다.
2. 제 생각에 그것은 "연못으로 뛰어들어."를 의미합니다.
3. 제가 그 소년이라면, 저는 당장 연못으로 뛰어들겠습니다.

Project Do It Yourself

1. "_____ _____ the mountain."

2. If I _____ soldiers to lead, I _____ _____ _____ _____
   _____ my messages.

3. For example, I _____ _____ a kite _____ face _____
   _____ a mountain to _____ _____ _____ _____ up
   the mountain.

1. "산 위로 올라가라."
2. 내가 병사를 지휘한다면, 나는 나의 메시지를 보내기 위해 연을 사용하겠다.
3. 예를 들어, 나는 병사들이 산 위로 올라가게 하려고 앞면이 산처럼 보이는 연을 날리겠다.

Link to the World

1. Hangeul _____ _____ _____ King Sejong.

2. _____ _____, many people _____ _____ _____
   _____ this new _____ _____.

3. _____, King Sejong _____ _____ _____ _____ people
   _____ Hangeul.

4. _____ _____ him, we _____ _____ _____ _____
   Hangeul now.

5. If we _____ _____ Hangeul, we _____ _____ _____
   _____ easily.

1. 한글은 세종대왕에 의해 창제되었다.
2. 처음에는 많은 사람이 이 새로운 문자 체계를 사용하는 것을 원하지 않았다.
3. 하지만, 세종대왕은 사람들이 한글을 사용하도록 돕기 위해 열심히 노력했다.
4. 그분 덕택에, 우리는 지금 한글로 무엇이든 표현할 수 있다.
5. 우리가 한글을 모른다면, 우리 자신을 쉽게 표현할 수 없을 것이다.

※ 다음 우리말을 영어로 쓰시오.

Express Yourself C1

1. 머리가 별로 덮인 소년은 그 여자의 몸짓을 이해하지 못합니다.

➡ _____

2. 제 생각에 그것은 "연못으로 뛰어들어."를 의미합니다.

➡ _____

3. 제가 그 소년이라면, 저는 당장 연못으로 뛰어들겠습니다.

➡ _____

Project Do It Yourself

1. "산 위로 올라가라."

➡ _____

2. 내가 병사를 지휘한다면, 나는 나의 메시지를 보내기 위해 연을 사용하겠다.

➡ _____

3. 예를 들어, 나는 병사들이 산 위로 올라가게 하려고 앞면이 산처럼 보이는 연을 날리겠다.

➡ _____

_____

Link to the World

1. 한글은 세종대왕에 의해 창제되었다.

➡ _____

2. 처음에는 많은 사람이 이 새로운 문자 체계를 사용하는 것을 원하지 않았다.

➡ _____

3. 하지만, 세종대왕은 사람들이 한글을 사용하도록 돕기 위해 열심히 노력했다.

➡ _____

4. 그분 덕택에, 우리는 지금 한글로 무엇이든 표현할 수 있다.

➡ _____

5. 우리가 한글을 모른다면, 우리 자신을 쉽게 표현할 수 없을 것이다.

➡ _____

MEMO

MEMO

MEMO

영어 기출 문제집

적중 100

1학기

정답 및 해설

천재 | 정사열

중 3

영어 기출 문제집

적중 100

1학기

정답 및 해설

천재 | 정사열

중 3

Laugh First and Then Think

시험대비 실력평가   p.08

01 discovery 02 ②   03 ④   04 ⑤
05 were eager to finish   06 ③
07 darkness   08 ①

01 '처음으로 어떤 것을 발견하는 행위'란 뜻의 '발견 (discovery)'이 적절하다.

02 • 그 고양이와 그 개 사이의 우정은 매우 특이하다. • 몇몇 사람들은 돼지, 이구아나 심지어 뱀과 같은 특이한 애완동물을 키운다.

03 학위를 받기 위해서 공부하는 가장 높은 수준의 교육 기관

04 배에서 일하는 사람

05 '어서 ~하고 싶어 하다'는 'be eager to+동사원형'을 사용한다.

06 (A) 7월 16일에 한국어 말하기 대회가 미국 캘리포니아에서 열렸다. (B) 그 소년은 반 학생들 앞에서 연설을 했다.

07 '형용사 – 명사' 관계이다. 형용사에 '–ness'를 붙여 명사로 만들 수 있다.

08 (A) 그 대문은 사람들이 공원에 들어가는 것을 막는다. keep+목적어+from V-ing: …가 ~하지 못하게 하다 (B) Leonardo da Vinci의 그림들은 많은 돈의 가치가 있다.

서술형 시험대비   p.09

01 (1) bored   (2) repeatedly   (3) A number
   (4) received
02 award
03 (1) navy, 해군   (2) magnet, 자석
   (3) invent, 발명하다   (4) ceremony, 의식, 식
04 not only, but also, invention, useful enough
05 (1) (a)ccept   (2) (h)umor   (3) (e)conomics
   (4) (f)illed   (5) (i)maginative

01 (1) 지루하지 않게 기내에 게임을 가지고 와라. 사람이 지루하다는 의미로 'get bored'를 사용한다. (2) 동사 sang을 수식하는 부사(repeatedly)가 적절하다. (3) '많은 학생들'이란 의미로 a number of students를 사용한다. (4) 과거 시점인 '지난(last) 크리스마스'가 있으므로 과거동사 received가 적절하다.

02 '업적을 기리기 위해 주어지는 상이나 기타 인정의 표시'의 의미로 award가 적절하다.

03 (1) 배와 함선으로 이루어진 군대 (2) 다른 철을 끌어당기는 금속 조각 (3) 새로운 것을 만들거나 디자인하거나 생각해 내다 (4) 특별한 전통을 가진 공식적인 공개 행사

04 A뿐만 아니라 B도: not only A but also B, 발명: invention, 충분히 유용한: useful enough

05 (1) 이 회사의 직원들은 고객들로부터 어떠한 선물도 받지 않았다. (2) 나는 유머 감각이 좋다고 생각한다. (3) 나는 은행원이 되기 위해 대학에서 경제학을 공부할 것이다. (4) 큰 상자는 가난한 사람들을 위한 따뜻한 옷으로 가득 차 있다. (5) 그 동화 작가는 상상력이 매우 풍부하다.

교과서
Conversation

핵심 Check   p.10~11

1 I'm really looking forward to it.
2 (D) → (B) → (C) → (A)

01 '기대하다'의 의미로 forward를 포함하는 것은 'look forward to'이다.

교과서 대화문 익히기

Check(√) True or False   p.12~13

1 T 2 F 3 T 4 F 5 F 6 T 7 T 8 T

교과서 확인학습   p.15~17

Get Ready 2
(1) solved a lot of, I'm sure, award / think so / keep, crossed
(2) winner, award / to get, prize / I'm sure, Good luck
(3) looking forward to / make, laugh, get the prize
(4) keep my fingers crossed

Start Off – Listen & Talk A
1. can't wait for / What, going to do / practiced, for / looking forward to / Actually, a little worried, afraid, make, mistake / Don't worry, do, job, my fingers crossed
2. take part in / m going to, end / forward, seeing / sure, win / do your best, keep my fingers crossed

are you coming / going, for me to try / sure, do great, keep, crossed / perform, other / sounds fun, looking forward, watching, stage

Start Off – Speak Up

looking forward to, model, ready / so, nervous / do well, keep, crossed

Step Up – Real-life Scene

field trip, talent show / like, do, jokes / looking forward to it / show, sure / worry, do great, keep my fingers crossed / Let, show, Guess / sound like / show / make, laugh out loud

Fun Time

m going to / sounds great, m really looking forward to

enter, m worried about / keep my fingers crossed

Express Yourself A

1. Can you tell me, invention / a pair of special, clean, floor / win a prize, keep

2. interesting, cutting board, feeder / not only, board but also, feeder, at the same time / idea / looking forward, using

시험대비 기본평가
p.18

01 keep my fingers crossed

02 ③   03 ⑤   04 ②

01 상대가 하는 일이 잘 되기를 기원하면서 '행운을 빌어!'라고 할 때 'I'll keep my fingers crossed (for you)!'라고 한다.

02 빈칸 뒤의 말이 결과의 접속사 so로 연결되어 '그러니 네가 상을 탈 거야.'라고 말하는 것으로 보아 빈칸은 Best Joker상을 타는 이유가 나오는 것이 타당하다.

03 그 상을 받고 싶다는 G의 말에 대한 대답으로 '네가 이번에는 그 상을 탈 거라고 확신해.'라고 말하는 것이 적절하다.

04 '준비가 됐니?'라는 말에 그런 것 같다고 말한 다음 but으로 이어지는 문장으로 보아 앞 문장과 대조되는 단어가 오는 것이 적절하다.

시험대비 실력평가
p.19~20

01 (A) seeing   (B) crossed   02 ③

03 ⑤   04 ④

05 the game Kick a Shoe and perform a funny dance with some other mothers   06 ⑤

07 I'm really looking forward to using it.

08 ④   09 ⑤   10 ④

11 I'm looking forward to your game.

01 (A) 전치사 to 뒤의 동사를 동명사로 바꾸어야 한다. (B) '동사(keep)+목적어(my fingers)+목적보어'의 5형식 구문으로 목적어와 수동의 관계일 때는 과거분사(crossed)가 적절하다.

02 소윤의 엄마가 경기에 뛰기를 원한다는 내용은 언급되어 있지 않다.

03 ⑤번은 'look forward to+동명사/명사' 형태를 취한다. watch를 watching으로 바꾸어야 한다.

04 (A)는 행운을 빌어주는 표현이나, ④번은 긴장한 실내에게 긴장을 풀어주는 표현이다.

05 'Kick a Shoe' 게임에 참가하고, 다른 엄마들과 코믹 댄스를 할 것이다.

06 빈칸 다음에 '너는 동시에 두 가지를 할 수 있어.'라고 말하는 것으로 보아 도마와 새 모이통 둘 다 사용 가능하다는 것을 알 수 있다.

07 '~을 기대한다'의 의미로 'be looking forward to -ing'를 이용한다.

08 주어진 문장은 '내가 나의 연기의 한 부분을 보여 줄게.'라는 의미로 'Guess who?' 앞에 들어가는 것이 적절하다.

09 Jimin이 몇 번이나 장기 자랑에 참가했는지는 대화에서 언급되어 있지 않다.

10 빈칸 다음의 엄마가 '그날 무엇을 할 거니?'라는 말로 보아 ④가 가장 자연스럽다.

11 '~을 기대하고 있다'는 'be looking for+명사/동명사'를 사용한다.

서술형 시험대비
p.21

01 (A) I'm (really) looking forward to it.
   (B) I'll keep my fingers crossed!

02 He talked like his English teacher.

03 It is not only a cutting board but also a bird feeder.

04 I'm afraid I'll make a mistake.

05 I can't wait for the sports day.

01 (A) 기대를 표현하는 말은 'be looking to+명사/동명사'를 사용한다. (B) 기원을 표현하는 말은 'keep one's fingers crossed'를 사용한다.

02 질문: 대화에서 Jimin은 누구처럼 말했는가?

03 'A뿐만 아니라 B도'의 의미로 'B as well as A'는 'not only A but also B'를 사용한다.

04 빈칸 앞에 '사실은, 전 조금 걱정이 돼요.'라고 말하는 것으로 보아 '실수할까봐 겁나요.'라는 말이 적절하다.

05 '~가 기다려진다'라는 표현은 'I can't wait for+명사'를 이용한다.

Grammar

핵심 Check
p.22~23

1 (1) strong enough (2) to win (3) for young students

2 (1) intensely (2) but (3) are they

시험대비 기본평가
p.24

01 (1) popular enough to win the award

(2) are easy enough to sing

(3) brave but also very nice

(4) is not only lovely but also smart

02 (1) Their music is great enough to make their fans excited.

(2) Their fans are excited enough to cry out.

(3) Pinocchio is not only popular but also very nice.

(4) I know not only the meaning of "eager" but also the meaning of "eagerness".

03 (1) The singer is tall enough to reach the shelf.

(2) The flower is big enough to cover the woman's face.

---

01 (1), (2) '~할 만큼 충분히 …한'의 문장은 '형용사/부사 +enough to+동사원형'의 형태로 쓴다. (3), (4) '~뿐만 아니라 …도 역시'의 문장은 'not only ~ but also …'의 형태로 쓴다.

02 (1) 'enough'는 형용사/부사 뒤에 위치한다. (2) 'enough' 다음에 to부정사를 쓴다. (3) 'not only ~ but also …'에 be동사의 보어로 둘 다 형용사를 써야 한다. (4) 'not only ~ but also …' 사이에 두 어구의 형태를 일치시킨다.

03 '~할 만큼 충분히 …한'의 문장은 '형용사/부사+enough to+동사원형'의 형태로 쓴다.

시험대비 실력평가
p.25~27

01 ⑤ **02** ③ **03** ④ **04** ⑤

05 ⑤ **06** ③

07 The room is big enough to accommodate up to 100 people. **08** ④

09 (1) He was so diligent that he could finish the work. 또는 He is so diligent that he can finish the work.

(2) Tom as well as his parents is eating chicken. 또는 His parents as well as Tom are eating chicken.

---

10 The puzzle was easy enough for me to solve.

11 ①

12 (1) nice enough (2) too (3) to fight

(4) wear it (5) it can run **13** ①, ④

14 This building is strong enough to survive a heavy storm.

15 The book is interesting enough to read several times.

16 ④ **17** ⑤

18 The river is deep enough for a huge ship to sail on.

19 ③ **20** (1) lovely (2) strong

---

01 enough는 형용사와 부사는 뒤에서, 명사는 앞 또는 뒤에서 수식한다. 형용사 'shy'를 앞에서 수식하는 단어로 'enough'를 사용할 수 없다. ⑤에는 'too'가 적절하다.

02 의미가 올바른 것은 ②, ③, ⑤이나 어법까지 적절하게 쓰인 문장은 ③이다. ③ 나뿐만 아니라 Oliver도 독일어를 학생들에게 가르친다. ① 나와 Oliver 둘 중 한 사람이 독일어를 학생들에게 가르친다. ② 나뿐만 아니라 Oliver도 독일어를 학생들에게 가르친다.(teach → teaches) ④ 나와 Oliver 둘 다 독일어를 학생들에게 가르치지 않는다. ⑤ 나와 Oliver 둘 다 독일어를 학생들에게 가르친다.(teaches → teach)

03 형용사 'warm'을 뒤에서 수식하면서 'to부정사'와 짝을 이루는 단어로 'enough'가 적절하다.

04 'enjoy'는 동명사를 목적어로 하는 동사이므로, 'not only 동명사 but also 동명사'의 형태로 써야 한다.

05 ①~④: (원인) 날씨가 매우 추웠다. (결과) 우리는 교실에 머물렀다. ⑤는 '날씨가 너무 추워서 우리는 교실에 머물 수 없었다.'의 뜻으로 의미가 전혀 다르다.

06 첫 번째 문장에서 접속사 'that'과 함께 쓸 수 있는 것은 'so'이다. 두 번째 문장에서 형용사 'sad'를 앞에서 수식하면서 'to부정사'와 함께 쓸 수 있는 것은 'too'이다.

07 '~할 만큼 충분히 …한'의 문장은 '형용사/부사+enough to+동사원형'의 형태로 쓴다.

08 'so+형용사/부사+that+주어+(can)+동사원형'은 '형용사/부사+enough to+동사원형'의 형태로 문장을 전환한다.

09 (1) 주절과 that절의 시제를 맞춘다. (2) 'as well as' 앞에 있는 주어의 수에 동사를 맞춘다.

10 'enough to'를 사용하여 문장을 만들 때, 문장의 주어와 'to부정사'의 주어가 다를 경우, 부정사의 의미상 주어 'for+목적격'을 부정사 앞에 넣는다. 이때 문장의 주어가 'to부정사'의 목적어 자리에 중복되어 나타나지 않도록 목적어를 쓰지 않아야 한다.

11 'Not only ~ but also …'가 주어로 쓰일 경우 동사의 수의 일치는 'but also'와 쓰인 주어에 맞춰야 하므로 ①의 동사 'are'를 'is'로 쓰는 것이 올바르다.

12 (1), (2) 부사 'enough'는 형용사나 다른 부사를 뒤에서 수식한다. (3) '형용사/부사+enough to+동사원형'의 형태로 문장을 쓴다. (4) that절에서는 목적어를 생략하지 않는다. (5) 접속사 'that' 다음에는 '주어+동사'의 형태가 오는 것이 올바르다.

13 ② John이 아니고 Mary가 ③ Mary와 John 둘 다 아닌 ⑤ John 또는 Mary 둘 중 한 명이

14 '~할 만큼 충분히 …한'의 문장은 '형용사/부사+enough to+동사원형'의 형태로 쓴다.

15 '~할 만큼 충분히 …한'의 문장은 '형용사/부사+enough to+동사원형'의 형태로 쓴다.

16 ④ '그는 너무 힘이 세서 그 모든 책을 나를 수 없었다.'는 내용상 어색하므로 'too strong' 대신 'strong enough'를 쓰는 것이 자연스럽다. (그는 그 모든 책을 나를 수 있을 만큼 충분히 힘이 세다.) ① 그는 너무 어려서 학교에 갈 수 없었다. ② 날씨가 너무 더워서 우리는 수영장에 갔다. ③ 그녀는 진실을 지지할 만큼 용감했다. ⑤ 그 상자는 어린이가 들어 올릴 수 있을 만큼 가볍다.

17 상관접속사 'both A and B'가 주어일 때. 그 주어는 복수이다. 그러므로 동사는 'were'가 적절하고, 형용사 'hungry'를 뒤에서 수식하면서 to부정사와 함께 쓸 수 있는 단어로 'enough'가 적절하다.

18 '~할 만큼 충분히 …한'의 문장은 '형용사/부사+enough to+동사원형'의 형태로 쓴다.

19 • 그는 매우 똑똑하다. • 그는 500 조각 퍼즐을 맞출 수 있다. → '그는 500 조각 퍼즐을 맞출 수 있을 정도로 똑똑하다.'에 적절한 문장은 ③이다.

20 두 단어가 짝을 이루어 하나의 접속사 역할을 하는 상관접속사에서는, 사용된 두 어구의 형태를 일치시킨다. 첫 번째 문장은 'heavy'와 같은 형용사인 'lovely'가 적절하고, 두 번째 문장은 be동사의 보어인 형용사 'strong'이 적절하다.

서술형 시험대비
p.28~29

01 (1) Eric is not only kind but also smart.
(2) Not only Jake but also you are a student.
(3) She was not only hardworking but also honest.
(4) Not only you but also he runs fast.
(5) Not only you but also he is going to join our club.

02 (1) This invention is useful enough to make your life much easier.
(2) Your smile is bright enough to light up the classroom.
(3) You not only make us happy but also help us (to) get along well.

03 (1) You can use it as a table for playing table tennis as well as as a door.

(2) She was kind enough to show me how to use chopsticks.

04 (1) Mark visited not only his mother but also his friends.
(2) This building is strong enough to survive a heavy storm.
(3) He is tall enough to touch the ceiling.
(4) They sell not only eggs but also milk.
(5) The box is too heavy for the girl to move.

05 The water is clean enough for us to drink.

06 (1) but also as a cup holder
(2) but also for storing things
(3) but also as lights

07 (A) He is a painter as well as a teacher.
(B) She looks not only friendly but also wise.

08 (1) He is tall enough to be a basketball player.
(2) Sumin ran fast enough to get there on time.
(3) The girl was brave enough to speak in front of many people.
(4) It is warm enough to play outside.
(5) He's cheerful enough to make us feel happy.

01 '~뿐 아니라 …도 역시'의 문장은 'not only ~ but also ...'의 형태로 쓴다. 상관접속사가 주어를 연결할 때에는 but also와 함께 쓰인 주어에 동사의 수를 맞춘다.

02 (1), (2) '~할 만큼 충분히 …한'의 문장은 '형용사/부사+enough to+동사원형'의 형태로 쓴다. (3) '~뿐 아니라 …도 역시'의 문장은 'not only ~ but also ...'의 형태로 쓴다.

03 (1) 'not only ~ but also ...'는 '... as well as ~'로 바꾸어 쓸 수 있다. (2) 'so+형용사/부사+that+주어+(can)+동사원형'은 '형용사/부사+enough to+동사원형'의 형태로 문장을 전환한다.

04 (1) 'not only ~ but also ...'의 문장에서 but은 생략하지 않는다. (2) 'enough to+동사원형'의 형태로 쓴다. (3) 'enough tall'로 형용사 'tall'을 뒤에서 수식하면서 to부정사와 같이 쓰는 것이 자연스럽다. (4) 상관접속사를 쓸 때는 두 어구의 형태가 같아야 하는데, 'They sell milk.'가 자연스러우므로, 전치사 'to'를 쓰지 않는다. (5) 'too ~ to ...'에서 문장의 주어와 to부정사의 목적어가 같을 때 그 목적어는 쓰지 않는다.

05 'enough to'를 사용해서 문장을 쓸 때 문장의 주어와 to부정사의 행위자가 다르면 to부정사 앞에 의미상 주어를 'for 목적격'의 형태로 쓴다.

06 두 단어가 짝을 이루어 하나의 접속사 역할을 하는 상관접속사는 짝을 이루는 두 어구의 형태를 일치시켜야 한다. (1) 'as an umbrella'와 'as a cup holder' (2) 'for going up and down'과 'for storing things' (3) 'as shoes'와 'as lights'

07 두 단어가 짝을 이루어 하나의 접속사 역할을 하는 상관접속사

에서는 사용된 두 어구의 형태를 일치시킨다. 첫 번째 문장은 직업을 나타내는 'a teacher - a painter'가 적절하고, 두 번째 문장은 동사 'look'의 보어인 형용사 'wise - friendly'가 적절하다.

08 (1) 형용사 'tall'을 뒤에서 수식하면서 to부정사와 같이 쓰려면 'enough'를 쓰는 것이 자연스럽다. (2) 'enough'는 형용사/부사의 뒤에 위치한다. (3) '그 소녀는 많은 사람들 앞에서 말할 수 있을 만큼 충분히 용감하다'라고 하는 것이 문맥상 자연스러우므로 'too'를 'enough'로 바꾸어 쓴다. (4), (5) 'enough to부정사'의 형태가 올바르다.

교과서 Reading

확인문제
p.30

1 T 2 F 3 T 4 F 5 T

확인문제
p.31

1 T 2 F 3 T 4 F 5 T 6 F

교과서 확인학습 A
p.32~33

01 Ig Nobel
02 happens, backward
03 did research
04 enough to
05 Maybe
06 how about
07 one
08 are awarded for, laugh, think
09 by honoring the unusual, the imaginative
10 are presented by
11 is, filled with, laughable
12 for
13 To save, instead of
14 laugh out loud
15 won an award
16 succeeded in floating
17 a sense of humor
18 bring, to
19 in, for
20 keeps running away
21 Not only, but also, makes
22 a number of, keep, from getting bored
23 two words each
24 an eight-year-old girl called
25 worth less than
26 Throwing, is
27 ends with, did
28 do not receive
29 great honors like
30 a lot more fun

교과서 확인학습 B
p.34~35

1 The Ig Nobel Prize
2 "What happens when you walk backward while you are carrying a cup of coffee?"
3 Han Jiwon, a Korean high school student, did research on this topic in 2015.
4 Is this research project good enough to win a Nobel Prize?
5 Maybe not.
6 But how about an Ig Nobel Prize?
7 He won one in 2017 for this fun research.
8 The Ig Nobel Prizes are awarded for discoveries that "first make one laugh and then think."
9 They were started in 1991 by AIR magazine to increase people's interest in science by honoring the unusual and the imaginative.
10 The prizes are presented by real Nobel winners in Sanders Theater at Harvard University.
11 The room is usually filled with people who are eager to cheer for the brave scientists with their "laughable" research.
12 The U.K. Navy won the Ig Nobel Prize for Peace in 2000.
13 To save money, the Navy made its sailors shout, "Bang!" instead of using real bombs.
14 Is that funny enough for you to laugh out loud?
15 Andre Geim also won an award that year.
16 He succeeded in floating a live frog in the air by using magnets.
17 "In my experience, if people don't have a sense of humor, they are usually not very good scientists," he said when he accepted his award.
18 If that still does not bring a smile to your face, how about this?
19 In 2005, Gauri Nanda won the Ig Nobel Prize in Economics for inventing an alarm clock.
20 It keeps running away until the sleeper finally gets out of bed.
21 Not only the winners' fun studies but also the ceremony for the Ig Nobel Prizes makes people laugh.
22 There are a number of interesting things that keep people from getting bored.
23 The opening and closing speeches are just two words each: "Welcome. Welcome." and "Goodbye. Goodbye."
24 If someone talks for too long, an eight-year-old girl called Miss Sweetie Poo shouts repeatedly, "Please stop! I'm bored."

25 Each winner receives ten trillion Zimbabwean dollars, which is worth less than one U.S. dollar.

26 Throwing paper planes is another fun tradition.

27 The Ig Nobel Prize ceremony ends with the words, "If you didn't win a prize — and if you did — better luck next year!"

28 The winners do not receive lots of money.

29 And the awards are not great honors like the Nobel Prizes.

30 But the Ig Nobel Prizes make science a lot more fun!

시험대비 실력평가
p.36~39

01 ⑤　　　02 ③　　　03 ④　　　04 ⑤

05 ③　　　06 shouting → shout

07 funny enough for you to laugh

08 He won it in 2000.　　09 ③　　10 ③, ④

11 are → is　　　　12 ③　　　13 ②

14 won a prize　　　15 ④　　　16 ②

17 awarded　　　　18 ④

19 ⑤　　　20 running　　21 using magnets

22 (A) with　(B) did　(C) like

23 Unless you won a prize

24 (A) Ig Nobel　(B) Nobel　(C) Ig Nobel

25 ③　　　　26 The Ig Nobel Prizes

27 ⓐ unusual people　ⓓ imaginative people

01 ⓐ on: ~에 관하여, ⓑ for: (이유·원인을 나타내어) ~으로

02 ③번 다음 문장의 But에 주목한다. 주어진 문장의 내용과 상반되는 내용을 뒤이어 소개하고 있으므로 ③번이 적절하다.

03 "first make one laugh and then think"로 고치는 것이 적절하다.

04 돈을 아끼기 위해, 해군에서는 선원들에게 진짜 폭탄을 사용하는 대신에 "쾅!"이라고 소리치게 했다고 하는 것이 적절하다. ② fake: 가짜의, blow: 강타, ④ artificial: 인공적인

05 be eager[anxious/dying] to 동사원형 = be eager[anxious/dying] for 명사[동명사] = long to 동사원형 = long for 명사[동명사]: ~하고 싶은 생각이 간절하다, be anxious about: ~에 대해 염려하다

06 사역동사(made)의 목적격보어이므로 shouting을 원형부정사 shout로 고치는 것이 적절하다.

07 so ~ that ... can = enough to

08 영국 해군이 이그노벨상을 탄 것과 같은 해에 탔다고 했으므로, 2000년에 탔다.

09 ⓑ와 ③: 살아 있는(형용사), ① 살다[생존하다](동사), ② 생

방송[생중계/실황]으로(부사), ④ (공연이) 라이브의, 실황인(형용사), ⑤ (기록이나 기억에) 남다(동사)

10 ⓐ와 ①, ②, ⑤: 반복해서, ③, ④: 갑자기

11 금액을 나타내는 ten trillion Zimbabwean dollars는 단일 개념으로 생각해서 단수동사로 받는다.

12 만일 누군가가 너무 오랫동안 말을 하면 Miss Sweetie Poo가 "Please stop! I'm bored."라고 외친다고 했으므로, 수상 연설을 길게 해야만 한다는 것은 이그노벨상 시상식의 재미있는 전통에 해당하지 않는다.

13 very는 원급을 강조하는 말이고, 나머지는 다 비교급을 강조하는 말이다.

14 'did'는 'won a prize'를 대신하는 대동사이다.

15 (B)와 ④: ~와 (똑)같이[마찬가지로], …처럼(전치사), ①과 ③ (~을) 좋아하다(동사), ② 비슷한(형용사), ⑤ ~한대로[처럼](접속사)

16 돈을 아끼기 위해, 해군에서는 신원들에게 진짜 폭탄을 사용하는 대신에 "쾅!"이라고 소리치게 했다고 하는 것이 적절하다. ①과 ⑤: ~에 더하여, ~뿐 아니라, ③ ~에 덧붙여, ~와 마찬가지로, ④ ~에도 불구하고

17 present: (특히 공식적인 의식을 통해) 주다, 수여[증정]하다, award: <사람에게 상·장학금 등을> (심사하여) 수여하다, 주다

18 '시상식 시기'는 알 수 없다. ① 진짜 노벨상 수상자들, ② Sanders Theater at Harvard University, ③ '웃기는' 연구를 한 용감한 과학자들을 열렬히 격려하고자 하는 사람들, laughable: 웃기는, 터무니없는, ⑤ 영국 해군

19 '사람들이 유머 감각이 없다면, 그들은 대개 별로 훌륭한 과학자가 아니다'라는 앞 문장의 Andre Geim의 말과 어울리는 말로는 ⑤번이 적절하다. ① 안락, 편안, ② 후회, ③ 존경, ④ inner: 내면의

20 keep ~ing: 계속해서 ~하다

21 '자석을 이용해서' 그 일을 했다.

22 (A) '이그노벨상 시상식은 ~로 끝난다.'고 해야 하므로 with가 적절하다. end with: (…으로) 끝나다, end up: 결국 (어떤 처지에) 처하게 되다, (B) 'won a prize'를 대신하는 대동사이므로 did가 적절하다. (C) 노벨상과 '같은'이라고 해야 하므로 like가 적절하다. like: ~와 같은, alike: [형용사] (명사 앞에는 안 씀) (아주) 비슷한

23 unless = if ~ not

24 비록 '이그노벨'상의 상금이 많지 않고 수상자들이 '노벨'상 수상자들처럼 훌륭한 영광을 얻는 것도 아니지만, '이그노벨'상은 과학을 훨씬 더 재미있게 만든다.

25 ⓐ와 ③: 부사적 용법의 부사 수식 용법, 나머지도 다 부사적 용법이지만 ① 판단의 근거, ② 목적, ④ 결과, ⑤ 원인

26 '이그노벨상'을 가리킨다.

27 the+형용사 = 복수 보통명사

01 (A) awarded   (B) honoring

02 Is this research project good enough to win a Nobel Prize?

03 (A) Ig Nobel Prize   (B) fun

04 Real Nobel winners present the prizes in Sanders Theater at Harvard University.

05 save money

06 To save money, the Navy made its sailors shout, "Bang!" instead of using real bombs.

07 unless people have a sense of humor

08 (A) floating   (B) a sense of humor

09 The ceremony for the Ig Nobel Prizes as well as the winners' fun studies makes people laugh.

10 (1) 개회사와 폐회사는 단지 두 마디이다.

   (2) 만일 누군가가 너무 오랫동안 말을 하면, Miss Sweetie Poo라고 하는 여덟 살짜리 여자아이가 "제발 멈춰요! 지루해요."라고 계속 외친다.

   (3) 각 수상자는 미국의 1달러보다 가치가 낮은 10조의 짐바브웨 달러를 받는다.

   (4) 종이비행기를 날린다.

11 Maybe this research project is not good enough to win a Nobel Prize.

12 interest in science

---

01 (A) 이그노벨상이 '수여된다'고 해야 하므로 awarded가 적절하다. award: ~에게 [상벌·장학금 따위]를 주다, 수여하다, reward: 보상[보답/사례]하다, (B) '높이 평가함으로써'라고 해야 하므로 honoring이 적절하다. honor: 존경하다, ignore: 무시하다

02 enough는 형용사를 뒤에서 수식한다.

03 그는 한국의 고등학생이었고, 2015년에 그가 했던 '재미있는' 조사 때문에 2017년에 '이그노벨상'을 받았다.

04 Real Nobel winners를 주어로 하여 고치는 것이 적절하다.

05 돈을 아끼기 위해, 해군에서는 선원들에게 진짜 폭탄을 사용하는 대신에 "쾅!"이라고 소리치게 했다.

06 '돈을 아끼기 위해, 해군에서는 선원들에게 진짜 폭탄을 사용하는 대신에 "쾅!"이라고 소리치게 한 것'을 가리킨다.

07 unless = if ~ not

08 Andre Geim은 자석을 이용해서 살아 있는 개구리를 공중에 '띄우는 데' 성공했고 이그노벨상을 받았다. 그는 수상 연설에서 '유머 감각'을 좋은 과학자의 필수적인 자질로 언급했다.

09 not only A but also B = B as well as A: A뿐만 아니라 B도

10 뒤에 이어지는 내용 네 가지를 쓰면 된다.

11 'Maybe this research project is not good enough to win a Nobel Prize.'에서 'Maybe not.'만 남긴 것이다.

12 *AIR* 잡지는 특이하고 창의적인 사람들을 높이 평가함으로써 '과학에 대한 사람들의 흥미'를 늘리기 위해 그것들을 시작했다.

---

01 unusual   02 ③   03 worried   04 ⑤

05 ①   06 ④   07 laughing → laugh

08 ⑤   09 ③   10 ④   11 ③

12 ⑤

13 Not only Marie Curie but also her daughter was awarded the Nobel Prize.

14 ③   15 ③

16 by email as well as on the phone

17 (1) Ted was kind enough to carry my bag.

   (2) Vivian worked hard enough to save lots of money.

   (3) The yard is so big that we can ride bikes in it.

18 ②   19 who[that] is   20 ②

21 by   22 so, that, can

23 (B) ②, ④, ⑤   (C) ①, ③   24 ③, ④

25 ⑤   26 ②

27 This invention is so useful that it can make your life much easier.

28 ④

---

01 반의어 관계이다. 유용한 - 쓸모없는 : 일반적인 - 특이한

02 (a) 우리는 비가 왔기 때문에 수영장에서 나와야 했다. (b) 그 나라의 대통령은 전쟁을 끝내고 평화를 가져오기를 희망했다.

03 '일어날지도 모르는 문제나 불쾌한 일들에 관해 생각하고 있기 때문에 불행한'의 의미를 갖고 본문의 단어 worry를 활용한 형용사 'worried'가 적절하다.

04 액체의 위에 있고 가라앉지 않다

05 하기를 자랑스러워하는 어떤 것

06 imaginative는 '상상력이 풍부한'이라는 뜻이고, '가상의'는 'imaginary'를 사용한다.

07 사역동사 make는 목적보어 자리에 동사원형을 사용한다.

08 '준비됐니?'라는 말에 B가 '음, 그런 것 같아, 하지만 자신 있어'라고 말하는 것은 어색하다. '준비되었지만 긴장이 되다 또는 불안하다'라는 의미가 오는 것이 자연스럽다.

09 사역동사 let은 목적보어 자리에 동사원형을 사용한다. to show를 show로 바꾸어야 한다.

10 대화의 첫 문장 '수학여행 장기 자랑에서 무엇을 할 거니?'라는 물음에 대한 대답에서 '장기 자랑을 기대하기'라는 것을 알 수 있다.

11 수업 시간에 선생님들이 말하는 것을 흉내 내고 농담도 할 사람은 미소가 아니라 지민이다.

12 주어진 문장의 'that'은 원인과 결과를 나타내는 'that'이다. 이와 같이 쓰인 것은 ⑤이다. ①, ② 명사절을 이끄는 접속사 ③, ④ 관계대명사

13 'Not only ~ but also …'가 주어로 쓰일 경우 수의 일치는 'but also'와 쓰인 주어에 맞춘다.

14 ③ '방은 내가 책을 읽을 수 있을 정도로 충분히 어두웠다.'의 뜻으로 어색한 문장이다.

15 a. jump → jumps, c. such → so, e. making → to make

16 'not only ~ but also …'는 '… as well as ~'로 바꾸어 쓸 수 있다.

17 (1), (2) '~할 만큼 충분히 …한'의 문장은 '형용사/부사 +enough to+동사원형'의 형태로 쓴다. (3) 'so+형용사/부사 +that+주어+동사'의 형태로 '매우 ~해서 …할 수 있다'라는 의미의 문장을 쓴다.

18 turn off the light: 불을 끄다

19 주격 관계대명사와 be동사가 생략되어 있다.

20 ⓑ와 ①, ④: 동명사, ②, ③, ⑤: 현재분사

21 ⓐ 행위자를 나타내는 by, ⓑ by ~ing: ~함으로써

22 ~ enough to = so ~ that … can

23 (B)와 ②, ④, ⑤: 'a+보통명사'를 받은 대명사, (C)와 ①, ③: 일반인을 나타내는 대명사

24 ⓐ와 ①, ②, ⑤: 마침내, 결국, ③ 무엇보다도, ④ 적어도

25 ⑤ Gauri Nanda가 발명한 자명종은 잠자는 사람을 계속 쫓아다니는 것이 아니라, 잠자는 사람이 결국 침대 밖으로 나올 때까지 계속 도망을 다닌다.

26 ⓐ와 ② (자격·기능 등이) ~으로(전치사), ① [이유·원인] ~이므로, ~이기 때문에(접속사), ③ [보통 'as ~ as …'로 형용사·부사 앞에서] …와 같은 정도로('as ~ as …'에서, 앞의 as가 지시부사, 뒤의 as는 접속사), ④ [때] ~일 때(접속사), ⑤ [비례] ~함에 따라, ~할수록(접속사)

27 ~ enough to = so ~ that … can

28 not only[just/simply/merely] A but also B = B as well as A = not only[just/simply/merely] A but B as well: A뿐만 아니라 B도, not A but B: A가 아니라 B

단원별 예상문제
p.48~51

01 float   02 ③   03 Break a leg

04 ②

05 He's going to talk like his teachers do in class and tell some jokes.

06 ③   07 and → or, one thing → two things

08 I'll keep my fingers crossed

09 ④   10 ⑤

11 not only putting → not only for putting   12 ③

13 (1) Tommy is not only strong but also wise.

(2) She has not only knowledge but also courage.

(3) I'm good at not only dancing but also singing.

(4) Not only you but also he wants to see the movie.

14 What happens when you walk backward while you are carrying a cup of coffee?

15 ②, ⑤

16 AIR magazine started them in 1991

17 ③   18 successful   19 ④

20 (A) laugh   (B) think   21 ⑤

22 ①, ②, ③   23 to throw   24 ④

01 반의어 관계이다. 뒤로 - 앞으로 : 가라앉다 - 뜨다

02 '폭발할 물질로 만들어진 무기'란 의미로 '폭탄'이 적절하다

03 'Break a leg!(행운을 빌어!)'라는 표현은 주로 공연이나 행사, 경기 등을 앞두고 있는 사람에게 '행운을 빌어!'라고 격려할 때 자주 쓰인다.

04 지민이 '수업 시간에 선생님들이 말하는 것을 흉내 내고 농담도 할 거야.'라는 말에 → (E) 그것이 기대된다는 말이 오고 → (A) 쇼에 대한 걱정을 말하고 → (D) 긴장을 풀어주며 행운을 비는 표현이 나오고 → (B) 감사의 대답이 온다. 그래서 네 번째 오는 대화는 (B)가 적절하다.

05 질문: 지민은 장기 자랑에서 무엇을 할 것인가? - 지민은 수업 시간에 선생님들이 말하는 것을 흉내 내고 농담도 할 것이다.

06 대화의 흐름상 긴장한 상대방에게 행운을 비는 말이나 긴장을 풀어주는 표현이 오는 것이 적절하다. ③번의 '포기하지 마!'라는 의미는 들어가기에 어색하다.

07 첫 문장은 '이것은 도마니, 아니면 새 모이통이니?'라는 의미로 and를 or로 바꾸어 준다. 그리고 도마일 뿐만 아니라 새 모이통이기도 하다고 했기 때문에 동시에 두 가지를 할 수 있다.

08 '행운을 빌어!'라고 할 때 'I'll keep my fingers crossed!'라고 한다.

09 민지의 엄마가 농구를 할 것을 기대하고 있는 것은 아니다.

10 ⑤번은 빨리 상을 받고 싶다는 의미고, 나머지는 상대에게 행운을 빌어주는 표현이다.

11 '~뿐 아니라 …도 역시'의 문장은 'not only ~ but also …'의 형태로 쓰고 상관접속사에 쓰인 두 어구의 형태를 일치시켜야 한다. 이때 'but also'에서 'You can use it for controlling the TV.'가 적절한 문장이므로 'not only' 부분을 for+동명사의 형태로 바꾸어 써야 한다.

12 not only 대신 not just[simply, merely]를 쓸 수 있다.

13 (1)~(3) '~뿐 아니라 …도 역시'의 문장은 'not only ~ but also …'의 형태로 쓰고 상관접속사에 쓰인 두 단어의 모양을 일치시켜야 한다. (4) 상관접속사에 주어가 쓰인 경우 'but also' 뒤의 주어에 동사의 수를 일치시킨다.

14 '커피 한 잔을 들고 가면서 뒤로 걸을 때 무슨 일이 일어날까?'를 가리킨다.

15 ⓑ와 ②, ⑤: 관계대명사, ① 지시형용사, ③ 접속사, ④ 지시대명사

16 AIR magazine을 주어로 하여 고치는 것이 적절하다.

17 ⓐ in: [성질·능력·기예 등의 분야를 한정하여] ~에서, ⓑ for: [이유·원인] ~ 때문에, ~으로 (인하여)

18 succeed in ~ing = be successful in ~ing

19 위 글은 '초청장'이다. ② 요약, 개요, ③ (신문·잡지의) 글, 기사, ⑤ 광고

20 이그노벨상을 타기 위해서는 사람들을 '웃게' 만드는 것이 사람들을 '생각하게' 만드는 것보다 더 중요하다.

21 누가 상을 수여할지는 알 수 없다. ① In 1991. ② First make one laugh and then think. ③ Thursday, September 14, 2017 6:00 PM. ④ In Sanders Theater at Harvard University.

22 keep/stop/prevent/prohibit A from ~ing: A가 ~하지 못하게 하다, ④ 허락하다, ⑤ 격려[고무]하다, 용기를 북돋우다

23 to부정사를 진주어로 해서 바꿔 쓸 수 있다.

24 개회사와 폐회사는 각각 단지 두 마디이다.

서술형 실전문제 p.52~53

01 I'm looking forward to watching you on the stage.

02 talent show, talk like, tell some jokes, looking forward to

03 I'm looking forward to seeing you at the race.

04 (a) was named (c) have (c) was awarded

05 good enough

06 the unusual and the imaginative

07 (A) laugh (B) think

08 (A) makes (B) is (C) is

09 There are a number of interesting things that[which] keep people from getting bored.

10 It is "Goodbye. Goodbye."

01 '~을 기대한다'의 의미로 'be looking forward to+동명사'를 사용한다.

02 지민과 미소는 장기 자랑에 대해 이야기하고 있다. 지민은 수업 시간에 선생님들이 말하는 것을 흉내 내고 농담도 할 것이다. 미소는 그의 쇼를 기대하고 있다.

03 Soyun이 100미터 달리기를 할 것이라는 말에 네가 경주에서 달리는 모습을 보는 것이 기대된다는 표현이 적절하다.

04 (1) be named after: ~의 이름을 따서 짓다 (2) 선행사가 복수 명사 people이므로 동사는 'have'로 쓰는 것이 올바르다. (3) 'Not only ~ but also ...'가 주어로 쓰일 경우 동사의 수의 일치는 'but also'와 쓰인 주어에 맞춰야 한다.

05 밑줄 친 ⓐ는 이 연구 과제가 이그노벨상을 받을 만큼 '충분히 훌륭할까'?를 의미한다.

06 the+형용사 = 복수 보통명사

07 AIR 잡지는 과학에 대한 사람들의 흥미를 늘리기 위해 1991년에 그것들을 시작했다. 만약 어떤 발견이 먼저 '웃기고' 나서 다음에 '생각하게' 만들 수 있다면, 그것은 그 상을 수상할 수 있다.

---

08 (A) not only A but also B에서는 B에 동사의 수를 일치시키고, 위 문장에서는 the ceremony가 B에 해당하므로 makes가 적절하다. (B) which의 선행사는 ten trillion Zimbabwean dollars이고, 돈은 단수 취급하므로 is가 적절하다. (C) 동명사가 주어일 때 단수 취급 하므로 is가 적절하다.

09 keep A from ~ing: A가 ~하지 못하게 하다

10 폐회사는 '안녕. 안녕'이다.

창의사고력 서술형 문제 p.54

|모범답안|

01 (A) A: I'm going to go camping with my parents.
   B: Wow! That sounds great.
   A: Yeah, I'm really looking forward to it.
   (B) A: I'm going to have a basketball game next week, but I'm worried about it.
   B: Don't worry. You'll do great. I'll keep my fingers crossed.
   A: Thank you.

02 (1) He is clever enough to understand the novel.
   (2) He is rich enough to buy the building.
   (3) He speaks not only English but also Chinese.
   (4) He is interested in not only basketball but also volleyball.

단원별 모의고사 p.55~60

01 ④   02 eagerness   03 ③

04 ②   05 ①   06 ⑤   07 ④

08 ④   09 (A) crossed (B) watching

10 (1) to talk like his teachers do in class
   (2) to tell some jokes   11 ③

12 Do I sound like our English teacher?

13 He is popular as well as nice.

14 She is both beautiful and lovely.

15 She is neither smart nor creative.

16 ④   17 ①, ④   18 ③

19 We were brave enough to face the strong enemy.

20 Ted is so old that he can talk about the topic.

21 He has not only knowledge but also experience.

22 I must look after the children as well as feed the animals.

23 (1) cutting a pizza
   (2) but also for picking up a piece of pizza

24 (1) Not only she but also you have to leave here.

　(2) Not only I but also my brothers like to play with dogs.

　(3) Not only I but also my best friend is from Busan.

25 ⓐ an Ig Nobel Prize

　ⓑ 커피 한 잔을 들고 가면서 뒤로 걸을 때 무슨 일이 일어날까?

26 makes → make　　　　　27 ④　　　　28 ①

29 a sense of humor

30 (A) an alarm clock　　(B) gets out of bed

31 the number of → a number of / keeps → keep

32 which is worth less than one U.S. dollar

---

01 ④번은 '1,000,000,000,000이라는 수'란 의미로 1조를 가리킨다. 'trillion'이 적절하다. 'million'은 '백만'이다.

02 '형용사-명사' 관계이다. 행복한-행복 : 열렬한-열망

03 '당신이 계획한 것을 성취하다'라는 의미로 '성공하다'가 적절하다.

04 춤 대회에 나가게 되어 걱정이 된다는 친구에게 긴장을 풀어주는 ②번의 대답이 가장 적절하다.

05 G의 말에 우리를 항상 웃게 만든다고 했기 때문에 Best Joker 상을 받기를 기대한다는 말이 자연스럽다.

06 민호는 항상 우리를 웃게 만든다는 A의 말에 B가 '걱정하지 마. 너는 잘 거야.'로 대답하는 것은 어색하다.

07 ④번은 대화의 흐름상 실수할까봐 겁난다고 했기 때문에 '거의 걱정이 되지 않는다.'라는 의미의 'little'을 '조금 걱정이 된다.'라는 의미의 'a little'로 바꾸는 것이 적절하다.

08 G의 마지막 말인 '무대에 선 엄마 모습을 보는 것이 기대돼요.'라는 말로 볼 때 ④에 들어가는 것이 적절하다.

09 (A)는 동사 keep의 목적보어 자리로 목적어인 my fingers의 수동 동작을 나타내는 과거분사 crossed가 적절하다. (B)는 look forward to(전치사) 뒤에 동명사 watching이 적절하다.

10 Jimin은 장기 자랑에서 수업 시간에 선생님이 말하는 것처럼 말하고, 농담을 할 것이다.

11 (A)는 대동사로 앞 문장의 동사 talk을 대신한다.

12 일반동사 의문문으로 'sound like our English teacher'와 중복되는 부분이 생략되어 있다.

13 '~뿐 아니라 …도 역시'의 문장을 'as well as'를 사용하여 쓸 때 강조하는 단어('…도 역시'에 해당하는 말)를 먼저 쓴다.

14 'both A and B'는 'A와 B 둘 다'의 뜻이다.ㅌㅏㄴㅏㄷㅏ

16 'not only ~ but also …'의 상관접속사에 쓰인 두 단어의 모양을 일치시켜야 한다. 일반동사 'sing'은 부사와 함께 써야 하므로 형용사 happy는 부사 happily로 쓰는 것이 적절하다.

17 'too ~ to …'를 사용하여 문장을 만들 때, 문장의 주어와 'to부정사'의 주어가 다를 경우, 부정사의 의미상 주어 'for 목적격'을 to부정사 앞에 넣는다. 이때 문장의 주어가 'to부정사구'의 목적

어 자리에 중복되어 나타내지 않도록 목적어를 쓰지 않아야 한다. 'so ~ that'을 사용할 때는 목적어를 생략하지 않는다.

18 a. to put → for putting, b. dance → danced, d. could → can

19 'so+형용사/부사+that+주어+(can)+동사원형'의 문장은 '형용사/부사+enough to+동사원형'의 형태로 전환할 수 있다.

20 'so+형용사/부사+that+주어+(can)+동사원형'의 문장은 '형용사/부사+enough to+동사원형'의 형태로 전환할 수 있다.

21 'not only ~ but also …'는 '… as well as ~'로 바꾸어 쓸 수 있다.

22 'not only ~ but also …'는 '… as well as ~'로 바꾸어 쓸 수 있다.

23 (1) 전치사 다음에는 동명사구를 쓴다. (2) 'not only for 동명사'이므로 'but also for 동명사'로 쓴다.

24 'Not only ~ but also …'가 주어로 쓰일 경우 동사의 수의 일치는 'but also'와 쓰인 주어에 맞춘다. (1) you (2) my brothers (3) my best friend가 주어이고 이 주어에 동사의 수를 일치시킨다.

25 ⓐ '이그노벨상', ⓑ "What happens when you walk backward while you are carrying a cup of coffee?"를 가리킨다.

26 주격 관계대명사 that의 선행사가 복수형인 discoveries이기 때문에 make로 고치는 것이 적절하다.

27 ⓐ와 ①, ③, ④, ⑤: 부사적 용법, ②: 명사적 용법

28 상은 '진짜 노벨상 수상자들'에 의해 수여된다.

29 Andre Geim에 따르면, 매우 훌륭한 과학자가 되기 위해서는 대체로 '유머 감각'이 필요한 조건이다.

30 Gauri Nanda는 잠자는 사람이 결국 침대 밖으로 나와야만 끌 수 있는 '자명종'을 발명했기 때문에, 2005년에 이그노벨 경제학상을 받았다.

31 '많은' 재미있는 것들이라고 해야 하므로 a number of로 고치는 것이 적절하다. the number of: ~의 수, a number of: 많은, that의 선행사가 a number of interesting things이므로 keep으로 고쳐야 한다.

32 be worth: ~의 가치가 있다

Lesson 4

Dreaming of My Future

01 laughed at   02 ②   03 ⑤
04 ③   05 be afraid of   06 ③
07 allowance   08 ①

01 '당신이 누군가나 어떤 것이 어리석다고 생각하는 것을 보여주다'란 뜻의 '비웃다(laugh at)'가 적절하다.

02 명사로 '판사', 동사로 '판단하다'라는 뜻을 가진 단어는 'judge'가 적절하다. • 판사는 그에게 3년형을 선고했다. • 피부색이 다르다는 이유로 사람을 판단하는 것은 아주 잘못이다.

03 '지구의 대기 또는 태양계 너머의 지역'의 의미로 '우주(space)'가 적절하다.

04 위험하거나 어려운 상황에서 두려움을 조절하는 능력: 용기 (courage)

05 '~을 두려워하다'는 'be afraid of'를 사용한다.

06 (A) 컴퓨터에 새 프로그램을 설치했니? (B) 그 무용수는 그녀의 뛰어난 춤 실력으로 선생님을 감동시켰다.

07 '동사 – 명사'의 관계다. 동사에 접미사 '-ance'를 붙여 명사로 만들 수 있다.

08 (A) 월트 디즈니는 역사상 중요한 문화계 인물이다. (B) 그 수치는 OECD 평균 6,741달러보다 낮다.

01 (1) Thanks to (2) engineers (3) Later (4) laughter
02 disappointed
03 (1) (c)areer (2) (h)idden (3) (r)ecognizes
04 (1) face, 직면하다 (2) expert, 전문가
(3) permission, 허락 (4) manager, 관리자
05 (1) (g)et (2) (c)olored (3) (c)ompetition

01 (1) 형의 충고 덕분에(thanks to), 민호는 의사가 될 수 있었다. (2) 'How many+복수명사'로 'engineers'가 적절하다. (3) 나중에(later), 그 가난한 소년은 대통령이 되었다. (4) 접속사 that 다음에 '주어+동사'의 문장이 와야 한다. 명사가 주어가 되어야 하므로 동사 'laugh'를 'laughter(웃음)'로 바꾸어 준다.

02 '어떤 것이 예상했던 것만큼 좋지 않거나 어떤 일이 일어나지 않았기 때문에 슬픈'의 의미로 'disappointed(실망한)'가 적절하다.

03 (1) career: 직업 (2) hidden: 숨겨진 (3) recognize: 인정하

다. 주어가 3인칭 단수이므로 동사 뒤에 '-s'를 쓴다.

04 (1) 어려운 상황을 처리하다 (2) 한 분야에서 높은 수준의 지식 또는 기술을 가진 사람 (3) 누군가에게 무엇을 하도록 허용해주는 행위 (4) 조직을 통제할 책임이 있는 사람

05 (1) 당신은 추위를 극복하기 위한 당신만의 방법을 갖고 있나요? (2) 미국 전체 인구의 8분의 1은 유색 인종의(흑인) 노예였습니다. (3) 철자 맞추기 대회는 미국의 철자 대회야.

Conversation (교과서)

1 ②   2 ⑤

교과서 대화문 익히기

1 F   2 T   3 F   4 T

교과서 확인학습   p.70~71

Get Ready 2

(1) look down, the matter / to take, that idea, that, should / sorry to hear that

(2) disappointed / preparing, competition, record, What / keep practicing, sure, get better and better

(3) to be, cook, laughs at, give up / never give up, good at cooking, cook

Start Off – Listen & Talk A

1. look, Why, disappointed / lost, because of, mistake / makes mistakes / practice / practice makes perfect

2. are you disappointed / give, presentation / Take, easy, speech, a little, presentation / more slowly / help, understand

Start Off – Listen & Talk B

look down, disappointed / lost, competition / sorry to hear that, hard / maybe, enough, cooking tips / How about getting useful / try, for, advice / remember, dishes

Why, disappointed / failed, audition, keep trying / Don't give up, better

disappointed / won't let, enter / sorry to hear, against / to study, worried about / parents, to be / Not yet, talk with / how much, Why don't you sing, in front of / Thank you for

1. disappointed / magician like, failed, competition, give up / Practice hard, get better, better, to keep trying / your advice

2. come in, Are, interested in designing / product designer, design / it's, to practice drawing, Reading, magazines / keep that in mind

look down, Why are you disappointed / lost, because / Don't be, happen, anyone / practice more / if, You know

---

시험대비 기본평가   p.72

01 are, disappointed   02 ⑤   03 ③
04 ②

01 'disappoint'는 '실망시키다'라는 동사로 사람이 실망한 것은 과거분사 'disappointed'를 사용한다.

02 상대방이 걱정스러운 표정으로 뭔가에 불만족하거나 실망하고 있는 것을 보고 사용하는 표현으로 Why are you disappointed? = What's wrong? = What's the problem? = Is there anything wrong? = What happened? = Why the long face? 등을 사용할 수 있다.

03 '절대 포기하지 마.'라는 소녀의 대답으로 보아 빈칸에는 '내가 꿈을 포기해야 한다고 생각하니?'라고 묻는 것이 적절하다.

04 미래를 위해 롤 모델을 가져야 하는지 충고를 구하고 있는 표현이다.

시험대비 실력평가   p.73~74

01 ④   02 (b) / because of → because
03 ③   04 ②   05 ②   06 ④
07 audition   08 ⑤   09 ④   10 ①
11 practice makes perfect

01 내가 실수를 해서 우리가 축구 시합에서 졌다고 말하고 나서 충

고를 구하는 말로 '더 연습을 해야 할까?'라는 ④가 적절하다.

02 (b)는 'I made'로 '주어+동사'가 있으므로 접속사 'because'가 적절하다. because of는 뒤에 명사(구)가 와야 한다.

03 상대방에게 충고를 구하는 표현으로 'Do you think I should ~?'가 적절하다.

04 충고를 명심하겠다는 표현이 적절하다.

05 요리 대회에서 떨어졌다는 말에 대해 '그것 참 안됐구나.'라는 표현이 적절하다. pleased를 sorry로 바꾸어야 한다.

06 '모든 실패는 성공으로 다가서는 한 걸음이다.'라는 조언이 가장 자연스럽다.

07 누군가가 배우, 음악가, 무용수 등으로 직업을 얻기 위해 하는 짧은 공연.

08 Ryan이 노래를 몇 곡을 만들었는지는 대화에 언급되어 있지 않다.

09 동사 'love'를 수식하는 부사가 필요하기 때문에 'how many'를 'how much'로 바꾸어야 한다.

10 ② 행함이 없는 믿음은 쓸모가 없다. ③ 충고는 해 줄 수 있으나, 행동하게 할 수는 없다. ④ 습관은 제2의 천성이다. ⑤ 어려움에 처했을 때 누가 진정한 친구인지 알게 된다.

11 '내가 더 연습해야 한다고 생각하니?'라는 말에 '음, 그래.'라고 답하고 있기 때문에 연습을 해야 한다는 의미로, 주어진 단어를 이용하여 '연습이 완벽을 만든다.'가 적절하다.

서술형 시험대비   p.75

01 Because they want him to study hard and be a doctor.
02 (A) Why are you so disappointed
   (B) Do you think I should
03 I'm sorry to hear that.
04 Are you interested in designing things?
05 it is more important to practice drawing every day

01 질문: 왜 Ryan의 부모님은 그가 슈퍼스타 101에 참가하는 걸 반대하는가?

02 (A) 'so'는 'disappointed'를 수식하는 부사로 'Why are you so disappointed'라고 쓴다. (B) 'Do you think I should ~?'는 '너는 내가 ~해야 한다고 생각하니?'라는 의미의 표현이다.

03 유감이나 동정을 나타내는 '그것 참 안됐구나.'의 의미로 'I'm sorry to hear that.'을 사용한다.

04 '~에 관심이 있다'는 표현은 'be interested in'을 이용한다. 전치사 in 다음에는 동명사 designing이 적절하다.

05 '가주어(It) ~ 진주어(to부정사)' 구문을 이용한다.

핵심 Check   p.76~77

1 (1) Having (2) Turning
2 (1) that (2) what (3) What

시험대비 기본평가   p.78

01 (1) Having no money

  (2) Walking on[along] the street

  (3) what you want

  (4) What we need

02 (1) Feeling tired, he sat on a bench.

  (2) Watching the news, she called her mom.

  (3) Let me tell you what(= the thing that[which]) I heard yesterday.

  (4) Show me what(= the things that[which]) you have in your pocket.

03 (1) (Being) Surprised at his test result

  (2) Feeling happy with what you are doing

01 (1), (2) 때, 이유, 동시동작, 연속상황, 조건 등의 뜻을 나타내는 부사구를 현재분사(동사원형+-ing)를 써서 간략하게 나타낸다. (3), (4) '~하는 것'의 의미로 선행사를 포함한 관계대명사 what을 명사절(주어, 목적어, 보어)로 쓴다.

02 (1) 접속사와 주어가 없으므로 동사 Feel을 분사구문 Feeling으로 쓰는 것이 적절하다. (2) 과거분사로 시작하는 분사구문은 주절의 주어와 수동 관계를 이루어야 한다. 주절의 주어인 그녀가 뉴스를 보는 것은 능동 관계이므로 Watching으로 쓰는 것이 적절하다. (3) that 앞에 선행사가 없고 동사 heard의 목적어가 없으므로 선행사를 포함한 관계대명사 'what'을 쓰거나 관계대명사 that 앞에 선행사를 넣는다. (4) 선행사 the things가 있으므로 선행사를 포함한 관계대명사 what을 쓰는 것은 옳지 않다. 그러므로 선행사 the things를 삭제하거나 관계대명사 what을 that 또는 which로 쓰는 것이 적절하다.

03 (1), (2) 접속사를 생략하고 접속사절의 반복 주어를 생략한 다음 접속사절의 동사를 현재분사(Ving)로 바꾼다. 단, Being은 보통 생략한다.

시험대비 실력평가   p.79~81

01 ④   **02** ②   **03** ①, ④   **04** ④

05 ④

06 I'm sorry, but this is not what we ordered.

07 ②   **08** ⑤   **09** ④

---

10 (1) What he said is true.

  (2) I know what you did yesterday.

11 This bag is what I want to buy.

12 (1) eating (2) Cooking (3) doing (4) Saying

  (5) Get

13 cried loudly, feeling sad   **14** ③

15 what you can do today   **16** ②

17 (1) what I want (2) what I want   **18** ①

19 They crossed the street, dancing to the music.

  (Dancing to the music, they crossed the street.)

20 ④   **21** ②

01 ④는 진주어가 필요하므로 that이 적절하다. ①, ③ 선행사를 포함한 관계대명사 what ②, ⑤ 의문사 what

02 주어진 문장은 '그는 다이어트 중이기 때문에, 빵을 조금도 먹지 않는다.'라는 뜻이 적절하므로, 분사구문을 '이유(as 또는 because)'로 써야 하며, 또한 주절의 시제가 현재이므로 부사절의 시제도 현재로 쓴다.

03 주어진 문장은 '그는 산을 올라가는 중에, 회색곰과 마주쳤다.'라는 뜻이 적절하므로, 분사구문을 부사절로 쓸 때, 동시동작의 접속사 as나 while을 쓴다.

04 what은 선행사를 포함하는 관계대명사이므로 앞에 명사(선행사)가 나오면 안 된다. ④번 문장에서 선행사 all 또는 관계대명사 what 둘 중의 하나를 선택하여 쓴다. → Leaving this crowded city is all (that) I want. (또는 what I want)

05 '접속사+주어+동사'의 부사절은 분사구문(V-ing)으로 바꾸어 쓸 수 있다. 이때, 분사구문 앞에 접속사는 생략하지 않아도 된다. 단, 주어만 생략하는 것은 올바르지 않다.

06 '이것은 우리가 주문한 것이 아니다.'라고 쓰는 것이 적절하므로 동사 is not 다음에 'what we ordered'를 보어로 쓴다.

07 첫 번째 문장의 보어절에서 선행사와 목적어 둘 다 없을 때 쓸 수 있는 것은 선행사를 포함한 관계대명사 what이다. 두 번째 문장에서는 선행사 the things가 있고 관계사절에 목적어가 없으므로 목적격 관계대명사 that 또는 which를 쓰는 것이 적절하다.

08 선행사를 포함한 관계대명사 what은 'the thing(s) that[which]'로 바꿀 수 있다. 관계대명사 that은 선행사 the book을 꾸며 줄 수 있으나 what은 선행사를 가질 수 없다.

09 주어 he가 뉴욕에 머무르는 것은 능동의 동작이므로, 'As he was staying in New York' 또는 'Staying in New York'으로 쓴다. ⑤는 'As she was tired after the long walk' 'Being tired after the long walk' 또는 being을 생략한 'Tired after the long walk'로 쓸 수 있다.

10 (1) That he said는 선행사가 없으므로 What he said로 쓰는 것이 적절하다. (2) which를 선행사를 포함하는 관계대명사 what으로 바꾼다.

11 첫 번째 문장의 the thing과 두 번째 문장의 목적어 it을 사용하여 선행사를 포함하는 목적격 관계대명사로 문장을 만든다.

12 (1), (3). (4) 접속사가 없으므로 동사가 아닌 분사구문을 써야 한다. (2) 과거분사의 분사구문은 주절의 주어와 분사가 수동 관계일 때 사용한다. 주절의 주어 he가 요리하는 것은 능동 관계이므로 Cooking이 적절하다. (5) 접속사가 있는 문장이므로, 분사구문이 아닌 명령문을 쓰는 것이 올바르다.

13 The boy 다음에 동사 cried와 부사 loudly를 쓴 후, 분사구문에서 분사 feeling의 보어로 sad를 쓰는 것이 적절하다.

14 My brother got the thing that[which] he wanted.(선행사를 수식하는 관계사) 또는 My brother got what he wanted. (선행사를 포함한 관계사) 형태로 쓴다.

15 '오늘 할 수 있는 것'을 what을 이용하여 쓴다.

16 분사구문의 부정은 'not+분사'의 형태로 쓴다. 그러므로 'Not feeling well'로 쓰는 것이 적절하다.

17 (1)번 대화에서 Is this bed what you want?(네가 원하는 것)에 대한 대답으로 what I want(내가 원하는 것)를 쓰는 것이 적절하고, (2)번 대화에서 질문에 대한 답을 '그것이 바로 내가 원하는 것이야.'로 할 때 'what I want'를 쓰는 것이 적절하다.

18 첫 번째 빈칸은 선행사가 없는 목적격 관계대명사가 필요하므로 'what'을 쓰고, 두 번째 빈칸은 선행사가 있는 목적격 관계대명사가 필요하므로 which 또는 that을 쓴다.

19 분사구문은 부사구로 주절의 앞이나 뒤 둘 다에 쓸 수 있다.

20 접속사를 써서 'When I opened the box, I found a gift in it.' 또는 분사구문으로 'When opening the box, I found a gift in it.', 'Opening the box, I found a gift in it.'으로 쓸 수 있다.

21 c. What you did was very brave. (what절이 추상적인 개념이므로 단수 취급) d. As the letter was written in Chinese 또는 Written in Chinese

---

01 (1) Don't always believe what you see.
   (2) Never put off what you can do today.
   (3) What is the most important is your health.
   (4) I'm not interested in what he showed to me.
   (5) What I got used to in Korea was eating spicy food.
02 (1) Watching TV, he fell asleep.
   (2) Singing a song, she danced happily.
   (3) Working as a pilot, he travels a lot.
03 (1) She left the room, singing a song.
   (2) There being no tickets left, we couldn't go to the concert.

---

04 (1) She walked in the park, eating bread. 또는 Walking in the park, she ate bread.
   (2) Is this cap what you wanted?
   (3) This key is what I was looking for.
   (4) Having no money, I can't help you.
   (5) Humming a song, I vacuumed the floor.
   (6) I hope he remembers what I did for him.
05 Not knowing what to say, I just stood around like a fool.
06 Eating an apple, Amy walked her dog. / Amy walked her dog, eating an apple.
07 (1) Writing on the board
   (2) Holding a flower
   (3) Swimming in the pool
08 (1) Climbing a mountain, I fell down.
   (2) Disliking watching TV, he only listens to music.
   (3) Not having time to see the movie "Frozen", I know who the Olaf is.
   (4) Dad took me to the kitchen, showing me what he had cooked.

01 (1) Don't always believe the things that you see. (2) Never put off the things that you can do today. (3) The thing that is the most important is your health. (4) I'm not interested in the things that he showed to me. (5) The thing that I got used to in Korea was eating spicy food. 선행사 the thing 또는 the things와 관계대명사 that을 결합하여 what이 있는 문장을 쓴다.

02 (1), (2), (3) 모두 분사구문이 주어와 능동의 관계이므로 현재분사로 시작하는 문장으로 쓴다.

03 (1) 접속사를 생략하고 접속사절의 반복 주어를 생략한 다음 접속사절의 동사를 현재분사(V-ing)로 바꾼다. 단, Being은 보통 생략한다. (2) 부사절과 주절의 주어가 다를 때는 부사절의 주어를 생략하지 않고 사용한다.

04 (1) 두 절을 접속사로 연결하거나 한 절을 분사구문으로 쓴다. (2) this cap은 선행사가 아니고 문장의 주어이므로, 보어절에 선행사를 포함한 관계대명사가 필요하다. (3) 관계대명사 what이 있으므로 관계사절의 목적어는 쓰지 않는다. (4) 명령문이 올 수 없으므로, 동사가 아닌 분사구문 'Having'을 쓰는 것이 적절하다. (5) 분사구문의 주어와 주절의 주어가 일치하므로 분사구문의 주어 I를 삭제한다. (6) what이 remembers와 did의 목적어가 되도록 한다.

05 분사구문을 만들 부사절이 부정문이면 'not+현재분사'의 형태로 쓴다. 해석: 무슨 말을 해야 할지 몰라서, 나는 바보처럼 멍하니 서 있었다.

06 동시동작을 현재분사(동사원형+-ing)를 써서 문장을 완성한다.

07 (1), (2), (3) '~하면서'의 의미를 가진 동시동작의 분사구문을

쓴다. 모두 주절의 주어와 분사구문의 동작이 능동관계이므로 현재분사의 분사구문을 쓴다.

08 (1) 접속사를 생략하고 부사절의 반복 주어를 생략한 다음 부사절의 동사를 현재분사(V-ing)로 바꾼다. 단, Being은 보통 생략한다. (2) 분사구문을 만들 때 동사원형에 -ing를 붙인다. (3) 분사구문을 만들 때 부사절이 부정문이면 'not+현재분사(V-ing)'의 형태로 쓴다. (4) 연속동작의 접속사 and와 (주어) 동사를 현재분사(V-ing)'의 형태로 쓴다.

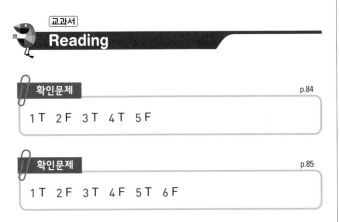

Reading

확인문제 p.84

1 T 2 F 3 T 4 T 5 F

확인문제 p.85

1 T 2 F 3 T 4 F 5 T 6 F

교과서 확인학습 A
p.86~87

01 Hidden Figures
02 last weekend
03 African-American
04 in the 1960s as
05 space experts, to get over difficulties
06 three, hidden figures
07 showed a talent in
08 got upset
09 where Katherine had been
10 bathroom
11 COLORED bathrooms
12 just to use
13 Hearing this
14 had courage to talk
15 break down
16 character
17 wasn't allowed to
18 to give her permission
19 can't change
20 have no choice but to
21 in a hundred years
22 Which one
23 impressed, what
24 stood up for
25 what impressed me most
26 first African-American woman engineer
27 the last
28 were installed, would lose
29 new programming language
30 taught it
31 was asked to
32 I'm not accepting
33 to program
34 alone
35 are ready
36 Thanks to
37 wasn't afraid of, as a chance

38 what I need to learn
39 how to face challenges
40 tears and laughter

교과서 확인학습 B
p.88~89

1 The Hidden Figures of NASA
2 I watched the movie Hidden Figures last weekend.
3 It was a movie about three African-American women who worked at NASA.
4 They began their career in the 1960s as "human computers."
5 However, they dreamed of becoming space experts at NASA and tried hard to get over difficulties.
6 Katherine Johnson was one of the three "hidden figures" in this movie.
7 She worked hard and showed a talent in math, and her manager Al Harrison recognized her ability.
8 One day, he got upset when Katherine was missing from her desk for too long.
9 Al asked where Katherine had been, and she answered.
10 Katherine: The bathroom.
11 There are no COLORED bathrooms in this building.
12 I have to run half a mile away just to use the bathroom.
13 Hearing this, I felt really sorry for her.
14 However, I was glad that she had courage to talk to the manager about the problem.
15 This made Al Harrison break down the "Colored Ladies Room" sign.
16 Mary Jackson was the character I liked the most of the three.
17 She wanted to learn more about rocket science, but she wasn't allowed to go to a white school.
18 So, she asked a judge to give her permission.
19 Mary: I can't change the color of my skin.
20 So … I have no choice but to be the first.
21 Your Honor, of all the cases you'll hear today, which one will matter in a hundred years?
22 Which one will make you the "first?"
23 The judge was impressed by what she said and finally gave her permission.
24 Mary stood up for herself and for other African-Americans.

25 That was what impressed me most in the movie.

26 Finally, she became the first African-American woman engineer at NASA.

27 Dorothy Vaughan was the last "hidden figure."

28 When IBM computers were installed at NASA in 1961, she was worried the "human computers" would lose their jobs.

29 She studied a new programming language, FORTRAN.

30 She also taught it to her team members.

31 Later, when she was asked to be the leader of a new IBM team, she made a suggestion.

32 Dorothy: I'm not accepting the offer if I can't bring my ladies with me.

33 We need a lot of people to program that machine.

34 I can't do it alone.

35 My girls are ready.

36 Thanks to Dorothy, her team members could become programmers.

37 She wasn't afraid of change and used it as a chance.

38 That's what I need to learn from her.

39 Watching this movie, I could learn how to face challenges in life.

40 I won't forget the tears and laughter of Katherine, Mary, and Dorothy.

시험대비 실력평가
p.90~93

01 ②   02 ⑤   03 ④   04 ②

05 건물에 유색 인종 전용 화장실이 없어서 단지 화장실을 사용하기 위해 Katherine이 반 마일을 달려가야 했던 사실

06 ④   07 permission

08 (A) black   (B) white   09 ④

10 (A) last   (B) experts   (C) hard

11 three African-American women

12 ①, ③, ④   13 ②, ③   14 I should[could]

15 ③   16 ⑤   17 ⑤   18 ③

19 ④   20 ①   21 hidden figure

22 ③   23 to go to a white school   24 ②

01 앞에 나오는 내용과 상반되는 내용이 뒤에 이어지므로 However가 가장 적절하다. ③ 그러므로, ④ 즉[말하자면], ⑤ 게다가, 더욱이

02 (A)와 ⑤: 인물, ① (~일 거라고) 생각[판단]하다(동사), ② (특히 공식적인 자료로 제시되는) 수치, ③ (아라비아) 숫자, (숫자의) 자리, ④ 계산하다(동사)

03 그들은 NASA에서 '우주 전문가'가 되기를 꿈꾸었다. astronaut: 우주 비행사

04 ⓐ show a talent in: ~에 재능을 보이다, ⓑ feel sorry for: ~을 안쓰럽게[안됐다고] 여기다

05 앞에서 Katherine이 말한 내용을 가리킨다.

06 이 글은 'Katherine의 대답이 Al Harrison으로 하여금 '유색 여성 화장실' 표지판을 부수게 만들었다'는 내용의 글이므로, 제목으로는 ④번 '"유색 여성 화장실"은 더 이상 없다'가 적절하다. ⑤ strict: 엄격한

07 직접목적어이므로 명사 형태로 쓰는 것이 적절하다.

08 '흑인' 학생이 '백인' 학생들과 함께 수업을 받도록 허락한 최초의 판사를 의미한다.

09 finally, eventually, after all, at last, in the end, in the long run: 결국, ④ 적어도

10 (A) '지난' 주말이라고 해야 하므로 last가 적절하다. latest: 최근의, (B) 우주 '전문가'라고 해야 하므로 experts가 적절하다. experts: 전문가들, exports: 수출품, (C) '열심히' 노력했다고 해야 하므로 hard가 적절하다. hardly: 거의 ~ 아니다

11 African-American: 아프리카계 미국인

12 ⓑ와 ②, ⑤: 부사적 용법, ①, ④: 명사적 용법, ③: 형용사적 용법, relieved: 안도하는, 다행으로 여기는

13 ⓐ와 ②, ③: 현재분사, ①, ④, ⑤: 동명사

14 '의문사 to부정사'는 '의문사+주어+should[can]'를 사용하여 고치는 것이 적절하다.

15 ⓒ 다음 문장의 it에 주목한다. 주어진 문장의 a new programming language, FORTRAN을 받고 있으므로 ③번이 적절하다.

16 ⑤는 NASA의 IBM 팀을 가리키고, 나머지는 다 인간 컴퓨터(계산원)들을 가리킨다.

17 Dorothy Vaughan wasn't afraid of change and used it as a chance.

18 Katherine이 너무 오래 자리를 비웠을 때 '화가 났다'고 하는 것이 적절하다. ① 부끄러운, ④ 안도하는, 다행으로 여기는, ⑤ 쑥스러운, 어색한, 당황스러운

19 ④번 다음 문장의 This에 주목한다. 주어진 문장에서 언급한 내용(그 문제에 대해 그녀가 상사에게 말한 것)을 받고 있으므로 ④번이 적절하다.

20 그 영화의 세 명의 '숨겨진 인물들'이 누구인지는 알 수 없다. ② She showed a talent in math. ③ He was Katherine's manager. ④ Because Katherine was missing from her desk for too long. ⑤ Because there were no COLORED bathrooms in the building and she had to run half a mile away just to use the bathroom.

21 Katherine Johnson은 Al Harrison으로 하여금 '유색 여성 화장실' 표지판을 부수게 만든 '숨겨진 인물'이었다.

22 ⓐ와 ③: 중요하다(동사), ① (고려하거나 처리해야 할) 문제[일/사안], ② (세상의 모든 것을 구성하는 일반적인) 물

질, properties: 속성, ④ (특정 종류의) 물질[물건/성분], reading matter: 읽을거리, ⑤ (걱정·고민 등의 원인이 되는) 문제[일]

23 ⓑ의 permission은 '(흑인 학생이) 백인 학교에 다닐 수 있는' 허락을 가리킨다.

24 위 글은 '일화(逸話, 에피소드, 세상에 널리 알려지지 아니한 흥미 있는 이야기)'이다. ① 수필, ③ (책·연극·영화 등에 대한) 논평[비평], 감상문, ④ (신문·잡지의) 글, 기사, ⑤ 독후감

서술형 시험대비 p.94~95

01 the movie *Hidden Figures*
02 nineteen sixties 03 overcome
04 Because there were no colored bathrooms in the building.
05 When[As] I heard this 06 to break → break
07 same 08 being, be
09 That was what impressed me most in the movie.
10 (A) rocket science (B) engineer
11 unless I can bring my ladies with me
12 She wasn't afraid of change and used it as a chance.
13 (A) new programming language
   (B) programmers

01 '영화 히든 피겨스'를 가리킨다.
02 연대는 두 자리씩 끊어 읽는 것이 적절하다.
03 get over = overcome: ~을 극복하다
04 건물에 유색 인종 전용 화장실이 없었기 때문이다.
05 'Hearing this'는 '이것을 듣고서'라는 의미의 분사구문으로, 부사절로 고칠 때는 접속사 When이나 As를 사용하는 것이 적절하다.
06 사역동사 made의 목적격보어이므로 동사원형인 'break'로 고치는 것이 적절하다.
07 과거에 유색 인종들은 인종차별에 직면했다. 예를 들어 심지어 Katherine 같이 똑똑한 여성도 백인들과 '같은' 화장실을 사용할 수 없었고, 별도의 다른 화장실을 사용하도록 강요받았다.
08 have no choice but to = cannot help ~ing = cannot but 원형: ~할 수밖에 없다
09 선행사를 포함하는 관계대명사 what을 사용하는 것이 적절하다.
10 Mary Jackson은 백인 학교에서 '로켓 공학'에 대해 더 많이 배웠고, NASA에서 최초의 아프리카계 미국인 여성 '공학자'가 되었다.
11 if ~ not = unless
12 앞 문장의 내용을 가리킨다.
13 Dorothy Vaughan은 '새로운 프로그래밍 언어'인 포트란을 공부했고, 그녀의 팀원들에게 그것을 가르침으로써 그들이 '프로그래머'가 될 수 있도록 도와준 히든 피겨스였다.

영역별 핵심문제 p.97~101

01 expert 02 ③ 03 ⑤ 04 ①
05 against 06 ② 07 cooker → cook
08 ② 09 ⑤ 10 ② 11 ④
12 ② 13 ②
14 Left alone in the room, the baby began to cry.
15 ② 16 ③ 17 ④
18 (1) David는 그녀가 말한 것을 기억하고 있다.
   (2) 그것이 네가 배워야만 하는 것이다.
   (3) 중요한 것은 네가 최선을 다했다는 것이다.
19 ③
20 Al asked where Katherine had been 21 ③
22 ② 23 ④
24 (A) the permission (B) stood up 25 ②
26 by myself 27 change
28 while he was decorating some cupcakes
29 ②, ⑤

01 반의어 관계다. 용기 : 비겁함 - 초보자 : 전문가
02 (a) 분노는 당신이 부당하게 대우를 받았을 때 스스로를 옹호할 수 있도록 도와주기 때문에 좋은 것일 수도 있습니다. (b) 교사들, 기자들, 그리고 공무원들은 값비싼 선물을 받을 수 없다.
03 법정에서 범죄자들이 어떻게 처벌 받아야 하는지를 결정하는 사람
04 매우 빠르게 이동하며 우주 여행에 사용되는 큰 원통 형태의 물체
05 '계획이나 활동에 동의하지 않는'의 의미를 가지는 'against(반대하여)'가 적절하다.
06 'audition'은 '오디션'이고, '관객'은 'audience'이다.
07 cooker: 요리 기구, cook: 요리사
08 실망한 이유를 묻는 말에 → (B) 이유를 설명하고 → (D) 위로하는 말을 한 후, 발표 때의 문제점을 말해 주고 → (C) 충고를 구하는 말을 한다. 마지막으로 (A) 충고를 구하는 말에 대한 대답이 오는 것이 적절하다.
09 '내 미래를 위해 롤 모델을 가져야 한다고 생각하니?'라는 물음에 '모형 비행기를 만드는 것은 쉽지 않다.'고 말하는 것은 어색하다.
10 부모님이 경연대회에 참석하는 것을 반대한다는 내용이기 때문에 'for'를 'against'로 바꾸어야 한다.
11 위 대화는 가수가 되고 싶은 자신의 꿈을 부모님에게 어떻게 보여 줄 것인가에 관한 내용이다.
12 Ryan의 부모님은 그의 성적에 대해 걱정을 한다.
13 주어진 문장과 ②: 선행사를 포함한 관계대명사 what, ①, ③, ④, ⑤: 의문사 what
14 동사 leave는 '남기고 가다'라는 뜻이며, 아기는 홀로 '남겨진' 상태이므로 수동의 분사구문으로 쓴다.
15 As it rained, we didn't play soccer outside. 또는 분사구문을 사용하여 It raining, we didn't play soccer outside.

16 a. Walking along the street, I saw a big cat. b. Living in America, he speaks English very well. d. They sat on the beach, looking at the rising sun.

17 ④는 의문사 what ①, ②, ③, ⑤는 선행사를 포함한 관계대명사 what.

18 (1), (2), (3) 선행사를 포함한 관계대명사는 '~하는 것'으로 해석되며 문장의 목적어, 보어, 주어로 쓰인다.

19 선행사와 목적어가 없으므로 선행사와 목적어 둘 다로 쓰일 수 있는 것을 써야 한다. that은 선행사가 없으므로 적절하지 않고, ①, ④는 목적격 관계대명사가 생략된 것으로 볼 수 있다.

20 'where Katherine had been'은 동사 'asked'의 목적어이므로 간접의문문 순서로 쓰는 것이 적절하다.

21 Al Harrison은 그녀의 능력을 '알아차렸다.' envy: 부러워하다

22 ⓐ와 ②: (소송) 사건, ①, ⑤: (특징한 상황의) 경우, ③ (질병, 부상) 사례[환자], ④ 용기, 통, 상자

23 이 글은 '"최초"가 되는 것 이외에는 선택이 없었던 Mary Jackson이 마침내 NASA 최초의 아프리카계 미국인 여성 공학자가 된' 내용의 글이므로, 제목으로는 ④번 '최초가 되는 것 이외에는 선택이 없었던 여성'이 적절하다.

24 Mary Jackson은 백인 학교에 다니도록 '허락'을 받았고, 그곳에서 로켓 공학에 대해 더 많이 배웠다. 그리고 그녀는 자신과 다른 아프리카계 미국인들의 '편에 섰다.'

25 Dorothy '덕분에', 그녀의 팀원들은 프로그래머가 될 수 있었다고 하는 것이 적절하다. Thanks to: ~ 덕분에, ① ~에도 불구하고, ③ ~보다는[대신에], ④ ~ 면에서[~에 관하여], ⑤ ~ 대신에

26 alone = by oneself: 혼자

27 '변화'를 가리킨다.

28 'decorating some cupcakes'는 '컵케이크에 장식하며'라는 의미의 동시동작을 나타내는 분사구문으로, 부사절로 고칠 때는 접속사 While을 사용하여 진행형으로 고치는 것이 적절하다.

29 ⓑ와 ②, ⑤: 관계대명사, ① 의문형용사, ③ 의문대명사, ④ [감탄사적] 의문형용사

단원별 예상문제
p.102~105

01 competition　　　　　02 ③
03 Why the long face?　　04 (A) – (C) – (B)
05 He should practice drawing every day and read design magazines.
06 ③　　　07 ⑤　　　08 ④　　　09 ②
10 (1) 감기에 걸려서, 그는 일찍 잠자리에 들었다.
　　(2) 공항에 도착해서, 그녀는 그녀의 부모님에게 전화를 걸었다.
　　(3) 물을 많이 마시면, 너는 더 건강해 질 거야.
11 ③, ④

12 (1) Make what[the things that] your family will love.
　　(2) Design what you dream of.
　　(3) I will not forget what he said.
　　(4) She told me about her job, drawing some product designs.
　　(5) You can be what you act.
13 (1) That's what I want to read.
　　(2) That's what I was looking for.
　　(3) That's not what I have in mind.
14 career　　　15 ③　　　16 missed → missing
17 ②　　　　18 answer　　　19 ⑤
20 The judge was impressed by what she said and finally gave her permission.
21 ③

01 '동사-명사'의 관계다. 받아들이다 - 수용 : 경쟁하다 – 시합, 대회

02 '직장 생활 동안 하는 일련의 직업' 의미로 'career(경력, 직장 생활)'가 적절하다.

03 상대방의 걱정, 슬픔이나 불만족, 실망의 원인에 대해 물을 때 사용되는 일반적인 표현으로 'Why are you disappointed?' = What's the problem? = Is there anything wrong? = What happened? = Why the long face? 등이 있다.

04 (A) 물건 디자인하는 데 관심 있는지 묻는 말에 → (C) 긍정의 대답과 제품 디자이너가 되고 싶다고 말하고, 디자인 학교에 가야 하는지 조언을 구하는 질문에 대해 → (B) 가는 것이 도움이 되고, 매일 그림을 연습하는 것이 중요하다고 말하고 디자인 잡지를 읽는 것도 또한 도움이 된다는 말이 이어지는 것이 자연스럽다.

05 질문: 소년은 제품 디자이너가 되기 위해 무엇을 해야 할까?

06 빈칸 다음에 '여자'의 대답이 '아뇨. 매일 열심히 연습하면 점점 더 나아질 거예요.'인 것으로 보아 마술 대회에서 떨어졌다는 말 다음에 부정적인 말이 오는 것이 자연스럽다.

07 주어진 문장은 '온라인 요리 영상에서 유용한 조언들을 얻는 게 어때?'라는 의미로 '알았어. 시도해 볼게.'라는 대답 앞인 ⑤에 들어가는 것이 적절하다.

08 오늘 우울해 보인다는 말 다음에 상대방의 걱정, 슬픔이나 불만족, 실망의 원인에 대해 물어보는 것이 자연스럽다.

09 실수로 경기에 진 사람이 상대방에게 충고를 구하는 내용으로 ②번의 질문이 가장 적절하다.

10 (1) As[Because] he had a cold, he went to bed early.
(2) When[As] she arrived at the airport, she called her parents. (3) If you drink a lot of water, you will be healthier.

11 접속사 while 대신 as를 쓸 수 있다. 분사구문에서 접속사는 생략하지 않고 사용할 수 있다.

12 (1) what은 선행사를 포함하고 있으므로 선행사 'the things'

또는 관계사 what 둘 중 하나만 쓴다. (2) that은 선행사가 필요한 관계대명사이나 그 앞에 선행사가 없으므로, 선행사를 포함한 관계대명사 what으로 쓴다. (3) what이 선행사와 목적격 관계대명사의 역할을 하고 있으므로, 관계사절의 목적어 it을 쓰지 않는다. (4) 주어진 문장에 접속사 and가 있으므로, 분사구문이 아닌 동사 drew 또는 and를 없애고 분사 drawing만 쓴다. (5) which는 선행사가 필요한 관계대명사이나 그 앞에 선행사가 없으므로, 선행사를 포함한 관계대명사 what으로 쓴다.

13 선행사를 포함한 관계대명사는 '~한 것'으로 해석되며 명사절 역할을 하여 문장의 보어로 쓸 수 있다.

14 career: 직업, 직장 생활, 어떤 사람이 삶의 오랜 기간 동안 하는 일, 직업

15 ⓑ와 ③: (자격·기능 등이) ~로(서)(전치사), ① ~한 대로(접속사), ② [보통 as ~ as ...로 형용사·부사 앞에서] …와 같은 정도로(앞의 as는 지시부사, 뒤의 as는 접속사), ④ ~이기 때문에(접속사), ⑤ 가령 ~와 같은(전치사)

16 missing: (제자리나 집에 있지 않고) 없어진[실종된]

17 ⓑ와 ②, ④: 형용사적 용법, ①: 부사적 용법, ③, ⑤: 명사적 용법

18 그의 질문에 대한 Katherine의 '대답'이 그로 하여금 '유색 여성 화장실' 표지판을 부수게 했다.

19 선행사를 포함하는 관계대명사 'what'을 쓰는 것이 적절하다.

20 be impressed by: ~에 의해 깊은 인상을 받다, what: 선행사를 포함하는 관계대명사

21 Mary Jackson은 최초가 될 수밖에 없었다. Mary Jackson couldn't but be the first. stand up for = support: ~을 지지하다

서술형 실전문제　　　p.106~107

01 Do you think I should practice more?

02 dream, enter, against, doctor, disappointed, advises, show, how much, thanks, advice

03 (1) ㉠ →to do　(2) ㉣ →what　(3) ㉤ →seeing

04 (1) Singing a song　(2) Drinking milk
　(3) Lucy read a book　(4) David kicked a ball

05 to go

06 first woman → first African-American woman

07 (A) first　(B) supported

08 installed → were installed

09 She wasn't afraid of change and used it as a chance.

10 While I was watching this movie

---

01 'Do you think I should ~?'는 '너는 내가 ~해야 한다고 생각하니?'라는 의미이다.

03 (1) ㉠ '~해야 할'의 의미로 things을 꾸미는 to부정사의 형용사적 용법을 쓰는 것이 적절하다. (2) ㉣ 목적격 관계대명사에

선행사가 없으므로 선행사를 포함한 관계대명사 what을 쓴다. (3) ㉤ 주절 이후에 접속사가 없으므로 '~하면서'의 의미로 분사구문 seeing을 쓰는 것이 적절하다.

04 (1), (2) 주절이 뒤에 있으므로, 분사구문을 사용하여 문장을 쓴다. (3), (4) 분사구문이 앞에 있으므로, 주절을 과거시제를 사용하여 쓴다.

05 be allowed to 부정사: ~하는 것이 허용되다

06 Mary Jackson은 NASA에서 최초의 '아프리카계 미국인' 여성 공학자가 되었다.

07 Mary Jackson은 판사로 하여금 흑인 학생이 백인 학생들과 함께 수업을 받도록 허락한 최초의 인물이 되도록 만든 숨겨진 인물이었다. 그녀는 또한 자신뿐만 아니라 다른 아프리카계 미국인들의 편에 섰다. stand up for = support: ~을 지지하다

08 NASA에 IBM 컴퓨터가 '설치되었을' 때라고 해야 하므로, 수동태로 고치는 것이 적절하다.

09 be afraid of: ~을 두려워하다, use A as B: A를 B로 사용하다, 대명사 it: 앞에서 언급된 'change'를 가리킨다.

10 'Watching this movie'는 '이 영화를 보면서'라는 의미의 동시동작을 나타내는 분사구문으로, 부사절로 고칠 때는 접속사 While을 사용하여 진행형으로 고치는 것이 적절하다.

창의사고력 서술형 문제　　　p.108

|모범답안|

01 (1) A: Why are you disappointed?
　　 B: I lost the dance competition. Do you think I should practice harder?
　　 A: Yes, I think so.(Sure. Don't give up.)

　 (2) A: Why are you disappointed?
　　 B: I fought with my friend. Do you think I should talk to my friend about it?
　　 A: Yes, I think so.

02 (A) designer　(B) what you dream of
　 (C) magician　(D) what you see

단원별 모의고사　　　p.109~114

01 ④　　02 hidden　03 ③　　04 ⑤

05 How about getting useful tips

06 ⑤　　07 ①　　08 ②

09 (C) - (A) - (D) - (B)　　10 ④　　11 keep

12 ⑤

13 Because his parents won't let him enter Superstar 101.

14 ③　　15 ①, ③　　16 ④　　17 ②

18 (1) decorating some cupcakes
　 (2) saying his famous lines

(3) doing some magic tricks

(4) showing me his news reports

(5) controlling robots

19 (1) what you see　(2) what is true

(3) what you cannot do

20 새 IBM 팀의 리더가 되어달라는 요청　21 ④

22 It was a new programming language.　23 ⑤

24 courageous / courageous　25 ③

26 ②　27 ①　28 ④　29 ③

30 ⑤

01 ④번은 '무언가를 하기 위해 필요한 기술이나 자질'을 의미하는 'ability'에 대한 설명이다. 'courage'는 'the ability to control your fear in a dangerous or difficult situation'이다.

02 유의어 관계이다. 용기 : 숨겨진

03 '기계나 장비를 제자리에 놓고 사용할 준비가 되도록 하다'는 의미로 'install(설치하다)'이 적절하다.

04 ⑤ '마술 수업을 들어야 한다고 생각하니?'라고 충고를 구하는 말에 '당신과 같은 마술사가 되고 싶어.'라고 대답하는 것은 어색하다.

05 'how about'은 뒤에 동명사를 취한다. get을 getting으로 바꾸어 준다.

06 우울해 보인다는 말 다음에 상대방의 걱정, 슬픔이나 불만족, 실망의 원인에 대해 물어보는 말이 자연스럽다.

07 대화의 첫 문장에 '왜 실망하고 있나요?'라고 묻는 것으로 보아 '슬퍼 보이지 않는다.'는 말은 어색하다. 'sad'를 'happy'로 바꾸어야 한다.

08 말이 약간 빨랐다는 말에 대해 더 천천히 말해야 한다고 생각하는지 묻는 것이 자연스럽다.

09 실망한 이유를 묻는 질문에 → (C) 오디션에서 떨어졌다는 대답을 하고 → (A) 그 말에 유감을 표현한다. → (D) 계속 노력해야 하는지 충고를 구하는 질문을 하고 → 마지막으로 (B) 충고에 대한 긍정의 답을 하는 것이 자연스럽다.

10 주어진 문장에 'also(또한)'라는 첨가의 부사가 사용되었기 때문에 앞 문장에도 도움이 되는 내용이 오는 것이 적절하다.

11 'in mind'와 함께 사용이 되어 '~을 명심하다'라는 의미로 'keep'이 적절하다.

12 빈칸 다음에 Ryan의 부모님이 그의 성적에 대해 걱정한다고 말하는 것으로 보아 ⑤가 적절하다.

13 'Ryan은 왜 실망하고 있는가?'라는 물음에 대한 답은 '그의 부모님이 슈퍼스타 101에 참가하는 것을 허락하지 않아서.'이다.

14 (A)는 '~에 반대하여'의 의미이다. ③ 1959년, 티베트 사람들은 중국 통치에 반대하는 운동을 일으켰습니다. ① 나는 마하트마 간디의 동상에 기대어 서 있었습니다. ② 그들은 화재에 대비하여 예방책을 취했다. ④ 그의 빨간 옷이 눈과 대비를 이루며 선명히 두드러져 보였다. ⑤ 당신은 비용 대비 이득을 따져 봐야 한다.

15 ① This is the thing that she likes. 또는 This is what she likes. ③ He read a newspaper, and drank[as he was drinking] coffee. 또는 He read a newspaper, drinking coffee.

16 '비록 나는 운동을 많이 하지만, 여전히 살이 찌고 있다.'라는 뜻이 가장 적절하므로 접속사 Though를 쓴 문장이 가장 가까운 뜻이다.

17 주어와 접속사가 있는 부사절의 형태 또는 주절과 분사구문의 형태로 쓰는 것이 적절하다. He said good-bye as he waved his hand. 또는 He said good-bye, waving his hand.

18 글의 흐름상 적절한 구절을 골라 분사구문의 형태로 쓴다. (1) 그는 컵케이크에 장식하며 그의 직업에 대해 말해 주었습니다. (2) 그는 자신의 유명한 대사를 말하면서 그의 직업에 대해 말해 주었습니다. (3) 그녀는 몇 가지 마술을 보여 주며 그녀의 직업에 대해 말해 주었습니다. (4) 그는 그의 뉴스 보도를 저에게 보여 주면서 그의 직업에 대해 말해 주었습니다. (5) 그녀는 로봇을 조종하면서 그녀의 직업에 대해 말해 주었습니다.

19 선행사를 포함한 관계대명사 what을 '~하는 것'의 의미로 명사절(목적어)로 쓴다.

20 'to be the leader of a new IBM team'을 가리킨다.

21 ④ 못 보고 지나치다, 빠뜨리고 못 보다, ⓑ 직면하다, ① 직면하다, 맞서다, ② ~에 대처하다, ③ 다루다, ⑤ ~을 다루다, 상대하다

22 포트란은 '새로운 프로그래밍 언어'였다.

23 앞에 나오는 내용과 상반되는 내용이 뒤에 이어지므로 However가 가장 적절하다. ① 게다가, 더욱이, ② 따라서, 그러므로, ③ 비슷하게, 마찬가지로, ④ 그 결과

24 'be 형용사 enough to부정사'는 'be so 형용사 as to부정사' 구문으로 고치는 것이 적절하다. 참고: 'have the 추상명사 to부정사' 구문은 'be 형용사 enough to부정사' 구문이나 'be so 형용사 as to부정사' 구문으로 고칠 수 있다.

25 전반부의 'he got upset'을 통해 'unpleasant'를, 본문 끝의 'This made Al Harrison break down the "Colored Ladies Room" sign.'을 통해 'sympathetic'을 찾을 수 있다. unpleasant: 불쾌한, sympathetic: 동정적인, 동조하는, 공감하는, ① upset: 속상한, disappointed: 실망한, ② nervous: 초조한, ④ bored: 지루한

26 ⓐ in: (시간의 경과를 나타내어) ~ 후에[~ 만에/~ 있으면], ⓑ stand up for: ~을 지지하다

27 ①번 다음 문장의 So에 주목한다. 주어진 문장의 결과를 나타내고 있으므로 ①번이 적절하다.

28 (A)와 ④: (소설 등의) 등장인물, ① 성격, 기질, ② 개성, ③ 문자(letter), ⑤ 인격, 품성

29 위 글은 Dorothy가 새로운 변화를 두려워하지 않고 도전하여 목적을 이루는 이야기이므로 ③이 적절하다.

30 Dorothy 덕분에 몇 명의 팀원들이 프로그래머가 될 수 있었는지는 대답할 수 없다. ① In 1961. ② She was worried the "human computers" would lose their jobs. ③ No. ④ She suggested bringing her team members with her.

The Frog Prince Continued

Reading

교과서 확인학습 A	p.120~122

01 Frog Prince
02 Characters
03 Scene
04 jumping
05 Stop jumping
06 can't stop
07 anymore
08 What's wrong with
09 I don't like it when
10 feel like running, as
11 hundreds of, were better off
12 That's it
13 Scene
14 To himself, into
15 How
16 turn me back into, ever after
17 look like, let you save
18 want
19 come in
20 Where
21 If
22 turn me back into, live happily
23 serve
24 is made of cookies, by the name of
25 I do
26 runs away
27 Could you, so
28 on my way, give it a try
29 will be okay
30 what a fool, stuck, unhappily
31 turns into
32 giving me a second chance, how I should live
33 keep my fingers crossed
35 smiling
36 have you been
37 else, did
38 even
39 looking forward to
40 hand in hand

교과서 확인학습 B	p.123~125

1 The Frog Prince Continued

2 Characters: Frog Prince, Princess, Witch 1, Witch 2, Fairy

3 Scene 1: In a room

4 (*Prince comes in, jumping around.*)

5 Princess: Stop jumping around, honey.

6 Prince: Well, I just can't stop.

7 Princess: You're not a frog anymore.

8 Prince: What's wrong with you? You don't go down to the pond these days.

9 Princess: I don't like it when you jump around in the room. Go out to kill monsters and save our people.

10 Prince: I don't want to go out and kill anything. I just feel like running away. (*Picking up a book*) Listen! "They lived happily ever after. The end." I'm living my life as the book says, but we're not happy. What's the problem?

11 Princess: What's the problem? There are hundreds of problems! Sometimes I think we were better off when you were still a frog.

12 Prince: Still a frog .... Yes! That's it! (*Goes out*)

13 Scene 2: On the mountain

14 Prince: (*To himself*) I need to find the witch, who will turn me back into a frog. (*Shouting*) Ms. Witch, Ms. Witch. Where are you? Please help me!

15 Witch 1: (*Coming out of the house*) Hi, Prince. How are you feeling?

16 Prince: I'm glad to meet you. I'm the Frog Prince. I hope you can turn me back into a frog so I can live happily ever after.

17 Witch 1: Frog Prince, you say? That's funny. You don't look like a frog. Well, it doesn't matter. If you're a prince, you're a prince. And I won't let you save Snow White. Here, eat the rest of this apple.

18 Prince: No, thank you. That's not what I want! (*Runs away*)

19 (*Prince and Witch 2 come in.*)

20 Prince: Ms. Witch, Ms. Witch. Where are you? Please help me! I'm the Frog ....

21 Witch 2: If you're a frog, I'm the King of France.

22 Prince: No, I'm not a frog. I'm the Frog Prince. But I need a witch to turn me back into a frog so I can live happily ever after. Can you do it?

23 Witch 2: Let's talk about it inside. I will serve you a delicious lunch. Come in

24 Prince: Thank you for inviting me. Oh, this house is made of cookies and candies. Wait a minute. Do you know any children by the name of Hansel and Gretel?

25 Witch 2: Yes, Prince, I do. (*With her mouth watering*) They are not fat enough yet, but you are ....

26 (*Prince runs away and finds a fairy.*)

27 Prince: I'm glad to meet you, Ms. Fairy. I am the Frog Prince. Could you turn me back into a frog so I can live happily ever after?

28 Fairy: Well, I'm on my way to see Cinderella, but I'll give it a try. It's my first time, you know. (*Fairy turns Prince into a wheel.*)

29 Fairy: Oops! Sorry, but don't worry. Everything will be okay.

30 Prince: (*To himself*) Oh, what a fool I've been! I want to be sitting at home with the Princess, living happily ever after. But instead, I'm stuck here under this cart and I'll live unhappily ever after.

31 (*The clock hits twelve, and the wheel turns into Prince.*)

32 Prince: I can't believe this. Thank you for giving me a second chance. Now I know how I should live my life. (*Goes out*)

33 Fairy: (*Waving her hand*) You learned a good lesson. I'll keep my fingers crossed.

34 Scene 3: In the Frog Prince's house

35 (*Prince runs in, smiling.*)

36 Princess: Where have you been? I've been worried. Your clothes are a mess.

37 Prince: (*Looking at Princess*) You believed me when no one else in the world did. You loved me even when I was a frog. From now on, I will make you happier.

38 Princess: I'm glad to hear that. I'll make you even happier.

39 Prince: Great! I'm looking forward to our bright future. Ha-ha ....

40 (*They run to the pond together, jumping hand in hand.*)

서술형 실전문제
p.126~127

01 (1) feel like   (2) feel like

02 (1) wheel, 바퀴   (2) frog, 개구리   (3) princess, 공주
(4) fairy, 요정

03 (1) (c)art   (2) (s)erved   (3) (I)nstead

04 (1) Listening to music, she wiped the window.
(2) Hearing the news, she began to cry.
(3) Leaving now, you won't be late.

05 which → what   06 running

07 to jump → jumping

08 (A) jumps around   (B) doesn't want

09 (A) *himself*   (B) How   (C) look like

10 to save

11 Because he thinks he can live happily ever after (if he becomes a frog again).

01 (1) 해석: 여러분은 종종 더운 여름날에 아이스크림을 먹고 싶어한다. (2) 해석: 너무 추워서 나는 우리가 마치 북극에 있는 것처럼 느껴져!

02 (1) 지면 위로 차량이 부드럽게 움직이도록 차량 아래에 고정되어 있는 원형 물체 (2) 물속이나 물가에 사는, 점프하기 위한 긴 뒷다리를 가진 작은 녹색의 동물 (3) 왕이나 왕비의 딸, 또는 그들의 가까운 여성 친척 중 한 명 (4) 마법의 힘을 가진 날개가 있는 작은 사람같은 상상 속의 생명체

05 목적격 관계대명사 which의 선행사가 없고, 선생님이 말씀하신 것으로 해석하면 자연스럽기 때문에 선행사를 포함한 관계대명사 what을 쓰는 것이 적절하다.

06 feel like -ing: ~하고 싶다, ~하고 싶은 기분이다

07 '주변을 뛰어다니지 마세요.'라고 해야 하므로, to jump를 jumping으로 고치는 것이 적절하다. stop+to부정사: ~하기 위해 멈추다, stop+~ing: ~을 그만두다

08 공주는 왕자가 방 안에서 '이리저리 뛰어다니는 게' 마음에 안 들어 왕자더러 나가서 괴물들을 죽이고 백성을 구하라고 말하지만, 왕자는 밖에 나가서 아무것도 죽이고 '싶지 않다.'

09 (A) '혼잣말로'라고 해야 하므로 himself가 적절하다. to oneself: 혼잣말로, (B) How are you feeling?: 기분이 어때요? (C) look+형용사, look like+명사: ~처럼 보이다

10 let+목적어+원형부사 = allow+목적어+to부정사

11 앞으로 행복하게 살 수 있을 것이라고 생각하기 때문이다.

단원별 예상문제
p.128~132

01 ②   02 shout   03 ①

04 water, water

05 am looking forward to watching

06 ④   07 ④   08 rest, rest

09 (1) better off   (2) run away   (3) From now on

10 ⑤   11 ④

12 (1) which was closed because it was Sunday
(2) which is located near my school
(3) who is good at kung fu

13 ⑤

14 My dad will not let me stay up all night.

15 ③   16 ⑤   17 ⑤   18 ③

19 ⑤   20 ②   21 ④   22 ④

23 ②　　　24 ③　　　25 ⑤　　　26 ②
27 Do you know any children by the name of Hansel and Gretel?
28 ④　　　29 how foolish I've been!　　30 ③

01 ②번은 '크고, 추하고, 무서운 상상 속의 생명체'의 뜻을 가지고 있는 'monster'에 대한 설명이다. 'dinosaur'에 관한 설명은 'a very large type of animal that used to live millions of years ago'가 적절하다.

02 유의어 관계다. 구하다 : 외치다, 소리치다

03 '대개 무언가를 다치게 하거나 손상시키기 위해 물건이나 사람을 힘을 가해 빠르게 손을 대다'

04 • 부엌에서 나는 냄새에 우리 입 안에 군침이 돌았다. • 비는 자연에서 물의 순환에 의한 결과이다.

05 앞으로 다가올 일에 대한 기대감을 표현하는 말로 'I'm looking forward to+명사/동명사'를 사용한다.

06 • hand in hand: 손에 손을 잡고. • turn ... into ~: …을 ~로 바꾸다 • by the name of: ~라는 이름의

07 모두 반의어 관계이고, ④번은 '외치다'라는 뜻의 유의어 관계이다.

08 take a rest: 휴식을 취하다 the rest: 나머지. • 휴식을 취하는 것은 좀더 활기차고 활동적으로 해 줄 것이다. • 남은 휴가 동안, 우리는 디즈니랜드에 갈 거야!

09 (1) 그는 3년 전보다 훨씬 잘 살고 있다. than이 있기 때문에 'good'의 비교급을 사용해야 한다. (2) 만약 낯선 어른이 여러분에게 오거나 부른다면, 도망치세요. (3) 이제부터, 우리는 어떠한 일본 제품도 판매하지 않을 것입니다.

10 보기와 ⑤번의 'as'는 '~하듯이'의 뜻으로 쓰인 접속사이다. ① ~함에 따라, ② ~이기 때문에, ③, ④ ~할 때

11 ④번은 분사구문이므로 현재분사이다. ①, ②, ⑤ 전치사의 목적어로 쓰인 동명사 ③ 보어로 쓰인 동명사

12 접속사와 대명사를 관계대명사의 계속적 용법을 사용하여 같은 의미로 바꿀 수 있다.

13 'What (a) 형용사+명사+주어+동사!' 어순으로 감탄문을 쓴다.

14 'let+목적어+원형부정사'는 'allow+목적어+to부정사'로 쓸 수 있다. 주어진 단어 중 'to'가 없기 때문에 let을 이용하여 문장을 완성한다.

15 stop 동명사: ~하기를 멈추다, stop to부정사: ~하기 위해 멈추다. • 나는 복통이 있다. 나는 먹는 것을 멈추어야 한다. • 한 소년이 장난감을 찾고 있었다. 그래서 나는 그를 돕기 위해 멈추었다.

16 ⑤ 관계대명사의 계속적 용법은 관계사 앞에 쉼표(,)를 쓰고 that은 사용하지 않는다.

17 ⑤의 by는 of로 쓰는 것이 적절하다. be made by: ~에 의해 만들어지다, be made of: ~로 만들어지다

18 보기에 쓰인 'did'는 앞선 'tell the truth'를 대신하는 대동사이

다. ③의 'did'는 앞선 'moved slowly'를 대신하는 대동사이다. ①, ②, ④, ⑤: 일반동사 'did'

19 선행사를 포함하는 관계대명사 what이 적절하다.

20 ②는 Ms. Witch를 가리키고, 나머지는 다 Prince를 가리킨다.

21 '자신을 다시 개구리로 바꿔주는 것에 대한 대가로 왕자가 마녀 1에게 무엇을 지불할지'는 대답할 수 없다. ① It is on the mountain. ② He wants to meet a witch. ③ He wants her to turn him back into a frog. ⑤ Because he doesn't look like a frog.

22 ⓐ와 ④: ~하는 것처럼(접속사), ① ~이기 때문에(접속사), ② (자격·기능 등이) ~로(서)(전치사), ③ [보통 'as ~ as ...'로 형용사·부사 앞에서] …와 같은 정도로, 마찬가지로('as ~ as ...'에서, 앞의 as는 지시부사, 뒤의 as는 접속사), ⑤ ~하는 동안에(접속사)

23 위 글은 '희곡'이다. ① (신문·잡지의) 글, 기사, ③ 전기, ④ 수필, ⑤ (책·연극·영화 등에 대한) 논평[비평], 감상문

24 ③ 'Princess' doesn't go down to the pond these days.

25 ⓐ turn A into B: A를 B로 바꾸다, ⓑ be made of: ~으로 만들어지다(물리적 변화), be made from: (화학적 변화)

26 '당신이 개구리라면 나는 프랑스의 왕이라는 말'은 왕자의 말을 '믿지 않는다.'는 의미이다. 'doubtful: 의심을 품은, ① 흥분한, ③ 지루한, ④ 우울한, ⑤ 만족한

27 by the name of: ~라는 이름의

28 시계가 12시를 치자 바퀴가 왕자로 바뀐 것이므로, '두 번째 기회'를 주셔서 감사하다고 하는 것이 적절하다. ③ identity: 신원, 신분, 정체, ⑤ an attractive personality: 매력적인 성격

29 'what+a+형용사+명사'는 'how+형용사[부사]'로 고칠 수 있다.

30 요정은 왕자를 바퀴로 바꿨다.

Pictures Speak a Thousand Words

시험대비 실력평가
p.136

01 (c)urious   02 ②   03 ⑤   04 ④
05 be covered with   06 ③   07 close

01 '무언가에 대하여 알거나 배우기를 원하는'의 뜻인 'curious(호기심 많은, 궁금한)'가 적절하다.

02 'letter'는 '편지', '글자, 문자'의 의미를 지닌다. • 전통적인 편지(mail)는 어떤 사람이 손으로 쓴 편지(letter)이기 때문에 특별한 의미를 포함합니다. • 오래 전에, 우리는 우리 자신의 글자(letter)를 가지고 있지 않았습니다.

03 '어떤 후보자에 대하여 선호를 표시하다'라는 의미로 '투표하다(vote)'가 적절하다.

04 '당신의 애정이나 우정을 보여주기 위하여 양팔로 다른 사람을 안는 행위'의 뜻으로 '포옹(hug)'이 적절하다.

05 '~로 덮이다'는 'be covered with'를 사용한다.

06 (A) 나이아가라 폭포는 정말로 멋진 광경이다. (B) 그는 배우로서 그의 숨겨진 재능을 보여주었다.

07 1. crossing 2. lit 3. oil 4. son 5. except

서술형 시험대비
p.137

01 (1) lots of (2) wait for (3) except for
   (4) look after
02 Braille
03 (1) hire (2) misunderstanding (3) rather
04 (1) ring, 반지 (2) discover, 발견하다 (3) oil, 기름
   (4) translate, 번역하다
05 (A) (f)oreign (B) (h)unters (C) (s)oldier

01 (1) 이 가게에는 많은 멋진 신발이 있다. 'lot'을 이용하여 '많은'의 의미를 나타낼 때는 'lots of'가 적절하다. (2) 우리는 식당에서 20분 동안 그를 기다려야 했다. '~를 기다리다'는 'wait for'를 사용한다. (3) 나는 잘 지내고 있고, 미세먼지를 제외하면 날씨도 좋아. '~을 제외하고'는 'except for'를 사용한다. (4) 이웃이 고양이를 돌보아 달라고 부탁했다. '~를 돌보다'는 'look after'가 적절하다.

02 '시각 장애인들이 만져서 읽는 돋우어진 패턴을 사용하는 인쇄 체계'로 '점자(Braille)'가 적절하다.

03 (1) hire: 고용하다 (2) misunderstanding: 오해 (3) rather: 다소

04 (1) 손가락에 끼는 둥근 형태의 보석 (2) 전에 알지 못하던 것을 찾아내다 (3) 요리를 위하여 사용되는 식물이나 동물로부터 만들어진 걸쭉한 액체 (4) 구어 또는 문어를 다른 언어로 바꾸다

05 (A) 한국 사람들은 인구가 더 많은 다른 외국들보다도 더 많은 물을 쓰고 있습니다. (B) 인간은 가장 위대한 사냥꾼이고 항상 고기를 먹어왔다. (C) 그는 제복을 입고 있기 때문에 군인임에 틀림없다.

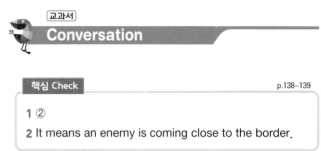

Conversation

핵심 Check
p.138~139

1 ②
2 It means an enemy is coming close to the border.

교과서 대화문 익히기

Check(√) True or False
p.140

1 T 2 F 3 T 4 T

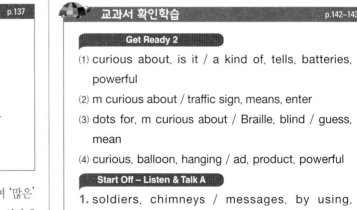

교과서 확인학습
p.142~143

Get Ready 2

(1) curious about, is it / a kind of, tells, batteries, powerful
(2) m curious about / traffic sign, means, enter
(3) dots for, m curious about / Braille, blind / guess, mean
(4) curious, balloon, hanging / ad, product, powerful

Start Off – Listen & Talk A

1. soldiers, chimneys / messages, by using, chimneys / m curious about, system / smoking chimneys / What, mean
2. enemy, smoke at all, do / Smoke, chimney / rising, What does, mean / It means, close, border

Start Off B

is crossing, border, dark, soldiers going to do, messages, about / light, chimneys / light, chimneys / It means, battle

m curious about, language / Let, show, expression /
What, mean / It means

hidden secrets / curious about, secrets / yourself /
Let's see, letters / one, means, Latin / awesome,
Any other / tells, rich / understand / spend lots of,
to buy, kind / the rich, that kind / Exactly, speak a
thousand

1. gesture, curious about / it means, pond / Why,
   think so / lots of, pointing, pond

2. So, gesture mean / It means, chicken / should
   bring, to get, right / I think so

3. What, gesture mean / Turn it off / What makes /
   The other hunter, close / see

시험대비 기본평가   p.144

01 It means, not enter   02 ④

03 ③   04 ⑤

01 'It means ~.'는 '그것은 ~을 의미한다.'라는 의미로 정의를 내리는 표현이다. 조동사 must의 부정은 뒤에 not을 사용하고 동사원형 enter를 쓴다.

02 궁금증을 표현하는 말로 'I am curious about ~', 'I'm curious if/whether 주어+동사 ~', 'I would like/want to know ~', 'I'd be very interested to know ~', 'Can you tell me about ~?' 등이 있다.

03 'I'm curious ~.' 등으로 상대방이 궁금증을 표현하거나 의미를 물어보면 'This/It means ~.(그것은 ~을 의미한다.)' 또는 'It is ~.(그것은 ~이다.)' 등의 표현을 사용하여 상대방이 궁금해하거나 알고 싶어 하는 것의 의미나 정의를 설명하는 표현을 쓰는 것이 적절하다.

04 'I'm curious about ~'은 '나는 ~이 궁금해'라는 의미로 궁금증을 표현하는 것이다.

시험대비 실력평가   p.145~146

01 ③, ⑤   02 (d) / Other → The other[Another]

03 ④   04 ②   05 ⑤   06 ④

07 batteries   08 ②   09 for   10 ③

11 this painting

01 빈칸 앞의 대화가 '그것은 "그것을 꺼."를 의미해.'라고 궁금증을 설명해주는 말을 하고, 그 말에 대해 '정말?'이라고 놀라움을 표현하고 있기 때문에 그 말을 한 이유를 물어보는 것이 타당하다.

02 'other'는 뒤에 복수명사가 온다. 단수명사 'hunter'와 함께 사용될 수 있는 단어는 'the other' 또는 'another'이다.

03 '메시지를 보내기 위해서 병사들은 무슨 일을 할까?'라는 물음 뒤에 그것에 관한 궁금함을 표현하는 말이 오는 것이 자연스럽다.

04 빈칸 (B) 다음의 말이 '그것은 전투가 시작되었음을 의미해.'라는 것으로 보아 빈칸은 의미를 묻는 말이 오는 것이 자연스럽다.

05 적이 없을 때도 연기를 피운다고 했으므로 글의 흐름상 굴뚝 한 곳에서 나오는 연기는 'No enemy.(적이 없음.)'를 나타낸다.

06 '그들은 연기를 전혀 피우지 않아, 그렇지?'라는 부정의문문으로 'Yes'는 '아니'로 해석한다.

07 라디오, 장난감, 자동차와 같은 것에 전기를 공급하는 물체

08 나머지는 모두 궁금증을 표현하는 말이고, ②번은 놀라움을 나타낼 때 사용하는 표현이다.

09 (a)는 '~은 무엇을 위한 거니?'라는 의미로 'What ~ for?' 구문이고, (b)는 의미상 '시각장애인을 위한'의 의미로 전치사 'for'가 적절하다.

10 그림에 숨겨진 또 다른 비밀에 관한 말로 보기 (C) 앞의 "Okay."와 뒤의 "I don't understand."가 부자연스럽기 때문에 (C)에 들어가는 것이 적절하다.

11 it은 인칭대명사로 주어인 This painting을 가리킨다.

서술형 시험대비   p.147

01 They mean "Jan van Eyck was here. 1434."

02 (A) I'm curious about them.   (B) It means

03 What makes you think so?

04 They mean they just saw an enemy.

05 They are sending messages to the king by using
   the chimneys.

01 질문: 여자아이가 찾은 글자는 무엇을 의미하는가?

02 (A) 궁금증을 나타내는 표현으로 'be curious about'을 사용하고 'secrets'는 복수형이므로 복수대명사 'them'을 사용한다. (B) 'It means ~.(그것은 ~을 의미한다.)'라는 의미로 정의를 표현하는 말이다.

03 'Why do you think so?'와 같은 의미로 'What makes you think so?'를 사용할 수 있다.

04 'They mean+주어+동사' 어순을 이용한다.

교과서

Grammar

핵심 Check   p.148~149

1 (1) were   (2) would

2 (1) whose   (2) whose   (3) enjoy

01 (1) If I were[was] a duck
   (2) What would you do
   (3) whose dog is carrying a doll
   (4) whose dog wants a hot dog

02 (1) If I had wings, I would fly in the sky.
   (2) What would you do if you were a fish?
   (3) Koko is the boy whose bag is on a big cat.
   (4) The girl whose cat is dancing is Didi.

03 (1) If I had a lot of money, I could travel around the world.
   (2) If I were[was] tall, I could be a basketball player.

01 (1), (2) 현재 사실에 대한 가정은 'If+주어+동사 과거형, 주어+조동사 과거형(would/should/could/might)+동사원형'의 형태로 쓴다. (3) 'Bubu is the boy.' 문장에서 선행사 the boy 뒤에 소유격 관계대명사 문장을 이어 쓴다. (4) 'Lala is the girl.' 문장에서 선행사 the girl 뒤에 소유격 관계대명사 문장을 이어 쓴다.

02 (1) 가정법 과거 문장은 주절에 조동사의 과거형을 쓴다. (2) 가정법 과거 문장은 If절에 과거동사를 쓴다. (3) 선행사가 사람일 때 소유격 관계대명사는 of which를 쓰지 않고 whose를 쓴다. (4) 사람이 선행사이므로 소유격 관계대명사는 whose를 쓴다.

03 (1), (2) 현재 사실에 대한 가정은 'If+주어+동사 과거형, 주어+조동사 과거형(would/should/could/might)+동사원형'의 형태로 쓴다.

01 ④   02 ①
03 There was a queen whose daughter was cursed by an evil fairy.
04 ①   05 ③   06 ②
07 Miso is a girl whose dog is jumping rope.
08 If I had a lot of money, I could buy that car.
09 ③, ⑤
10 (1) If I had a monkey, I could play with it.
     또는 If I have a monkey, I can play with it.
   (2) The boys whose mom is a lawyer live next door.
11 ⑤
12 (1) would build   (2) knew   (3) whose   (4) who
   (5) whose
13 ④
14 If I were[was] a bird, I would fly over the mountain.

15 The animal whose name begins with z is a zebra.
16 ④   17 ④   18 ⑤
19 If I met the President, I would shake hands with him[her].
20 (1) would / would   (2) were / were[was]
21 she doesn't work with him, is not[isn't] very disappointed with him

01 선행사가 사물일 때 소유격 관계대명사로 whose와 of which 둘 중의 하나를 쓴다. 이때 whose는 무관사의 명사를 써야 하므로 the+명사가 있는 경우는 of which를 쓴다.

02 선행사가 사물일 때 소유격 관계대명사로 whose와 of which 둘 중의 하나를 쓴다. 이때 whose는 무관사의 명사를 써야 하고, the+명사가 있는 경우는 of which를 쓴다.

03 두 문장에서 a queen과 소유격 Her는 동일 인물이므로 소유격 관계사 whose로 연결하여 쓴다.

04 ② drove → drive ③ can → could ④ wins → won ⑤ will → would

05 ③ 건강 상태가 좋아서, 나는 너와 운동할 수 있다. ①, ②, ④, ⑤ 건강 상태가 좋다면, 나는 너와 운동할 텐데. (건강 상태가 좋지 않아서, 나는 너와 운동할 수 없다.)

06 '내가 너라면'이 적절하므로 둘 다 'were'를 쓴다.

07 선행사 a girl 뒤에 소유격 관계대명사를 이어서 쓴다.

08 가정법과거는 현재 사실과 반대되므로 직설법 부정은 가정법 긍정으로 쓰고, 동사는 과거시제로 쓴다.

09 우리는 충분한 시간이 없기 때문에 더 오래 머무를 수 없다. = 우리가 충분한 시간이 있다면, 더 오래 머무를 텐데. (가정법과거) *with: ~이 있다면, without: ~이 없다면 (if절을 대신할 수 있다.)

10 (1) 가정법 과거형 또는 조건절의 형태로 주절과 if절을 맞추어 쓴다. (2) 동사 lives의 주어는 The boys이므로 live로 쓴다. 또는 The boy whose mom is a lawyer lives next door. 로 고쳐도 좋다.

11 가정법 과거의 주절은 '조동사의 과거형+동사원형'으로 쓴다. lent → would lend

12 (1) 가정법 과거의 주절은 '조동사의 과거형+동사원형'으로 쓴다. (2) 가정법 과거 문장은 If절에 과거동사를 쓴다. (3) 관계대명사의 선행사 'a friend'가 family를 소유하는 것이 자연스럽다. (4) 관계대명사 다음에 동사가 이어지는 것이 주격 관계대명사 문장이다. (5) 관계대명사의 선행사 animals가 명사 lives를 소유하는 것이 자연스럽다.

13 현재 사실에 대한 가정은 'If+주어+동사 과거형, 주어+조동사 과거형(would/should/could/might)+동사원형'의 형태로 쓴다.

14 현재 사실에 대한 가정은 'If+주어+동사 과거형, 주어+조동사 과거형(would/should/could/might)+동사원형'의 형태로 쓴다.

15 The animal is a zebra 문장에서, 선행사 The animal 뒤에 소유격 관계대명사 whose를 사용하여 문장을 이어 쓰고 술부 is a zebra를 쓴다.

16 현재 사실에 대한 가정은 'If+주어+동사 과거형, 주어+조동사 과거형(would/should/could/might)+동사원형'의 형태로 쓴다.

17 두 문장에서 A girl과 소유격 Her는 동일 인물이므로 소유격 관계사 whose로 연결하여 쓴다.

18 첫 번째 문장은 'They taste like apples.'에서 주어 They로 관계대명사를 만들었기 때문에 which 또는 that을 쓴다. 두 번째 문장은 'Its smell is so sweet.'에서 소유격 Its로 관계대명사를 만들었기 때문에 whose를 쓴다.

19 현재 사실에 대한 가정은 'If+주어+동사 과거형, 주어+조동사 과거형(would/should/could/might)+동사원형'의 형태로 쓴다.

20 (1) 주절에 조동사의 과거형을 쓴다. (2) '네가 오리라면', '내가 오리라면'의 뜻에는 were가 적절하다.

21 가정법과거의 문장은 현재 사실에 대한 반대를 가정한 문장이므로, 가정법 문장이 부정이면 직설법 문장은 긍정으로, 가정법이 과거시제이면 직설법은 현재시제로 쓴다.

서술형 시험대비
p.154~155

01 (1) I have a friend whose brother enjoys skateboarding.
   (2) The boy who[that] is dancing on the floor is my brother.
   (3) He wants to ride a bike which[that] I bought yesterday.
   (4) Do you like the house whose roof looks like a hat? 또는 Do you like the house of which the roof[the roof of which] looks like a hat?
   (5) The boy whose cat is spinning a hula hoop is Jeje.

02 (1) If I had strong arms, I could climb trees.
   (2) If I had a long nose, I could use it to take a shower.
   (3) If I had a beautiful voice, I would sing on the tree.

03 (1) If I were[was] an English teacher, I would play word games every day.
   (2) If I were[was] on the moon, I could jump much higher.

04 (1) Were he rich, he could travel to Europe.
   (2) The boy who[that] is talking to Mary is my cousin.

   (3) He lent me the book which[that] I want to read.
   (4) I stayed at the house whose walls are white. 또는 I stayed at the house of which the walls[the walls of which] are white.
   (5) If I were you, I would take a swimming lesson.

05 (1) would give (2) would dance with them
   (3) would get my feet

06 were[was], could sing and dance

07 (1) he doesn't talk to her. (또는 he won't talk to her)
   (2) Were he at home

08 (1) The boy whose cell phone is ringing loudly doesn't understand the man's gesture.
   (2) The girl whose feet are in the water doesn't understand the man's gesture.
   (3) The boy whose hand the woman is pulling doesn't understand her gesture.
   (4) The boy whose bag the monkey is pulling doesn't understand its gesture.

01 (1) 두 문장에서 a friend와 소유격 His는 동일 인물이므로 소유격 관계대명사 whose로 연결하여 쓴다. (2) 두 문장에서 The boy와 주어 He가 동일 인물이므로 주격관계대명사 who 또는 that으로 연결하여 쓴다. (3) 두 문장에서 a bike와 목적어 it이 동일하므로 목적격 관계대명사 which 또는 that으로 연결하여 쓴다. (4) 두 문장에서 a house와 소유격 whose가 동일하므로 소유격 관계대명사 whose로 연결하여 쓴다. (5) 두 문장에서 The boy와 소유격 His는 동일 인물이므로 소유격 관계대명사 whose로 연결하여 쓴다.

02 현재 사실에 대한 가정은 'If+주어+동사 과거형, 주어+조동사 과거형(would/should/could/might)+동사원형'의 형태로 쓴다.

03 가정법 과거는 현재 사실과 반대되므로 직설법 부정은 가정법 긍정으로 쓰고, 동사는 과거시제로 쓴다.

04 (1) rich는 형용사이므로 be동사 were로 가정법 문장을 쓴다. (2) 관계대명사가 주어 역할을 하는 문장이므로 소유격이 아닌 주격 관계대명사를 쓴다. (3) 관계대명사가 목적어 역할을 하는 문장이므로 소유격이 아닌 목적격 관계대명사를 쓴다. (4) 선행사 the house가 walls를 소유하는 문장이므로 소유격 관계대명사 whose나 of which를 쓴다. (5) 가정법 과거의 주절은 '조동사의 과거형+동사원형'으로 쓴다.

05 가정법 과거의 주절은 '조동사의 과거형+동사원형'으로 쓴다.

06 현재 사실에 대한 가정은 'If+주어+동사 과거형, 주어+조동사 과거형(would/should/could/might)+동사원형'의 형태로 쓴다.

07 (1) 가정법 과거는 현재 사실과 반대되므로 직설법 문장으로 표

현할 때 긍정은 부정문으로, 과거시제는 현재시제로 쓴다. (2) 'If 주어 were ~'로 표현한 가정법은 if를 생략하고 were를 문두로 도치할 수 있다.

08 (1) 두 문장에서 The boy와 소유격 His는 동일 인물이므로 소유격 관계사 whose로 연결하여 쓴다. (2) 두 문장에서 The girl과 소유격 Her는 동일 인물이므로 소유격 관계사 whose로 연결하여 쓴다. (3) 두 문장에서 The boy와 소유격 his hand의 his는 동일 인물이므로 소유격 관계사 whose로 연결하여 쓴다. (4) 두 문장에서 The boy와 소유격 his bag의 his는 동일 인물이므로 소유격 관계사 whose로 연결하여 쓴다.

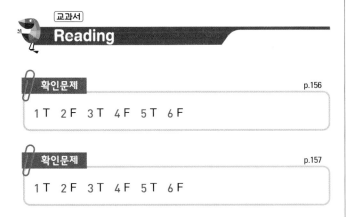

교과서 Reading

확인문제   p.156

1 T   2 F   3 T   4 F   5 T   6 F

확인문제   p.157

1 T   2 F   3 T   4 F   5 T   6 F

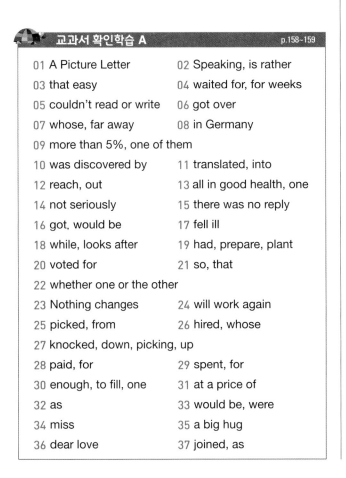

교과서 확인학습 A   p.158~159

01 A Picture Letter
02 Speaking, is rather
03 that easy
04 waited for, for weeks
05 couldn't read or write
06 got over
07 whose, far away
08 in Germany
09 more than 5%, one of them
10 was discovered by
11 translated, into
12 reach, out
13 all in good health, one
14 not seriously
15 there was no reply
16 got, would be
17 fell ill
18 while, looks after
19 had, prepare, plant
20 voted for
21 so, that
22 whether one or the other
23 Nothing changes
24 will work again
25 picked, from
26 hired, whose
27 knocked, down, picking, up
28 paid, for
29 spent, for
30 enough, to fill, one
31 at a price of
32 as
33 would be, were
34 miss
35 a big hug
36 dear love
37 joined, as

교과서 확인학습 B   p.160~161

1 A Picture Letter from a Mother of Three
2 Speaking to family members or friends in a foreign country is rather easy and simple today.
3 But before the days of phones and the Internet, it was not that easy.
4 People just sent a letter and waited for a reply for weeks.
5 And it was a lot harder if they couldn't read or write.
6 This letter shows how people got over these difficulties.
7 It was written in 1973 by a woman whose husband was far away.
8 She lived in Sicily, an Italian island, while her husband worked in Germany.
9 At the time, more than 5% of the people in Italy could not read or write, and she was one of them.
10 This letter was discovered by Sicilian writer Gesualdo Bufalino.
11 Here's how he translated the pictures into words.
12 My dear love, I miss you so much, and I reach my arms out toward you, together with our three kids.
13 We are all in good health except for the little one.
14 He's a little sick, but not seriously.
15 I already sent you a letter, but there was no reply, so I am sad about it.
16 If I got a letter from you, I would be very happy.
17 Your mother fell ill, and I'm going to visit her in the hospital with some money and food.
18 I'll go there with our middle son while the oldest looks after the youngest.
19 I had two workers prepare our field and plant seeds for 150,000 lire.
20 I voted for the DC.
21 The PCI lost so many seats that it almost seems dead.
22 But whether one or the other wins, it's the same.
23 Nothing changes for us poor people.
24 We worked yesterday, and we will work again tomorrow.
25 We picked lots of olives from our olive trees this year.
26 I hired a man whose sons are good workers.
27 He knocked the olives down, and his two sons helped him, picking them up from the ground.
28 I paid him 27,000 lire for the work.
29 I spent 12,000 more for the olive press.

30 I got enough oil to fill a large pot and a small one.

31 I can sell it at a price of 1,300 lire a liter.

32 My love, my heart thinks of you as Christmas is coming.

33 I would be so happy if you were with me.

34 We all miss you so much.

35 I'm sending you a big hug from me and our three little kids.

36 Goodbye, dear love.

37 My heart is yours, joined to you as our two rings are.

시험대비 실력평가
p.162~165

01 ②, ④, ⑤   02 ④   03 ⑤   04 hired

05 일꾼이 올리브를 쳐서 떨어뜨리면 그의 두 아들이 땅에서 올리브를 주우면서 그를 도와주는 일

06 per   07 ②   08 ①   09 ⑤

10 ①   11 ⓑ so ⓒ that

12 one hundred (and) fifty thousand   13 ④

14 (A) missed   (B) three kids

15 joined   16 ②   17 joined

18 As[Because, Since] I don't get a letter from you, I'm not very happy. 또는 I don't get a letter from you, so I'm not very happy.

19 ①, ③

20 (A) nothing   (B) worked   (C) will work

21 ②   22 there was no reply

23 If I got a letter from you, I would be very happy.

24 ④   25 ②, ④   26 ⑤

01 ⓐ와 ②, ④, ⑤: 동명사, ①, ③: 현재분사

02 이 글은 '전화와 인터넷 시대 이전에 외국에 있는 가족이나 친구와 대화하는 것이 그렇게 쉽지 않았다'는 내용의 글이므로, 제목으로는 ④번 '예전에 해외에 있는 사람들에게 말하는 것의 어려움'이 적절하다.

03 ⑤ 이 글만 읽고서는 읽거나 쓸 수 없는 사람들이 외국에 있는 사람들과 어떻게 대화했는지는 대답할 수 없다. ① No, it is rather easy and simple today. ② No, it was not that easy. ③ They just sent a letter and waited for a reply for weeks. ④ It took weeks.

04 hire: 고용하다

05 일꾼과 그의 두 아들이 한 일을 쓰는 것이 적절하다.

06 ⓒ의 a는 '(가격·양·비율을 나타내어) ~당'이라는 뜻으로, 'per(~당[마다])'로 바꿔 쓸 수 있다.

07 ⓐ by: ~가 한(수동형 문장에서 행위자, 창작자 등을 나타냄), ⓑ translate A into B: A를 B로 번역하다, 해석하다

08 주어진 문장의 It에 주목한다. ①번 앞 문장의 This letter를 받고 있으므로 ①번이 적절하다.

09 Gesualdo Bufalino는 그녀의 '그림들'을 '글'로 번역했다. ② illiterate: 글을 (읽거나 쓸 줄) 모르는, 문맹의

10 have+사람+동사원형

11 so ... that ~ = so ... as to ~: 너무 …해서 ~하다

12 보통 3자리씩 끊어서 읽고, 천의 자리에 thousand를 붙여서 읽는 것이 적절하다. one hundred (and) fifty thousands(X)

13 '세 아이와 함께 당신을 향해 내 팔을 쭉 뻗고 있어요. 막내를 제외하고는 우리 모두 건강해요.'라는 내용을 나타내는 그림으로는 ④번이 적절하다.

14 한 여성이 멀리 떨어져 있는 남편을 '그리워하며' 그녀와 그들의 '세 아이'가 어떻게 지내고 있는지를 알려주는 편지를 썼다.

15 "I join my heart to you"의 수동태 형태로 '(my heart is) joined to you'로 쓰인 것이다. 분사구문의 형태로 볼 수 있다. joined: 연결된 채로

16 '나와 우리 세 아이의 큰 포옹을 보내요. 내 마음은 당신의 것이에요. 우리들의 두 반지처럼 당신과 연결된 채로요'라는 내용을 나타내는 그림으로는 ②번이 적절하다.

17 are 뒤에 'joined'가 생략되었다.

18 가정법 과거 문장은 현재 사실과 반대되는 상상이나 가정을 나타내는 것이므로, 직설법으로 고칠 때는 현재시제를 사용하는 것이 적절하다.

19 look after = take care of = care for: ~을 돌보다, ② ~을 닮다, ④ ~을 찾다, 구하다, ⑤ ~의 안부를 묻다, 문안하다

20 가난한 사람들에게는 '아무 것도 바뀌지 않고' 그들은 어제도 '일했고', 내일도 다시 '일할' 것이기 때문이다.

21 ⓐ와 ②: 그리워[아쉬워]하다, ① (치거나 잡거나 닿지 못하고) 놓치다[빗나가다], ③ (식사 등을) 거르다, ④ (기회를) 놓치다, ⑤ (어디에 참석하지 않아서 그 일을) 놓치다

22 '(편지를 보냈는데) 답장이 없는 것'을 가리킨다.

23 현재 사실과 반대되는 상상이나 가정을 나타내는 가정법 과거 문장으로 쓰는 것이 적절하다.

24 ⓐ [교환] ~에 대하여, ~의 금액[값]으로, ⓑ at a price of: ~의 가격으로

25 ⓒ와 ②, ④: (가격·양·비율을 나타내어) ~당, ① (사람의 이름 앞에 쓰여) ~라는 사람, ③ 단수 명사 앞에 쓰여 그 부류를 통칭함, ⑤ 글 속에 처음 언급되는 단수형 명사 앞에 쓰임.

26 글쓴이가 올리브 기름(올리브유)을 팔아 얼마를 벌었는지는 알 수 없다. ① Yes. ② A man whose sons are good workers. ③ 27,000 lire. ④ The writer got enough oil to fill a large pot and a small one.

01 This letter shows how people got over these difficulties

02 Sicilian writer Gesualdo Bufalino discovered this letter.

03 (A) her husband   (B) in Germany

04 stretch   05 We are all in good health

06 kid   07 (A) 27,000   (B) 12,000   (C) 1,300

08 the olives   09 She spent 39,000 lire.

10 I already sent a letter to you

11 will → would

12 (A) fell ill   (B) some money and food

13 for   14 to prepare   15 as

16 As[Because, Since] you are not with me, I'm not so happy. 또는 You are not with me, so I'm not so happy.

01 shows의 목적어를 간접의문문의 순서(how+주어+동사)로 쓰는 것이 적절하다.

02 Sicilian writer Gesualdo Bufalino를 주어로 해서 능동태로 고치는 것이 적절하다.

03 '독일'에서 일하는 '그녀의 남편'에게 편지를 썼다.

04 reach ~ out = stretch ~ out: (손 등을) 내밀다, 뻗다

05 be in good health: 건강 상태가 좋다

06 세 아이(three kids) 중 막내 '아이'를 가리킨다.

07 그림 편지의 '일꾼이 올리브를 쳐서 떨어뜨리면 그의 두 아들이 땅에서 올리브를 주우면서 그를 도와주는 것을' 나타내는 가운데 그림을 참조하여 (A)에는 '27,000'을, '올리브 압착'을 나타내는 오른쪽 그림을 참조하여 (B)에는 '12,000'을, '큰 항아리 하나와 작은 항아리 하나를 채울 만큼의 충분한 기름'을 나타내는 왼쪽 그림을 참조하여 (C)에는 '1,300'을 쓰는 것이 적절하다.

08 '올리브'를 가리킨다.

09 올리브나무에서 올리브를 따는 비용 27,000리라+올리브를 압착하는 비용 12,000리라 = 39,000리라

10 send는 to를 사용하여 3형식으로 고친다.

11 가정법 과거 문장이므로, 주절의 시제를 'would'+동사원형으로 고치는 것이 적절하다.

12 그녀의 시어머니께서 '병이 드셔서' 병원에 계시기 때문에, 그녀는 '약간의 돈과 음식'을 가지고 병원을 방문할 예정이다. mother-in-law: 시어머니

13 ⓐ [교환] ~의 금액[값]으로, ⓑ vote for: ~에 (찬성) 투표를 하다

14 have+사람+동사원형 = get+사람+to부정사

15 ⓐ as Christmas is coming: 크리스마스가 다가오면서, ⓑ ~처럼

16 가정법 과거 문장은 현재 사실과 반대되는 상상이나 가정을 나타내는 것이므로, 직설법으로 고칠 때는 현재시제를 사용하는 것이 적절하다.

01 hug   02 ②   03 ⑤   04 ①

05 expression   06 ③

07 (a) board → border   08 ④   09 ②

10 ③   11 ⑤   12 ⑤

13 (1) I didn't know the singer, I couldn't shake hands with him

(2) he were[was] smart, he would prepare for the game in advance

14 ①   15 ⓓdon't → didn't   16 ③

17 ③   18 could see, were[was] taller

19 (1) would use kites to send my messages

(2) whose face looks like a mountain

(3) whose bag is full of fruit

20 ②

21 more than 5% of the people in Italy who could not read or write

22 ③   23 ⑤   24 reply   25 ③

26 ①   27 picking them up from the ground

28 were[was]   29 its gesture

01 유의어 관계이다. 고용하다 – 포옹하다, 안다

02 (a): 당신은 추위를 극복하기 위한 당신만의 방법을 갖고 있나요? (b): 이것이 존경할 만한 정치인을 뽑는 것이 중요한 이유이다.

03 한 여자가 결혼한 남자

04 '위원회, 법정 등의 구성원으로서의 지위'의 뜻으로 'seat(의석)'이 적절하다.

05 '특별한 의미를 가지는 단어들의 그룹'의 의미를 가지는 'expression(표현)'이 적절하다.

06 'whether'는 부사절 접속사로 사용되면 '~이든 아니든'의 의미가 된다. 명사절 접속사일 때는 '~인지 아닌지'로 해석한다.

07 board: 판, 위원회, border: 국경

08 그 당시의 사람들이 어떤 종류의 개를 기르고 싶어했는지는 알 수가 없다.

09 위 대화는 Jan van Eyck의 그림 속에 숨겨진 비밀을 발견하여 그림을 통해 화가가 전달하고자 하는 메시지를 파악할 수 있는지에 관한 내용이다.

10 (C) '이 점들이 무엇을 위한 거니?'라고 궁금증을 표현하는 말이 오고 → (B) 궁금증에 대한 설명이 오고, Braille의 용도를 이야기해 준다. (A) 마지막으로 알았다는 대답이 오는 것이 자연스럽다.

11 '난 수화가 궁금해'라는 A의 말에 대해, B가 '수화가 뭐니? 내가 표현 하나를 알려줄게.'라고 말하는 것은 어색하다.

12 가정법 과거의 문장이 '만일 그가 춤을 잘 춘다면'이므로 직설법 문장은 '그는 춤을 못 추기 때문에'로 쓰는 것이 적절하다. 'not poor'를 'poor' 또는 'not good'으로 쓴다.

13 가정법 과거는 현재 사실과 반대되므로 직설법 문장을 가정법으로 표현할 때 긍정은 부정문으로, 부정은 긍정문으로 쓰고, 현재 시제는 과거시제로 쓴다.

14 ①은 두 문장을 연결하는 접속사와 주어 역할을 하는 주격 관계 대명사가 필요하므로 which 또는 that을 쓴다. ②, ③, ④, ⑤ 는 소유격 관계대명사 whose를 쓴다.

15 가정법 과거 문장이므로 if절의 동사를 과거시제로 쓴다.

16 ③은 의문사 whose이다. ①, ②, ④, ⑤는 소유격 관계대명사 whose이다.

17 c. have → had d. won't → wouldn't e. will → would

18 현재 사실에 대한 가정은 'If+주어+동사 과거형, 주어+조동사 과거형(would/should/could/might)+동사원형'의 형태로 쓴다.

19 (1) 가정법 과거의 주절은 '조동사의 과거형+동사원형'으로 쓴다. (2) 선행사 a kite가 명사 face를 소유하는 것이 자연스러우므로 whose를 쓴다. (3) 선행사 The boy가 명사 bag을 소유하는 것이 자연스러우므로 whose를 쓴다.

20 선행사가 사물인 경우에는 소유격을 whose나 of which로 쓸 수 있지만, 사람인 경우에는 of which로 쓸 수 없다. ① overcome: 극복하다, ③ over: ~ 이상, ④ the Italians: 이탈리아 사람들, ⑤ 관계부사 'how'를 'the way'로 바꿔 쓸 수 있다. 그러나 'the way how'와 같이 선행사와 관계부사를 함께 쓸 수는 없다.

21 '읽거나 쓸 수 없었던 5% 이상의 이탈리아 사람들'을 가리킨다.

22 글의 마지막에서 '그가 그림들을 어떻게 글로 번역했는지는 다음과 같다.'고 했으므로, 뒤에 올 내용으로는 'Gesualdo Bufalino가 그림 편지들을 글로 번역한 내용'이 가장 적절하다.

23 ⓐ와 ⑤: 부정대명사로 가산 명사를 반복하는 것을 피하기 위해 쓰임. ① 하나(의), ② (과거·미래의) 어느 한, ③ 같은, ④ 일반 사람, 누구나

24 ⓑ의 letter는 '편지'를 가리킨다.

25 글쓴이는 남편에게 이미 편지를 보냈지만, 답장이 없어서 슬프다고 했으므로, 처음으로 편지를 보내고 있다는 ③번은 옳지 않다. ④ mother-in-law: 시어머니.

26 ①번 다음 문장의 He에 주목한다. 주어진 문장의 a man을 받고 있으므로 ①번이 적절하다.

27 이어동사 picking: '주우면서'라는 의미로 동시 동작을 표현한다. 이어동사 picking up의 목적어가 인칭대명사 them이므로 picking과 up 사이에 them을 쓰는 것이 적절하다.

28 가정법 과거이므로 'were'로 쓰는 것이 적절하다. if절에 쓰이는 be동사의 과거형은 보통 'were'를 사용하지만, 구어체에서는

주어가 'I' 또는 3인칭 단수인 경우 'was'를 쓰기도 한다.

29 '원숭이의 몸짓'을 가리킨다.

단원별 예상문제
p.174~177

01 (a)live　　　02 ②
03 It means "Do not[Don't] enter." 또는 It means (that) you must not enter here.
04 (C) – (A) – (B) – (D)
05 They are for sending messages to the king.
06 ③　　　07 ②　　　08 ④　　　09 ⑤
10 ③　　　11 ①
12 (1) Is there any student whose name was not called?
　(2) Mike is the boy whose hair is very short.
　(3) The house whose windows are very big is my uncle's.
　(4) My sister is the girl whose cat is eating a fish.
　(5) Do you know the old man whose shoes are red and blue?
13 (1) I know a boy whose mother grows bananas.
　(2) The boy whose dog is barking is my cousin.
　(3) The girl whose hat is covered with flowers is a great dancer.
　(4) If you were with me(또는 Were you with me), I could show you my painting.
　(5) If I were a fish, I could swim in the water.
14 Speaking to family members or friends in a foreign country
15 ②　　　16 ④　　　17 ①　　　18 out
19 ③　　　20 don't → doesn't
21 ②, ③, ⑤

01 반의어 관계다. 아픈-건강한 : 죽은-살아 있는
02 '어떤 것을 사용할 준비가 되도록 하다'라는 의미로 'prepare(준비하다)'가 적절하다.
03 그림은 진입 금지를 나타내는 표지판이다.
04 '병사들이 5개의 굴뚝으로 무엇을 하고 있니?'라는 물음에 → (C) 왕에게 메시지를 보내고 있다는 답을 하고 → (A) '정말?' 이라고 놀라움을 표현한 다음, 그 체계에 대한 궁금증을 표현하며, 좀 더 말해달라고 부탁을 하는 말에 대해 → (B) '연기 나는 굴뚝 두 개가 보이지?'라는 물음을 통해 그 체계에 대한 질문을 하고 마지막으로 → (D) 긍정의 답을 하며 그것이 무엇을 의미하는지 묻고, 소녀의 마지막 말이 오는 것이 적절하다.
05 질문: 그 굴뚝들은 무엇을 위한 것이라고 생각하는가?
06 G의 빈칸 다음 말에서 굴뚝 하나에서 연기가 나오면 적이 없다는 것을 의미한다고 했으므로, '만약 적이 없다면, 그들은 연기

를 전혀 피우지 않아, 그렇지?'라는 B의 물음에 대해 '아니, 연기를 피워.'라는 대답이 적절하다.

07 주어진 문장은 '그것은 "Jan van Eyck가 여기 있었다. 1434."를 의미해.'라는 뜻으로 (B)에 오는 것이 적절하다.

08 남자의 마지막 말에 '그 여자는 연못을 가리키고 있어.'라고 말하는 것으로 보아 ④번이 자연스럽다.

09 ⑤번은 '이 집은 수 천 개의 비밀을 가진 것으로 유명해.'라는 말에 대해 '정말? 그것은 네가 비밀을 찾아야 하는 것을 의미해.'라고 말하는 것은 자연스럽지 않다.

10 빈칸 다음에 '그럼 그 소년은 과일을 얻기 위해 닭을 한 마리 가져와야 하는구나, 맞지?'라고 말하는 것으로 보아 ③이 적절하다.

11 선행사 The house 뒤에 its doors의 관계이므로 whose doors로 쓴다.

12 (1) 두 문장에서 any student와 소유격 His는 동일 인물이므로 소유격 관계사 whose로 연결하여 쓴다. (2) 두 문장에서 The boy와 소유격 His는 동일 인물이므로 소유격 관계사 whose로 연결하여 쓴다. (3) 두 문장에서 The house와 소유격 Its가 동일하므로 소유격 관계사 whose로 연결하여 쓴다. (4) 두 문장에서 the girl과 소유격 Her는 동일 인물이므로 소유격 관계사 whose로 연결하여 쓴다. (5) 두 문장에서 the old man과 소유격 His는 동일 인물이므로 소유격 관계사 whose로 연결하여 쓴다.

13 (1) 선행사 a boy가 mother를 소유하는 문장이므로 주격이 아닌 소유격 관계대명사 whose를 쓴다. (2) 선행사가 사람일 때는 소유격 관계대명사로 of which가 아닌 whose를 쓴다. (3) 선행사 The girl이 문장의 주어이므로 동사는 are가 아닌 is를 쓴다. (4) 한 문장에 두 개의 절이 있을 때 접속사가 필요하므로 If you were with me, 또는 if를 생략한 도치문장 Were you with me로 쓴다. (5) 가정법 과거의 주절은 '조동사의 과거형+동사원형'으로 쓴다.

14 '외국에 있는 가족이나 친구와 대화하는 것'을 가리킨다.

15 ⓑ와 ①, ⑤: 지시부사('그렇게'), ②, ④: 지시형용사, ③: 접속사

16 ④ a lot(much/even/still/far): 비교급을 강조하는 부사('훨씬'), ④ rather: 다소, 약간.

17 주어진 문장의 We에 주목한다. ①번 앞 문장의 'I'와 'our three kids'를 받고 있으므로 ①번이 적절하다.

18 reach ~ out: '(손 등을) 내밀다, 뻗다,' 목적어가 명사일 경우에는 목적어를 out 다음에 쓰는 것도 가능하다.

19 그녀의 남편으로부터 왜 답장이 없었는지는 알 수 없다. ① There were three kids. ② No. ④ She will visit the hospital with her middle son. ⑤ The oldest will look after the youngest.

20 The boy가 주어이므로 don't를 doesn't로 고치는 것이 적절하다.

21 right away = right now = at once = immediately: 즉시, ① 머뭇거리며, 망설이며, ④ 순차적으로

---

01 It tells people their batteries are very powerful.
02 Pictures speak a thousand words
03 hidden secrets, Latin, means, the rich, rich
04 (1) ㉠ → was created   (2) ㉡ → (to) use
    (3) ㉢ → couldn't
05 (1) If I didn't have any money, I couldn't buy the new shoes.
    (2) If Suji were[was] here, I could tell her the story.
06 (1) If I were you, I would set the alarm clock.
    (2) If I were you, I would write it by hand.
    (3) If I were you, I would search it on the Internet.
07 picking up them → picking them up
08 olive oil   09 whose
10 (A) is   (B) while   (C) how
11 it was a lot harder if they couldn't read or write.

01 'tell+간접목적어(people)+직접목적어(their batteries are ~)' 어순으로 쓴다.

02 그림을 통해 여러 가지 숨겨진 사실들을 알 수 있다는 내용이므로 'Pictures speak a thousand words(그림이 천 마디 말을 하지.)'가 적절하다.

04 (1) 주어 Hangeul과 동사 'create'는 수동 관계이므로 수동태를 쓴다. (2) help의 목적보어는 원형부정사 또는 to부정사를 쓴다. (3) 가정법 과거를 써야 하므로 조동사를 과거형으로 쓴다.

05 가정법 과거는 현재 사실과 반대되므로 직설법 문장을 가정법으로 표현할 때, 긍정은 부정문으로, 부정은 긍정문으로 쓰고, 현재시제는 과거시제로 쓴다.

06 현재 사실에 대한 가정은 'If+주어+동사 과거형, 주어+조동사 과거형(would/should/could/might)+동사원형'의 형태로 쓴다.

07 picking up의 목적어가 인칭대명사 them이므로 picking과 up 사이에 them을 쓰는 것이 적절하다.

08 '올리브기름(올리브유)'을 가리킨다.

09 소유격 관계대명사 'whose'가 적절하다.

10 (A) 동명사 Speaking이 문장의 주어이므로 is가 적절하다. (B) 뒤에 '주어+동사'가 있으므로 while이 적절하다. during+기간을 나타내는 명사, while+주어+동사, (C) 뒤에 완전한 문장이 이어지고 있으므로 관계부사 how가 적절하다.

11 'Speaking to family members or friends in a foreign country'를 가리키는 'it'을 주어로 해서 쓰는 것이 적절하다.

|모범답안|

01 (1) A: What does this sign mean?

B: It means you must not ride a bike here.

(2) A: What does this sign mean?

B: It means you must drive slowly here.

02 (1) I would see a doctor

(2) I wouldn't wait for him anymore

(3) I wouldn't hurry

(4) I wouldn't quit the job

03 (A) in the pond   (B) gesture

(C) Step back from the pond

단원별 모의고사   p.181~185

01 ④   02 border   03 ④   04 ⑤

05 ②   06 No enemy   07 ①   08 ③

09 Because only the rich could have that kind of dog at that time.

10 (A) They mean they just saw an enemy.

(B) Now the enemy is crossing the border in the dark.

(C) It means the battle has started.

11 ②   12 ⑤   13 ②   14 ②

15 I have a brother whose job is a fire fighter.

16 (1) If I were[was] God   (2) If I traveled to the past

17 ④

18 (A) a foreign country

(B) phones and the Internet

19 the way how → the way 또는 how   20 ②

21 ⓑ twenty-seven thousand   ⓒ twelve thousand

ⓓ one thousand three hundred

22 ②   23 ③

24 (A) a letter   (B) the hospital

25 oldest → middle   26 ③   27 pot

01 ④번은 '당신을 걱정하게 만들 만큼 나쁘거나 위험한 방법으로'를 의미하는 'seriously'에 대한 설명이다. 'ill'에 대한 설명은 'suffering from an illness or disease'이다.

02 유의어 관계이다. 궁금한 : 경계, 국경

03 '지구의 표면'의 의미로 'ground(땅, 지면)'가 적절하다.

04 ⑤: 이 글자가 무엇을 의미하는지 묻는 말에 이 편지가 파란 잉크로 쓰였다고 말하는 것은 어색하다.

05 '메시지를 보내기 위해서 병사들은 무슨 일을 할까?'라는 물음에 대한 답으로 ②번이 적절하다.

06 대화의 흐름상 굴뚝 한 곳에서 연기가 나오면 적이 없다는 것을 의미한다.

07 '~에 대해 궁금해 하다'는 'be curious about'을 사용한다.

08 G의 첫 번째 대화에서 '그 비밀들은 어디에 있니?'라고 묻는 것으로 보아 그림 속에 비밀이 숨겨져 있다는 것을 알 수 있다.

09 질문: 왜 사람들은 사진 속의 남자가 매우 부자였다고 생각하는가?

10 봉수대의 연기는 적이 성에 접근하는 위치에 따라 굴뚝의 연기 개수가 많아진다는 것을 알 수 있다.

11 이 남자의 몸짓은 무엇을 의미하는지 묻는 말 다음에 궁금증을 표현하는 말이 적절하다.

12 ①~④: were ⑤ had

13 'The man is good at playing soccer.' 문장에서, 선행사 'The man' 뒤에 소유격 관계대명사 whose를 사용하여 문장을 이어 쓰고 술부 'is good at playing soccer'를 쓴다.

14 현재 사실에 대한 가정은 'If+주어+동사 과거형, 주어+조동사 과거형(would/should/could/might)+동사원형'의 형태로 쓴다. *fall in love with: ~와 사랑에 빠지다 (수동형으로 쓰지 않는다.)

15 'I have a brother.'의 문장을 쓰고, 선행사 a brother 뒤에 소유격 관계대명사 문장을 이어 쓴다.

16 현재 사실에 대한 가정은 'If+주어+동사 과거형'으로 쓴다.

17 이 글은 '읽거나 쓸 줄 모르는 한 여자가 독일에서 일하는 남편에게 그림으로 쓴 편지를 시실리의 작가 Gesualdo Bufalino가 글로 번역했다'는 내용의 글이므로, 주제로는 ④번 '읽거나 쓸 줄 모르는 한 여자가 외국에 있는 남편에게 보낸 그림 편지'가 적절하다. ② illiterate: 글을 (읽거나 쓸 줄) 모르는, 문맹의, ③ illiteracy rate: 문맹률

18 사람들, 특히 문맹인 사람들이 '전화와 인터넷' 시대 이전에 '외국'에 있는 가족이나 친구와 대화하려고 노력할 때 겪었던 어려움들을 의미한다.

19 관계부사 'how'를 'the way'로 바꿔 쓸 수 있지만, 'the way how'와 같이 선행사와 관계부사를 함께 쓸 수는 없다.

20 ⓐ와 ①, ②, ④: 현재분사, ③, ⑤: 동명사

21 천의 자리에서 끊어서 읽으면서, 그 자리에 thousand를 붙여서 읽는 것이 적절하다. ⓑ 십 단위와 단 단위 사이에 보통 하이픈으로 연결하는 것이 적절하다. twenty-seven thousands(×), ⓒ twelve thousands(×), ⓓ one thousand three hundreds(×)

22 땅에서 올리브를 주운 것은 '일꾼'이 아니라 그의 '두 아들'이다. 본문의 picking은 분사구문으로 행위자가 his two sons이고, ②번의 pick은 helped의 목적격보어로서 행위자가 목적어인 him이 된다.

23 ⓐ in good health: 건강하여, ⓑ look after: ~을 돌보다

24 그림 편지의 '편지 봉투' 문양을 참조하여 (A)에는 a letter를, '십자가 문양의 병원 표시'를 참조하여 (B)에는 the hospital을 쓰는 것이 적절하다.

25 글쓴이는 '둘째' 아들과 시어머니를 방문할 것이다.

26 ⓐ와 ①, ③, ④: 형용사적 용법, enough+명사+to부정사: 형용사적 용법, enough+형용사/부사+to부정사: 부사적 용법, ②: 부사적 용법, ⑤: 명사적 용법

27 '항아리'를 가리킨다.

교과서 파헤치기

Lesson
3

01 용감한	02 발견	03 대학, 대학교
04 뒤로	05 폭탄	06 뜨다
07 실수	08 존중하다; 명예	
09 창의적인, 상상력이 풍부한		10 아마도
11 수여하다; 상	12 개막	13 발명, 발명품
14 웃기는	15 의식, 식	16 저장하다
17 가치; ~의 가치가 있는		18 받아들이다
19 자석	20 열렬한, 간절히 바라는	
21 반복적으로	22 응원하다	23 전통
24 공연하다	25 실제로, 사실은	26 경제학
27 해군	28 수여하다	29 관심
30 연구, 조사; 조사하다		31 선원
32 유용한	33 1조	34 드문, 특이한
35 ~ 대신에	36 계속 ~하다	37 ~에 성공하다
38 큰 소리로 웃다	39 ~에 참여하다	
40 A가 ~하지 못하게 하다		
41 ~을 (열렬히) 하고 싶어 하다		
42 ~에서 떠나다, 나가다		43 행운을 빌다

01 accept	02 opening	03 backward
04 discovery	05 eager	06 repeatedly
07 perform	08 economics	09 float
10 peace	11 honor	12 bomb
13 brave	14 award	15 ceremony
16 invention	17 while	18 laughable
19 actually	20 unusual	21 navy
22 magnet	23 maybe	24 mistake
25 sailor	26 tradition	27 research
28 trillion	29 useful	30 worth
31 imaginative	32 interest	33 university
34 receive	35 less than	36 instead of
37 succeed in	38 take part in	39 laugh out loud
40 keep -ing	41 get out of	42 be eager to
43 keep A from -ing		

1 live, 살아 있는   2 award, 수여하다   3 sailor, 선원
4 trillion, 1조   5 accept, 받아들이다   6 magnet, 자석
7 navy, 해군   8 backward, 뒤의   9 discovery, 발견

10 float, 뜨다, 띄우다   11 research, 연구, 조사
12 invent, 발명하다   13 eager, 열렬한, 간절히 바라는
14 honor, • 명예 • 존경하다
15 imaginative, 창의적인, 상상력이 풍부한
16 university, 대학

Get Ready 2

(1) solved a lot of, I'm sure, win, award / think so / keep, crossed
(2) winner, award / to get, prize / I'm sure, get, prize, Good luck
(3) looking forward to / make, laugh out loud, get the prize
(4) get, award, keep my fingers crossed

Start Off – Listen & Talk A

1. can't wait for / What, going to do / practiced, for a few weeks / looking forward to / Actually, a little worried, afraid, make, mistake / Don't worry, do, job, my fingers crossed
2. take part in / m going to run, end / looking forward, seeing / sure, win / do your best, keep my fingers crossed

Start Off – Listen & Talk B

are you coming / going to play, for me to try / sure, do great, keep, fingers crossed / going to perform, other mothers / sounds fun, looking forward, watching, stage

Start Off – Speak Up

looking forward to, model, ready / so, nervous / do well, keep my fingers crossed

Step Up – Real-life Scene

field trip, talent show / going to, like, do in class, jokes / looking forward to it / show, sure / worry, do great, keep my fingers crossed / Let me show, act, Guess / sound like / going to show / make, laugh out loud

Fun Time

m going to travel / sounds great, m really looking forward to
going to enter, m worried about / Don't worry, keep my fingers crossed

Express Yourself A

1. Can you tell me, invention / a pair of special, clean, floor / win a prize, keep, crossed
2. looks interesting, cutting board, feeder / not only, board but also, feeder, at the same time / idea / really think so / looking forward, using

35

Get Ready 2

(1) G: You solved a lot of problems in class. I'm sure you'll win the Class Brain award.

B: Do you really think so?

G: Of course. I'll keep my fingers crossed for you, Sangjun!

(2) B: The winner of the Oh So Sweet award will get some candies.

G: Oh, I want to get the prize.

B: I'm sure you'll get the prize this time. Good luck, Jiu!

(3) B: I'm looking forward to the Best Joker award this time.

G: Ha-ha. You always make us laugh out loud. So you'll get the prize, Yunki. Good luck.

B: Thank you.

(4) B: Minji, you're a happy girl. I think you'll get the Ms. Cheerful award. I'll keep my fingers crossed!

G: Oh, thank you, Jiho.

Start Off – Listen & Talk A

1. G: Mom, I can't wait for the sports day.

W: What are you going to do on that day, Minji?

G: I'm going to play basketball for my class. We've practiced hard for a few weeks.

W: Oh, I'm looking forward to your game.

G: Actually, I'm a little worried. I'm afraid I'll make a mistake.

W: Don't worry. You'll do a good job. I'll keep my fingers crossed!

2. W: Soyun, are you going to take part in any races on the sports day?

G: Sure. I'm going to run a 100 meter race at the end of the day.

W: Wow, I'm looking forward to seeing you at the race.

G: But, Mom, I'm not sure I'll win the race.

W: Just do your best. I'll keep my fingers crossed!

Start Off – Listen & Talk B

G: Mom, are you coming to the sports day?

W: Sure. I'm going to play the game Kick a Shoe. This will be the first time for me to try it.

G: Don't worry. I'm sure you'll do great. I'll keep my fingers crossed for you!

W: Thank you. I'm also going to perform a funny dance with some other mothers.

G: That sounds fun. I'm looking forward to watching you on the stage.

Start Off – Speak Up

A: I'm looking forward to the model airplane contest tomorrow. Are you ready?

B: Well, I think so, but I'm nervous.

A: You will do well. I'll keep my fingers crossed!

Step Up – Real-life Scene

Miso: We're going on a field trip next Tuesday. What are you going to do in the talent show, Jimin?

Jimin: I'm going to talk like our teachers do in class and tell some jokes.

Miso: Wow! I'm really looking forward to it.

Jimin: Will everyone like my show? I'm not sure.

Miso: Don't worry. I'm sure you'll do great. I'll keep my fingers crossed!

Jimin: Thank you, Miso. Let me show you one part of my act. Guess who? "Goood Jooob!"

Miso: Ha-ha, you sound like our English teacher.

Jimin: Do I? I'm going to show you more at the show.

Miso: Great! You always make us laugh out loud.

Fun Time

A: I'm going to travel to Jejudo next week.

B: Wow! That sounds great.

A: Yeah, I'm really looking forward to it.

A: I'm going to enter the dance contest next week, but I'm worried about it.

B: Don't worry. You'll do great. I'll keep my fingers crossed.

A: Thank you.

Express Yourself A

1. G: Can you tell me something about your invention?

B: They are a pair of special shoes. You can also clean the floor with them.

G: Great! I'm sure you'll win a prize. I'll keep my fingers crossed!

2. B: This looks interesting. Is this a cutting board or a bird feeder?

G: It is not only a cutting board but also a bird feeder. You can do two things at the same time.

B: That's a great idea!

G: Do you really think so?

B: Yes. I'm really looking forward to using it.

01 Ig Nobel Prize

02 happens, backward while, carrying

03 did research on, topic

04 research, enough to win

05 Maybe not   06 how about

07 won, fun research

08 awarded for, laugh, think

09 interest, honoring, unusual, imaginative

10 are presented by, winners

11 filled with, cheer, laughable

12 won, for, in   13 To save, instead of

14 enough, laugh out loud   15 also won, award

16 succeeded in floating, using

17 sense, humor, accepted, award

18 bring, to, face, how

19 in, for inventing, alarm

20 keeps running away, out   21 Not only, but, makes

22 number, keep, from, bored

23 opening, closing, words each

24 called, shouts repeatedly, bored

25 trillion, which, worth less

26 Throwing, is another, tradition

27 ends with, win, did

28 winners, receive lots of

29 awards, great honors like   30 a lot more fun

01 Ig Nobel Prize

02 happens, backward while, carrying

03 did research, topic   04 good enough to win

05 Maybe   06 how about

07 won one, fun reserch

08 are awarded for discoveries, laugh, think

09 to increase, interest, by honoring the unusual, the
    imaginative

10 are presented by real Nobel winners

11 is, filled with, eager to cheer, laughable

12 won, for

13 To save, made, shout, instead of using

14 funny enough, laugh out loud

15 won an award

16 succeeded in floating, by using magnets

17 a sense of humor, when, accepted, award

18 bring, to, how about

19 in, for inventing

20 keeps running away, gets out of

21 Not only, but also, makes, laugh

22 a number of, keep, from getting bored

23 opening, closing speeches, two words each

24 an eight-year-old girl called, repeatedly

25 ten trillion, which, worth less than

26 Throwing, is, tradition

27 ends with, win, prize, did   28 do not receive

29 great honors like   30 a lot more fun

1 이그노벨상

2 "당신이 커피 한 잔을 들고 가면서 뒤로 걸을 때 무슨 일이
   일어날까?"

3 한국의 한 고등학생인 한지원은 2015년에 이 주제에 관해
   연구했다.

4 이 연구 과제는 노벨상을 받을 정도로 훌륭할까?

5 아마도 아닐 것이다.

6 하지만 이그노벨상은 어떤가?

7 그는 이 재미있는 연구로 2017년에 상을 탔다.

8 이그노벨상은 '먼저 웃기고 나서 다음에 생각하게 하는' 발견에
   수여된다.

9 그것은 특이하고 창의적인 사람들을 높이 평가함으로써 과학에
   대한 사람들의 흥미를 늘리기 위해 AIR 잡지에 의해 1991년에
   시작되었다.

10 그 상들은 하버드 대학의 Sanders 극장에서 진짜 노벨상
   수상자들에 의해 수여된다.

11 그 방은 대개 '웃기는' 연구를 한 용감한 과학자들을 열렬히
   격려하고자 하는 사람들로 가득 찬다.

12 영국 해군은 2000년에 이그노벨 평화상을 탔다.

13 돈을 아끼기 위해, 해군에서는 선원들에게 진짜 폭탄을
   사용하는 대신에 "쾅!"이라고 소리치게 했다.

14 그것이 당신이 큰 소리로 웃을 정도로 우스운가?

15 Andre Geim도 그해에 상을 탔다.

16 그는 자석을 이용해서 살아 있는 개구리를 공중에 띄우는 데
   성공했다.

17 그는 상을 받을 때, "내 경험상, 사람들이 유머 감각이 없다면,
   그들은 대개 별로 훌륭한 과학자가 아니다."라고 말했다.

18 그것이 아직도 당신의 얼굴에 미소를 띠게 하지 않는다면,
   이것은 어떤가?

19 2005년에 Gauri Nanda는 자명종을 발명해서 이그노벨
   경제학상을 받았다.

20 그것은 잠자는 사람이 결국 침대 밖으로 나올 때까지 계속
   도망을 다닌다.

21 수상자들의 재미있는 연구뿐만 아니라 이그노벨상 시상식도
   또한 사람들을 웃게 만든다.

22 사람들이 지루해하지 않도록 하는 재미있는 것들이 많이 있다.

23 개회사와 폐회사는 단지 두 마디이다: "환영합니다. 환영합니다."와 "안녕. 안녕."

24 만일 누군가가 너무 오랫동안 말을 하면, Miss Sweetie Poo라고 하는 여덟 살짜리 여자아이가 "제발 멈춰요! 지루해요."라고 계속 외친다.

25 각 수상자는 10조의 짐바브웨 달러를 받는데, 그것은 미국의 1달러보다 가치가 낮다.

26 종이비행기를 날리는 것은 또 다른 재미있는 전통이다.

27 이그노벨상 시상식은 "만일 당신이 상을 타지 못했다면 – 그리고 만일 탔다면 – 내년에는 좀 더 많은 행운이 있기를!" 이라는 말로 끝이 난다.

28 수상자들은 많은 상금을 받지 않는다.

29 그리고 그 상은 노벨상같이 훌륭한 영광은 아니다.

30 하지만 이그노벨상은 과학을 훨씬 더 재미있게 만든다!

본문 TEST Step 4-Step 5 p.19~23

1 The Ig Nobel Prize

2 "What happens when you walk backward while you are carrying a cup of coffee?"

3 Han Jiwon, a Korean high school student, did research on this topic in 2015.

4 Is this research project good enough to win a Nobel Prize?

5 Maybe not.

6 But how about an Ig Nobel Prize?

7 He won one in 2017 for this fun research.

8 The Ig Nobel Prizes are awarded for discoveries that "first make one laugh and then think."

9 They were started in 1991 by *AIR* magazine to increase people's interest in science by honoring the unusual and the imaginative.

10 The prizes are presented by real Nobel winners in Sanders Theater at Harvard University.

11 The room is usually filled with people who are eager to cheer for the brave scientists with their "laughable" research.

12 The U.K. Navy won the Ig Nobel Prize for Peace in 2000.

13 To save money, the Navy made its sailors shout, "Bang!" instead of using real bombs.

14 Is that funny enough for you to laugh out loud?

15 Andre Geim also won an award that year.

16 He succeeded in floating a live frog in the air by using magnets.

17 "In my experience, if people don't have a sense of humor, they are usually not very good scientists,"

18 he said when he accepted his award.

19 If that still does not bring a smile to your face, how about this?

20 In 2005, Gauri Nanda won the Ig Nobel Prize in Economics for inventing an alarm clock.

21 It keeps running away until the sleeper finally gets out of bed.

22 Not only the winners' fun studies but also the ceremony for the Ig Nobel Prizes makes people laugh.

23 There are a number of interesting things that keep people from getting bored.

24 The opening and closing speeches are just two words each: "Welcome. Welcome." and "Goodbye. Goodbye."

25 If someone talks for too long, an eight-year-old girl called Miss Sweetie Poo shouts repeatedly, "Please stop! I'm bored."

26 Each winner receives ten trillion Zimbabwean dollars, which is worth less than one U.S. dollar.

27 Throwing paper planes is another fun tradition.

28 The Ig Nobel Prize ceremony ends with the words, "If you didn't win a prize   and if you did — better luck next year!"

29 The winners do not receive lots of money.

30 And the awards are not great honors like the Nobel Prizes.

31 But the Ig Nobel Prizes make science a lot more fun!

구석구석지문 TEST Step 1 p.24

Self-study Guide

1. words
2. showed, eagerness to learn
3. get, meaning
4. not only, but also

Express Yourself C

1. Stairs
2. These, Magic
3. not only, going, but also, storing
4. useful enough to make, much easier

Link to the World

1. Nobel Prize
2. named after, Swedish scientist
3. is awarded to, who, great work
4. all the winners, the youngest
5. at the age of, had fought, children's rights

6. received, three times

7. Not only, but also, was awarded

구석구석지문 TEST Step 2 · p.25

Self-study Guide

1. New words again!

2. He showed great eagerness to learn new things.

3. Oh, I get the meaning of "-ness."

4. Now I know not only the meaning of "eager" but also the meaning of "eagerness."

Express Yourself C

1. Magic Stairs

2. These are Magic Stairs.

3. You can use them not only for going up and down but also for storing things.

4. This invention is useful enough to make your life much easier.

Link to the World

1. The Nobel Prize

2. The Nobel Prize was named after Alfred Nobel, a Swedish scientist.

3. It is awarded to people who have done great work for the world.

4. Of all the winners, Malala Yousafzai is the youngest.

5. She won the Nobel Prize at the age of 17 because she had fought for women's and children's rights.

6. The Curie family received the Nobel Prize three times.

7. Not only Marie Curie but also her daughter was awarded the Nobel Prize.

단어 TEST Step 1 · p.26

01 알아보다, 인정하다		02 직업, 직장 생활
03 대회, 시합	04 숨겨진, 비밀의	05 능력
06 감명을 주다, 깊은 인상을 주다		07 소송, 사건
08 (상황에) 직면하다	09 판사	10 마술사
11 전문가	12 허락	13 조종하다
14 (중요한) 인물, 숫자		15 웃음(소리)
16 시합, 경기	17 (연극, 영화 등의) 대사	
18 발표	19 유용한	20 받아들이다
21 중요하다, 문제가 되다		22 용기
23 기록	24 색깔이 있는, 유색 인종의	
25 관리자, 경영자	26 제의, 제안	27 장식하다
28 등장인물	29 옷걸이	30 실망한
31 설치하다	32 ~에 반대하여, ~에 맞서	
33 허락하다	34 나중에, 후에	35 기분이 상하다
36 ~을 옹호하다, 지지하다		37 포기하다
38 ~을 부수다	39 ~을 극복하다	40 ~ 덕분에
41 ~을 준비하다	42 ~을 비웃다	43 ~할 수밖에 없다

단어 TEST Step 2 · p.27

01 ability	02 hidden	03 impress
04 courage	05 accept	06 decorate
07 colored	08 career	09 against
10 character	11 disappointed	12 presentation
13 case	14 record	15 magician
16 figure	17 permission	18 recognize
19 control	20 install	21 judge
22 later	23 matter	24 offer
25 lose	26 expert	27 face
28 match	29 line	30 competition
31 useful	32 speech	33 manager
34 laughter	35 give up	36 thanks to
37 stand up for	38 look down	39 keep ~ in mind
40 get over	41 keep -ing	42 laugh at
43 break down		

단어 TEST Step 3 · p.28

1 colored, 유색 인종의   2 hidden, 숨겨진, 비밀의

3 figure, (중요한) 인물, 거물   4 baker, 제빵사

5 face, (상황에) 직면하다   6 allow, 허락하다

7 laughter, 웃음(소리)   8 career, 직업, 직장 생활

9 engineer, 기술자, 엔지니어　10 courage, 용기

11 permission, 허락　12 expert, 전문가

13 judge, 판사　14 manager, 관리자, 경영자

15 space, 우주　16 record, 기록

Get Ready 2

(1) look down, the matter / to take dance classes, that idea, that, should / sorry to hear that

(2) disappointed / preparing for, competition, record, What / keep practicing, sure, get better and better

(3) to be, cook, laughs at, give up / never give up, good at cooking, cook

Start Off – Listen & Talk A

1. look, Why, disappointed / lost, because of, mistake / makes mistakes / should practice more / practice makes perfect

2. are you disappointed / give, presentation / Take, easy, speech, a little, presentation / more slowly / help, understand, better

Start Off – Listen & Talk B

look down, disappointed / lost, cooking competition / sorry to hear that, tried hard / maybe, enough, learn more cooking tips / How about getting useful, from, online / try, for, advice / welcome, remember, dishes

Start Off – Speak Up

Why, disappointed / failed, audition, keep trying / Don't give up, better

Start Up – Real-life Scene

disappointed / won't let, enter, singing competition / sorry to hear, against / to study hard, worried about my grades / parents, to be / Not yet, talk with / how much, Why don't you sing, in front of / Thank you for

Express Yourself A

1. look happy, disappointed / magician like, failed, competition, give up / Practice hard, get better, better, it's, to keep trying / your advice

2. come in, Are, interested in designing things / product designer, design / it's, to practice drawing, Reading, magazines will also help / keep that in mind

Learning Diary– Listen & Speak 1

look down, Why are you disappointed / lost, because, made, mistake / Don't be, happen, anyone / practice more / if, You know

Get Ready 2

(1) G: You look down today. What's the matter?

B: I want to take dance classes, but my father doesn't like that idea. He thinks that boys should play sports.

G: I'm sorry to hear that.

(2) G: Why are you disappointed?

B: I'm preparing for the ski jumping competition, but my record is not good. What should I do?

G: I think you should keep practicing more. I'm sure you'll get better and better.

(3) B: I want to be a cook, but everybody laughs at me. Do you think I should give up my dream?

G: No, never give up. I think you're really good at cooking. You'll be a great cook!

B: Thank you.

Start Off – Listen & Talk A

1. B: You don't look happy. Why are you disappointed?

G: We lost the basketball game because of my mistake.

B: Come on. Everyone makes mistakes.

G: Do you think I should practice more?

B: Well, yes. You know, practice makes perfect.

2. G: Why are you disappointed?

B: I didn't give a good presentation.

G: Take it easy. Your speech was a little fast, but I liked your presentation.

B: Do you think I should speak more slowly?

G: Yes. It will help your classmates understand you better.

Start Off – Listen & Talk B

G: Junsu, you look down today. Why are you disappointed?

B: I lost the cooking competition.

G: I'm sorry to hear that. I know you tried hard.

B: Yeah, but maybe that wasn't enough. Do you think I should learn more cooking tips?

G: Yes. I think they will help. How about getting useful tips from cooking shows online?

B: Okay. I'll try. Thank you for your advice, Mina.

G: You're welcome. Just remember I'm a fan of your dishes.

Start Off – Speak Up

B: Why are you disappointed?

G: I failed the audition for the Mapo Youth Band. Do you think I should keep trying?

B: Sure. Don't give up. You'll do better next time.

G: Thank you.

Jisu: Why are you so disappointed, Ryan?

Ryan: My parents won't let me enter Superstar 101, a singing competition.

Jisu: I'm sorry to hear that. Why are they against it?

Ryan: They want me to study hard and be a doctor. They're always worried about my grades.

Jisu: Did you tell your parents you really want to be a singer?

Ryan: Not yet. Do you think I should talk with them about it?

Jisu: Yes. Just show them how much you love singing. Why don't you sing the songs you made in front of them?

Ryan: Okay. I'll try. Thank you for your advice, Jisu.

Express Yourself A

1. W: You don't look happy. Why are you disappointed?

B: I want to be a wonderful magician like you, but I failed the magic competition. Do you think I should give up?

W: No. Practice hard every day and you'll get better and better. It's important to keep trying.

B: Okay, I'll try. Thank you for your advice.

2. W: Please come in. Are you interested in designing things?

B: Yes, I want to be a product designer. Do you think I should go to design school?

W: I think that will help, but it's more important to practice drawing every day. Reading design magazines will also help you.

B: Thank you. I'll keep that in mind.

Learning Diary– Listen & Speak 1

B: You look down today, Minji. Why are you disappointed?

G: We lost the soccer game because I made a mistake.

B: Don't be so sad. It can happen to anyone.

G: Do you think I should practice more?

B: Well, yes. I can help you if you want. You know, I'm a good soccer player.

G: Really? Thank you, Seho.

본문 TEST Step 1 — p.33~35

01 Hidden Figures, NASA
02 watched, movie, last weekend
03 African-American women who worked
04 career in, as human
05 experts, get over difficulties

06 one, hidden figures, movie
07 hard, talent, recognized, ability
08 got upset, missing, for
09 where Katherine had been 10 The bathroom
11 There are, COLORED bathrooms
12 have, half, away, use
13 Hearing, felt, sorry   14 had courage to talk
15 made, break down, sign
16 character, most, three
17 learn, wasn't allowed to
18 judge, give her permission
19 can't change, color, skin   20 no choice but to
21 cases, which, matter, years
22 Which one, make
23 impressed, what, finally, permission
24 stood up, herself, other
25 what impressed me most
26 first African-American woman engineer
27 the last, hidden figure
28 installed, worried, would lose
29 new programming language
30 taught it, members
31 asked to, made, suggestion
32 accepting, offer, bring, with
33 need, lot, to program   34 can't do, alone
35 are ready
36 Thanks to, become programmers
37 afraid of, as, chance   38 what, need to learn
39 how to face challenges
40 won't forget, tears, laughter

본문 TEST Step 2 — p.36~37

01 Hidden Figures
02 watched, last weekend
03 African-American women, worked at
04 in the 1960s as
05 of becoming space experts, to get over difficulties
06 three, hidden figures
07 showed a talent in, recognized her ability
08 got upset, was missing
09 where Katherine had been 10 bathroom
11 There, COLORED bathrooms
12 half a mile, just to use
13 Hearing this, felt, sorry
14 However, had courage to talk
15 break down   16 character
17 wasn't allowed to, white school

18 to give her permission　　19 can't change, skin

20 have no choice but to

21 cases, in a hundred years　22 Which one

23 impressed, what, finally gave, permission

24 stood up for herself, other

25 what impressed me most

26 first African-American woman engineer

27 the last

28 were installed, would lose

29 new programming language

30 taught it

31 was asked to, made, suggestion

32 I'm not accepting, offer　　33 lot, to program

34 alone　　　　　　　　　35 are ready

36 Thanks to

37 wasn't afraid of, as a chance

38 what I need to learn

39 Watching, how to face challenges

40 tears and laughter

---

1 NASA의 숨겨진 인물들

2 나는 지난 주말에 〈히든 피겨스〉라는 영화를 보았다.

3 그것은 NASA에서 일했던 세 명의 아프리카계 미국인 여성들에 대한 영화였다.

4 그들은 1960년대에 '인간 컴퓨터(계산원)'로 일을 시작했다.

5 하지만 그들은 NASA에서 우주 전문가가 되기를 꿈꾸었고 어려움을 극복하기 위해 열심히 노력했다.

6 Katherine Johnson은 이 영화에서 세 명의 '숨겨진 인물들' 중 한 명이었다.

7 그녀는 열심히 일했고 수학에서 재능을 보였으며, 그녀의 상사인 Al Harrison은 그녀의 능력을 알아차렸다.

8 어느 날, 그는 Katherine이 너무 오래 자리를 비웠을 때 화가 났다.

9 Al은 Katherine에게 어디에 갔었는지 물었고 그녀는 대답했다.

10 Katherine: 화장실요.

11 이 건물에는 유색 인종 전용 화장실이 없어요.

12 저는 단지 화장실을 사용하기 위해 반 마일을 달려가야 해요.

13 이 말을 듣고서, 나는 그녀가 정말 안됐다고 느꼈다.

14 그러나 나는 그 문제에 대해 상사에게 말한 그녀의 용기를 보고 기뻤다.

15 이것은 Al Harrison으로 하여금 '유색 여성 화장실' 표지판을 부수게 만들었다.

16 Mary Jackson은 셋 중에 가장 나의 마음에 드는 인물이었다.

---

17 그녀는 로켓 공학에 대해 더 많이 배우고 싶었지만 백인 학교에 다니는 것이 허락되지 않았다.

18 그래서 그녀는 판사에게 허락해 달라고 요청했다.

19 Mary: 저는 제 피부색을 바꿀 수 없어요.

20 그래서… 저는 '최초'가 되는 것 이외에는 선택이 없어요.

21 판사님, 당신이 오늘 들을 모든 사건 중에서, 백 년 뒤에 어느 것이 중요할까요?

22 어느 것이 판사님을 '최초'로 만들까요?

23 판사는 그녀가 말한 것에 감명을 받고 마침내 그녀에게 허락해 주었다.

24 Mary는 그녀 자신과 다른 아프리카계 미국인들의 편에 섰다.

25 그것은 영화에서 나를 가장 감동하게 한 점이었다.

26 마침내 그녀는 NASA에서 최초의 아프리카계 미국인 여성 공학자가 되었다.

27 Dorothy Vaughan은 마지막 '히든 피겨(숨은 인물)'였다.

28 1961년 NASA에 IBM 컴퓨터가 설치되었을 때, 그녀는 '인간 컴퓨터(계산원)'들이 직업을 잃을까봐 걱정했다.

29 그녀는 새로운 프로그래밍 언어인 포트란을 공부했다.

30 그녀는 또한 그것을 그녀의 팀원들에게 가르쳤다.

31 나중에 그녀가 새 IBM 팀의 리더가 되도록 요청받았을 때, 그녀는 제안했다.

32 Dorothy: 저는 저의 여성 팀원들을 데려올 수 없다면 그 제안을 받아들이지 않겠습니다.

33 그 기계의 프로그램을 짜기 위해서는 많은 사람이 필요합니다.

34 저는 그것을 혼자 할 수 없습니다.

35 제 여성 팀원들은 준비가 되어 있습니다.

36 Dorothy 덕분에, 그녀의 팀원들은 프로그래머가 될 수 있었다.

37 그녀는 변화를 두려워하지 않고 그것을 기회로 이용했다.

38 그것이 내가 그녀에게서 배울 필요가 있는 점이다.

39 이 영화를 보면서, 나는 삶에서 어떻게 도전에 직면해야 하는지 배울 수 있었다.

40 나는 Katherine, Mary, 그리고 Dorothy의 눈물과 웃음을 잊지 않을 것이다.

---

1 The Hidden Figures of NASA

2 I watched the movie *Hidden Figures* last weekend.

3 It was a movie about three African-American women who worked at NASA.

4 They began their career in the 1960s as "human computers."

5 However, they dreamed of becoming space experts at NASA and tried hard to get over difficulties.

6 Katherine Johnson was one of the three "hidden figures" in this movie.

7 She worked hard and showed a talent in math, and her manager Al Harrison recognized her ability.

8 One day, he got upset when Katherine was missing from her desk for too long.

9 Al asked where Katherine had been, and she answered.

10 Katherine: The bathroom

11 There are no COLORED bathrooms in this building.

12 I have to run half a mile away just to use the bathroom.

13 Hearing this, I felt really sorry for her.

14 However, I was glad that she had courage to talk to the manager about the problem.

15 This made Al Harrison break down the "Colored Ladies Room" sign.

16 Mary Jackson was the character I liked the most of the three.

17 She wanted to learn more about rocket science, but she wasn't allowed to go to a white school.

18 So, she asked a judge to give her permission.

19 Mary: I can't change the color of my skin.

20 So … I have no choice but to be the first.

21 Your Honor, of all the cases you'll hear today, which one will matter in a hundred years?

22 Which one will make you the "first?"

23 The judge was impressed by what she said and finally gave her permission.

24 Mary stood up for herself and for other African-Americans.

25 That was what impressed me most in the movie.

26 Finally, she became the first African-American woman engineer at NASA.

27 Dorothy Vaughan was the last "hidden figure."

28 When IBM computers were installed at NASA in 1961, she was worried the "human computers" would lose their jobs.

29 She studied a new programming language, FORTRAN.

30 She also taught it to her team members.

31 Later, when she was asked to be the leader of a new IBM team, she made a suggestion.

32 Dorothy: I'm not accepting the offer if I can't bring my ladies with me.

33 We need a lot of people to program that machine.

34 I can't do it alone.

35 My girls are ready.

36 Thanks to Dorothy, her team members could become programmers.

37 She wasn't afraid of change and used it as a chance.

38 That's what I need to learn from her.

39 Watching this movie, I could learn how to face challenges in life.

40 I won't forget the tears and laughter of Katherine, Mary, and Dorothy.

구석구석지문 TEST Step 1   p.45

Express Yourself C

1. had a good time with
2. told me, decorating
3. what he said, what your family love
4. had a good time with
5. told me about, saying his famous lines
6. what he said, what you act

After You Read A

1. made my manager break down, sign
2. asked the judge to allow, to study
3. to prepare for change

Link to the World

1. What, at this restaurant
2. make various Italian dishes
3. is difficult, your job
4. many things to do other
5. have to buy fresh meet, every day
6. wash the dishes, keep my kitchen clean
7. Are, happy with
8. tough job, what I do
9. feel proud, seeing people enjoy

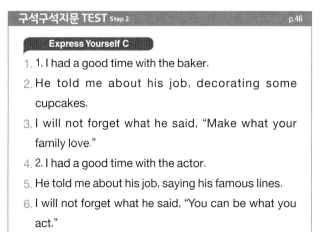

구석구석지문 TEST Step 2   p.46

Express Yourself C

1. 1. I had a good time with the baker.
2. He told me about his job, decorating some cupcakes.
3. I will not forget what he said, "Make what your family love."
4. 2. I had a good time with the actor.
5. He told me about his job, saying his famous lines.
6. I will not forget what he said, "You can be what you act."

1. Katherine Johnson: I made my manager break down the "Colored Ladies Room" sign.
2. Mary Jackson: I asked the judge to allow me to study at a white school.
3. Dorothy Vaughan: I studied a new programming language to prepare for change.

1. Q1 What do you do at this restaurant?
2. A1 I make various Italian dishes and desserts.
3. Q2 What is difficult about your job?
4. A2 I have so many things to do other than cooking.
5. I have to buy fresh meet and vegetables every day.
6. I also wash the dishes and keep my kitchen clean.
7. Q3 Are you happy with your job?
8. A3 Yes, I am. It's a tough job, but I love what I do.
9. I feel proud, seeing people enjoy my dishes.

Lesson
5

단어 TEST Step 1   p.47

01 아무것도, 어떤 일도		02 믿다
03 수레	04 (손을) 흔들다	05 맛있는
06 충분히	07 요정	08 통통한, 살찐
09 백성, 국민	10 밝은, 눈부신	11 찾다
12 바보, 멍청이	13 기회	14 괴물
15 침이 고이다, 침을 흘리다		16 옷, 의복
17 치다, 때리다	18 안에, 안으로	19 대신에
20 구하다	21 죽이다	22 교훈, 단원
23 중요하다, 문제되다		24 바퀴
25 대접하다	26 마녀	27 엉망진창
28 공주	29 개구리	30 나머지
31 외치다	32 꼼짝 못 하는, 움직일 수 없는	
33 불행하게	34 걱정하다	35 지금부터 죽
36 손에 손을 잡고	37 혼자	38 줍다, 집어 들다
39 도망가다, 달아나다		
40 ~에 가는 길(도중)에		41 더 잘 살다
42 ~라는 이름의	43 한번 해 보다, 시도하다	

단어 TEST Step 2   p.48

01 cart	02 monster	03 delicious
04 enough	05 believe	06 fairy
07 fat	08 witch	09 mess
10 save	11 stuck	12 bright
13 fool	14 people	15 serve
16 hit	17 inside	18 still
19 instead	20 clothes	21 kill
22 wave	23 matter	24 chance
25 even	26 rest	27 shout
28 pond	29 unhappily	30 water
31 lesson	32 princess	33 worry
34 funny	35 hand in hand	36 not ~ anymore
37 on one's way to		38 be better off
39 hundreds of	40 from now on	41 run away
42 jump around	43 to oneself	

단어 TEST Step 3   p.49

1 rest, 나머지   2 shout, 외치다   3 delicious, 맛있는
4 stuck, 꼼짝 못하는   5 lesson, 교훈   6 witch, 마녀
7 cart, 수레   8 invite, 초대하다   9 monster, 괴물
10 pond, 연못   11 princess, 공주   12 frog, 개구리

13 wheel, 바퀴   14 fairy, 요정   15 wave, (손을) 흔들다
16 hit, 치다, 때리다

01 Frog Prince Continued
02 Characters, Princess, Fairy
03 Scene, in, room   04 in, jumping around
05 Stop jumping around   06 just can't stop
07 a frog anymore
08 wrong, down, pond these
09 around, kill monster, save
10 feel, away, after, as
11 hundreds of, better off
12 Still, it, out
13 Scene, On, mountain
14 himself, witch, turn, back
15 out of, How, feeling
16 meet, into, ever after
17 like, matter, let, save   18 what, want, away
19 come in
20 Where, Please, help   21 If, frog, France
22 turn, back, live happily
23 Let's, inside, serve, delicious
24 made of, by, name
25 With, watering, fat enough 26 runs away, finds
27 Could, turn, so, after
28 on, way, try, into   29 worry, will be okay
30 what, fool, stuck, unhappily
31 hits, turns into
32 chance, how, should live
33 Waving, lesson, keep, crossed
34 In, Prince's house   35 runs in, smiling
36 been, worried, clothes, mess
37 believed, else, did, on
38 glad, hear, make, even
39 looking forward, bright future
40 to, jumping, in hand

01 Frog Prince Continued
02 Characters, Princess, Fairy
03 Scene, In   04 jumping around
05 Stop jumping   06 can't stop
07 anymore
08 What's wrong with, these days

09 I don't like it when, kill monsters, save
10 feel like running away, Picking up, as
11 hundreds of, were better off when, were still
12 That's it   13 Scene, On
14 To himself, turn, into   15 out of, How
16 turn me back into, so, live happily ever after
17 look like, doesn't matter, let you save, rest
18 want   19 come in
20 Where   21 If
22 turn me back into, live happily
23 Let's, serve, delicious
24 for inviting, is made of cookies, by the name of
25 I do, fat enough   26 runs away
27 Could you, so
28 on my way, give it a try, turns, into
29 don't worry, will be okay
30 what a fool, living happily, stuck, unhappily
31 turns into
32 giving me a second chance, how I should live
33 Waving, lesson, keep my fingers crossed
34 Prince's house   35 smiling
36 have you been, clothes, mess
37 else, did, From now on
38 even
39 looking forward to, bright future
40 jumping hand in hand

1 계속된 개구리 왕자
2 등장인물: 개구리 왕자, 공주, 마녀 1, 마녀 2, 요정
3 장면 1: 방 안에서
4 (왕자가 이리저리 뛰어다니며 등장한다.)
5 공주: 여보, 이리저리 뛰어다니지 마세요.
6 왕자: 저, 나는 단지 멈출 수 없을 뿐이에요.
7 공주: 당신은 이제 개구리가 아니에요.
8 왕자: 당신한테 무슨 문제가 있어요? 요즘 당신은 연못으로 내려가지도 않잖아요.
9 공주: 나는 당신이 방 안에서 이리저리 뛰어다니는 게 마음에 안 들어요. 나가서 괴물들을 죽이고 우리 백성을 구하세요.
10 왕자: 나는 밖에 나가서 아무것도 죽이고 싶지 않아요. 나는 단지 멀리 뛰어다니고 싶을 뿐이오. (책을 집어 들고) 들어 봐요! "그들은 그 후로 행복하게 살았다. 끝." 나는 책에서 말한 것처럼 내 인생을 살고 있지만, 우리는 행복하지 않아요. 뭐가 문제일까요?
11 공주: 뭐가 문제냐고요? 수백 가지 문제가 있어요! 가끔 나는 당신이 아직 개구리일 때 더 잘 살지 않았나 생각해요.
12 왕자: 아직 개구리라 …. 그래! 바로 그거요! (퇴장한다.)

45

13 장면 2: 산속에서

14 왕자: (혼잣말로) 나는 마녀를 찾아야 해. 그녀가 나를 다시 개구리로 바꿔 줄 거야. (소리치며) 마녀님, 마녀님. 어디 계세요? 저 좀 도와주세요!

15 마녀 1: (집 밖으로 나오며) 안녕, 왕자님. 기분이 어때요?

16 왕자: 당신을 만나서 기뻐요. 저는 개구리 왕자예요. 저는 당신이 저를 다시 개구리로 바꿔줘서 제가 앞으로 행복하게 살 수 있게 되기를 원해요.

17 마녀 1: 개구리 왕자라고 했어요? 그거 웃기는군요. 당신은 개구리처럼 보이지 않아요. 음, 그건 중요하지 않아요. 당신이 왕자라면 왕자인 거죠. 그리고 나는 당신이 백설공주를 구하도록 놔두지 않을 거예요. 여기, 이 사과의 나머지를 먹어요.

18 왕자: 고맙지만 됐어요. 그건 제가 원하는 게 아니에요! (도망간다)

19 (왕자와 마녀 2가 등장한다.)

20 왕자: 마녀님, 마녀님. 어디 계세요? 저 좀 도와주세요! 저는 개구리 ….

21 마녀 2: 당신이 개구리라면 나는 프랑스의 왕이에요.

22 왕자: 아니요, 저는 개구리가 아니에요. 저는 개구리 왕자예요. 하지만 저를 다시 개구리로 바꿔 줘서 제가 앞으로 행복하게 살 수 있게 해 줄 마녀가 필요해요. 그렇게 해 주실 수 있나요?

23 마녀 2: 안에서 그것에 관해 이야기해 봅시다. 내가 당신에게 맛있는 점심을 대접할게요. 들어와요.

24 왕자: 저를 초대해 주셔서 감사합니다. 오, 이 집은 과자와 사탕으로 만들어져 있네요. 잠깐만요, 당신은 헨젤과 그레텔이라는 이름의 아이들을 혹시 알아요?

25 마녀 2: 그래요, 왕자님, 알고 있어요. (그녀가 군침을 흘리면서) 그 애들은 아직 충분히 살이 찌지 않았지만, 당신은 ….

26 (왕자는 도망치다가 요정을 발견한다.)

27 왕자: 만나게 되어 기쁩니다, 요정님. 저는 개구리 왕자예요. 저를 다시 개구리로 바꿔 앞으로 행복하게 살 수 있게 해 주실 수 있나요?

28 요정: 음, 저는 신데렐라를 만나러 가는 길이지만, 한번 해 볼게요. 아시다시피 이건 제가 처음으로 해 보는 거예요. (요정이 왕자를 바퀴로 바꾼다.)

29 요정: 이런! 미안하지만 걱정하지 마세요. 모든 게 잘될 거예요.

30 왕자: (혼잣말로) 오, 내가 얼마나 바보였던가! 앞으로 행복하게 살면서 집에서 공주와 함께 앉아 있고 싶구나. 하지만 대신에 여기 이 수레 아래에 붙박여 있고 앞으로 불행하게 살게 되겠구나.

31 (시계가 12시를 치자 바퀴가 왕자로 바뀐다.)

32 왕자: 믿을 수가 없네. 두 번째 기회를 주셔서 감사합니다. 이제 나는 내 인생을 어떻게 살아야 할지 알겠어요. (퇴장한다)

33 요정: (손을 흔들며) 좋은 교훈을 배웠군요. 행운을 빌어요.

34 장면 3: 개구리 왕자의 집 안에서

35 (왕자가 미소를 지으며 뛰어 들어온다.)

36 공주: 어디 있었어요? 걱정했잖아요. 옷이 엉망진창이네요.

37 왕자: (공주를 바라보며) 당신은 세상 어느 누구도 나를 믿지 않을 때 나를 믿어 주었어요. 당신은 내가 개구리일 때 조차도 나를 사랑해 주었죠. 이제부터는 내가 당신을 더 행복하게 해 주겠어요.

38 공주: 그 말을 들으니 기뻐요. 제가 당신을 훨씬 더 행복하게 해 줄게요.

39 왕자: 좋아요! 난 우리의 밝은 미래를 기대할게요. 하하….

40 (그들은 서로 손을 잡고 함께 연못으로 뛰어간다.)

본문 TEST Step 4 - Step 5　　　　　　　　　　　p.59~64

1 The Frog Prince Continued

2 Characters: Frog Prince, Princess, Witch 1, Witch 2, Fairy

3 Scene 1: In a room

4 (*Prince comes in, jumping around.*)

5 Princess: Stop jumping around, honey.

6 Prince: Well, I just can't stop.

7 Princess: You're not a frog anymore.

8 Prince: What's wrong with you? You don't go down to the pond these days.

9 Princess: I don't like it when you jump around in the room. Go out to kill monsters and save our people.

10 Prince: I don't want to go out and kill anything. I just feel like running away. (*Picking up a book*) Listen! "They lived happily ever after. The end." I'm living my life as the book says, but we're not happy. What's the problem?

11 Princess: What's the problem? There are hundreds of problems! Sometimes I think we were better off when you were still a frog.

12 Prince: Still a frog …. Yes! That's it! (*Goes out*)

13 Scene 2: On the mountain

14 Prince: (*To himself*) I need to find the witch, who will turn me back into a frog. (*Shouting*) Ms. Witch, Ms. Witch. Where are you? Please help me!

15 Witch 1: (*Coming out of the house*) Hi, Prince. How are you feeling?

16 Prince: I'm glad to meet you. I'm the Frog Prince. I hope you can turn me back into a frog so I can live happily ever after.

17 Witch 1: Frog Prince, you say? That's funny. You don't look like a frog. Well, it doesn't matter. If you're a prince, you're a prince. And I won't let

you save Snow White. Here, eat the rest of this apple.

18 Prince: No, thank you. That's not what I want! (*Runs away*)

19 (*Prince and Witch 2 come in.*)

20 Prince: Ms. Witch, Ms. Witch. Where are you? Please help me! I'm the Frog ....

21 Witch 2: If you're a frog, I'm the King of France.

22 Prince: No, I'm not a frog. I'm the Frog Prince. But I need a witch to turn me back into a frog so I can live happily ever after. Can you do it?

23 Witch 2: Let's talk about it inside. I will serve you a delicious lunch. Come in

24 Prince: Thank you for inviting me. Oh, this house is made of cookies and candies. Wait a minute. Do you know any children by the name of Hansel and Gretel?

25 Witch 2: Yes, Prince, I do. (*With her mouth watering*) They are not fat enough yet, but you are ....

26 (*Prince runs away and finds a fairy.*)

27 Prince: I'm glad to meet you, Ms. Fairy. I am the Frog Prince. Could you turn me back into a frog so I can live happily ever after?

28 Fairy: Well, I'm on my way to see Cinderella, but I'll give it a try. It's my first time, you know. (*Fairy turns Prince into a wheel.*)

29 Fairy: Oops! Sorry, but don't worry. Everything will be okay.

30 Prince: (*To himself*) Oh, what a fool I've been! I want to be sitting at home with the Princess, living happily ever after. But instead, I'm stuck here under this cart and I'll live unhappily ever after.

31 (*The clock hits twelve, and the wheel turns into Prince.*)

32 Prince: I can't believe this. Thank you for giving me a second chance. Now I know how I should live my life. (*Goes out*)

33 Fairy: (*Waving her hand*) You learned a good lesson. I'll keep my fingers crossed.

34 Scene 3: In the Frog Prince's house

35 (*Prince runs in, smiling.*)

36 Princess: Where have you been? I've been worried. Your clothes are a mess.

37 Prince: (*Looking at Princess*) You believed me when no one else in the world did. You loved me even when I was a frog. From now on, I will make

you happier.

38 Princess: I'm glad to hear that. I'll make you even happier.

39 Prince: Great! I'm looking forward to our bright future. Ha–ha ....

40 (*They run to the pond together, jumping hand in hand.*)

단어 TEST Step 1 　　　　　　　　　　　p.65

01 근사한, 멋진, 엄청난, 어마어마한　　02 전쟁, 전투
03 땅, 지면　　04 ~을 향하여　　05 교통
06 굴뚝　　07 광고　　08 강한, 강력한
09 가까이, 근접하여　　10 번역하다, 해석하다
11 준비하다　　12 호기심이 많은, 궁금한
13 다소, 약간　　14 답장　　15 남편
16 죽은, 쓸모없는　　17 치다, 두드리다　　18 발견하다
19 숨은, 숨겨진　　20 포옹; 포옹하다　　21 오해
22 진지하게, 심각하게
23 큰 소리로, 시끄럽게　　24 ~처럼 보이다
25 적군, 적대자　　26 좌석, 의석　　27 군인
28 정확하게　　29 투표하다, 선출하다
30 국경, 경계　　31 점자　　32 표현
33 고용하다　　34 상품, 제품
35 이겨내다, 극복하다　　36 ~을 돌보다
37 ~로 덮이다　　38 ~의 가격으로　　39 ~을 제외하고
40 ~에 (찬성하는) 투표를 하다　　41 ~에 조심하다
42 즉시, 당장　　43 ~ 대신에

단어 TEST Step 2 　　　　　　　　　　　p.66

01 traffic　　02 awesome　　03 letter
04 battle　　05 translate　　06 dead
07 enemy　　08 discover　　09 light
10 loudly　　11 exactly　　12 curious
13 expression　　14 husband　　15 toward
16 chimney　　17 seriously　　18 rather
19 prepare　　20 hidden　　21 soldier
22 border　　23 product　　24 sign language
25 hire　　26 misunderstanding
27 hug　　28 knock　　29 seat
30 pond　　31 foreign　　32 gesture
33 pull　　34 vote　　35 instead of
36 except for　　37 look after　　38 be careful with
39 step back　　40 right away
41 be covered with　　42 at a price of
43 get over

단어 TEST Step 3 　　　　　　　　　　　p.67

1 dead, 죽은　　2 toward, ~을 향하여　　3 reply, 답장
4 foreign, 외국의　　5 ground, 땅, 지면　　6 hire, 고용하다
7 husband, 남편　　8 ill, 아픈, 병든　　9 prepare, 준비하다
10 seat, 의석　　11 vote, 투표하다, 선출하다　　12 oil, 기름
13 ring, 반지　　14 translate, 번역하다, 해석하다
15 discover, 발견하다　　16 hug, 포옹

대화문 TEST Step 1 　　　　　　　　　　　p.68~69

Get Ready 2

(1) curious about, is it standing / a kind of, tells, batteries, powerful
(2) m curious about / traffic sign, means, enter
(3) dots for, m curious about / Braille, blind / guess what, mean
(4) curious, balloon, hanging / ad, product, powerful

Start Off – Listen & Talk A

1. soldiers, with, chimneys / messages, by using, chimneys / m curious about, system / smoking chimneys / What, mean / saw, enemy
2. enemy, smoke at all, do / Smoke, chimney, enemy / rising, What does. mean / It means, close, border

Start Off B

is crossing, border, dark, soldiers going to do, messages, curious about / light, chimneys / light, chimneys / It means, battle, started

Start Off – Speak Up

m curious about, language / Let, show, expression / What, mean / It means

Step Up – Real-life Scene

hidden secrets / curious about, secrets / Find, yourself / Let's see, letters / one, means, Latin / awesome, Any other secrets / tells, rich / understand / spend lots of, to buy, kind at that time / the rich, that kind, right / Exactly, speak a thousand

Express Yourself A

1. gesture, curious about / it means, into, pond / Why, think so / lots of bees, pointing, pond
2. So, gesture mean / It means, chicken / should bring, to get. right / I think so
3. What, gesture mean, curious about / Turn it off / What makes, so / The other hunter, close / see

Get Ready 2

(1) G: I'm curious about that robot. Why is it standing there?

B: It's a kind of ad. It tells people their batteries are very powerful.

(2) G: What's this? I'm curious about it.

B: It's a traffic sign. It means "Do not enter."

G: Oh, I see.

(3) G: What are these dots for? I'm curious about them.

B: Oh, they are Braille. They are for blind people.

G: I see. Now I can guess what they mean.

(4) G: I'm curious about that balloon. Why is it hanging there?

B: Oh, that. It's an ad. It says the product is very powerful.

Start Off – Listen & Talk A

1. B: What are the soldiers doing with the five chimneys on TV?

G: They are sending messages to the king by using the chimneys.

B: Really? I'm curious about the system. Can you tell me more?

G: Well, do you see the two smoking chimneys?

B: Yes. What do they mean?

G: They mean they just saw an enemy.

2. B: If there's no enemy, they don't smoke at all, do they?

G: Yes, they do. Smoke from one chimney means "No enemy."

B: Now smoke is rising from three chimneys. What does that mean?

G: It means an enemy is coming close to the border.

Start Off B

B: Now the enemy is crossing the border in the dark. What are the soldiers going to do to send messages? I'm curious about that.

G: They will light four chimneys.

B: When they light all five of the chimneys, what does that mean?

G: It means the battle has started.

Start Off – Speak Up

B: I'm curious about sign language.

G: Are you? Let me show you one expression. Look.

B: What does it mean?

G: It means "Hello."

Step Up – Real-life Scene

B: This painting has some hidden secrets in it.

G: Really? I'm curious about them. Where are the secrets?

B: Find one yourself.

G: Let's see. ... Oh, I see some letters here.

B: You found one! It means "Jan van Eyck was here. 1434." It's Latin.

G: That's awesome! Any other secrets?

B: Okay. This dog tells us the man here was very rich.

G: I don't understand.

B: They had to spend lots of money to buy a dog of that kind at that time.

G: I see. Only the rich could have that kind of dog, right?

B: Exactly. Pictures speak a thousand words, you know.

Express Yourself A

1. W: What does this woman's gesture mean? I'm curious about it.

M: I think it means "Jump into the pond."

W: Why do you think so?

M: The boy has lots of bees on his head. And the woman is pointing at the pond.

2. W: This woman doesn't want a dollar. So what does her gesture mean?

M: It means she wants a chicken.

W: Then the boy should bring a chicken to get the fruit, right?

M: I think so.

3. W: What does this man's gesture mean? I'm curious about it.

M: It means "Turn it off."

W: Really? What makes you think so?

M: The other hunter there is coming close to an animal.

W: Oh, I see.

01 Picture Letter from, of

02 Speaking, foreign, rather, simple

03 before, days, that easy

04 sent, waited for, reply

05 lot harder, couldn't, write

06 how, got over, difficulties

07 by, whose, far away

08 island, while, worked in

09 more than, one of

10 was discovered by, writer

11 how, translated, into words

12 miss, reach, out toward   13 in, expect for, little

14 little sick, not seriously   15 sent, there, reply so

16 got, from, would be   17 fell ill, going, with

18 with, while, looks, youngest

19 had, prepare, plant seeds

20 voted for   21 so, that, almost seems

22 whether, other wins, same

23 Nothing changes, poor

24 worked, will work again   25 picked lots, from, this

26 hired, whose, workers

27 knocked, down, picking, up

28 paid, for, work   29 spent, for, press

30 enough, to fill, pot   31 sell, at, price, lire

32 heart, of, as, coming   33 would be, if, were

34 all miss, so   35 sending, big hug, little

36 dear love   37 heart, yours, joined, as

---

28 paid, for   29 spent, for, press

30 enough, to fill, one   31 at a price of

32 as   33 would be, were with

34 miss   35 a big hug, little kids

36 dear love   37 joined, as

1 세 아이의 엄마가 보낸 그림 편지

2 오늘날 외국에 있는 가족이나 친구와 대화하는 것은 다소 쉽고 간단하다.

3 하지만 전화와 인터넷 시대 이전에는 그것이 그렇게 쉽지 않았다.

4 사람들은 단지 편지를 보내고 답장을 몇 주 동안 기다렸다.

5 그리고 그들이 읽거나 쓸 수 없었다면 그건 훨씬 더 힘들었다.

6 이 편지는 사람들이 이런 어려움을 어떻게 극복했는지 보여 준다.

7 그것은 남편이 멀리 떨어져 살았던 한 여자에 의해 1973년에 쓰여졌다.

8 그녀의 남편은 독일에서 일한 반면, 그녀는 이탈리아의 섬인 시실리에서 살았다.

9 그 당시에는 5% 이상의 이탈리아 사람들이 읽거나 쓸 수 없었고, 그녀도 그들 중 한 명이었다.

10 이 편지는 시실리의 작가 Gesualdo Bufalino가 발견하였다.

11 그가 그림들을 어떻게 글로 번역했는지는 다음과 같다.

12 사랑하는 여보, 난 당신이 정말 그립고, 우리 세 아이와 함께 당신을 향해 내 팔을 쭉 뻗고 있어요.

13 막내를 제외하고는 우리 모두 건강해요.

14 그 아이는 약간 아프지만 심각하진 않아요.

15 난 당신에게 이미 편지를 보냈지만, 답장이 없어서 그것 때문에 나는 슬퍼요.

16 당신에게서 편지를 받는다면, 나는 정말 행복할 거예요.

17 당신의 어머니께서는 병이 드셨고, 나는 약간의 돈과 음식을 가지고 병원에 있는 어머니를 방문할 예정이에요.

18 큰애가 막내를 돌보는 동안 둘째와 함께 그곳에 갈 거예요.

19 나는 150,000리라에 두 일꾼을 시켜 우리 밭을 준비하고 씨앗을 심게 했어요.

20 나는 DC에 투표했어요.

21 PCI는 매우 많은 의석을 잃어서 거의 죽은 것처럼 보여요.

22 하지만 이쪽이 이기건 저쪽이 이기건, 상황은 똑같아요.

23 우리 가난한 사람들에게는 아무 것도 바뀌지 않지요.

24 우리는 어제도 일했고, 내일도 다시 일할 거예요.

25 우리는 올해 올리브나무에서 올리브를 많이 땄어요.

26 나는 아들들이 훌륭한 일꾼인 한 남자를 고용했어요.

27 그가 올리브를 쳐서 떨어뜨리면 그의 두 아들이 땅에서 올리브를 주우면서 그를 도왔어요.

01 A Picture Letter

02 Speaking, foregin country is rather, simple

03 before, that easy

04 sent, waited for, for weeks

05 a lot harder, couldn't read or write

06 got over

07 was written in, whose, far away

08 while, worked in Germany

09 more than 5%, one of them

10 was discovered by, writer

11 how, translated, into

12 miss, reach, out toward

13 all in good health except for, one

14 a little, not seriously

15 already, there was no reply

16 got, would be   17 fell ill, with

18 while, looks after, youngest

19 had, prepare, plant seeds

20 voted for   21 so, that

22 whether one or the other, the same

23 Nothing changes   24 will work again

25 picked, from   26 hired, whose, workers

27 knocked, down, picking, up from

28 나는 그 일을 위해 그에게 27,000리라를 지급했어요.

29 올리브 압착을 위해 12,000리라를 더 썼어요.

30 나는 큰 항아리 하나와 작은 항아리 하나를 채울 만큼 충분한 기름을 얻었어요.

31 리터당 1,300리라의 가격으로 팔 수 있을 것 같아요.

32 여보, 크리스마스가 다가오면서 내 마음은 당신을 떠올려요.

33 당신이 나와 함께 있다면 난 정말 행복할 거예요.

34 우리는 모두 당신을 매우 많이 그리워해요.

35 나와 우리 세 아이의 큰 포옹을 보내요.

36 잘 있어요, 여보.

37 내 마음은 당신의 것이에요, 우리들의 두 반지처럼 당신과 연결된 채로요.

---

1 A Picture Letter from a Mother of Three

2 Speaking to family members or friends in a foreign country is rather easy and simple today.

3 But before the days of phones and the Internet, it was not that easy.

4 People just sent a letter and waited for a reply for weeks.

5 And it was a lot harder if they couldn't read or write.

6 This letter shows how people got over these difficulties.

7 It was written in 1973 by a woman whose husband was far away.

8 She lived in Sicily, an Italian island, while her husband worked in Germany.

9 At the time, more than 5% of the people in Italy could not read or write, and she was one of them.

10 This letter was discovered by Sicilian writer Gesualdo Bufalino.

11 Here's how he translated the pictures into words.

12 My dear love, I miss you so much, and I reach my arms out toward you, together with our three kids.

13 We are all in good health except for the little one.

14 He's a little sick, but not seriously.

15 I already sent you a letter, but there was no reply, so I am sad about it.

16 If I got a letter from you, I would be very happy.

17 Your mother fell ill, and I'm going to visit her in the hospital with some money and food.

18 I'll go there with our middle son while the oldest looks after the youngest.

19 I had two workers prepare our field and plant

seeds for 150,000 lire.

20 I voted for the DC.

21 The PCI lost so many seats that it almost seems dead.

22 But whether one or the other wins, it's the same.

23 Nothing changes for us poor people.

24 We worked yesterday, and we will work again tomorrow

25 We picked lots of olives from our olive trees this year.

26 I hired a man whose sons are good workers.

27 He knocked the olives down, and his two sons helped him, picking them up from the ground.

28 I paid him 27,000 lire for the work.

29 I spent 12,000 more for the olive press.

30 I got enough oil to fill a large pot and a small one.

31 I can sell it at a price of 1,300 lire a liter.

32 My love, my heart thinks of you as Christmas is coming.

33 I would be so happy if you were with me.

34 We all miss you so much.

35 I'm sending you a big hug from me and our three little kids.

36 Goodbye, dear love.

37 My heart is yours, joined to you as our two rings are.

Express Yourself C1

1. whose, is covered with, doesn't understand

2. means, Jump into

3. were, would jump into, right away

Project Do It Yourself

1. Climb up

2. had, would so kites to send

3. would fly, whose, looks like, make the soldiers climb

Link to the World

1. was created by

2. At first, didn't want to use, writing system

3. However, tried hard to help, use

4. Thanks to, can express anything with

5. didn't know, could not express ourselves

51

Express Yourself C1

1. The boy whose head is covered with bees doesn't understand the woman's gesture.
2. I think it means "Jump into the pond."
3. If I were the boy, I would jump into the pond right away.

Project Do It Yourself

1. "Climb up the mountain."
2. If I had soldiers to lead, I would so kites to send my messages.
3. For example, I would fly a kite whose face looks like a mountain to make the soldiers climb up the mountain.

Link to the World

1. Hangeul was created by King Sejong.
2. At first, many people didn't want to use this new writing system.
3. However, King Sejong tried hard to help people use Hangeul.
4. Thanks to him, we can express anything with Hangeul now.
5. If we didn't know Hangeul, we could not express ourselves easily.

적중 100
영어 기출 문제집
정답 및 해설

천재 | 정사열